THE PRINCE OF FIRE

PITT SERIES IN RUSSIAN AND
EAST EUROPEAN STUDIES

THE PRINCE OF FIRE

An Anthology of Contemporary Serbian Short Stories

Edited by Radmila J. Gorup
and Nadežda Obradović

With a Foreword by Charles Simic

UNIVERSITY OF PITTSBURGH PRESS

Published by the University of Pittsburgh Press, Pittsburgh, Pa. 15261
Copyright © 1998, University of Pittsburgh Press
All rights reserved
Manufactured in the United States of America
Printed on acid-free paper
10 9 8 7 6 5 4 3 2 1

Library of Congress Cataloging-in-Publication data
are located at the end of this book.

A CIP catalog record for this book is available from the British Library.

The authors of these stories have graciously consented to have them
translated and included in this anthology.

"The Great Rebellion at the Stuln Nazi Camp," copyright by David
Albahari. Translation by Ellen Elias-Bursać copyright © 1996 by
Northwestern University Press.

CONTENTS

FOREWORD

Ah, the Serbs! Until recently no one knew very much about them in the United States, and now almost everybody has opinions, which like all opinions that have their source in newspapers and television broadcasts, are not only superficial, but often plain wrong. A book of contemporary Serbian stories ought to make things clearer, or more likely, it may make their historical predicament even more baffling for the reader. That is as it should be. The difference between journalism and literature is that the first specializes in simplifying complex issues while the latter makes complex issues even more multifarious. Given the political, religious, and ethnic history of the Balkans, how could it ever be any different?

The primary problem any literature confronts is how to go about representing reality. If that reality includes two world wars, several civil wars (depending on how you count), communism, fascism, nationalism, genocide, and occupation by foreign armies and a dozen other horrors and atrocities to choose from, then the writer is faced not only with an aesthetic, but also a moral problem. To live in such times and to attempt to convey, by whatever literary means one has at one's disposal, what it is like to experience the unimaginable and the unthinkable, is the issue here.

The narrative strategies employed by the writers included in the anthology range between the following two positions:

On one hand, there are writers who roughly continue the long realist tradition, which in Serbia, as elsewhere, had its beginnings in the late nineteenth century. I have in mind here writers like Pavlović, Šćepanović or Mihailović, and a few others, whose stories almost all take place in a

rural setting and are distinguished by a strong feeling for a particular region, its local dialect and customs. They differ from socialist realists of an earlier epoch in that they do not idealize peasant life. In fact, what we have is a violent, blood-and-guts vision of rural life. Theirs is a harsh realism verging on the grotesque. Bad conscience, evil done to the innocent, and powerlessness to change the world are frequent subjects. There's never any doubt in most of these stories that their characters live in a time of astonishing cruelty and injustice. Here's a realism that holds up a funhouse mirror to the world and believes that only its terrifying distortions can be trusted to represent accurately what one has seen and heard.

At the other extreme, we find writers like Pavić, Albahari, Basara, Kiš, Pištalo, Mitrović, Prodanović, and Savić, who practice a Serbian version of magic realism. They mix reality and fantasy in the same story with an irreverence and exhilaration that often reads as a deliberate critique of realism and its claim to tell the truth. These writers have obviously studied and have been influenced by the works of Borges, García Márquez, Schultz, Gombrowicz, Bulgakov, Cortázar, Barthelme, Pyncheon, and Coover. Dream, myth, and folk tale play as much a part in their stories as the experience of living in the city, going to movies, and listening to jazz. Elaborate experiments with form are characteristic of their writing. They've been called postmodernist, and in the last couple of years they have been engaged in a fierce polemic with their counterparts, the so-called traditionalists. The issue, as always in literature, is the choice of tradition, local or foreign, and the divergent ways in which stories can be told. The traditionalists tend to believe in the possibility of an unconscious, native genius, while postmodernists see the writing of stories as a self-conscious act, an act of criticism of the "reality" in realism. Nevertheless, their intention, too, is a more truthful representation of the world they find themselves living in.

Readers of this anthology are lucky to have both. What William Trevor says is true: "Of all literary forms, the short story belongs most unequivocally to the twentieth century." The richness and variety of the stories in this collection may be the result of this polarization and passionate intellectual argument, but is equally due to the amount of sheer talent present on all sides. Regardless of their aesthetic premise, this is a collection of well-told stories that can stand with the best short story collections

anywhere. Danilo Kiš and Milorad Pavić already have international reputations. Svetislav Basara, David Albahari, and a number of others deserve the same. They create literature in the most difficult of historical circumstances and have done so, as we discover here, in many original and memorable ways.

Charles Simic

INTRODUCTION

The genre of the short story has a long and important tradition in Serbian literature. Serbian writers courted this medium before attempting to master the novel, and consequently the novel developed more slowly than the short story in Serbian letters.

The life of the contemporary Serbian short story is associated with the avant-garde journals in which stories are usually published. Consequently, the genre is perceived as a testing ground for new narrative techniques. In that sense, the contemporary Serbian short story is a genuine reflection of contemporary Serbian literature as a whole. Moreover, every author included in this collection has also written poetry or novels or both.

Serbian literature did not experience a revolutionary break with its past traditions, even though it had to exist under a communist regime after World War II. Before the war, there was a strong surrealist movement in Serbia, whose proponents made up the prewar leftist avant-garde. Many of these leftist prewar poets and writers, like Dušan Matić and Marko Ristić, survived the war and were able to take up positions in the postwar literary establishment in Yugoslavia. The political repression that marked other spheres of postwar life made a loop around the arts, and the doctrine of socialist realism never took root in Yugoslavia on the same scale as in the USSR and the other East European countries.

In the wake of Yugoslavia's break with Stalin in 1948, Yugoslav writers began to enjoy greater creative freedom. In subsequent years, a large number of Western literary works were translated and appeared in

Yugoslav journals. Since the 1950s, Yugoslav writers have been able to follow Western literary trends and Western critical theory.

The works of Miodrag Bulatović and Antonije Isaković represent a turning away from the uniformity of themes and styles of the late 1940s and early 1950s. Bulatović combined realistic prose with elements of fantasy, and that freed the author from the requirement of providing realistic descriptions or respecting cause and effect in his narratives. In the 1960s and 1970s, a new trend emerged called the New Style Prose. A synthesis of the traditional and the modern, this prose attempted to present the changes in society by employing the style of documentary realism and by exploiting the language of various milieus and regions as a poetic device. This generation of writers finally consolidated the ties between contemporary Serbian literature and its prewar tradition.

Starting with the mid-1970s, modern Serbian writers have shown a tendency toward subjective prose. Good prose, according to Henry James, reproduces life. Contemporary Serbian writers do not wish to reproduce life, at least not in the traditional fashion. They shun the realistic story. Instead of employing a prose style that relies on observation, a linear narrative, and psychological motivation, they emphasize narrative form itself and the process of narration. Many writers use a technique that spans the real and the imaginary, relying on the language of dreams, lyricism, and the phantasmagoric.

Younger writers, only a few of whom are included in this anthology, are responding to the challenges of modern media and film. They show a preference for the very short, plotless story that has neither a rigid structure nor a fixed stylistic profile.

Ever since the 1960s, the quality of the Serbian prose has been rising steadily. The 1970s and 1980s saw the emergence of several internationally recognized writers: Bulatović, Kiš, Kovač, Pekić, and Pavić. But the group of outstanding talents is much larger than those just named.

Thus the contemporary Serbian short story is characterized by impressive achievements and an astonishing variety. Everyone seems to be telling a story in her or his own way. There is no single dominant model of storytelling. Like contemporary South American literature, Serbian prose today represents a felicitous synthesis in which postmodernist and traditional elements interact. It deserves to be made accessible to a larger Anglophone reading public.

The past always informs the present, and even after so many years, the traumatic events of the last world war weigh heavily on the conscience of the Serbian writers presented in this anthology. The Serbs, numerically a small nation, have experienced a disproportional share of historical tragedies, and the memory of these experiences is assimilated in contemporary literature. The tragedy of the present-day civil war in the former Yugoslavia makes it even more poignant.

While history in this selection is not presented in an objective and epic fashion, it is nevertheless there, internalized and deconstructed on the level of individual protagonists. Events taking place in the Balkans for several years now are presented on international television and newspapers daily. Public curiosity about the Serbs in particular has been fanned by a variety of conflicting media reports on the past and present of the Serbian nation. Stereotyped images have been established about the Serbs in the public consciousness. An anthology of contemporary Serbian short stories may help restore a more realistic and differentiated view about the region and about its present tragic conflict among the reading public.

A majority of the authors selected for the anthology belong to the generation born between around 1930 and 1960. The older writers of the group include those who appeared on the literary scene in the 1960s and became well known, nationally and internationally, in the 1970s and 1980s. The younger ones, who started to publish in the late 1970s, are beginning to gain wide recognition. While the cutoff point is to some extent arbitrary, the editors believe that the present anthology can serve as a continuation of *The New Writing in Yugoslavia*, edited by Bernard Johnson (Baltimore: Penguin Books, 1970). However, even though we have tried to include the most prominent contemporary writers, for a variety of reasons some very well-known writers could not be included.

This project took several years to accomplish, and many individuals deserve credit for it. I first would like to thank my dear friend and co-editor Nadežda Obradović for all of her help, primarily for encouraging me to undertake this work. My thanks also go to all the authors and their families, who granted us free copyright so that this project could be realized. I would like to express my deep gratitude to my colleagues and friends who translated the stories, some more than one. They are Bogdan Rakić, Dragan Milivojević, Stephen M. Dickey, Paul M. Foster, Christina

Pribićević-Zorić, Alice Copple-Tošić, Henry R. Cooper Jr., Ellen Elias-Bursać, Edward D. Goy, Vasa D. Mihailovich, Karolina Udovički, Višeslav Simić, Amanda Blasko, Biljana Šljivić-Šimšić, Anita Lekić, Vida Janković, Ann Clever, Gordana B. Todorović, Robert Gakovich, the late Veselin Šćekić, Snežana Dabić, Darka Topali, Charles Simic, Radmila J. Gorup, and Hallie Stein.

Finally, it has been a pleasure to work with the University of Pittsburgh Press and the editors Catherine Marshall and Jane Flanders.

Radmila J. Gorup

THE PRINCE OF FIRE

Aleksandar Tišma

Aleksandar Tišma (b. 1924) is a poet, prose writer, and essayist. He has published several collections of short stories: *Wrongs* (1961), *Violence* (1965), *Dead Angle* (1973), *Return to Peace* (1977), *The School of Atheism* (1978). His novels are entitled *Following the Black-Haired Girl* (1969), *The Book on Blam* (1972), *Fugitives* (1981), *Oaths and Plots* (1983), *Capo* (1987). *The Wide Door* (1988), and *Those We Love* (1990).

In his best works Tišma successfully accomplishes a synthesis of tradition and modern writing techniques. The essence of his prose is an atypical narrative about typical, ordinarly occurrences, while the historical is always given indirectly and without an epic perspective.

THE WHOLE SELF

True, my uncle was an overproud genius of sorts, but he was not crazy. I say this despite the interpretations the family is wont to dole out with the conventional dispiritedness of those confronting something that transcends the bounds of ordinary understanding. In doing what he did, Uncle was obeying a monstrously overdeveloped conceit and, in my view, an inordinate sense of compassion.

When he was introduced to my aunt, at a party for young ladies during the holidays, she was already engaged to a very ambitious director of a sugar refinery just outside town, a man who would later become a member of Parliament and who, in World War II, would be hanged by the Germans from a post in front of the administration building of the very company he had run so successfully for two decades. Uncle bore no resemblance whatsoever to this adroit businessman, with his quick little eyes and movements. Uncle was a giant of a man, not tall so much as broad-shouldered, with a big head of unruly curly hair that would have made him look quite wild had it not been for the steady, calm, round brown eyes peering out from underneath, between the high arched brow and fleshy cheeks with the short straight nose. He was very quiet, but there really was no need for him to talk much. He told Aunt that he was thinking of abandoning his theology studies in order to devote himself to his "own writing," and he recited a couple of verses of what at the time was modern French poetry, thus enhancing the impression that nature had been so generous in creating. After seeing him several times, Aunt announced to the family that she was breaking off her engagement.

The family found this hard to accept. My grandfather was a wholesaler

and could not imagine having a twenty-year-old theologian for a son-in-law—and that was before he knew that the fellow was planning to leave the priesthood without ever actually joining it. The girl was subjected to the full range of pressures known to the middle classes at the time: she was whisked off to a spa, forbidden to see him, cajoled, threatened, slapped, and her freedom of movement restricted. The pressure continued for four and a half months—all of that summer and early autumn—whereupon Aunt swallowed twenty sachets of sleeping powder. They found her unconscious in her white room upstairs in Grandfather's house, and it took days of stomach pumping, injections, and shock treatment to revive her. The poisoning left her with a damaged and weakened heart for the rest of her short life.

The family was frightened for her, naturally, but then, after the exhausting battle to save the sinful woman's life, they were disgusted by her. They now handed her over to her seducer without objection, discarding her like something that upon first use, as it were, had proved perishable and therefore worthless. Uncle left the seminary and the capital, and rented a room for the two of them on the outskirts of town. Thereafter, and until the end, he supported my aunt by giving foreign language lessons, devoting all his free time to his "own work."

Today it is impossible to say anything specific about that work because Uncle never published any of it, and whatever he had in manuscript he ultimately burned. All we have to rely on, therefore, is what we were occasionally told by Aunt, who, after a certain punitive rupture in relations, was invited back into the homes of some of the more tenderhearted members of the family, including my mother. But even Aunt had no real facts to offer—she was so sure of the worth and future success of Uncle's work that all you could get out of her were exclamations. Did her faith in something that was never to be indicate a certain blindness, even a certain limitation, perhaps? She was no expert on literature, of course, but she did have a good clear head on her shoulders—as absolutely everyone in the family acknowledged—and she was blind only to the extent that she transposed her confidence in Uncle's human worth and character unreservedly onto his deeds. Rightly so, too, in my opinion, because what else lends value to a work if not the character of its creator? There are instances, of course, where the personal element, even when bolstered by a strong will, is not enough, but the exception merely proves the rule.

Given its initial attitude, which it felt it had to justify, the family was

naturally skeptical about Aunt's effusiveness. As an ever present member of the family, I was forced, as it were, to follow from various vantage points how Uncle's work was, or was not, progressing.

In response to my mother's usually repeated invitations, Aunt would come, fragile and beautiful, looking girlishly youthful, despite the pallor caused by her infirmity. She would sit down on the edge of the armchair, casting a dreamy, yearning look over the back of the chair, sipping her café au lait and chatting breathlessly—even animated conversation was a strain on her lungs—and then, often for no particular reason, as if unable to suppress a thought that had been weighing on her mind the entire time, she would burst out with: "Ratko is working on a play now." And then, closing her blue, always slightly wet, compassionate eyes, she would add: "I'm sure it will be wonderful!"

And months or years later, Father would suddenly ask Mother, not without a bite to his words: "What ever happened to that wonderful play of Ratko's?" He did not expect an answer, of course. In the meantime, Aunt had long since stopped mentioning the play, announcing some long story or poem instead.

So much for Aunt. What about Uncle? How did he bear the non-fulfillment of his ideas? That is to say, if he did bear it, because of the grumbling (as he did for nearly fifteen years); was he not then really crazy? I think his silent perseverance shows the opposite to be true. It is maniacs who impatiently, unscrupulously, often even cunningly, push their products—their patents or poems or prophesies—onto the community of normal men, attributing failure to the unreadiness of that same community to accept them, seeking a remedy not within themselves but in the guise of new patrons. Uncle, however, did not foist his writings onto anyone; he never even showed them—except once, and that was the first time and the last and not done for his own sake; no, he himself rejected his writings, all of them, one by one, thus proving himself to have a very critical eye. But why then, if he kept rejecting everything, did he not give up sooner? Again, part of the answer can be found in Aunt's incidental comments, and still more, I think, in her boundless faith as victim and invalid, which left him obligated. "Ratko doesn't care when he will succeed. He doesn't even care whether he will succeed. He just cares about finding the right form in which to express himself."

To express himself. But which self? The self of the apostate and pen-

Aleksandar Tišma

niless language teacher, the self of the uncorrupted worker and uncorrupted husband in the midst of a pack of filthy egotists, the self of the handsome, strapping zealot surrounded by provincial gnomes, or the self of a man helpless in the face of society's needs and those of nature? Probably all of them together, the whole self at once, because Aunt, who kept changing the descriptive genre of his writing, finally began talking about "the work" without indicating anything more, a big book requiring long years of labor.

At this point, the burden of effort that went into this strangely uncommon marriage began to leave visible traces on Uncle himself. He was still enormous, strong, and handsome, even though his mop of hair was streaked with gray—he had passed the thirty-five-year mark. In other words, he was strong and good-looking, but underneath that external frame, that shield of armor, that sculpting, there seemed to be a growing hollowness. He still wore the suits of his youth—he had no money to buy new ones—and though they hung lightly and spotlessly from the unchanged gigantic frame of his body, they looked as if they had been worn so thin from the friction of the same repeated movements that they would disintegrate like cigarette ash. He walked down the street ramrod straight, marching like a wound-up toy soldier, his earthy dark face towering above the heads of passers-by, his big chestnut-colored eyes fixed on a sight visible to him alone. He often failed to recognize us, and we would turn around to look at him.

Aunt alone still saw him that way, but she obviously did not see how others saw her: impoverished and enfeebled by a confined life, a life without respite for the irrevocably captured former beauty. Admittedly, even when the conversation turned to more mundane matters, she did not hide the fact that theirs was a hard life, which meant it was getting harder because of rising costs, because of the dwindling number of students, because of the various formal obstacles the authorities placed in their way. But in describing their difficulties, it was as if she was vaunting them— her eyes shone feverishly bright, her short breath was convulsed with emotion. Ratko works terribly hard. Ratko makes up for lost time at night. Ratko is burning himself out. Masked as concern, was this not the best possible news, a step toward accomplishing the supreme and only important goal?

My aunt's slightly comic courage, by now tedious and even unnoticed

by us, was shattered by a crime. His pupils banged on their teacher's door in vain; the neighbors—whose narrow lives made them suspicious—broke in only to find Aunt in bed with her head smashed, and Uncle, fully dressed, lying on his back next to her bed, with his veins slashed. And lots of blood on the floor and lots of ashes by the stove.

Needless to say, the incident left the public shocked—as anyone can see who cares to leaf through the November 7 and 8, 1938, issues of our local paper, the *Herald*. But the articles—which, while not particularly detailed, were written in the cheapest kind of journalese—also showed a total absence of any real surprise or doubt, a response that was entirely in keeping with my own recollections. For fifteen years, Uncle's haughty yet unfounded ambition had astonished people, and now, in hindsight, it seemed dreadful but natural that the only way this continuing mania could have ended was in the very worst paroxysm of self-destruction. Of course, there was also another victim here: Aunt, who had no eccentricity other than being blind to his; but was that not sufficient to condemn her to ruin as well? In a fit of deep, dark despair, when he decided to cut short his life, this madman dragged down with him whoever was close to him—indeed, the only person close to him: my aunt.

Only one detail jarred slightly with this generally accepted picture, as witness the closing paragraph in the *Herald*'s first report, which mentions the conclusions of the police investigation. There was a certain deliberateness about the scene in which the dead couple was discovered: the woman's head smashed with a single calculated swing of the axe, obviously delivered while she was peacefully asleep; the burning of the papers and slashing of the veins, which requires the utmost resolve on the part of the suicide, because it gives him time to reconsider even after having taken the fatal step. All this seemed to call into question the theory of suicide in a moment of despair, taking the life of the other person as well; it pointed to a different, unknown, but deliberate motive.

But since the facts of the drama and distribution of the roles were so vividly clear, the investigation did not make any detailed examination of what was a purely academic contradiction; in its second report, the *Herald* did not even mention it. It merely published the statements of those questioned: my father and my mother's brother, both of whom enumerated Uncle's offenses, which had been so fatal for my poor aunt; then the neighbors, who talked mostly about the couple's financial straits;

and finally one of Uncle's childhood friends, a singing teacher in the local school, a bachelor and closet alcoholic who had moved to our town long after Uncle and had developed the habit of visiting him every Saturday afternoon, his last remaining friend. He was the only person to offer, apart from general, already known information, something new. Two months earlier, Uncle had entrusted him with a fragment of one of his huge literary works in progress, which he asked his friend to send, under his name, to a publisher he knew for an expert opinion. Four days before the tragedy, the friend had told Uncle of the publisher's negative reply. He told him the news in his own apartment and had returned the manuscript. This detail simply confirmed the accepted view: suicide out of despair, which in a moment of insane resolve had necessitated taking the life of the innocent, peacefully sleeping woman as well.

Many years later, however, I learned from a nephew of that same friend (by then deceased)—the nephew being a man my own age whom I chanced to meet on the coast—one other detail which I think confirms the hypothesis that this had been a crime of mercy—or to be more precise, that Uncle had not been in the grips of anger or despair, with himself as the main target, but rather that his primary goal had been to kill Aunt, with suicide playing only a subordinate role as the by-product of that main act. It was she, not himself, that Uncle wanted to spare the humiliation of failure. Long before the event, he had probably begun to doubt his own ability to accomplish this "all-embracing work"—as shown by his touchingly helpless move to submit it for an opinion under someone else's name. Finally, by the time he had spilled her blood and his own, he had already known the reply for four days. But I have yet to report what detail it was that, during my conversations with the nephew of Uncle's friend—those long evening talks which I arranged apprehensively—leaped out like a white stone popping out of a clenched fist in the dark, shining for a second in the moonlight, only to hit the floor, showing how close all things are to the ground. The detail in question was the fact that the deaths had taken place on the night before Saturday, which was the day of the weekly visit of Uncle's friend, who certainly had no idea of the effect of his news on my aunt and thus might repeat it in front of her.

Now you may wonder: why, instead of killing the woman he faithfully loved, as well as himself, whom she faithfully loved, didn't Uncle

simply ask his friend to hold his tongue and forget the whole story regarding the publisher? The reason, I think, was that he had an overriding inner need for purity. And also perhaps he was afraid of how Aunt would be affected not so much by the news itself as by his own now listless, indifferent acceptance of that news—an acceptance he would be unable to conceal—and she would then have to realize something that hitherto even he had only begun to understand, something he might have been able to bear on his own: that their splendidly sacrificed life was a delusion.

By killing her before she came to realize this, by killing her while she was asleep, he could tell himself that he was finishing something she herself had bravely attempted to do fifteen years earlier, and that by connecting the two acts, hers and his own, into their final irreversible outcome, he was annulling that failure, that delusion shared between them, for which he himself bore the blame.

Translated by Christina Pribićević-Zorić

Aleksandar Tišma

Milorad Pavić

Milorad Pavić (born in 1929 in Belgrade) is the best-known contemporary Serbian prose writer. Pavić is also a poet, as well as expert on the Serbian baroque and symbolist literature, theoretician, translator, university professor, and member of the Serbian Academy of Arts and Sciences.

Pavić began his university career at the Sorbonne and the Jagić Institute for Slavic Philology in Vienna. He currently teaches at the University of Belgrade. Pavić first published his scholarly works and poetry, then moved to prose fiction. He has published ten studies in literary history, several books of poetry and four collections of short stories: *The Iron Curtain* (1973), *Saint Mark's Horses* (1976), *Borzoi* (1979), *New Belgrade Stories* (1981), and *The Inverted Glove* (1989); and five novels: *The Dictionary of the Khazars* (1984), *Landscape Painted with Tea* (1988), *The Inner Side of the Wind* (1991), *The Last Love in Constantinople* (1993), and *The Hat Made of Fish Skin* (1996). In 1993 Pavić published a play, *For Ever and a Day*, which appeared in English in 1997.

Pavić's works are greatly respected both at home and abroad. *Landscape Painted with Tea* was translated into eleven languages, and *Dictionary of the Khazars,* a best-seller in France and England and one of the year's seven best works of fiction in the United States in 1988, was translated into twenty-three. *The Inner Side of the Wind* was published in the United States and several European countries in 1993.

Pavić's prose is characterized by the increasing inclusion of the fantastic into the realistic narrative. This gives an impression of an inexhaustible text and it is highly regarded by writers of hyperfiction.

THE WEDGEWOOD
TEA SET

In the story you are about to read, the protagonists' names will be given at the end instead of the beginning.

At the capital's mathematics faculty, my younger brother, who was a student of philology and military science, introduced us to each other. Since she was searching for a companion with whom to prepare for Mathematics I, we began studying together, and as she did not come from another town as I did, we studied in her parents' big house. Quite early each morning, I passed by the shining Layland-Buffalo car, which belonged to her. In front of the door I would stoop down and look for a stone, put it in my pocket, ring the doorbell, and go upstairs. I carried no books, notebooks, or instruments; everything stayed at her place and was always ready for work. We studied from seven to nine, then we were served breakfast and would continue till ten; from ten to eleven we would usually go over the material already covered. All that time, I would be holding the stone in my hand. In case I should doze off, it would fall on the floor and wake me up before anyone noticed. After eleven she would continue to study, but not I. So we prepared for the mathematics exam every day except Sunday, when she studied alone. She very quickly realized that I could not keep up with her and that my knowledge lagged more and more behind hers. She thought that I went home to catch up on the lessons I had missed, but she never said a thing. "Let everyone like an earthworm eat his own way through," she thought, aware that by teaching another she wasn't teaching herself.

When the September term came, we agreed to meet on the day of the examination and take the exam together. Excited as she was, she didn't have time to be especially surprised that I didn't show up and that I did not take the exam, either. Only after she had passed the exam did she ask herself what had happened to me. But I didn't appear till winter. "Why should every bee gather honey, anyway?" she concluded, but still asked herself sometimes, "What's he up to? He is probably one of those smile-carriers, who buys his merchandise in the East, and sells it in the West, or vice versa . . ."

When Mathematics II was on the agenda, she suddenly met me one morning, noticing with interest the new patches on my elbows and the newly grown hair, which she had not seen before. It was again the same. Each morning I would come at a certain hour, and she would descend through the green and layered air, as if through water full of cool and warm currents, open the door for me, sleepy, but with that mirror-breaking look of hers. She would watch for one moment how I squeezed out my beard into the cap and how I took off my gloves. Bringing together the middle finger and the thumb, with a decisive gesture I would simultaneously turn them inside out, thus taking them both off with the same movement. When that was over, she would immediately go to work. She made up her mind to study with all her strength, which happened daily. With untiring will and regularity, she delved into all details of the subject, no matter if it was morning, when we started out fresh, after breakfast, or toward the end, when she worked a bit more slowly but not skipping a single thing. I would still quit at eleven, and she would soon notice again that I couldn't concentrate on what I was doing, that my looks grew old in an hour, and that I was behind her again. She would look at my feet, one of which was always ready to step out, while the other was completely still. Then they would change positions.

When the January term arrived, she had the feeling that I could not pass the exam, but she was silent, feeling a trifle guilty herself. "Anyway," she concluded, "should I kiss his elbow to make him learn? If he cuts bread on his head, that's his own affair . . ."

When I didn't show up then either, she was nevertheless surprised, and after finishing the exam looked for the list of candidates to check whether I was perhaps scheduled for the afternoon or some other day.

To her great surprise, my name wasn't on the list for that day at all—or any other day, for that matter. It was quite obvious: I hadn't even signed up for that term.

When we saw each other again in May, she was preparing Concrete. When she asked me if I was studying for the exams I had not taken before, I told her that I, too, was preparing Concrete, and we continued to study together as in the old times, as if nothing had happened. We spent the whole spring studying, and when the June term came, she had already realized that I would not appear this time, either, and that she wouldn't be seeing me till fall. She watched me pensively with beautiful eyes so far apart that there was space between them for an entire mouth. And naturally, things were the same once again. She took and passed the Concrete exam, and I didn't even bother to come. Returning home satisfied with her success, but totally puzzled as far as my position was concerned, she noticed that, in the hurry of the previous day, I had forgotten my notebooks. Among them she caught sight of my student's booklet. She opened it and discovered with astonishment that I was not a student of mathematics at all, but of something else, and that I had been passing my exams regularly. She recalled the interminable hours of our joint study, which for me must have been a great strain without purpose, a big waste of time, and she asked the inevitable question: what for? Why did I spend all that time with her studying subjects that had nothing to do with my interests and the exams that I had to pass? She started thinking and came to one conclusion: one should always be aware of what is passed over in silence. The reason for all that was not the exam but she herself. Who would have thought that I would be so shy and unable to express my feelings for her? She immediately went to the rented room where I lived with a couple of people my age from Asia and Africa, was surprised by the poverty she saw, and received the information that I had gone home. When they also gave her the address of a small town near Salonica, she took her Buffalo without hesitation and started off toward the Aegean coast in search of me, having made up her mind to act as if she had discovered nothing unusual. So it was.

She arrived at sunset and found the house she had been told about wide open, with a great white bull tied to a nail, upon which fresh bread was impaled. Inside she noticed a bed, on the wall an icon, below the

icon a red tassel, a pierced stone tied to a string, a top, a mirror, and an apple. A young naked person with long hair was lying on the bed, tanned by the sun, back turned to the window and resting on one elbow. The long ridge of the spine, which went all the way down the back and ended between the hips, curving slightly, vanished beneath a rough army blanket. She had the impression that the girl would turn any moment and that she would also see her breasts, deep, strong, and glowing in the warm evening. When that really took place, she saw that it was not a woman at all lying on the bed. Leaning on one arm I was chewing my moustache full of honey, which substituted for dinner. When she was noticed and brought into the house, she could still not help thinking of that first impression of finding a female person in my bed. But that impression, as well as the fatigue from a long drive, were soon forgotten. From a mirror-bottomed plate she received a double dinner: for herself and her soul in the mirror: some beans, a nut, and fish, and before the meal a small silver coin, which she held, as did I, under the tongue while eating. So one supper fed all four of us: the two of us and our two souls in the mirrors. After dinner she approached the icon and asked me what it represented.

"A television set," I told her. In other words, it is the window to another world which uses mathematics quite different from yours.

"How so?" she asked.

"Quite simple," I answered. "Machines, space crafts, and vehicles built on the basis of your quantitative mathematical evaluations are founded upon three elements, which are completely lacking in quantity. These are: singularity, the point, and the present moment. Only a sum of singularities constitutes a quantity; singularity itself is deprived of any quantitative measurement. As far as the point is concerned, since it doesn't have a single dimension, not width or height or length or depth, it can undergo neither measurement nor computation. The smallest components of time, however, always have one common denominator: that is the present moment, and it, too, is devoid of quantity and is immeasureable. Thus, the basic elements of your quantitative science represent something to whose very nature every quantitative approach is alien. How then should I believe in such a science? Why are machines made according to these quantitative misconceptions of such a short lifespan, three, four or more times shorter than the human ones? Look, I also have a

white 'buffalo' like you. Only, he is made differently from yours, which was manufactured at Layland. Try him out and you will see that in a way he is better than the one you own."

"Is he tame?" she asked, smiling.

"Certainly," I answered. "Go ahead and try."

In front of the door she stroked the big white bull and slowly climbed onto his back. When I also mounted him, turning my back to the horns and facing her, I drove him by the sea, so that he had two feet in the water and the other two feet on the sand. She was surprised at first when I started to undress her. Piece by piece of her clothing fell into the water; then she started unbuttoning me. At one moment she stopped riding on the bull and started riding on me, feeling that I was growing heavier and heavier inside her. The bull beneath us did everything that we would otherwise have had to do ourselves, and she could tell no longer who was driving her pleasure, the bull or I. Sitting upon the double lover, she saw through the night how we passed by a forest of white cypresses, by people who were gathering dew and pierced stones on the seashore, by people who were building fires inside their own shadows and burning them up, by two women bleeding light, by a garden two hours long, where birds sang in the first hour and evening came in the second, where fruit bloomed in the first and there was a blizzard behind the winds. Then she felt that all the weight from me had passed into her and that the spurred bull had suddenly turned and taken her into the sea, leaving us finally to the waves that would separate us . . .

However, she never told me a word about her discovery. In the fall, when she was getting ready to graduate and when I offered to study with her again, she was not the least bit surprised. As before, we studied every day from seven until breakfast and then until half past ten; only now she did not try to help me master the subject I was doing and also stayed after ten-thirty for half an hour, which separated us from the books. When she graduated in September, she wasn't surprised at all when I didn't take the examination with her.

She was really surprised when she did not see me any more after that. Not that day, nor the following days, weeks, or examination terms. Never again. Astonished, she came to the conclusion that her assessment of my feelings for her was obviously wrong. Confused at not being able to tell what it was all about, she sat one morning in the same room in which we

had studied together for years; then she caught sight of the Wedgewood tea set, which had been on the table since breakfast. Then she realized. For months, day after day, with tremendous effort and an immeasurable loss of time and energy, I had worked with her only in order to get a warm breakfast every morning, the only meal I was able to eat during those years. Having realized that, she asked herself another thing. Was it possible that in fact I hated her?

At the end, there is one more obligation left: to name the protagonists of this story. If the reader has not thought of it already, here is the answer. My name is the Balkans. Hers, Europe.

Translated by Darka Topali

Borislav Pekić

Borislav Pekić (1930–1992), one of the most popular writers in Yugoslavia, was born in Podgorica, Montenegro. As a high school student in Belgrade, Pekić was sentenced to fifteen years in jail for his democratic ideas. He served five years. After graduating from the University of Belgrade, he worked as a film script writer. He began to publish in the 1960s, after which he left for London. For the rest of his life, he shared his residence between London and Belgrade.

Pekić was a prolific writer, an immaculate and rich stylist. He left a large opus that includes, in addition to plays and essays, novels and short story collections: *Time of Miracles* (1965), *The Houses of Belgrade* (1970), *The Rise and Fall of Icarus Gubelkijan* (1975), *The Defense and the Last Days* (1977), *How to Quell the Vampire* (1977), *Rabies* (1983), *The Years Devoured by Locusts* (1988), *The Golden Fleece* (1978–1986), *The New Jerusalem* (1988), and *Atlantis* (1990).

Pekić was a member of the Serbian Academy of Arts and Sciences. His works appeared in many world languages. *The Time of Miracles* and *The Houses of Belgrade* were published in English in 1976 and 1978.

MEGALOS MASTORAS
AND HIS WORK

1347 A.D.

> The Muses gave us one more life,
> Only let us not praise them to excess,
> From one illusion creating two.
>
> Anonymous Greek poet

There are some men whose lives are traces of hot iron impressed into the ground. Wherever they walk, the ground burns beneath their feet. Long after they have passed, the smoke of scorched earth still hurts one's eyes. Each resembles a star, the birth of which we see—but do not hear —millions of years after it has gone out. The death of an old sun resembles the birth of a new one; the death of such a man is always the birth of something new and unknown.

They are creatures of Fire. Fire is their Element. It is their nature and destiny.

Demetrios Kyr Angelos, *kallitechnes*—an artistic woodcarver from Alea, the ancient Arcadian Tegea, on the Peloponnesus, was one such man. His legend lives on anywhere Greeks live, from Epiros in the north to Crete in the south. And in the Woodcarvers' Guild it can be heard in the shabbiest workshops in the dying Hellenic colonies of Ionia. Had he belonged to a more humble, less proud race, it might not have survived so long. But since the fall of Constantinople in 1453, when the protectress of the last Roman Empire, Divine Mother Maria Theotokos, abandoned them to the Mohammedan infidels, the Byzantines, like the ancient Israelites,

have preserved their history and lived it in their hearts, where no one can find it or persecute them because of it. Along with it, in their secret hearts, they keep rare tales that preserve their frozen history far below another, alien one.

All conquerors hope to write palimpsests, but rarely does one succeed in playing the Creator and beginning the world from Alpha to Omega. No matter how one scrapes the parchment, something inherited from an earlier life always remains. Defeated peoples live on, like cryptograms. Through that which is seen, deep under the contours and marks of a visible history there flows the invisible history of extinct races and dead tribes, which knows no end.

Thus was preserved the tale of Demetrios Kyr Angelos, the master woodcarver from Tegea.

All that remains of Tegea, the birthplace of Atalanta, heroine of the Argonauts and the divine illegitimate daughter of Artemis, are some excavated ruins scattered over a plateau in the heart of the Peloponnesus. And memories of the glorious battles with the Persians at Thermopylae and Plataea, as well as more shameful memories of the Peloponnesian wars at Leuktra and Mantinea, in which the Tegeans first participated on the side of the Spartans, and later against them. In the fifth century A.D., Alaric's Goths destroyed Tegea, but the Byzantines rebuilt it under the name Nikli. The resurrected city was the business center of Morea at that time. During the Latin invasion, in 1202, it was the location of the barony of the crusader Geoffroy de Villehardouin. Today the town bears the name of Alea. I have kept the oldest of the names, since the tale has something of the charm of the old Gothic sagas.

As in other tales that exist in more than one version, our story—like all good tales of old—strives to include events that, strictly speaking, do not belong in it, since they cross over into the domain of other legends. (It is as if someone wanted to tell the entire past in one and the same narrative breath, or as if the forced unification of unconnected images were the product of the past itself, when it returns and speaks for itself—thus resembling a naïve writer, who, in an attempt at all-inclusiveness, embellishes a tale with everything of any importance in life; soon, forced to choose, he realizes the impossibility of creating such a tale, not so much because there are too many diverging paths, but because they are mutually exclusive—one path deprives another of its significance—and so he

finishes with the even more naïve conviction that none is of any real importance, and his universal story remains the blank sheet of paper he began with.) Nevertheless, in this story one can discern elements that undoubtedly belong to Kyr Angelos's artistic career. And given a little patience and familiarity with the monstrous Latin-Ottoman-Byzantine structures of the fourteenth century, these elements can be sifted out of the apocryphal residue of time and the Greek tradition of exaggeration.

We will not be concerned with the archeological evidence. *Megalos mastoras,* the great master of woodworking, whose works would be prized possessions in the chambers of Hellenic aristocrats inhabiting the Fanari quarter of Constantinople, and who worked conscientiously for all—the heathen sultan's harem, the Latin usurpers, and the Regency of Christ in the Patriarchate—with an exalted freedom and unconcern stemming from his God-given talent, represents an accidental, incidental find in the course of my research in preparation for writing *The Golden Fleece.*

We will accept as truth all that I heard at the Hagios Nikolaos (Saint Nicholas, a church not far from the ruins of the temple of Athena in Alea) from an old monk, a hermit who went blind seeking the still unknown sins of his people, who had at first brought the Latins and then the Turks to the Greek Hellespont. Why would I choose, from among more believable, sober, and even more reliable tales I heard during a long fasting dinner in the cell of Father Pamphilios, to remember the most unusual and improbable? When the tale no longer belongs only to Kyr Angelos's life (whatever it may have been) but also to me, his first and undoubtedly his only biographer, you will understand my reasons more clearly.

At the beginnings of art, when it still possessed some meaning, the only people who knew how and who were allowed to tell stories were prophets and temple priests. At that time, tales came from the gods. They were messages transformed into the Word. Eternal and unchanging, they determined the lives of men. When the gods fell silent, the prophets and priests continued for some time to speak in their name. But the tales no longer had the power of destiny. They became false, although they had a certain charm lent to them by the falsehoods that lived on, which became the art of storytelling.

I heard things from Father Pamphilios of the Hagios Nikolaos that I had never heard from anyone else, although all other experts on Kyr

Angelos's life, including the curators of the museums in Alea and Athens, agreed that there was a mystery connected with the master's death.

His death was a long and painful one, but a joyful one as well, which is a contradiction. His last days were spent in a chair of his own making, although he had not yet reached an age that required rest; this is also a contradiction. He refused to confide in anyone about the reasons for his odd behavior, nor did he go into the details if anybody bothered him about it—which for the Greeks is more than a contradiction. When he died, he was cremated together with his chair, and I do not know how to characterize that.

Let the story speak for itself.

It was the Year of Our Lord 1347. A hundred and six more would pass before the fall of Constantinople and the demise of the Holy Byzantine Empire, and one hundred and forty-five more before the voyage of Christopher Columbus, which would open up the western routes to silver and gold.

But before Europe would be seized by "gold fever," she would have to survive another illness, fearfully called the Black Plague.

When, according to the Franciscan Michele de Piazza, twelve Genoese galleons brought the plague from Constantinople to Messina in Sicily in October 1347, it was not yet black. The putrid flesh of the sick did not darken. Rather the body, especially the face and lips, turned blue, and the French were correct when they named it *La mort bleue,* the Blue Death. The term *black* certainly came from a black comet which, heralding the demise of the Second Roman Empire, happened to be crossing the European sky at that time, or from a literal translation of the vulgate *atra mors.* The word *ater* denoted something black, later horrible or terrifying. The poetic color supplanted the other figurative meanings, but it told as little about the plague as each of its other names.

In 1333, fifteen years before Kyr Angelos's story begins, a terrible disaster struck ancient Cathay. All five elements—Fire, Water, Earth, Metal, and Air—turned on the yellow race. A drought in the form of a gaunt woman with dry breasts, who nourished herself with her own flesh, devastated the fertile valleys of the Kiang and Hoai, while heavy clouds gave birth to multitudes of locusts that utterly ravaged the regions of Houkuang and Honan. The Chin Chou mountain fell apart; another, Ki Ming Chan, dissolved, leaving in its place a lake formed by the

tears of dying dragons. Under the city of Canton, the earth spoke with a terrible voice, which no one could understand.

The misfortune then descended on India. A Flemish priest, informed by a friend from the papal curia in Avignon, described it thus: "At first everyone heard a music very pleasant to the ear, the source of which no one could determine. But then disaster struck. A storm raged for three days. On the first day, rats, frogs, locusts, snakes, lizards, and scorpions fell from the sky like rain. On the second day, thunder was heard: red-hot stones, riding on bolts of lightning, struck the earth. On the third day, the sky burst into flames and burned every remaining man and beast."

On the twenty-fifth of March 1345, at one o'clock in the afternoon, Saturn, Jupiter, and Mars converged in Aquarius. Those with any knowledge of the stars shuddered with fear. The convergence of Saturn and Jupiter brought death, that of Mars and Jupiter pestilence.

The greater events of history tend to overshadow the smaller ones, although lives of men, and sometimes even history itself, depend on those small, insignificant events. While Cathay and India suffered the catastrophe described in the reports of the Flemish monk, one man fell ill at the mouth of the Ganges. By profession he was a sailor, an adventurer—a merchant when he was able, when not, a pirate—but where he had come from, and on what ship he had arrived before he fell ill, no one knew. He was burning with fever and started raving. In his delirium he spoke of a foreigner who had hired him and who was black. But no one could find out whether the man himself was black or only wore black clothes. Purulent welts soon covered his body, and when they burst he died in agony, without revealing the name of his employer or saying anything else about him.

The workshop, *ergasterion,* had two rooms. The larger one in front, which one entered from a stone porch under a lush arbor, was where the assistants, journeymen, and apprentices worked; until two years before, Demetrios Kyr Angelos had also worked there. In the smaller room at the back, since then called with exaggerated pride the atelier, finished products awaited their commissioners.

Kyr Angelos had been locked in that back room for a few hours when the oldest assistant, Enas, knocked on the door cautiously, barely touch-

ing it, although even that was strictly forbidden. Whenever the master withdrew into his *ergasterion,* he was not to be disturbed with worldly matters, not even if someone in the house were dying. Death is also a worldly matter. Death more than anything else. Death is in fact the only thing that is certain to happen. It is always to be expected. Only art is spared from that reduction to insignificance. And art was taking place in the locked atelier of master Kyr Angelos.

"As if he were Skopas chiseling the wise owl for the Temple of Athena Alea," Enas thought, enraged by that act, which was not only artistic but ritualistic as well! He was dying of curiosity. Since Kyr Angelos had begun locking himself in his room two years before, no one had entered the master's cacodemonic atelier or knew what kind of commission he was working on.

All they could hear were noises. The *hylikon,* the divine material, defended its original form; wood strove to keep the shape given to it in Genesis. God apparently considered His work impeccable, and certainly there was nothing about it that could be improved. "Thou shalt not make unto thee any graven image" was God's commandment, one of the ten, the purpose of which was—naturally—to protect His authority and also His creative dignity, to protect His work, the divine art. It seems that Kyr Angelos did not hold the latter in high esteem. What for the Creator was finished, complete, and perfect, was for the master only material from which one should fashion something truly good, complete, and perfect. The will of man defied that of God, the divine will resisted that of man—just as the Byzantine will resisted the Latin, just as the Orthodox spirit could not bear the Roman Catholic precepts that the Frankish West had been pushing on them for two centuries already. And the noises from the atelier stemmed from that same battle of two powerful, opposed wills.

Unfortunately, they revealed nothing. Not even Enas's practiced ear could determine from them the shape or purpose of the object. Even haughty iconographers, who created the holiest of images, for which, in the Golden Age of Byzantium, fratricidal wars were waged and men were mutilated in the imperial hippodrome—both those for and against—did not object to showing their work before it was finished.

And a painter is *kallitechnes*—an artist! He does not belong to *technites*—the artisans—like Demetrios Kyr Angelos!

Enas knocked louder. Or at least he thought he did. The man standing behind him was not of the same opinion. He kicked the door with his dusty riding boot. He was nobly dressed and so was presumably permitted to behave that way, Enas concluded, withdrawing to a safe distance from the forbidden chamber.

The door opened just enough for one to see Kyr Angelos's rough fingers, broken fingernails, dirty face, and elderly grumpiness—nothing else. When he saw the visitor, his fingers and nails remained the same, but the grumpiness disappeared from his face and was replaced by an expression of bored indifference.

"*Eseis eiste*—Is it you?" he asked, and slipped through the crack of the door, gaunt, fatigued by work, dirty. He closed the door and locked it; now he could offer the visitor some hospitality.

"Let's go to the porch. We'll talk there."

His stern glance put the workshop back to work. The woodcarvers' tools began to draw angry, rebellious sounds from the wood, sounds that had been hidden in it while the tree was still only a seed, from which it had grown quietly and peacefully year after year until it was as tall as God wished, knowing nothing of the great artistry that would kill it.

"It's noisy in the workshop."

"I didn't come to talk, sir. I've been sent to take a look," said the man.

"Well, we'll get to that, too," Kyr Angelos answered, and he went out on the porch.

The visitor, if he wished to get what he wanted, had no choice but to follow him.

In the shade of the porch there was a long, narrow oak bench with palmetto carvings along the edges, the Seven Deadly Sins carved into the seat (which did not make it very comfortable), and curved legs in the shape of lion's paws. It had not been intended for outside use. Kyr Angelos's grandfather had made it in the crude and heavy Gothic style for a vagabond crusader in Geoffroy de Villehardouin's entourage. That follower of Christ had been on his way to the Holy Land and the tomb of the Savior, but found that he liked Greece better, although it was full of holy pagan graves. In the meantime, the Latin lord was strangled; he made it to some sort of grave, at least. And no one ever came for the damned bench.

"Please sit down."

"*Eycharisto*—thank you, but I did not come to sit."

"I know. You came to take a look."

Without regard for good manners, Kyr Angelos sat down. Finally, the visitor sat as well. He frowned.

"Is it hard?"

"Anything is softer than a saddle after three days on horseback."

"This bench was made for the Frankish dogs. And their damned drinking bouts last all night long. Imagine, sir, spending the night on such a chair."

"Kyr Angelos, I won't count last year, but this is the third time I've come this year. You said it would be ready by winter. I came, but it wasn't. You promised you would finish by spring. But it was not ready in the spring. You swore it would be ready by summer. Now it's summer. Is it ready?"

"No."

"I can't return to my master and tell him that."

"So what are you planning to do? Will you retire, or find some other line of work?"

The visitor controlled himself. He could not believe that this *katharma* —this trash, this old fool was mocking him. The old man knew with whom he was talking, as well as who his master was; he had simply not understood him.

"Kyr Angelos, are you working on it at all?"

"I haven't been doing anything else."

"I spoke with your assistant Enas."

"Then you know."

"I don't know anything, sir. Nobody knows anything. Nobody in the workshop knows what you're doing behind that locked door."

"I'm working on your commission."

"*Isos*—maybe. But maybe not. Maybe you're working on something for someone else."

"I've been commissioned to make something that no one in the world has. And in order to create something like that, one has to make something that no one has made before."

"And that's what you're doing?"

"Yes. For the second year already."

"In that time you could've furnished an entire court."

Megalos Mastoras *and His Work, 1347* A.D.   25

"Maybe—but not with pieces like *this*."

"Like what?"

"Like what I'm making for your lord."

"May I see it?"

"I said I'm working on it, not that it's finished."

The visitor got up. Kyr Angelos also rose, with effort.

"If I return and tell him what you've said, he will come for his commission himself. Do you know what that means, sir?"

"I do."

"And that doesn't worry you?"

"Why should it worry me?"

"It doesn't mean anything to you?"

"I've lived long enough."

"Don't think only about yourself. Think about your family."

"I don't have any."

"Then think about Tegea, your city."

"It's not my city."

The visitor hesitated.

"I'm going to ask you something, sir. I hope I'll get a sincere answer."

"If I happen to have one, I'll give it to you."

"Are all artists such rogues?"

"No, sir. Only the very great ones."

The visitor looked at him. In his glance there was surprise, at which he himself (a man used to all sorts of people) was surprised as well; there was also amazement, disbelief, and even a certain admiration. His next look, more indifferent, was directed toward the workshop where the noble wood at times creaked harshly, at others chanted soothingly, depending on the condition it was in, whether it had already submitted to the new form desired by Kyr Angelos, or whether it still lamented its original, divine form. His third look, pitiful, was aimed down over the wall on the city—a summer shower was washing its dilapidated, dirty roofs. Then he turned and left without a word, upright, slim, clothed in black.

Before he reached the gate, he was obscured by the heavy rainfall.

When the hoof beats of his black horse faded away, Kyr Angelos returned to his atelier and resumed work.

At summer's end, in the Year of Our Lord 1347, Kyr Angelos still had no good reason for not having finishing the commission. The black emissary insisted on seeing what progress had been made, what Kyr Angelos had accomplished, if he had accomplished anything at all, if he had even begun the commission. He threatened to contact the authorities in Alea or Mistras and to accuse him of breaking a contract.

"What accursed authorities?" Kyr Angelos wondered. Hardly any existed. Just two years before, one could still spit from the Peloponnesus across the Corinthian gulf and hit the barbarians, the Serbian spearmen who were spreading the tribal crown of Nemanjić all the way down to the Aegean coast! In Athens, in all of Attica, the heart of Hellenism, reigned the thieving Castilian kingdom of Mistras! And all around, on land and sea, there were marauding bands of Ottomans.

But the more he thought about the threat, the more Kyr Angelos became unsettled. The civil war between the great *domestikos* Ioannis Kantakouzenos and those who defended the divine right to the throne of the Palaiologos had just ended; the usurper had just been crowned emperor of all Byzantium; the land had just returned to some sort of peace. The civil authorities in Morea had still not recovered, and authorities are most dangerous when they are insecure. An agitated government is like a rabid dog. The treasuries were empty, prices were high, and taxes went uncollected for years. *Nekrike dulia*—the work of the devil! If the hungry state got hold of him, his workshop would go bankrupt.

"*Poli kalo*—very well, sir." He did not know the visitor's name, or that of his master, for that matter. "I see that I can't convince you that a work still not completed is less finished than one that has not been started. But you are not an artist, and I can't expect you to understand this. Come with me."

He unlocked his secret workshop, let the visitor inside, crossed himself, entered, and then locked the door behind them.

The room was shadowed in a soft half darkness and illuminated by a pearly light from two tall, narrow windows in the stone wall.

At first, the guest could see nothing. Then certain gray shapes appeared in the shadows, becoming darker and more distinct. He discerned a dowry chest leaning against a wall, with the classical scene of the wedding of Ulysses' son Telemachus and Nausikaa carved into it; a smooth-topped table in the shape of a Spartan shield supported by four water

nymphs, each with fins instead of feet; chairs and benches of different sizes, styles, fashions, from a Greek *klismos* and a massive Roman podium to portable tables that (due to lack of furniture) one carried along on visits, and which were sometimes combined with collapsible beds. He noticed several pieces of furniture that he had never seen before, the purpose of which he could only guess by their shapes. But even in the half darkness he immediately recognized the artistic beauty of those pieces, covered with a thin layer of summer dust.

He did not find what he was looking for.

Kyr Angelos lit the lamps in the consoles along the walls. The visitor saw the master's work in still greater splendor, but not the object that he had come so far to see.

"*Iste pragmatika kallitechnes*—you're truly an artist, Kyr Angelos," the visitor said, looking around. "I admit that I don't really understand beauty. All these things, beautiful or ugly, are not very useful to a man whose service to a lord without a home keeps him constantly on the road. But I can feel it."

"Doesn't your lord have a palace?"

"No. And he doesn't need one."

"And is it true that no one knows where he's from?"

"Some say he came from the east, but that's just talk."

"And where is he staying now?"

"In Constantinople. You've probably heard about that."

"I have. I had relatives there," said Kyr Angelos. "Will he soon be traveling again?"

"In October he's planning on going to Messina."

"Messina is crowded, rich, lavish, magnificent. "

"He likes crowded cities. Empty places terrify him. Unless, of course, you don't finish in time."

"And if I don't?"

"He'll visit Tegea. He won't be happy about the detour; that will delay his business in the West. But what can be done? I see that he'll have to come for his commission himself."

"Why?"

"Because, sir, I don't see it," the visitor answered sharply. "Because I don't see his commission."

Kyr Angelos hesitated only a moment; an idea that would torture him

during the coming months came to him softly, and he said, "You're stand-ing in front of it, *Kyrie*."

The object to which the master was pointing had confronted the vis-itor before, but only then did he recognize what it was—a chair.

In fact, it was not quite a chair, but something that might sooner or later become a chair, if work on it continued. For now, the only features that pointed in that direction were a back with closed sides and a roughly carved seat, whereas the rear part of the seat and the four legs were still held captive in the formless wood, which resembled a tree stump more than anything else. Around it, amid splinters and shavings, there lay a few chisels and cutting tools of various shapes and sizes.

"This?" asked the guest.

"Yes."

The visitor paced around the partial creation, looked at it carefully from all sides, touched whatever there was to touch, running the tips of his fingers in places over the thin, smooth surface of the wood, in others over the still unstripped bark that chafed them, and then stood up.

"I thought this was a stump that you rest on after work. But if this is what you agreed to make, then I am certain that my lord will have to come for the chair himself when it's ready, if it ever is. I can't take this to him."

"We didn't agree upon anything definite. He wanted the best chair in the world, and that's what he'll get."

Two years before, a mere oak stump from Dodona had stood here. Kyr Angelos was not a pagan. He did not believe that the Dodonian oak would repeat the miracle that had forced the stern of the ship Argo, which had been carved from the same wood, to speak with the bovine voice of Hera. The miracle would be the work of his hands. He took the hardest wood, Zeus's wood, because he knew that working in soft wood, no matter how skilled the hands, no matter how good the tools, did not offer the resistance necessary for great art. Soft wood, after enough work, reaches the point where nothing more can be touched, let alone a flaw corrected, without the whole piece falling apart. Oak, when it is brought to that point, when it reaches the limits of transformation beyond which even the slightest change destroys its beauty, remains—forever.

(I didn't make a chair, he thought, I sculpted a chair, *yomari*—you ass!)

"Although I spend my life on the go, I know that there are various

kinds of chairs. I've seen many of them in my travels. But I've never seen anything like this. Whose style is it in?"

"Mine," Kyr Angelos answered rudely.

During the reign of Empress Irene, the visitor had stood in the antechamber of a painter who was dying from the plague and listened to him as he raved. He was squabbling with God about whether it was permissible to paint icons. Around that time the Lord himself had settled the argument, granting victory to the Orthodox Church, which allowed the painting of saints' images, but this artist was an independent soul. He considered it to be a violation of the inexpressible essence of heaven. Spitting blood, he tried to prove to God that he had done great harm to himself. He wanted to bring him into the camp of the iconoclasts at any price.

"I thought these things are assembled from several pieces of wood."

"Did Phidias assemble Poseidon from several pieces of marble?"

"His Poseidon was a sculpture, sir."

"And my chair is a sculpture, sir."

"Oh, really?" the visitor responded caustically.

When he and his master had sought a woodcarver in Constantinople, they were told that the best woodcarver in the whole empire, and in all of Europe, was certainly Demetrios Kyr Angelos. No one had told them he was not talented or that he was *trellos anthropos*—a lunatic. Or maybe in the world of art both are the same recommendation, only expressed differently?

"If you want me to be completely honest, I'm not even doing that."

"No?"

"I'm only freeing it from the excess wood. I'm discovering it in this stump."

"You don't say!"

"The chair has been here forever, only without my help it can't get out."

"It can't?"

"No."

What would this *phantazmenos,* when he lay dying, argue with his Creator about? Probably something about his being sloppy and building the world out of poor materials, especially the flora, the material of which hinders chairs from coming out of stumps without the help of great talents!

"Do you intend to carve the arms in any particular fashion?"

"No."

"Will the legs end in animal paws, as on chairs in Frankish and Latin cities?"

"No."

"Then at least a design will be carved in its back?"

"No."

"Forgive my ignorance, sir," the visitor said impatiently, "which has been spared because the chair is not finished, and because it looks more than anything like the stump of a tree that's been struck by lightning, but what is it you're doing? What exactly is your style?"

"Sit down and you'll see," the master answered.

The visitor looked at the dusty unfinished seat. He hesitated. It would not have helped to brush away the dust, and the insolent master gave no sign that he would do it. He tucked his light traveler's *chlamyda* under his arm and boldly sat down. He adjusted himself in the chair, although he knew that this would rub the accursed dust into his cloak. He would have to tell his lord something when he returned. He could report little about the beauty of the form of the *object*—it was still too early to call it anything else—about what the "chair" looked like. But if he tried it out, he might be able to say what it was like to sit in it.

"*Ti lete ya auto*—What do you think?"

"It's comfortable," he admitted.

"Well, that's it," master Kyr Angelos told him.

That was his style.

And the visitor finally understood that much. It was harder to explain to him that it was time to go, because it was getting dark and the Morean roads had already been open graves for years.

Kyr Angelos almost had to lift him physically from the chair.

That summer was unbearably hot. But the heat did not merely descend from the yellow, blazing sky, as usual. It also rose up from the ground, which was warm from the bonfires designed to repel the plague, which had spread deep into the Peloponnesus. Everywhere people were dying, over a period of three to five days. Everywhere except for Tegea. For the time being, the Tegeans bore the heat and feared that the blue disease would finally reach them as well.

Kyr Angelos knew that it would not. Not yet. Not until he finished his work, *aristurgima*—his masterpiece. No one in the workshop knew what his certainty was based on, except maybe on artistic pride, but they all were ready to believe him, praying to God that he would never finish what he was working on, his masterpiece.

Unfortunately, everything comes to an end, and Kyr Angelos was where every artist longs to be, loathing the hour in which it will inevitably come.

He was almost done.

The sharp, loud, impatient noises from two years before—which bore witness to the fact that blows from a chisel, no matter how they are inflicted, cannot harm the desired form, that the wood only casts off excess layers of material, in which the future beauty is hidden—had been replaced by gentle, cautious, brief strokes with a plane between long, silent pauses.

Only the experienced Enas knew that behind the locked door there was a *mysterion,* a secret unfolding, which was holy for art, like what happens for the faith when a black curtain is lowered over the *iconostasis* to hide the miracle of turning wine to the blood of Communion. Until then, no matter what the master had been working on, there had not been an object. There had only been dead wood and a form that resembled an object.

There behind the door, as behind the black altar drapery, the wood came to life. Until then, every well-placed blow with the chisel had led to the object, and an ill-placed blow could be corrected; from then on, every blow had to be carefully planned, since the slightest mistake would return the object to nonexistence. That was not a physical nothingness; the object would remain but would no longer be able to be what it had been without that unnecessary blow—the only and final form of God-given essence. Equal to itself, formed by itself. *Aristurgima*—a masterpiece.

Enas was acquainted with the suffering of the artist, especially since he always made that ill-placed blow. And he became aware of it only too late, when he had already made the fatal error without which the piece would have been perfect. Kyr Angelos also noticed it, of course. The uninitiated customers never did. Not even the collectors. And there was no use in trying to explain to them. Because of the inaccessible secret behind the

locked door, which could not be discovered by study or practice—one either had it or not—Enas was reconciled to the fact that he would be a good, perhaps even renowned woodcarver, but he would never, never be *megalos mastoras* Demetrios Kyr Angelos.

In the master's progress toward the final form, the nature of which Enas did not know and which he could follow only from the sounds of the master's tools, there was an inexplicable flaw. It upset him. It did not agree with what his experience had taught him. It occurred after the last visit of the servant from Constantinople.

He kept noticing a certain freedom in his master's movements—almost carelessness—from the time the work started. The sounds of his chisel became accelerated, sudden, and even impatient. The condition of the object, which, after almost two years of labor, had to be nearing its final, untouchable form, could not in principle allow for such rashness. Mistakes had become irreparable.

This could only mean that Kyr Angelos had attained such mastery that his movements did not come from him, but from *thia didaskalia,* the divine teaching, from God himself, who directed them and who could make no error no matter how fast he worked. (The scant six days of Genesis were, after all, sufficient proof of this fact.) In the last three weeks, however, his work had slowed, stabilized, and now it again resembled the tedious caution that a mortal artist, even the greatest, had to obey during the completion of a work.

Enas dared to devote himself to these idle reflections. There was little work to be done, and what there was could be performed by any carpenter. Fearing the plague, customers no longer came from distant lands. Civil wars had emptied the coffers of even the richest Greeks and Latins, and the disease made them disinclined to spend money on such luxuries. After they stopped burying people individually and began covering them with lime and throwing them into mass graves, no one cared any longer whether he would die in a bed made by Kyr Angelos's anointed hand or on a doormat woven by an unskilled peasant. No one cared how he died, because everyone died in the same way; all that mattered was how one lived until that time.

There was a bankrupt silence in the workshop. Since the master had also quit working, there was nothing to be heard except the crackling of

fires in the distance at the crossroads in Tegea and the screams of vultures hurrying after the plague through the burning sky.

During the night the sky cooled. Tegea fell into a deep, deathlike sleep. The workshop also slept. Kyr Angelos sat on the porch, on the uncomfortable Frankish bench of his grandfather, and watched the flickering glow of the city fires, waiting.

It was believed that fire not only repelled the plague, but also betrayed its presence. In the proximity of the plague flames would die down, no matter how well stoked or fueled. Between fire and the plague—*limos* (in the vulgate, *panukla*)—there existed an apocalyptic, blood relation, whose roots were to be found in the Revelation of John. In the family of human miseries, war had brought fire, which had thrown the world into chaos. Chaos in turn gave birth to hunger, and also plague. Death came at last to unite them. However, as in every family, certain inexplicable conflicts were at work, which their common blood could not mitigate. Although their goals were the same—the only difference being that plague afflicts men, while fire destroys both men and objects—they hated each other. No one could expect much from their hatred, but that was all one could do except trust in God.

Before dawn, while it was still dark, a wind started up; the leaves stirred. *Pirkaya*—the fires—died down. Kyr Angelos paid no attention. Before sunrise the flames always weakened. The city watchmen and volunteers, who maintained the fires, would finally forget their duties and fall asleep.

At first he heard *diavlos,* the double flute, as if at that late time of night a shepherd was leading his sheep down the mountain. Even then, he did not get upset. But when he heard hoofbeats, he knew that the time had come for him to part with his *aristurgema*. He had not really made the decision. He left it for God to help him in this matter.

But God was silent.

The horses stopped before the gate. Since he had finished the chair, the gate had not been locked. It opened without creaking and a rider entered. The man behind him led in his own horse, closed the gate, and helped the rider to dismount.

Kyr Angelos got up from the bench.

He knew one of the visitors well. The other he had seen only once,

two years before, when they had negotiated the commission. The man was wearing the black suit of an aristocrat, without ornament or embroidery, without anything superfluous. His black apparel accented the weariness on a face of indefinite age. The moonlight touched it like a thin mask of plaster. *Anthropos apo allo kosmo*, thought Kyr Angelos—a man from the other world!

"Is my commission ready?"

The customer spoke Greek, but one could not tell where he came from by his accent. It was perfect, as if belonging to no particular region, or to all at once.

"*Malista*—it is, sir."

Kyr Angelos lit a torch and led his guest through the workshop, where his journeymen and apprentices were sleeping. The servant remained in the courtyard with the horses.

As he passed, the guest brushed the sleeping Enas with his boot, but he did not awaken. He only groaned painfully and turned his face to the other side.

Kyr Angelos ushered the guest into his chamber, locked the door behind them, and lit the torches in the consoles.

The *ergasterion* was half empty. Most of the objects in it had been removed. Along the walls, covered with heavy cloths, there were a few pieces of furniture whose purchasers had died.

Kyr Angelos stood there, hesitating. God kept silent. He was left to himself. He had spent two years on his work. He would never make anything like it again. He could not, even if he wanted to. Such things can be accomplished only once in a lifetime, and very few people achieve even that much. How many great masters are there who are never granted the creation of their own masterpieces?

The Peloponnesus was dying. The population of Constantinople had been reduced by two-thirds. And in Attica there were not even enough people to light the fires. Galleys waited in ports; thinking they were transporting the treasures of Greece, their crews instead ferried the pestilence over to Sicily and Sardinia, to Italy and Spain. He should rejoice at that. Latin papists would rot alive, just like the Greek Orthodox. But he did not rejoice. He felt no particular pity for them, but he did not rejoice, either.

It was not the material he was concerned about. He was not short of

Dodonian oak. There were other kinds of oak as well, even more precious. There was plenty of better wood. As for those rare, magic, blessed moments when everything comes easily—there would be such moments again. But one such moment could not replace another. One masterpiece could not replace another. Each one was special, a world in itself.

A few days before, he had gone to Mistras. He could not help it. He had delivered a table to a lover of antiquities who was ill with the plague. The man would never sit at that table. But he still wanted to see it before he became delirious and lost his aesthetic sense. He saw the table and died—more calmly than others, in less pain than he would have been without his table.

He would have to make up his mind. The gentleman in black was not hurrying him. But he certainly expected to see the object that had cost him so many ducats and two years of waiting.

The man was standing in the middle of the chamber, illuminated by torchlight that did not warm his face. The light reflected off his face, leaving it cold, tired, and sad. But most of all tired. For a man without a home, an *axenatos,* a wanderer, on the road, fatigue and even sorrow were nothing unusual.

Kyr Angelos started reluctantly toward the wall. Both he and God had a few moments to make their decisions. God—whether to help him; he—what to do.

This was his only true masterpiece. And his final one, because every masterpiece is a finality. Otherwise it is not truly great.

This was not the first, and certainly not the last plague epidemic. Before this one, another had broken out in Arabia and Egypt in 542, and had spread as far as Britannia. During the rule of the departed Emperor Justinian, people had died of the plague just as they were dying now. And they died even before that. Pericles had witnessed one epidemic, only he did not know what to call it. The world had survived. Even at that early time, people thought it meant the end of the world. Each time, people thought it was the end of the world. Many people died, it is true, the cities became empty, the cemeteries overcrowded, and only the wind traveled the roads, but the world had not become a desert. After a few decades everything returned to normal, and everything was as before. And even more people were born into the world than before the pestilence. To make a man, of course, one does not need any particular gift.

Everyone does it without bothering much about the quality of the product. Criminal and tsar, sage and fool are all born without concern for how their makers' talent influences the outcome. That's not art! Certainly not great art!

He could not do otherwise, he had to extend his arm toward his work and finally remove the cover from it.

A torch, poorly fixed, fell from the bronze mouth of a console. God has spoken, the carver thought delightedly, as he ran to it, picked it up from the floor, and placed it back in the console. He wiped his sooty hands against his robe, giving the Lord more time to explain his message, to tell him what to do.

However, it was apparently not God who needed more time. He had, it seemed, created this moment for Kyr Angelos and left him to do with it what he wished: He made no other sign.

As long as the chair remained on land, even if moved from one place to another (most probably in a covered horse cart—but would it really be covered?), nothing harmful could happen to it. Unless, of course, the driver drove recklessly along the edge of an abyss. It would certainly survive a minor fall. Not a big one. But destiny would decide that; no art could help there. Changes in the weather could not affect well-prepared oak, finished with special oils. But on the seas (and its owner traveled the world), in a storm, who would think about a chair? In such situations, people try to save their own lives and could not care less about furniture. Waves would rock the ship, tear it apart, shake it, toss it from side to side, and the unfastened chair would roll under the deck, colliding with hard ribs of the ship, crashing against its beams. It did not necessarily have to break. It was carved from one piece of wood, it was sculptured, not glued together. It did not have to fall to pieces. It was enough if it rubbed for a long time against a rough, hard surface. The chisel of misfortune would remove from it everything that the chisel of the artist—relying on instinct rather than skill—had meticulously created, and without which, once you sat on it, it would not be what it had been: the best chair in the world. It would be the *former* best chair in the world. It would be nothing. It would cease to exist.

But the plague would pass, like any other misfortune.

Kyr Angelos sighed, and started again toward the wall where the covered pieces of furniture were placed. He walked heavily, tiredly, letting

the feeling of profound despair come entirely over him, leaving him with nothing with which to defend himself.

"Everything has to come to an end, sir," said the stranger.

This cryptic expression of sympathy made Kyr Angelos check his hand, which had already taken hold of the cloth to remove it from the chair. He delayed the decision. His client was able to understand his suffering. Could he also be an artist?

"It's terrible when there's no end. When you are in a trade that by its nature knows no end. When you always work on one and the same thing, which is never done, and you always have to return to finish it, knowing that you'll never finish."

"Is there such a trade?"

"Life is like that."

"Life has its end, sir."

"Does it?"

"It does. For people."

The visitor smiled. "One has to be a man first . . . Do you part with your works with difficulty?"

"Not with all of them."

"But with this one, certainly."

Kyr Angelos caressed the cloth with his fingertips. He did not touch the object beneath, but only sensed its form. "This is the best thing I've ever made."

"But that's not why you have such difficulty parting with the chair. It's difficult for you because you know that you'll never make another one like it."

The woodcarver lowered his head. There was no use denying it. "Excuse my curiosity, which is in part provoked by your insight. Are you an artist as well?"

"Where did you get that idea?"

"You seem to be well acquainted with artists."

"That's true," said the stranger. "I used to know a few. But not any better than any of the other people whom I've met during my travels."

"Then you've seen how different they are from ordinary people. The latter can part with the things they've created and still remain human beings. But if you take from an artist his creation, nothing of him remains."

"I knew an icon painter in Constantinople. His name was Nicodemus.

He fell ill with the plague while working on an icon of the Virgin for a monastery in Thessalonika. Do you have any experience with the plague, sir?"

"I've seen it."

"But it's not in Tegea."

"I was in Mistras."

"And you weren't afraid?"

"No."

"Why not?"

"Because I hadn't finished the chair."

"The master Nicodemus didn't finish his Virgin, either. Unfortunately, unlike you, he got the plague."

"And the icon was never finished?"

"Oh, no. That's the point. He was in agony, he raved, he could barely move his fingers, but he kept painting up to the last moment. In the end, he ran out of paint. No one dared enter the house, no one wanted to prepare it for him."

"So how did he finish the picture?"

"With sweat, blood, and pus."

With his own sweat, with his own blood, with his own pus. Kyr Angelos suddenly felt himself able to cope with this situation. The stranger had unwittingly helped him to make up his mind.

"Don't jump to any conclusions. If conscience is the phenomenon that explains Nicodemus's behavior—although we could find the answer elsewhere—it's not the exclusive characteristic of your profession. I witnessed an event that might reassure you in your belief that conscientiousness belongs only to your kind. My business led me to the Crimea, in Capha, the city from which the Genoese merchants trade with the Scythians. I don't know the reason for the Tatar revolt, but one day they besieged Capha under the command of their Khan Kapchak Yannibey. The city was about to surrender when the besiegers were attacked by the plague, which had already decimated the population of Syria, Mesopotamia, and Armenia."

"How do you know about all of that, *Kyrie*?"

"I was passing through those parts on business."

"Trading?"

"You could say that, although I always considered it somehow artistic,

which makes me, in my own humble way, your *adelphos*—your brother. I said, the Tatars were attacked by the plague. Khan Yannibey also fell ill. He was dying in great pain and had almost crossed the threshold of death, when his military conscience spoke up—you call it artistic, but someone else would call it differently, according to his own profession. Wars are waged in order to defeat the enemy. And if you can't defeat your opponent, you should endeavor to kill as many enemy soldiers as possible and thus weaken the adversary for some future war. Before he died, the khan ordered his catapults to hurl infected corpses over the walls of Capha. The Genoese retreated to their galleys and sailed away. I arrived at Constantinople with them."

"He was a great military leader," Kyr Angelos admitted, knowing what he was going to do.

"Just as you are a great artist."

"You'll be able to judge for yourself," said the woodcarver, and he removed the cover.

At first glance, the chair merely had a strange appearance, and only to someone who had seen all the other chairs in the world and was able to notice imperceptible but important differences between them. For everyone else it was just a remarkably beautiful, but simple and obviously very carefully finished chair. One could see that it was shaped like a sculpture, that it was chiseled, not assembled from previously prepared parts, as was done in all workshops in Europe and in the East. Due to the tallow, which was prepared according to Kyr Angelos's recipe, its brown surface resembled healthy oriental skin.

The customer touched it. The oak felt hard deep under its carefully finished surface. The long meticulous treatment with various special solutions made the wood soft to the touch, yet resistant and firm. The chair seemed to effuse light; it was as if surrounded by a golden, shimmering aura, like those with which icon painters surround the heads of saints.

"Would you like to sit down?"

"Should I?"

"You can't tell whether a chair is good or not with your eyes. That's something your body has to feel."

"*Auto einai aletheia*—that's true," said the customer. Then he sat

down, threw his body back, and crossed his legs, resting his hands on the arms of the chair. His entire body relaxed. A few quivers passed over his face before it calmed as well. Finally, he closed his eyes.

"It's comfortable."

"It was made according to your measurements."

"I don't remember your taking them."

"There was no need for that. We're the same size."

"Did that help you?"

"Not really. We're the same size, but we each sit differently."

"I've been sitting so little that I hardly know how I sit anymore."

"Everyone sits in his own way, sir."

The guest rose. "*Eycharisto,* thank you," he said. "That's exactly what I wanted."

Kyr Angelos was sitting on the porch, under the arbor of lush vines, on his grandfather's Frankish bench. The darkness returned, but without its usual breath of freshness. The air was saturated with the bitter smell of bonfires and the spices that people threw into them. Everyone had his own mixture, as well as *prosephi*—a prayer that accompanied it, but the results were the same. None offered protection from the plague. The fires were low and the flames weak, no matter how much wood they threw on them. Down the street, beyond the wall of his garden, could be heard fading away the dull sound of the clappers that announced the approach of the horse cart onto which he had laid the body of his last apprentice, twelve-year-old Manolis. Children succumbed first; they could not resist for more than a couple of days, and Manolis died last and suffered longest.

Enas fell ill first, the morning after the chair was taken away. In a few weeks, no one was left alive in the workshop. The population of Tegea was reduced by half. In the evening, the horse carts were unable to collect all those who had died during the day; and in the morning, they could not collect all who had died during the night. Those had it best who went to bed healthy and thought that they were falling asleep instead of dying.

The sound vanished. It would not be heard again before morning. He would be alone until then. The clappers would rattle again at dawn. They

would rattle in front of his workshop as well, but he would have no one left to put on the horse cart. And just like now, the sound would disappear, only to return with daylight.

One day that too would stop. *Panikula,* the plague, would pass as it always had. It had passed in Pericles's time; it had passed in Justinian's time; it would pass in Kantakouzenos's time as well.

During the many days of the epidemic, he had not entered his atelier. But that day he had not forgotten about it. There was nothing to be afraid of anymore. He was alone with his masterpiece.

He took a torch from one of the consoles on the porch and entered the house, as he would enter a tomb. The front workshop was empty. Tools lay carefully arranged in their places. The mats on which his carvers had died had been left in place, reeking of the plague. None of them would have come to anything, with the exception of Enas, anyway.

Perhaps not even Manolis. But the boy had had a hand for wood. A hand and a feeling.

He entered the atelier and with the torch he lit a lamp that hung from the ceiling, then extinguished it in a bucket of water. Since he had taken leave of his last customer, nothing had changed in the room. A few covered pieces of furniture still stood along the walls. They would remain there forever. No one would ever come to take them. And if a fire were to follow the plague, no one would ever see them at all.

How many days, how many lives had been wasted in that room?

He began to remove the cloths. He uncovered a chest that opened from the side instead of the top. It would be better to say that one could unfold it. That was a new model, which he had invented by accident. It opened new possibilities for his trade. Pieces of clothing were usually put in a chest one on top of another. If one wanted to get something from the bottom, everything had to be removed. But in a chest that opened from the side, a plank could be placed in the middle of the chest and clothes arranged on top of it. One could immediately see what one needed and reach it more easily. Because it opened from the top, an Egyptian chest had to be small. A bigger one could keep more things, but they would be more difficult to reach. The new model could be as big as you wanted. Of course, there were limitations, but its height could expand to an average arm's length, since one could reach the contents by standing on tiptoe.

Some woodcarver would discover this as soon as it occurred to him that he could make a chest that opened from the side, and not from the top.

Some other woodcarver, but not him. His work was over. He had reached the end.

Just as the plague would reach its own end.

He also uncovered a table. Its top was in the shape of a Spartan shield and it was supported by the fins of four nymphs. Not even a connoisseur would be able to recognize it as a rarity. One versed in the Hellenic past would recognize the letter *lambda* Λ carved on the board, as the letter that decorated old Laconian shields and would misinterpret it as an ornament appropriate to the history of Sparta. But it was not just a letter, an ornament, a simple decoration. The table top could be disassembled along the length of the *lambda* and another board of the same shape (the shape of the letter *lambda,* only inverted: V) appeared from within. Thus the table's surface could be enlarged by a third.

When he was no more, someone would look a bit more carefully at the ornament and discover its secret. Then he would pass it on to other woodcarvers.

Some other woodcarver. Not him. His work was over. He had reached the end.

Just as the plague would reach its own end.

He did not even look at the other pieces of furniture. He only uncovered them. They were merely the best of their kind, but not unique.

One day, some other woodcarver would make the same kinds of pieces. Maybe even better ones.

Some other woodcarver. Not him. His work was over. He had reached the end.

Just as the plague would reach its own end.

One day, somewhere in the world, the plague would kill its last victim. His family would nurse him, touch him, wash him, give him drink, inhale the breath from his mouth, but would not succumb to the epidemic. The plague would try to do everything it could to them. In vain. It would not have enough strength to kill another man. It could only take as much as it had been granted. Just as it is with art. An artist can give as much as he has been granted. Which means everything. That was how much he, Kyr Angelos, had given—everything.

The blow of a chisel that gives the final touch to a unique, incomparable masterpiece, was for him what that last man would be for the plague. After that one, any further blow would damage both the work and the artist.

He had accomplished that final blow. To take a chisel now would be sacrilege. His work was over. He had reached the end.

Just like the plague.

Slowly, gently, with the tenderness of a mother, with both hands he removed the cover from it, from his own end, as if he were not removing dead matter from dead matter but living breath from living breath. He uncovered a chair. It looked exactly like the one the customer from Constantinople had taken with him. They were identical.

Kyr Angelos smiled wearily. Only he knew that they were not exactly identical.

There was an irresistible charm in those postponements, almost the same as the one that had kept him, while the chair had still had the indefinite form of Dodonian oak, from laying either hand or tool on it until he had spent enough time looking at the wood in which it was hidden. He had paced around the stump for a long time, examining it from all sides, his gaze passing through the still unstripped coarse, brown bark, deep into the pith, in which there was, instead of a pagan forest sprite or *phasma,* a chair being held captive, as if in the seed of the Creator, helpless without his touch. He had learned about it from long, tender caresses. He had crouched beside the wood, caressed it, the way that every woman would like to be caressed (which could have perhaps also kept his wife from leaving him), and with the tips of his fingers he gradually drew the form through useless layers of wood from the mist of nothingness. Only much later did he begin to free it from divine slavery, when he knew it as if it were already finished, already free.

Thus even now he refrained from sitting in the chair; his soul took the down payment of satisfaction that he was certain awaited him in the chair's life-giving embrace.

He never thought that he would be the one to sit in it. He had not kept the chair for himself—not even to deny it to someone whom he as a Greek, a Christian, and a human being had had so many reasons to

hate. That was not why he had slipped its fake double to the Black Lord. He could not part from his best, maybe his only real work. A man can renounce everything and remain a man. An artist cannot. Without his work he is nothing.

Later, sitting on the porch as his last apprentices lay dying, reproaching himself for thinking not of those children but of the chair, of the torment to which he had exposed himself in order to keep it, of the nights he had spent making the imitation, of the danger he ran that his customer would discover his deceit—all seemed to be futile, useless. A chair is not an artist's canvas, whose beauty exists independent of its use. The beauty of a chair lies mostly in its function, in the degree to which it successfully performs that function. The most beautiful chair, if one cannot sit in it, is merely a sculpture. It is not a *chair.* It has fulfilled one purpose, which is fulfilled by any successful statue, but not another, which is its essence. The one for which he had chafed his aged knees for months as he knelt beside the stump.

This led him to decide not to look at it any more, but to sit in it. Otherwise his sin would have made no sense. He knew that it would be beautiful, but he kept postponing the moment of epiphany until he had given the last of his apprentices to the grave diggers. The wait did not come easy to him, but he thought it un-Christian to enjoy himself while everyone around him suffered.

His last obstacle disappeared along with the young Manolis.

The way he paced around the chair, waiting to sit down in it, was now different from before. He withdrew to the atelier to view the chair behind closed doors, to marvel at it, to talk with it, to ponder the secrets of form that it proclaimed, yet knowing all the while nothing more could be expected of it. Maybe his wonder would become greater with time, maybe his thoughts about the relationship of *hylikon*—the material, and the forms in which it occurs, would grow deeper, and thus his artistic satisfaction more unrestrained. But unfortunately, all of that would unfold in the sphere of pleasures already tasted. He stood before something unknown. He could feel it, he awaited it with a lustful body, but did not come to know it. That difference spurred him to taste the anticipated pleasure as soon as possible and kept him from ruining even a single lascivious moment of expectation.

When he did finally sit down, tense, full of hope, he felt nothing. He felt only wonder, which he rejected immediately, turning it into anxiety and disappointment.

There could be no doubt, the chair was comfortable. And after all, the Black Lord's servant had felt that, too, when he sat down in the original one, from which Kyr Angelos had barely been able to get him up again and send him on his way. But the Black Lord had said the same thing about the fake that he had slipped him. Only this one had not kept him in it; he parted from it without difficulty. So the chair was comfortable. He might have said that he had never sat in such a comfortable chair. But he knew that without even trying it out. That was not what had made him sit in it.

Alas, he felt nothing of what had made him sit in it.

His body was stiff as a board. He *felt* the chair, which was the worst thing of all. Each muscle, each vein, even his skin. Relax, *ma ton theon*—for God's sake!—he told himself. Don't sit like you're at the tax collector's in Mistras! Surrender to the chair, give yourself over to its forms, trust in it! It was made for your body, it knew that before it received it. Have faith! The chair is yours! It's your friend!

He felt better immediately. His body sank down into the seat as if into another skin, his hands found the best position, in which they did not feel its arms. He felt as if he were floating. He sighed. This was still not the *real thing*, but it was the path to it. Relieved, he surrendered to sleep.

He dreamed of the sea. A galley was sailing into a harbor. Judging from its contours, the city was Latin. Somewhere on the Mediterranean. Genoa. Maybe Naples. Or even Messina in Sicily. He had become acquainted with these places while he had still believed that art could be learned, before he realized that everything was within him and had probably been there before him. On the deck there was the double of his chair, and sitting in it the gentleman in black. The chair was in good condition, but he did not care. That did not concern him any more. The galley sailed into the harbor. The Black Lord got up—the ease with which he did so indicated that the chair was not the real one—and as the sailors anchored the ship, he walked down a bridge onto the shore. By the dock a child was begging, a little gypsy in rags. The Black Lord patted him on the head and walked on.

A rattling awoke him. The sun had risen before the grave diggers. The plague had wearied them as well. He did not have any dead to offer. Soon the wooden noise faded away. It would return in the evening. Then the horse cart would not stop in front of the workshop. They would know that there was nothing for them in that house. Whoever had no family to carry him out, stayed inside. In every Tegean house, the last inhabitant was rotting. The grave diggers never entered a house. After a time they would throw torches through the windows. Fire, as was written, followed the plague. No one knew the reason for this practice. A street was infested by the plague no less than its houses. Spices were also burned in the houses. Fires burned in the yards, replacing the extinguished hearths. It did not help. The grave diggers waited for the corpses to be thrown out the windows or to be carried out on the doorsteps, first in sacks; when no more sacks appeared, they approached the house. They picked up the sacks with hooks attached to poles, put them on the horse carts, and left. But they never entered the homes.

The town was different now. It was another town, a village really, such as he had seen in Germany and Bohemia. Beyond the snowy fields, where he waited with a few families loaded up with bundles, he could see through a silent blizzard whitewashed walls and the tower of a small church whose bells were tolling frantically. The people were not allowed into the village. The inhabitants, armed with poles, pitchforks, and adzes, blocked the refugees' path. Whenever one of them approached, they hurled stones at him; he came from a region in which pestilence raged. The village, which was still untouched, was protecting itself. The blizzard stopped for a moment. Beyond the fields, in the door of an inn, he thought he saw a familiar face. But whose, he was unable to tell.

Only later did he realize that he was sitting, when the rattling faded and the silence woke him. He was feeling well. He had endured fatigue for a long time. The healing chair would bring him out of his languor. When he rose from it, he would be reborn. That, of course, was not the real reason why he sat in the chair, but was very, very close to it. He did not in fact know what he would do when he got up; there was no work, and he would not have taken on any—he had finished his task—but it was pleasant to know that he would get up rested. Not, as after torturing himself in other chairs, more weary than before.

Light penetrated the atelier at an angle. He could tell the time accord-

ing to the shadow on the wall. He had been an early riser when it made sense to get up early. It no longer did. He would get up, by God, because he was used to it; not because time or an obligation to finish something by a certain date forced him to do so, but because he was fed up with sitting.

Actually he hoped that he would not, that some other reason would lift him out of the chair. Any reason but that! That would disappoint him bitterly. It would admit the possibility that he had not succeeded. That he had not made a chair from which it would be painful to part. When he got up from the chair, it had to be done with effort, displeasure, and even the desperation that he had seen in the eyes of the Black Lord's servant when he had to lift him roughly, when the chair was still not even ready, when it was still imperfect.

Two men at the head of a procession carried purple banners with tassels interwoven with gold. The men walked ahead, the women followed. On the fronts, backs, and hoods of their gray novices' robes there were white crosses. In the square they cast off their robes, revealing bloody linen shirts; they formed a circle, threw themselves on the ground, and lay as if about to be crucified. Then they jumped up and, chanting, began to whip each other with leather thongs with iron tips. People were carried into the circle on stretchers and laid across the fallen robes. A mother brought a dead child. The robes purportedly had healing powers. He could not learn whether they really did. In the crowd he saw a familiar face. Or had he just thought so? He did not have time to make his way to it. The chanting stopped. The whipping also ceased. Everyone looked to the window of a house, where a girl was standing. A girl and a black cat. They all started toward the house. And he along with them. He did not want to go, but he went. The cat bristled. The girl withdrew from the window. She left it open. All around people lit torches.

He was stunned when he awoke again. Around him everything was dark. Moonlight shone through the windows. He had slept the whole day. He had not even heard the grave diggers' horse cart. He felt exhausted. Fortunately, his weakness did not stem from fatigue, but from bliss. The chair was alive. The chair imparted its life to him, repaid him the debt, and this exhaustion stemmed from an overabundance of that life.

Was that what he had expected from it, from his masterpiece? Perhaps it was. He was not sure. Maybe there would still be something else. Something more. Something final. Something impossible.

He was taking pleasure in his body, which, for the first time, by means of the chair, he felt to be his and his *alone,* and not as contact with the world, with the earth under his heels, the air against his face, a kiss on his lips when he was young, an object in his hands, even a face in his eye; then he remembered his dream. At first the sound of a flute, and then his dream.

It was *nukta fphantazmaton*—the night of ghosts. And it had to be a dream as well. The doors of the workshop were locked. Customers, had they any reason, could not have gotten in. But one visited him. He stood there, in the black clothes of an aristocrat, and was saying something to him. And he was saying something in return.

The Black Lord stood. Kyr Angelos sat. That, even regardless of the irresistibility of the chair, was already testimony to the fact that he was dreaming. Were he not, he would have risen out of respect. Like a polite man. Out of fear, like a thief or swindler. The Black Lord was talking about fatigue, about how he was weary and how he envied him, Kyr Angelos, because he could rest. He seemed not to notice the similarity between the chair that he, Kyr Angelos, was sitting in and the chair that had been sold to him, or he considered it unimportant.

Kyr Angelos wanted to be sure. (At the time, while he was asleep, he did not think he was dreaming.) He asked him whether he was satisfied with his work. The Black Lord answered that he was. That the chair was the most comfortable he had ever sat in.

"Then you shouldn't be tired."

"I thought the same thing."

"Maybe you don't sit for long enough?"

"Therein lies the problem. I sit, but the chair doesn't keep me in it."

That's *it!*—thought Kyr Angelos, with pride. That's the difference between a perfect chair and a merely good one! That's the difference between a work and a masterwork!

"Had it kept me, I wouldn't have come back here. Do you know how long the journey is from Norfolk to Tegea?"

"You've come from England?"

"I had considerable problems finding a ship."

"Why?"

"Most of the sailors are dead. In the end, my servant and I were the only ones left. We arrived at the Morean coast in a small boat."

Fear for his chair seized him. He thought the customer was coming to take it away. "So why have you come?"

"Do you remember when I told you about Nicodemus, who completed his icon as he was dying?"

"Yes."

"And about the Khan Yannibey, who, also about to die, finished his war, casting the plague-ridden Tatar bodies over the walls of Capha?"

"Yes."

"They were, each in his own calling, conscientious men, weren't they?"

"Yes they were."

"And you have brought your work to completion. When you made the chair for me, you wanted it to be the best in the world and you did not cease working until you created it. Why?"

"Because I can't work any other way."

"See then, Master Angelos—neither can I. Although I can see no end to my work, I always hope for it. And I, for one, do have a conscience."

"So you do too?" he asked, both horrified and exhilarated.

"*Malista*—of course. It seems that it is the curse of all artists."

Kyr Angelos gave a knowing smile. It was not a matter of the stranger's conscience, but of his own. It had returned the Black Lord to Tegea to remind him of his deceit. It had no need to do that. Or right. Art was above both. Above need, above right. Above everything.

Everything except God. But God would understand him. He was also a great artist.

Maybe not exactly the greatest, but certainly great.

His bliss had infused him with such languor that, in the evening, right after the horse cart passed, when he felt a dull aching somewhere in his body, he could not get up. Neither did he make an effort to do so. Any pain would pass more quickly and easily in the chair. It had healing powers. But no, it was not miraculous. He was an artist, not a magician. Yet it could heal, because it was perfect. It healed with its perfection.

Unfortunately, the aching did not subside, but sharpened so that he could now recognize it. His stomach muscles hurt. The pain, like a sluggish flatland river swollen by flood, spread throughout his body. It penetrated his armpits, below his thighs, to his throat, choking him and racking him with fits of coughing.

The pain increased his languor, the dry cough exhausted him; the ef-

fort that it took to suppress it by tensing his muscles took away his last bit of strength, but brought no relief. He could not have gotten up even if he had wanted.

And he did not. He did not want to.

He was oppressed by a thought to which he did not want to give final form as long as he was capable of withstanding the pains and giving them more benign explanations. One of the more harmless explanations was the plague. Maybe he had been infected at last. With the plague-ridden, dead city of Tegea surrounding his house, that would not have been a surprise. And that would not have frightened, upset, or embittered him. He had finished his work. For better or worse. Whether he had succeeded or not, nothing could be changed now.

Because, if he had not been infected, if the pains came from something else, his misfortune was much greater. Death defeated the plague. Death killed the plague. But a failure could never be erased. It would never die. It would remain, immortal.

He moaned, squirmed, changed positions, rubbing himself against the chair, because his weakness did not allow him to part from it. Neither his weakness nor his will. But nothing brought him relief. All he had gained was that the terrible thought became clear.

If he was not sick, if his pains did not come from the plague, then there was one source—the chair. His masterpiece. His *would-be* masterpiece!

No bodily pain, from which he was already screaming, could be stronger than the mute pain of the realization that he had failed. That everything had been futile! That he had not made the finest chair in the world, from which no one could get up once he sat down in it.

Den ine dikeo—it's not fair!

On the wall, light alternated with darkness; his pains were unrelieved. No matter how great they were, and they were so unbearable that he fell into a delirium and returned to them again, as if checking their origin, with diminishing hopes that they were caused by the plague, they were milder than the pain that was to come. The inevitability of the stronger pains sharpened them in advance, but never enough to surpass the pain of failure.

He was not comforted by the thought that maybe his sin was not unforgivable and that, had he completed his commission faithfully, not even

the Black Lord would have felt so much pleasure in the chair that he would have canceled his travels. Nothing could comfort him.

But when he came out of his delirium once again, for who knows what time, to face his pains, they were not there.

He was sitting in the dark and felt nothing. It was not an ordinary nothingness. It was the nothingness of bliss. Complete unification with his work.

This was what the work had been created for. This was the final, true measure of perfection. The measure of his, Kyr Angelos's, genius.

For several days, the grave diggers had heard the master screaming for help in his workshop. His screaming alternated with a howling that sometimes sounded exactly like that of a dog, and was in any case more unbearable than anything they had ever heard during executions by *skolops*, the Byzantine salted stake on which criminals were impaled. Later the wailing stopped, and they heard him laughing, talking with himself, joyfully shouting his thanks to the Lord.

And other Tegeans died from the plague. Two-thirds of Tegea already lay in the ditches; the remaining third was gasping for air in vain. But no one died so slowly, with such difficulty and such ease, so painfully and joyfully, dully, and somehow mysteriously as master Kyr Angelos.

The grave diggers knew him. There were few in Tegea for whom *xenos*, foreigners from all ends of the earth, would visit the city. Kyr Angelos was the most glorious among them. As he sat dying, no one dared to enter his house. But after he fell silent, and for three days no one heard either a yell or a joyful psalm from the workshop, they decided, more out of curiosity than respect, to violate their custom, to enter the house and take the corpse.

Protected by black hoods with small nosepieces that resembled birds' beaks, armed with long barbed boathooks so that they would not come into contact with the body, they went into the house, contaminated by the stench of the disease, and broke into the workshop.

Megalos mastoras Demetrios Kyr Angelos was dead.

His face had the dark-brown color of the chair, in which he had, it seemed, been sitting very comfortably. He appeared calm, content, almost happy. But he must have suffered. He was unclothed. He had evidently stripped off his robes in his agony. But the position in which he

sat gave no indication of suffering. Pleasure, if anything. The pus that had oozed from his welts made others ugly, but on him it seemed like a golden ointment and resembled *elayon,* a yellowish oil used for finishing wood, his secret alchemic mixture.

They thrust the hooks into his flesh to carry him away, and great was their surprise when the corpse fell to the floor, together with the chair.

They tried everything to separate him from it. In vain. It was as if his body had grown together with the chair.

That was a waste of time, so they gave up and tossed a torch through the window. Then they sat down on some rocks, away from the house, and waited for the fire to do their job for them. When the ashes cooled, they would search through the ruins, looking for any of the master's bones that had not been totally consumed by the fire. They would make amulets out of them.

Because anything that had passed through fire offered protection from the plague.

Translated by Stephen M. Dickey and Bogdan Rakić

Miodrag Bulatović

Miodrag Bulatović (1930–1991), one of the most important authors of his generation, was born in Montenegro. He started to write while still young and achieved instant celebrity with his first collection of short stories, *The Devils Are Coming*, published in 1956. He wrote several novels, including *The Wolf and the Bell* (1958), *The Red Cockerel* (1959), in which he treats individuals from the bottom of society, *Hero on a Donkey* (1964), in which he likens war to pornography, *War Was Better* (1968), *The Four-Fingered Man* (1975), and *Gullo, Gullo* (1983).

The war left an indelible impression on Bulatović. His prose works present a strange, brutal yet compassionate picture of man's existence.

Bulatovic's novels have been translated into most European languages. *The Red Cockerel* was published in English in 1962, *Hero on a Donkey* in 1970, and *War Was Better* in 1972.

THE LOVERS

My flesh is clothed with worms and clods of dust; my skin is broken, and become loathsome.

My days are swifter than a weaver's shuttle, and are spent without hope.

Job 7:5–6

The café was small and dingy. Olja and I sat in a corner so that neither Ananije nor Fotije, who were sitting a table or two away, could see us, not to mention Sima and Nikifor, who were sitting behind the door. The café was dark, and but for its small windows you would have thought you were in a dugout rather than an inn on the outskirts of the town from which few people left sober. Its dark-colored walls were very high, so that we could not see them properly; they towered above us, sheer as ramparts. Olja and I looked at each other. The people around us were whispering bits of fabric, murmuring or keeping silent over the tables. Olja whispered too, but I had nothing to say. The people looked gray, like clay or paper dolls, some suspended in midair, some not. Most of them were old men.

Olja asked whether I was afraid. I looked calmly in the mirror. It was a tissue of smoke, spider webs, and glass. All the faces I saw in it were wrinkled and sick except mine. I had a birthmark on my cheekbone that improved my appearance. My eyes were particularly fine. They glowed darkly in the hollows of my pale face; it was bound to be pale, for I was thinking about how to find something that would arouse my wonder

and enthusiasm. Fotije told me that airplanes were a very strange invention, and that one ought to take an interest in them. I became very fond of them, with the enthusiasm of a child. I made them from paper and cardboard, wood and tin. I thought it would be the pinnacle of my happiness when I took off from an airport. But I was disappointed. As soon as we left the ground I got sick. At that time, I did not know either Olja or Ananije. Ananije was standing, his figure reflected in the mirror. As long as I had known him, his face had been distorted and gloomy. He had a deformed foot that he dragged behind him, but I could not see it in the mirror for the smoke. Sima was standing stiffly beside him with a book. He was so tall that his shoulders broke through the mirror frame, and his head was somewhere above the glass. I was the only person who knew that Ananije and Fotije rehashed other people's poems and signed them with their own names. I found this out when they were drunk, but I never told anyone, as I always forgot. I used to write poems before I got interested in airplanes. Actually, I am a born poet, with a natural talent, but I don't like this kind of lying. I had a special gift for making verses and devising new and unusual rhymes, but I had no interest in work of any kind. I looked in the mirror and saw Olja's head beside my shoulder. I laughed at Olja and Ananije for being sad. I did not know what it meant to be either happy or sad. Even today I regard the world quite simply, as though I were looking at the most ordinary garden, though I am aware that I am better, wiser, and more handsome than all the people I know. Olja leaned her head on my shoulder.

Then I began to dream about boats. I lived in a world of shipwrecks, courageous captains, and sailors. I went to sea and embarked on a voyage. I did not come to my senses for nearly a month. When a mirror was held up to my face, I saw that I looked like a skeleton. I grieved for the loss of my beauty. My eyes no longer had that fine, alluring gleam. I fled from the water and began to wander aimlessly about the world. I went from town to town, from country to country. To the Spaniards I presented myself as a persecuted nobleman, to the French as the son of the king of Serbia, to the Dutch as an ear, nose, and throat specialist, and to the Danes, Norwegians, and Swedes as the leader of the Yugoslav Communists. All this seemed dull and uninteresting, though people usually believed me and regarded me as a Serbian genius. Last year, after ten years of wandering about the world, I returned to Belgrade to the pubs beside

the Sava, to my old acquaintances whose names I had already begun to forget. I celebrated my thirty-second birthday in my attic room, and as soon as I went out into the street, I noticed Olja.

I saw my fine hands in the mirror. One was stretched out on the table and the other rested on Olja's shoulder. Her eyes were so gentle and sad that it seemed to me tears could pour forth from them at any moment. I couldn't look at them, and I cried out several times, asking her to smile. I could see in the mirror how she was clinging to me. This gave me neither pleasure nor amusement. Fotije and Ljubica came toward the mirror. He was small, and she was so tiny that you could hardly see her among the tables. I liked Fotije because when he was drunk he used to say strange things. I smoothed my hair with my hands. I passed my hand caressingly under my chin. It seemed to me that my blood passed from my fingers into my cheeks.

Olja asked me whether I was afraid. She was sitting with her hands on her knees, petrified, looking at me. I answered that I had nothing to be afraid of. She asked me:

"What would you do if a robber pointed his gun at you?"

"I should probably be frightened," I answered. "And you?"

"I should be frightened too."

She asked me again. I answered that it was practically all the same to me, but that I should be sorry to die, especially as I was so young. She said she would weep and beg them to spare her life. I told her I should probably do the same.

Since I returned from my wanderings, I had become increasingly preoccupied with the fact that I must have an heir. I thought that this would calm me down and interest me more than planes and boats. Olja was whispering and looking in the mirror on the wall. She was a large girl with rosy cheeks, and I thought it would be a good idea to marry her. Ljubica went off with Fotije, and Sima with Ananije. A film clouded my eyes. In the mirror I could see only smoke and an empty space around the frame.

Then I asked Olja, "Would you like to marry me?"

We were looking at each other. I remembered that Ivana had looked just like that when I put the same question to her. Ivana had consented and said she would bear me a daughter. I changed my mind and sent her back to her mother, unmarried. She cried bitterly at the station. I asked

her why she was crying, though I knew it was because it was hard to see me leave. She said I had ruined her future. I said that the future was merely the present moment, when we were looking at each other, and therefore there was no need to cry. She looked at me. I promised to introduce her to Ananije, who would marry her at once, for women shunned him as though he were the devil. I told her that he would be pleased, because he was a virgin, although he was old. She looked at me. At last she confessed that she was crying for me. I believed her. The train was ready to leave. I left her on the platform, wrapped in a cheap cloak and steam. Later I realized why I had fled from her. I wanted a son, and she had told me she would bear me a daughter. What's more, she had diseased, staring eyes.

Olja and I were looking at each other. Her expression reminded me so much of Ivana that I almost got up. There was something inconceivably dark in the hollows of her eyes, something that kept dripping down her eyelashes.

Olja answered, "Am I worthy of you?"

Her answer pleased me. I embraced her and said quietly, "No, but I'll marry you in order to have a son, since you are healthy. I don't like small, thin women. I can't bear poor stock."

"But why do you want a son?"

"So that he may achieve all that I have been unable to achieve."

"Let it be as you say," she said.

Later I learned that Ivana had married a man who worked on the railroad. I didn't doubt this for a moment, because her home was near a railway station. Ananije decided that her husband was hurt because her child was not his, but still he was in love with her. Fotije told me that they were always on the move from one end of the country to the other. He also told me that Ivana had suffered a great deal on my account. I believed this too, because a lot of them yearned for me. But I've never found out what causes suffering. I told Ananije that it simply didn't exist and that people had invented it. Fotije answered that it was one of the finest things in life. Ananije said that without suffering there was neither love, happiness, nor creative activity. Olja looked steadily into my eyes. Then I asked them both if they would describe as suffering the feeling a man has when he is so hungry that he has pains in his stomach. They answered that this was only hunger and physical need. They explained that suffering was an

accumulation of happiness, longing, and pain. I told them that I did not believe in anything in the world, least of all in theories that were sick fancies. I added that it would be better if they abandoned their poetry and took a look at the crawling gait of human skulls seen from an airplane; or sailed out to sea at least as far as Rijeka, to feel below them the fathomless deep and, around them, emptiness; or chose a healthy woman and bred children by her; any of these things would be better than this perpetual talk about the heart and human suffering, and about the future of poetry and the secrets of the universe.

"Why are you looking at me so long?" I asked her.

"I don't know," she whispered.

"Look somewhere else for a while, not just at me. Look at the smoke."

"And what shall we do if it is a girl?"

"We'll both throw it in the river," I said, shaking with rage.

"In the river? What has come over you?"

"In the river, I say. Why are you looking at me like that? You and the child!"

She was clinging to my right side. I told her how I would teach my son right from childhood to fly a plane, to sail the seas, to study people, and to deceive them as a juggler did. She asked me what would become of us. Nothing, I said. I promised her that I would take off her rags and buy her fine clothes if I had the money, but that I wouldn't do so if I hadn't, and that her best plan was to listen to me. She said that she liked someone to order her about.

Fotije and Ananije were the same age as I, but they looked about forty. Olja was sitting beside me. They looked at me enviously. I felt that they were talking about us, but I had no idea what they were saying. They were smiling. While Olja was whispering something beside my shoulder, I was thinking that Ivana had done well for herself to marry that railroad man who moved her around. I remembered that I had left a brass ring with her.

An old man stood beside Olja. He was tall and thin, with a beard pointed toward his breast. At his side he carried a bundle of shoelaces and dozens of other trifles. I watched him. He was weeping, but there were no tears in his eyes. He was quite an ordinary old man. He stretched his large wrinkled hand toward me. I continued to watch him. He said quietly, "Give me something!"

He looked like Ivana's father, who was a watchman on the railroad. I

think Ivana's father was an inch or two taller than this man, and, what's more, a thief; once my wallet and handkerchief disappeared from my pocket. I asked what he wanted me to give him. He repeated, in an ordinary, quiet voice, "Just give me anything."

"Aren't you a poet?" I asked.

His voice was so quiet you could scarcely hear it. He went away. Then Ananije and Fotije came and told me that he was the most unhappy man in Serbia. They said he had been reduced to poverty and begging by love and suffering.

"Are you sure he wasn't a poet, Ananije?"

"He tried his hand at poetry, poor man," answered Fotije.

"Did he ever travel in an airplane? Did he ever swallow salt sea water?"

"The important thing is that he suffers, like any poet," said Ananije.

"But surely you aren't suffering, Ananije?"

"Yes, I am."

Ananije and Fotije were sitting in their old place. I thought what a pity it was that Belgrade and Serbia were so full of such daydreamers. There are fewer of them, I thought, in Montenegro and Macedonia. People are healthier there, because they really have to work for their bread. I didn't like this café scum—these people who sat in their tiny rooms and wrote poetry about love and social problems and mysticism; these ragged, bearded painters who wandered about the cafés, got drunk, quarreled, and fought. I liked healthy people like football players, because they were ordinary.

I asked Olja, "Do you like football players?"

She made no reply. I asked her, "Would you like me to take you to my home now? Do you want me to take you right now?"

She nodded.

The next day she became mine, and burst into tears.

I rarely dropped in to see Ananije and Fotije, my nearest neighbors, and still less to see Sima, Nikifor, and Akim, for I loathed poetry. I used to tell them that writing poems was not a healthy job, and that they ought to be put to work on some building as manual laborers to learn about the real world. We all lived on Karadjordje Street behind the cafés on the bank. I told them that what they needed was to be healthy, and that they were just ordinary invalids—the kind that filled up the clinics.

I went to Ananije to complain about Olja. Since she had become mine,

she had grown pale and withdrawn and looked at me very strangely. Ananije said that this was because she regretted the loss of her virginity. I asked him how she could regret her virginity after ten years of marriage. But Olja wept continually. Fotije told me that she was living through some difficult experience. I was interested to know what this was. Ananije said this was the pure, eternal Slavic suffering without which the very idea of self-respect was inconceivable, especially if he were an artist. I told him and Slavic suffering to go to the devil. Ananije and Fotije were surprised. I wanted a wife and son, and I had got illness and Slavic suffering. They looked at me. I said I would break her in two and throw her out of the house if she continued to act like this. Ananije said that Olja had a very deep feeling for poetry. I learned from Fotije that Ivana and her railroad man were in Aleksinac.

Olja wept constantly. I couldn't find any way to make her laugh. Circus and jugglers' tricks, with which I had conquered the world, didn't help me. We had a small attic room, like Ananije's. Some artists lived next door to us. I used to leave the house so that I wouldn't see them. I found congenial company among magicians, hypnotists, and football players. Actually I had only one wish: to have an heir. Such was the pattern of my days. When I returned home, I found Olja in a corner of the room. She stared at me for a long time and she seemed not to recognize me. I asked her what was the matter. She answered that nothing ailed her. We had nothing in the room but a table and a bed, which was quite enough for two healthy people.

We used to go out into the world for our daily bread, selling odds and ends. I stole whenever I could. Somewhere in Bosnia our hair began to turn gray. Olja asked me when we would go back home. I told her she was very ill. She asked me how much longer I would go on torturing her. I told her that she had dried up and that I liked her better when she was plump. Someone had stolen the few possessions we had in a bag and a bundle. She said, "We are done for!"

"No, we aren't," I said. "I'll rob somebody."

"Isn't that wrong?"

"Why should it be?"

I often remembered Ivana. Sometimes I felt that it would have been better if I hadn't left her. Fotije told me that her daughter was like me, and that this particularly displeased her husband. I didn't believe she had

grieved for me very long and it was all the same to her whom she moved around with. But along with this memory came the thought of her weeping at the station, and then I at once turned to Olja. I told her all about it, to arouse her jealousy.

Olja was growing more and more silent. My smile was still as beautiful as when I was younger. Wrinkles had improved my appearance and gray hairs made me look more serious. Finally Olja became almost mute. She answered me only when I asked her whether she still loved me.

I soon saw that there was no hope of ever having a son. I concluded that it was foolish to want one. Later I realized that it was definitely a form of illness to want anything. My most foolish desire had been for an heir. I explained to Ananije that it was disgusting to see oneself in anyone else. He answered that it was a noble and lofty desire, and that he had suffered deeply because he had no son. I began to reflect about suffering, for I was constantly hearing about it. I wanted to experience it. I began to think about what I should do in order to suffer. I thought about suffering day and night, and decided that it must be a pleasant sensation. Olja refused to describe it to me. She even appeared not to have heard me when I asked her.

I went to Ananije, and he told me that suffering was like a rainbow above a river. I said to him, "Tell me what I should do in order to suffer."

"Thrash Olja," he said.

"Hard, or just a little?" I asked.

"As hard as you can," he answered.

That morning I quarreled with the painters next door. They wanted to throw me out of the house. I went home and started to beat Olja. I watched her cringe under my switch and spit out blood through her teeth. When I was tired, I sat down, but still suffering had not come. I beat her some more. Olja made no protest.

I looked at a photograph on the wall of myself as a young man. My head was tilted to one side, since Ivana's head was alongside mine. I had cut it out before we parted at the station near the Morava. My eyes were large, dark, and merry, and smiled ruthlessly and self-confidently. I was unbelievably handsome.

Olja was lying on the floor. Her face was covered with blood. My picture had been enlarged and framed. I didn't want to have a picture of anyone else in the room. I gave Olja's picture to a man who had once

been madly in love with her and used to write her letters and poems. He thanked me and burst into tears. He asked me whether she was happy. He was gray-haired and could not walk without a cane. Olja whispered a curse from the floor. I wanted to spit at her, since her cursing reminded me of Ivana, who had once knelt in front of me and cursed the hour she had met me and fallen in love with me. Olja tried to get up.

I beat her every day to see if it would make me unhappy. Fotije came up with another suggestion, but it was so distasteful that I cursed him. I told him that he was an incurable lunatic. He wasn't hurt. He really didn't know how to take offense. If I had said such things to Akim or Sima, it would have led to a quarrel, or even to blows. Olja became more and more wizened and yellow.

For nearly two years I sought suffering, and as I didn't find it I decided to leave Olja and go off on my travels again. I wanted to wander through Serbia and Macedonia as a juggler. I had begun my life with juggling, and wanted to end it the same way. It seemed to me that it wasn't so bad to deceive others while one preserved one's own integrity.

Just as I was about to depart, Olja said to me, "You might at least wait until I die before you go."

"And what shall I do if you live a long time? You're tough, you'll live a long time." But I postponed my journey. For several days she was delirious constantly. She could not recognize me. I had many distasteful and unpleasant things to say to her. I remembered some of them only when her breathing began to fail and a strange light appeared in her eyes. But they weren't unpleasant or distasteful things, just quite ordinary remarks. Olja held her hand to her throat. She kept clenching her fingers in agony and pressing them to her face.

Such scenes disgusted me. I was once sick when I saw a young man in his death throes. He stretched himself on the ground, crossed his hands on his chest, screamed with pain, and then died just like anybody else.

Olja lay motionless on the floor; only her lips moved. That night I didn't dream at all, but before I fell asleep I reflected for a long time in an absent-minded sort of way that I had made a mistake when I married Olja and not Ivana.

By dawn Olja was stiff. She looked the same as usual. One arm was lying by her head. Shrunken and yellow, it looked like a worm. Only her

lips and eyelashes were visible above her scarf. I stood by the window and looked at her.

It was hard to believe that she wasn't awake. I thought about my trip to Macedonia. Olja looked peaceful lying there. I sang over her, quietly at first, then more and more loudly. I pretended to weep and lament. Only the elbow of her other arm peeped out from under the bedclothes. I threatened to kill myself and leave her to starve to death. She said nothing. I leaned against the door. I called out to her to wake up. Her eyelids were tightly shut and ridged like tiles on a roof. I remembered that old man who had sold odds and ends in the café.

The next day I called on Ananije and Fotije. They read me a lecture on suffering. I listened to them as usual. They persuaded me. I realized that I should begin to suffer only if I did something very unusual. I put Olja beside me on the bed. I caressed the top of her head. I tickled her under the arm. Her skin had begun to peel. When my fingers disappeared inside her, it seemed to me that her ribs moved. Yet even when I possessed her, suffering did not come. I stood in front of the mirror; the only thing I noticed was that I was a little paler. My face had a wonderful beauty that comes only with age. Olja was lying with her hands at her throat.

I was frightened that I should die without experiencing suffering and sorrow. To take my mind off this, I began to perform my juggler's tricks in front of the mirror. The only thing I had forgotten was how to mimic other people's voices. I started to cry, just so that I might hear something. It seemed to me that there was nothing finer than being in my room beside Olja. It was only when night fell that I went out for some food and brandy.

Two days later I called on Ananije. When Fotije and Ljubica had left, I told him everything. Ananije looked pale. He trembled slightly as I told my story. I told the story in my usual voice. He said to me, "You're a very strange and interesting man."

"What do you mean? Why strange? Why interesting?"

"If I were a prose writer, I should write a novel about you."

I told him that he was a very sick man and that I wanted to pee. He was surprised, and an even sadder expression came on his face.

I asked him, "Why do all your poems have such gloomy, tragic end-

ings? Why do you always write about death? It isn't the end of everything. You're old and experienced enough to know that—better than anyone else, in view of the fact that you think yourself a poet."

"If I knew anything else, I'd write about it," said Ananije.

"Look a little more closely at life," I said, "it isn't all bad. Everything in the world is quite normal. But your poems are gloomy because you were born sick. Isn't it so? It is because you have a deformed foot. Perhaps there is some hereditary weakness. What do you think?"

He looked at me; he was pale. I asked him, "And where on earth is the toilet in this tenement of yours, my dear Ananije? I was going along the street wondering where to drop in, and in the end I dropped in on you."

As I descended the stairs from the attic room, I noticed that I had forgotten half of my jugglers' tricks.

Olja was stiffer than ever. I packed for my journey. The darkness was weaving a curtain over the aperture of my window. Outside the door I heard a commotion.

"Who is there?" I called out.

"Your neighbors, the painters."

"What do you want?"

"Can you lend us a few dinars to buy some bread?"

"I have some, but I'm not giving you any. You never pay your debts. I've been lending you money for years, and you've never given me back a single dinar. You're a set of rotten swindlers, a thoroughly bad lot. I'm not such a fool as to feed such crazy gluttons."

I knew them well. They lived in attic rooms, too. They were all in rags and smeared with paint. They wore beards, so that people laughed at them and asked them if by any chance they were priests. I avoided them like the plague, especially since I'd heard they were louse-ridden and liked to steal.

"Something stinks in your room."

"Get lost!" I said.

"It's such an awful smell that you can hardly walk along the corridor. This is what we wanted to tell you; we haven't fallen so low as to ask you for money."

"If you can smell something, I can't. Get out of here!"

"You must be rotting alive. Let us in! We want to paint you."

"Go to the devil," I said. "You haven't come because of the smell, but to throw me out. There's no smell here. You've imagined it, it's a sick man's fancy."

"And how is your wife?"

"She's ill. She's asleep. She's all right. What are you asking about her for?"

"Because she's likely to be in a bad way, living with a cretin like you."

For a long time they hammered on the door with their fists, threatening to break it down if I didn't open it. They got an axe and began to smash the lock. But when I took out my gun from under the bed and shoved a bullet down the barrel, they fled.

Olja was lying quite peacefully. A street car was rocketing down Karadjordje Street. The car tracks shone before it, like two healthy thoughts lost in the night. Behind it, it left darkness and silence. It was too dark for me to see Olja. Under the boats, the Sava was heaving. Toward it, peacefully, flowed the Danube. I stood at the window. I decided I had better take my gun with me on my journey.

I hurriedly wrapped Olja in a blanket and took her to the cemetery. I buried her just before dawn. Beside a marble stone sleep came over me. I didn't dream at all. When I awoke the sun was high above the graves. I wondered if I had forgotten anything. It seemed as if I had lost something. I felt in my pockets: all my usual things were there. I fell asleep again and woke up as the sun was slowly sinking toward the Sava.

The grass was growing over the grave, and still I didn't go home. I made friends with the grave diggers. We started to steal food from the graves together. I completely forgot about my journey to Macedonia and my wish to end my days as a juggler. My only desire was that my conscience should prick me. This wish came to me only in the morning, after I had slept. During the day, all I wanted to do was satisfy my hunger. Before I closed my eyes I would laugh at my naïve, childish desire for suffering. I realized that I had made a mistake in not having married Ivana. Many days passed, and I came to the conclusion that my desire for an uneasy conscience and a journey to Macedonia was a sick fancy. I started to think about airplanes and parachutes.

Ananije came to the cemetery. Fotije and Ljubica followed him.

Ananije was tall and quite gray. He carried a stick and dragged his deformed, key-shaped foot behing him. Fotije was disturbed.

Ananije said to me, "I heard that you were here, so I came to see what you were doing."

"Nothing," I replied in my normal voice.

"What the devil are you looking for in a cemetery?" asked Fotije.

"I'm not looking for any devil," I answered. "Devils never come to the cemetery. Only vampires and bad poets come here."

"You will suffer from those vampires," said Ananije, "especially if you take food from graves; you're done for."

I told him that I could live without the food intended for the souls of the dead.

"You're in a bad way," said Ljubica.

They took me away. I could hardly stand on my feet, but I went off and looked around me as if everything were normal. The grave diggers waved to me. One of them whispered to me not to tell anyone that we had stolen food from the graves together. I noticed some birds on the fence beside the gate. They were fat and lazy and weren't afraid of anyone. Ljubica talked of the painters, who had lost all sense of morality and social behavior; and Ananije talked about Akim and Nikifor, who had begun to flatter some of the leading lights among the politicians. I walked slowly and wondered if I could demean myself enough to ask them for a crust of bread.

The next day, the painters turned me out of my flat. I went down to Serbia with a knapsack and a stick.

It's been a long time since I saw you, Olja. Sometimes you come to me in a dream. You walk, but you don't say anything. Your blood trickles between your teeth. I run after you and ask you, "How are you, Olja dear?"

You shake your head.

I ask you, "Do you still love me, Olja? Are you still madly in love with me?"

You weep and ask me how long I shall torture you.

I say, "Wait, I want to look in your eyes. Turn around, I'm your husband. Perhaps I could come with you to the underworld?"

The sky is bloody above your head. And it seems to me that you hold in your hands not shoelaces and odds and ends for sale, but a bundle of dead snakes.

As for me, I'm all right. I go about the world sightless and begging. I can tell night from day by human laughter. I cannot suffer, but a little well of pus forms in the hollows of my eyes when I remember how your lips rotted away.

Translated by Edward D. Goy

Dragoslav Mihailović

Dragoslav Mihailović (born 1930) works and lives in Belgrade as a professional writer. He studied at the University of Belgrade. In 1952, Mihailović was imprisoned for his political views and sent to the notorious prison camp, Goli Otok.

After his release in the late 1960s, he published a book of stories, *Goodnight, Fred* (1967) and his most important novel, *When the Pumpkins Blossomed* (1968, published in the United States in 1971). It was adapted for the stage and after ten performances banished at the insistence of President Tito. Mihailović's other works include the novels *Petrija's Wreath* (1975), *Čizmaši* (1983), *Goli Otok* (1990), *Evildoers* (1997), and collections of short stories, *Catch a Falling Star* (1983) and *Hunt for the Bedbugs* (1993).

Mihailović writes about suffering and mercy. His stories are projected against a historical background or mundane everyday reality.

CATCH A
FALLING STAR

> Go and catch a falling star,
> Get with child a mandrake root,
> Tell me where all past years are.

> John Donne

I was sick; after last night's fever my whole body hurt and you could have thrown me out with the trash. Still dressed, I lay down on the bed I had risen from on the morning of that dismal, smoky November day; I read for a while and briefly disappeared somewhere. And then I came back home.

I was approaching it from the main street, and the first thing I noticed was that all around a lot had changed. All our little street, which bore Njegoš's name, once so dusty and covered with cinders but now black-topped, was heavily settled, almost every free inch of it was being used for some kind of new building. The three or four shacks in the yard behind ours had been torn down, and in their place two or three larger structures had been squeezed in. And in the former gardens of the two old ladies Stanijas, the one in front of our house and the one across the street from us, where a plum orchard and a stand of corn once grew, there too were huddled not so much big as rather bulky, awkward buildings. Our house was supposed to be around here too, and, so I remember, whether inhabited or abandoned, greenish-gray, and peeling, would have

stuck out between these buildings like a hock of spit after a chest cold.

Well, I looked up, down, and all around and still didn't see it. All the same, even though everything had changed, I knew exactly where I was and didn't think for one second that I had gotten lost. In fact I felt as if I had been invited here after a long absence, and something was quivering in my chest.

And so I approached it.

Then, up close, I could see that the fence had been torn down. Our old blackened and rotting fences, with no one to replace them, had been removed in large sections so as to make a bigger entrance, as if for numerous guests for a wedding or an important holiday, let's say. And in fact the yard was full of all kinds of people—drowned, as it were, beneath the surface of a quiet murmur. They looked out toward me and even seemed to expect me.

I was a bit surprised. I wondered what was going on in this crowd and turned to look at it more closely. And so I was unable to look well at the gate—I didn't see it all covered in tile, nor did I notice that it wasn't even there, though it was probably still in place, with two long-necked poplars on either side of the lintel—and I was already in the yard. In the process, I stepped over a damp furrow of black earth that the fence had left, which means it had only recently been taken down.

At the back of the yard to the left, where the pigsty and the outhouse once stood, where the corner of our fence almost touched the back of the miller Nikodije's large building (he was a tall, handsome graying man, and his wife was a fat, almost immobile, secretive Hungarian, Wilma, who rarely came out and used to call over in her unreal, hoarse squeaking voice—their entrance, with its big iron door, and the mill actually faced out onto the main street), it looked now as if some sort of new construction had begun. On the ground in the form of a rectangle lay long, freshly hewn finished boards, which reminded me of the outline of a roof made up of two-by-fours, as if they were tracing the lines where the foundation would be dug. Clamped together, these boards were held down at the corners by heavy stones, while all along, as on notepaper, there lay similar, freshly hewn but somewhat narrower planks, which carpenters call roof supports. These would make the structure more stable.

But, for God's sake, this could not have been a foundation. One day, I concluded, there would most likely be a building here, but built a bit

strangely since it wasn't started from bottom to top, but like no other building ever built, from the roof and attic down.

Around the rectangle stood a few workers. They noticed me as soon as I walked in; they stopped their work—if they had been working—and, dressed in short, thick peasant jackets and tall shapeless fur hats of the kind I had seen in Banat and Bačka, hands dangling at their sides, they stood quietly. It occurred to me that they were probably waiting for someone's approval in order to continue their work. And as soon as they received it, they would get rid of the frame and on the same spot that was certainly the one marked out below, they would begin to dig the foundation.

I was truly moved. I smiled at them and wanted to hurry over to greet them in a sincere, brotherly way. But they were rather far from me (to get to them I would have to greet a lot of people in the same way) and I didn't recognize them—and on top of that, looking rather indifferent, they didn't indicate that they understood my wish, or that they had a similar desire. And so I refrained from going over, leaving my greetings for later.

I passed to where once upon a time our pear tree stood. It used to produce seeds bigger than a child's fist, and I looked to the right.

I did not catch sight of the *big, upper* house—they were both wattle-and-daub shacks, but this one differed from the *little, lower* one in that it had a floor and three (instead of two) *premises,* a kitchen and two rooms—but it must have been here somewhere, maybe just a little farther along than usual, because the whole yard was somehow overgrown, as if someone were pulling it apart on three sides like pie dough. Along the whole right side, from where the gate should have been, down to the little house, long uncovered tables were set up facing one another, here and there lengthened by rectangular curves in the form of the letter *N.* Guests were sitting on plain wooden benches; there were a lot of them, also dressed for winter—simply—the men in dark peasant jackets and fur hats and the women in kerchiefs (the fuller, warmer kind that Russian village women wear) tied under the chin and at the nape of the neck. It had to be late autumn, I thought, and winter would soon be here.

To my left, leaning on two sides against some pruned tree, probably that pear tree with the juicy fruit, was an arbor. I wasn't able to examine it, but it seemed to me carelessly and hastily built, like those at village

fairs, made of young, untrimmed logs for the beams and roof supports, without a peak, dried oak branches serving as eaves; dark leaves like old rags hung from the branches. Some women were scurrying about under the arbor, but I didn't have a chance to look at them more closely. Wisps of steam flew by, probably from kettles and pots where food was cooking. And here also, I suppose, were the stoves, with their pipes sticking up out of the arbor, maybe in the direction of old lady Stanija's plum orchard in front of our house, so that you couldn't smell the smoke. These people have to be fed, I thought.

However, I did not examine all this very well because at the moment, under the fruit tree next to the arbor, I caught sight of someone I recognized, a woman who might have been the daughter of my maternal uncle from Novi Sad. She had that same triangular, drawn face of my mother's family, well rounded in childhood but a bit fatty after thirty, with a meaty nose that gives it importance, but now without glasses and somehow sprinkled with ashes, with sad gray shadows around the mouth and between the brows, on the somewhat sunken cheeks and particularly in the eyes, the whole face painted as it were in gray, and, though without wrinkles, in some strange way elderly. How old, I wondered, was she?

Joyfully, though somewhat confused, I hurried over to her while I quickly examined the gray scarf covering her pretty abundant blond hair, and her dark gray or black dress covered over by an apron. Was that she? I asked myself with some doubt.

As she stood next to the fruit tree, wiping her hands on her apron, she looked into me. She was probably waiting for me. But her face showed no feeling whatever, and she continued to look at me as if, without any great interest, she awaited an explanation. And I, having approached her, refrained from embracing her and extended my hand, smiling.

"Hello," I said merrily, though my voice was also somewhat—in the vicinity it was not quiet; in fact, it seemed that everything was very noisy—muffled.

She grabbed my hand clumsily, twisting her wrist like a country woman unaccustomed to handshaking, while she looked up at me with concern and perhaps sadness, all the while as if I were a stranger. And I uttered my surname, quite inappropriately and stupidly as if at some reception.

"Oh," exclaimed the woman full of joy, holding on to me with her

twisted wrist. She pronounced my surname twice, without the "vić" at the end, the way they once used to call me in the army. Obviously, she either didn't know me at all or knew me only vaguely.

Then she motioned to me with her hand. "Let's go."

We set off.

The gray lady made me walk in front of her. We took a few steps in this way and then she disappeared somewhere, even though I was walking quite slowly. And so, unexpectedly and without noticing it, I lost her.

I continued on my way toward the little house—I still didn't see the large one, but that did not appear strange to me, though a short while before I had been with people and once had lived upstairs—as if in a corridor between the arbor and the building under construction on the left and the crowd of people at the tables on the right. I looked at the people, smiled, and tried to recognize someone from among them.

They still seemed to recognize me; for one moment, in letting me pass, they almost rose as before an elder. Nevertheless, they restrained themselves. I passed by them slowly, and that lasted and lasted and I continued to assure them with my smile that I was glad to see them. But it elicited no response. They only looked at me—there were men here and women and children, and all wore the same simple dress—with large, sad, deep eyes and enormous, darkened circles under their eyes like those of beaten, exhausted inmates of the Goli Otok concentration camps, and they let me pass in silence, without giving me even a simple sign that they wanted me to approach them.

I wondered who they were and how they could recognize me if I could not remember them. The thought gladdened me that perhaps they had come to greet me, but if that was so, why didn't they respond to my greeting? Passing my gaze over their faces one after another—somehow they all looked alike, and I did not see anyone's hands—I merely gave them an expressionless, distant, somewhat pleading smile, searching for a response.

Then it dawned on me: I was walking before them like a conceited young master returning to his estate. And since, no longer young, I had never been a master, I grew ashamed; and, sensing that I had carelessly folded my arms behind my back, I untwined my fingers and let my hands hang at my sides.

And so I reached the door.

And there again I spotted someone I knew.

In front of the house itself, almost jutting over the slab not quite two yards wide that we had once self-assuredly called a veranda (then it had been covered with a sheet metal roof supported by two trimmed poles leaning against the wall), was the end of the last table. At the head of the table, turned toward me, sat a man I recognized. But I could not remember from where. Still, he seemed to be a party functionary I had seen on TV and even met two or three times on the street—one of those self-satisfied, repulsive boys who serve in so-called high-level politics as goads and believe that *they are always there when they are needed,* who in the pernicious battle for power are called from the shadows only at turbulent moments when someone must be overthrown. For in such a campaign, according to their chosen role, wielding words like meat cleavers, they will exaggerate so that the overthrow of the wretch later appears to be not only humane but almost merciful.

I was a bit confused and forgot that I was looking at him, while he could not look at me. But in that crowd, which kept silent, even one such as he seemed unexpectedly attractive.

"Hello," I said, almost joyful. And I extended my hand.

He returned my greeting, glancing and smiling at me, still seated, then hastily turned his attention again to the table, where they were passing a bottle. He said something jocular to the person he was speaking with— I noticed that everyone at the table was chatting—and grabbed the bottle. And immediately took a swig.

Then from this close-up I realized that again I had made a mistake. He resembled my TV acquaintance, but it wasn't the same man. Mine was tall and, though on in years, powerful, with a squared head covered with thick, bristling, trimmed gray hair, and with powerful jaws that often clenched, with something brutal in his regular features that women still find attractive. Though from Serbia, aware of the notorious stereotype of Balkan peoples, he probably still cheerfully vaunted his pedigreed Dinaric background. This fellow here, on the other hand, while resembling him like a brother, was probably shorter, more the stature of someone from the Vojvodina. His head, though more rounded, was shaped like that of my acquaintance; it was also covered with short, spiky hair, but whiter at the ears and nape and darker at the crown; and his face was fat, full of veins, and its expression a bit dull. Like people everywhere

when they eat and drink, this one knows what he's doing, I thought maliciously.

The man was still struggling with the bottle, and I stood beside him, waiting to see if he would turn toward me. But he continued to chat with the people around him, no longer noticing me. And so, pondering whether I really knew him or had made a mistake, I continued into the house.

I leaped over that too high doorsill, which as children we had constantly tripped over, and entered the murky kitchen. I took my cap off—I noticed it was a shabby leather cap with earflaps of the kind I wore as a child—and turned to a woman who was waiting for me.

Younger and taller than the woman I'd met earlier, wearing a kerchief on her head, she stood discreetly at the door allowing me to pass.

I offered my hand. She took it. Then she said, "Forgive her for not waiting for you. The poor thing, she's completely deaf." Then she mumbled something I did not hear well but understood as: "and blind."

I nodded as if I understood, though I understood nothing, and turned to the interior of the building.

The wall between the kitchen and one of the rooms had been removed, and the dirt floor in what once had been a separate room had been lowered by almost a foot and a half, fleetingly bringing to mind the apartment in Košutnjak where I had lived briefly a few years ago. The entire rear wall was taken up by a big, high bed like those in Vlah* villages on which the whole family sleeps, with an overstuffed, fat, double-decker straw mattress supported by a wide plank.

In the huge bed, covered with an overlong white cloth—as if illuminated by something, everything down there could be seen clearly—lay a young girl, no bigger than my five-year-old daughter, but already gray, with hair as white as a sheep, with yellowish sunny highlights.

So much white, I thought for some reason, cannot be good. I expected something unusual and my heart clenched. Who was this?

Her head pressed against the wall, the little girl began to turn over. Like a real child, she first sat up, then mumbling and moaning, bent and squinting, she crossly turned toward me. And with astonishment, I recognized in her my aunt, never this gray, but now shrunken. Dead thirty

---

*Vlah: In Serbia the descendants of Romanian emigrants. (Translator's note)

Dragoslav Mihailović

years ago, she had taken care of me almost from my birth until I was six or seven; I thought she had given me birth, this woman whom I stopped calling Mother only after her death, when I was already an adult. Now she was strangely the same size as my eighty-four-year-old younger daughter, who was named after her.

Contorted and tossing her head just like her five-year-old grandniece and namesake, my aunt continued to sleep, perhaps whispering something. And above her firmly shut eyes I recognized her broad eyebrows and high, clear, luminous forehead, which drew my attention from her panting mouth and which made her almost beautiful, her entire noble, care-ridden face, which in past years I could recall only with the help of photographs. And I grasped that she was not just squinting that way but was truly blind and that she wasn't sleeping but dying. The people in the yard were waiting for her to die. And here I was invited after thirty years to attend her departure once again.

Twice in those years I had been invited to watch my father's death (each time knowing he had died, I knew he would also die again). But never hers. And so, knowing she was dead and that she would be so again before me, I remembered that then, too, she had been in the bed at the back of our middle room, with her head, however, turned away, and unintentionally hidden behind the old yellow kitchen cabinet, from which for three days her stifled moans had penetrated the house, and then there was the nightmarish, maddening three-hour death rattle of her breathing.

Well into my sixteenth year, as old as my son is now, though I had already been acquainted with death, I knew nothing of its consequences. And sensing that now one such consequence was occurring, the likes of which I did not want to know—"Her stomach is rotting," said old Dr. Tomić, "sometimes it takes two, sometimes four days,"—that evening I sneaked away quietly to the movies. And there I sometimes got carried away by the colored pictures of some comedy, sometimes I awoke at the noise of my sinking to sleep, not giving way to tears and denying that I believed in *that* back there.

But then that night, just before the event, with the same sensation I would have later as I watched how they carried off everything that came to hand *so that the others don't get it*—You're little, I'll put this away for you so that nobody steals it from you—in the darkness of the bedroom, awake but pretending to be asleep, I listened to the quiet deliberations of

my two Parcae. "Dada asked me," said the female voice quietly, "to take him till he finishes school. There was a brief silence, then the superstitious male voice asked: "You didn't promise anything, did you?" (If I die today, will someone decide my son's fate this way?)

Before noon of the following day, a wet November day, like this one today, they led me in to say goodbye. And then I could no longer see the person I loved, only the exhausted remains of a body that did not resemble its former self, a distorted face of a kind I would never like to look at, painfully leering lips that barely emitted the slowing rattle of her breathing, dully praying for mercy from the terrors to which God's creation is heir, and dreadfully protruding eyes, one of which seemed to look to the right, toward me, the other to the left, and both somewhere above, toward the attic, but neither saw anything and merely reflected a hellish, undeserved pain, surprise at an incomprehensible punishment, and the misery, abasement, and monstrosity of a life no longer capable of defending itself or wanting to.

Determined in my childish vanity to prove that I could stand anything, I kissed her icy hand and colorless forehead, and then, abandoned by my imagined strength, suddenly burst into tears and clenching my jaws began to call for help. So that I did not *interrupt* her dying, I was quickly led outside.

Now, watching her just as white, childishly curled up and shrunken on the huge bed, in a marvelous way I recalled everything and at the same time knew I would see all the same things again and yet somehow differently. And with a different sort of vanity, the vanity of those years that allegedly bring firmness and restraint, I wanted, calm and self-contained, to go and greet her. And again unable to hold back, as I had done thirty years before, I collapsed in groans and tears.

Crying back then, I hated death, threatened it, and looked for someone to blame. Now I sobbed, knowing its laws and requirements, hating no one and seeking no help, allowing everything to be as it was and only gagging on my own wormlike impotence. The woman next to me did not embarass me and I did not try to hold on to her, but I bent over, feeling the tears pouring from my eyes, sniffled with my mouth wide open and howled something. But I did not know what these howls were supposed to mean, nor did my tongue help me to compose myself and they

poured forth as an inarticulate, gut-deep, clenched-jaw "Aaaaaa," which had no shape and was directed at no one.

"Aaaaa," I howled, hearing also about me a drawn-out, high-pitched sound. "Aaaaa! Aaaaa!"

The sound, I felt, rose above me and at the same time fell somehow from up there, slowly as if to enfold me. It may even have been threatening to crush me. I still did not feel the pressure; I knew, however, that my mouth was gaping and my teeth were bared: what would happen, it dawned on me, if I sucked it in?

Suddenly I was no longer in that house. There was no one around me and I was lying by myself in some bed, perhaps the same sort of double-decker deathbed as the one right before me.

"Aaaaa! Aaaaa!" I still heard around me, and it was getting closer and terrifying me more and more.

What will I do now, I thought, beginning to feel spasms, what will I do, where will I go?

And somehow mechanically I clamped my mouth shut. My jaws were almost chattering, my lips pressed together, sticking.

At that, the painful, dangerous sound went out like a candle. In an instant a change had occurred.

Like a just disturbed swift stream, something near me began to clear. And I remembered—the overgrown yard, the uncovered tables with people at them, the white little girl in the huge bed who was dying—and I continued to tremble.

I was quivering. I pondered without conviction, like a dying man. But I knew at the same time that this was not it. And already the sky was opening wide above me and the light suddenly grew clearer.

Then beneath the just born, filtered morning rays, I was lying on the grass. My face was bathed with warm and mild, kind summer dew.

Translated by Henry R. Cooper Jr. and Gordana B. Todorović

Svetlana
Velmar-Janković

Svetlana Velmar-Janković, who was born in 1933 in Belgrade, is a prominent Serbian novelist and essayist who also writes plays for television and radio. Her most important works are a collection of short stories entitled *Dorćol, Names of Streets* (1981) and the novels *The Scar* (1956), *The Dungeon* (1990, published in English in 1996), and *The Bottomless* (1995). She won the Ivo Andrić Prize for *Dorćol*.

Velmar-Janković writes in a polished style. *The Dungeon* tells how victorious communists destroyed the Serbian middle class while at the same time trying to emulate its life style.

Velmar-Janković works and lives in Belgrade.

SIMA STREET

Today, Sima Nešić would be called an interpreter; in his time they called him Sima the *targuman*. But it is not such a big difference, since *targuman* means translator. Sima could translate from seven different languages and speak just as many. As a boy, he would roam for hours through the city's main trading district called the Dubrovnik Bazaar (today a section of Seventh of July Street between Prince Mihailo Street and Jugović Street). He walked past cramped little wooden shops listening to what Jews, Tzintzars, and Greeks shouted out loud or muttered to themselves as they traded—words and sentences that have been continually repeated by all the world's merchants from time immemorial. Sima listened to those strange and unfamiliar sounds; his ears adapted to them and gradually domesticated them. He realized that each language has its own melody, which—when you grasp its meaning—reveals not only the secrets of that particular language, but at least one of the secrets of communication in general. The laws that govern words began to interest him more than the laws governing people, and the more he learned about the ways of words, the more he seemed to know about the ways of men. As he grew, he spent more and more time playing the game of translating sentences from one language into another, and then into a third and fourth. He began to believe that much evil stemmed from the fact that people were unaccustomed to listening to or understanding each other—they simply did not pay enough attention to words. In the

The title refers to a Belgrade street named for Sima Nešić, a minor Serbian police official, who was killed in a well-known incident at a Belgrade public fountain in 1862.

young man's opinion, people should have been taught to handle words instead of guns. The first to hear this was his father, the hide merchant Pavle Nešić, who was shocked. And when his son declared that he would like to go abroad in order to study languages, he became deathly afraid. Being a practical and well-to-do man, Pavle Nešić sent his son to the School of Commerce in Vienna.

Every morning around ten o'clock, Sima the *targuman* stands again at the corner of Sima Street and Captain Miša Street, approximately at the place where, during his lifetime, an alley separated the Turkish and the Serbian police headquarters. Here Sima Street is empty and its noises are muffled by half-darkness. Passers-by are rare; when they squeeze between the parked cars, they seem to be splashed with shadows. The place is now dark because the sunlight is completely blocked out by the new building of the College of Natural Sciences and Mathematics. Underneath that large edifice, erected where both the Turkish and the Serbian police headquarters (and, later, the Glavnjača prison) once stood, there is a covered passageway with columns that leads to Students' Square. Sima the *targuman* now considers this another example of the misunderstanding of words: why should a building in which natural sciences and mathematics are taught block the sunlight and a view of the sky? But on that day, the third of June 1862, the place looked much different. It was early Sunday afternoon. Sima, the interpreter for the Serbian police, was standing next to an open window. The enormous sky over Kalemegdan radiated summer light, the smell of the Danube, and a protracted, subtle feeling of tranquillity. He listened to the meandering drawl of Sunday voices, which reached him from the central marketplace (Students' Park is now located where the central marketplace used to be). That soft whirlpool of noises forced itself on him and goaded him into selecting individual sounds and trying to discover their origins. He had come into his own (as one would have said then)—he had children; in five days he would turn thirty-two. But he still liked to play. With words, of course. Never before—it seemed to him—had he felt so keenly how similar that urchin of yesterday was to this dignified *targuman*. Just like that boy, Sima the *targuman* believed in the power of words; just like that boy, he knew the power of inner harmony, once it was attained. He felt that life would offer him an opportunity to do something that would reveal to others how essential words are in the process of communication. As an

interpreter, he accomplished a few things: he prevented misunderstandings. But that was not enough. He hoped that he might be offered a position as an envoy to a foreign land or be invited to teach at the *lycée*. Everything was possible that afternoon, and the world lay wide open before him. With the glittering June, he felt his youthful elation rise in his blood again. Glowing inwardly, Sima surveyed green gardens on the sloping banks of the Danube: he saw the upper stories of Turkish houses peeping from the greenery, and, close up, the roof of Dositej's School of Higher Learning rising above that crossroads of light.[1] In the distance, out of reach, the mists of the Danube drifted above the slopes. Everything looked so clean in the mild June air, so free of any foreboding. But then, suddenly a cry soared up from the bottom of the green expanse. The voices grew stronger, reached him, and became distinct: they were a bad omen. The distorted sounds contained threats and expressions of fear, and Sima felt that the mildness of the day was suddenly shattered.

Soon the news reached him: over there, on the slope, at the Čukur fountain, a Turkish soldier had wounded, or maybe even killed, a Serbian boy.

So Sima the *targuman* hurried toward the fountain. If there had been a misunderstanding, who could straighten it out better than he? If some misfortune had occurred, who could find the right word as quickly as he? The *targuman* walked hurriedly; right behind him was Djordje of Niš, a jokester who spoke an impossible dialect, and two gendarmes. They leapt over the contorted shadows of rose bushes and the drooping shadows of mulberry trees (so suitable for dreaming of love). But Sima was not thinking about love: he was thinking about the well-known Viennese banker, Tzintzar Sinna, for whom he had worked as a very young man. That banker, who had the face of an intelligent rat, would inspect his employees every morning as if sizing them up for the day's work (long experience seemed to urge him to anticipate changes in their biorhythms), and he would say: "When you are in the utmost hurry, slow down. If you don't, making a mistake is unavoidable." Sima was in a hurry now, and his strides grew longer and longer, madder and madder. The banker was warning him in vain. Sima did not slow down.

1. Dositej Obradović, 1742–1811, was a famous Serbian scholar and founder of the School of Higher Learning, which later developed into the University of Belgrade. (Translator's note)

He got there at the right moment. The crowd around the fountain grew more silent as it grew larger: a mute ring tightened around the Turkish soldiers. The boy was lying on the ground, wounded in the head and perhaps still alive. At his feet was a broken water jug. Water flowed from the fountain into the silence. Sima knew what he had to do. Politely making his way through the ring, he gave a sign to the gendarmes, and they quickly tied up the soldiers. Sima bent over the boy, sadness on his face. Then he raised his head. The sorrow was gone; now was the time for resolute action. He looked at no one in particular, although everyone in the ring felt as if Sima were looking straight at him (he had also learned that trick from the ratlike banker). He said that the boy should be taken away immediately; he might still be saved. As for the Turkish soldiers, they would go with him to the Serbian police headquarters; they would be tried before a Serbian court. Serbian citizens should keep their dignity. At the same time, speaking in Turkish, he told the soldiers not to resist.

This was not the first time that Sima the *targuman* saw words—*his* words—accomplish something: they reached people, calmed them down, and remained in their ears. And people obeyed him: the crowd, the soldiers, the gendarmes. The boy was carried away, the handcuffed soldiers walked ahead of Sima, between the gendarmes, dozens of reflections flickered like eyes from the garden greenery, the townspeople followed Sima at a distance, and the sky was translucent, spacious, and bright.

In his imagined watchtower at the corner of Captain Miša and Sima Streets, Sima the *targuman* now always shakes his head as he watches that silly *targuman,* who—many decades before—walked with the handcuffed Turkish soldiers and a group of peaceful townspeople, suddenly strengthened by his confidence in the power of words. Sima knows what that young fool will tell him in passing: it is easy for Sima to shake his head now. Since the day he died, he has had an entire century plus a few decades more to think over everything that happened. But as a young *targuman,* he didn't have it so easy then and there, he didn't have a single moment for reflection. He had to be prepared for anything. All eyes and ears, he walked behind the Turkish soldiers and thought about nothing. He felt numb inside. But he nevertheless saw light in the spacious sky, dimmer in the vanishing June evening. The dust was drowsy, and fragrances of linden trees, mulberry trees, wild mint, and sage blended together. Only the mildness was gone, extinguished. Although Sima

walked through well-known alleys, he felt that he had entered a region where he had never been before. And again he was in a hurry (there was no reason for it), and, hurrying, he erroneously took a shortcut, the wrong one, the one that led by the Turkish police headquarters. (The problem is that bankers are usually right.) At the windows of the Turkish building (which also served as a barracks), he suddenly noticed soldiers aiming their rifles at him, at all of them; he realized their evil intention and shouted a warning. As he shouted, the arrested Turkish soldiers broke away and ran toward their barracks. Djordje of Niš rushed after them, the crack of rifle fire could be heard, and the townspeople started to draw back. Sima walked toward the soldiers who were shooting at him. He saw black smiles on their faces, and—in impeccable Turkish—he began calling to them, telling them to hold their fire, to stop, that what they were doing could lead to a disaster. His words collided with the swirling air, with the shattered light, with the shots. The soldiers fended off his words furiously, as if they were some kind of accursed disease. Sima the *targuman* shouted louder and louder; rifle fire answered him more and more rapidly. Then he could no longer feel his legs and body—he became bodiless. Only his head, which had suddenly become wobbly, sank to the bottom of the shallow darkness.

Sima the *targuman* now stands again at the corner of the street named after him, uncertain which turn to take: the one to the left, the shorter one, toward Višnjić Street, or the one to the right, the longer one, toward Francuska Street. The house that Milan Bogdanović[2] frequently visited is on the left; the house in which Slobodan Jovanović[3] lived is on the right. The two men thought differently in politics, but they were both perfect stylists and shared a sense of historical paradox; they might help him express what has been bothering him for more than a century: how is it that his genuine desire for harmony caused so many deaths? (For the first time in his life, Sima the *targuman* is having difficulties with words.) Immediately after Sima was killed, Djordje of Niš was seriously wounded; he died a few hours later. On the slopes above the Sava and the Danube, old hatreds flared up. The Serbs quickly seized their arms and

2. Milan Bogdanović, 1892–1964, was a well-known Serbian Marxist literary critic, renowned for his eloquence. (Translator's note)
3. Slobodan Jovanović, 1869–1958, a famous Serbian historian and jurist, was considered one of the finest masters of historical portraiture. (Translator's note)

attacked the city gates, which were manned by the Turks. The Turks began to retreat into the Kalemegdan Fortress, and the battle (in the words of the British envoy Gregory, who supported the Serbian cause at the famous session of the House of Commons, on May 17, 1863, in London) the battle lasted the entire night. The next day, just before noon, in the opaque June glow, foreign consuls met with Ashir, the pasha of Belgrade, and Ilija Garašanin, president of the Ministerial Council, and they reached a mutual agreement and put together the Armistice Convention, effective immediately. So one could again walk the hushed streets of Belgrade with a feeling of relative security. The historical comedy was thus postponed until the following day. The following day was Tuesday, the fifth of June,* a dazzling, magic day, full of deep light. From the direction of the Stamboul Gate (located between the present Monument of Prince Mihailo and the National Theater), a procession moved toward Palilula Cemetery, in Tašmajdan. The entire Serbian population of Belgrade, anyone who could move and was not bedridden, was in that procession. They were attending the funeral of Sima Nešić, the *targuman* with excellent prospects, braver than a hero of legend, his parents' only son, the handsome interpreter who spoke seven languages. They were attending the funeral of Sima Nešić, who was riddled with bullets, and of Djordje of Niš, who was also riddled with bullets. Sobs and liturgical chants blended with the thick heat of the morning, the water from the moat at the Stamboul Gate stank, no one lamented aloud, and sweat trickled from beneath the top hats of the officials. Flocks of large storks and wild ducks circled swiftly over Terazije and the Venice pond. There was not the slightest breath of wind under the sky. They walked toward the outskirts of the city, toward Terazije, on the hard, hot dirt road (it is Kolarac Street today). They reached a small tailor's shop and stopped at the place where today, in Kolarac Street, is a branch of the Belgrade Bank and the entrance to the underground walkway in front of the "Albania" building. With his head bowed, the tailor waited to join them. Forbidden portents hid in the dust. And then, with a whistling sound, a bomb fell right from the sunny sky. The cannonball was perfectly round, not very big, and it exploded right under Sima's coffin. The Turkish guns started to thunder from the direction of Kalemegdan. The bombardment of Belgrade had

---

* All dates are given according to the Julian calendar.

begun. It lasted for four hours and turned into a hotly disputed international issue. Foreign correspondents later tried to maintain that the bombardment was not particularly heavy, because the poorly armed Turks were poor marksmen. Bombs exploded one after another (admittedly, in intervals, not as they did in 1915, or 1941, or 1944; however, this was also a sort of a beginning). The coffin containing Sima the dead *targuman* was dropped on the hard ground, and the lid slipped a bit, although no one noticed it. The whole crowd scattered, storks and wild ducks included. Through the crack in his coffin, only the peaceful *targuman* Sima Nešić, whom they would not allow to rest, stared with his right eye at the sun, which had reached its zenith.

At his corner, Sima now shakes his head again. But he is not inclined to reproach himself anymore: he reproaches Mr. Longworth, the British consul in Belgrade. This gentleman's reports to his government almost obliterated Sima's role in history. Being a Turkophile, he was convinced that the Turks were "good-natured people" who were "rightly annoyed by the rebellious attitude of the Christian population."** Accordingly, he notified his government that the riots of the third of June were incited by the Serbs, not the Turks. Fortunately, both at that time and later, some British gentlemen and others thought differently, so that the truth about his death, slightly distorted, has become historical fact. But even that is unimportant now. His name has been preserved, admittedly not as a proper noun but rather as a modifier of another noun, written in white letters on a dark blue street sign: *Sima Street*. The *targuman* reads this inscription on the sign several times; he listens attentively to its sound, already somewhat unfamiliar: its meaning evades him and fades away, sharing the inevitable fate of repetition. Suddenly, he is confused: does Sima Street have anything to do with Sima the *targuman*?

Translated by Bogdan Rakić

** See M. F. Hristić, *Srbija i Engleska pre pola veka* (Belgrade: Geca Kon, 1910), 145.

Svetlana Velmar-Janković

Živojin Pavlović

Živojin Pavlović (born 1933), a prolific Serbian author, is a film director, novelist, short story writer, and essayist. His collections of stories include *The Curving River* (1963), *Two Evenings in the Fall* (1970), *The Gypsies' Cemetery* (1972), *I Killed the Bulls* (1985), and *Symmetry* (1997). His novels are *Dolls* (1965), *Cain and Abel* (1969), *The Stench of the Body* (1982), *The Wall of Death* (1985), *Hunt at the Tigers* (1985), *The Almond Tree* (1988), *Fair on Saint Archangel's Day* (1990), *Lapot* (1992), *Wild Wind* (1993), *They Exist No More* (1995), and *The Blood of Plants* (1995).

Pavlović has received international recognition both for his writings and his films.

THE QUESTION

Around three months ago, my cow gored me in the belly, and it made me think, "There must be a God!"

Just like everybody else in my village, preacher, I ain't—well—what you'd call *religious*. When there's a holiday, we take off; we celebrate our patron saints, there's no doubt about that. And when there's a funeral or a baptism we always call you—you know that yourself. But like the others, I always say, "While you're alive—you're alive, but after that—who cares?"

That's how we all are, and I was, too. Till this last winter, when Belka got me with her horn, it's sharp as a knife. My spleen busted open like a fish's air sack. If it wouldn't of been for Doctor Mikajlo, God bless his ass, well, I'd of went off to meet my maker, preacher; and for you and for Sredoje "the Mongrel," the one who does all the village grave diggin', well there'd of been a whole lotta work to do! My old lady, Bosiljka, would of kneaded the dough for flatbread and baked cheese pie with last year's cheese and brung down some apples from the cellar fer the kids. And the left shoulder of that boar we slaughtered last winter and cured the meat in the smokehouse, so we'd have meat this spring when the fasts are over. She'd of brung down a slab of bacon for cookin' beans, too, preacher, she'd of took it off the hook for you, my old Bosiljka. All that so you'd sing me a requiem, say me a prayer, and send me off to the heavenly kingdom accordin' to the regulations, preacher! Accordin' to our regulations, the people's and the church's, like they say . . .

Damn, that Doctor Mikajlo's got a fast hand, I tell ya—he's the son of

the dead beekeeper Dragutin from Novo Korito. He got the best grades in all his doctor studies, that's right! I tell you, he's got a quick hand and a quicker mind, God grant him a long and peaceful life. He cut me open as soon as they put me in that white car and took me in the Vranovac hospital and threw me on the operatin' table like a dead carcass. He slit me open with a knife, opened me up like a sack, took out my spleen, sewed me up, and here I am! But I wonder, preacher, what do they do with all those pieces of meat in that operatin' ward, where do they put all those hands and feet and guts? Do they throw 'em out for the cats—God forgive me—or do they haul 'em over to the Gypsy Cemetery and bury 'em in small holes the size of a shoe or glove, dependin' on what they're buryin'? I wonder, preacher—(Don't get mad 'cause I don't say "Father"; I can't say that, son, you're young, just a kid, God bless you, a lot younger than me. You could be my son, or my Zoran's classmate; so how can I call you "Father"?) Anyway, I wonder and ask myself at night, when I can't sleep, in the dead of night when the dogs in Zjapina all start barkin' at werewolves and vampires and evil spirits. I wonder, I rack my brains tryin' to figure out if there's a God or not . . .

Because if there ain't, then why did my Belka up and stick me in the belly with her horn and tear my guts open on *that* day, the fourteenth of March, Holy Sunday, twenty years after what I done to Ljuba? Huh? Twenty years exactly, not a day more or less. Hell, it's almost enough to make you doubt the cow's the one that did it; it's almost enough to make you believe, preacher, that Gornjak's spirit was in the beast, and that God sent him, Belka I mean, to take revenge . . .

But if there *is* a God, then why didn't the Holy Father leave me all in one piece, instead of havin' Doctor Mikajlo take out some of my guts? And why, for instance, didn't that same spleen keep on livin' without me? And if there's a God, why didn't he want that to happen? And here I am, livin' with no spleen. I get around, and even eat and drink, sonny, just like before; nothin's wrong with me, thank God. I got enough to eat, my family's healthy and well, and, you know, we're gonna buy a tractor, on credit. And I've had an Opel sittin' in my yard for three years—like they say, I don't even go to take a piss on foot anymore. But still, since that day, the fourteenth of March, I mean, I ain't been able to get no sleep.

So I'm asking, preacher: if there's a God and if he gave me my life, like they say, then why don't he let me sleep? And why all of this now, after

so long? Why can't I get no peace and shut my eyes for at least one night? I sit up all night long and think and ponder about how I'm here and Ljuba's gone. I keep thinkin' and rackin' my brains, my head's about to split open, it's swollen up like a ripe tomato, but I can't find no answer nowhere, preacher, only that I'm thinkin' about God more and more. I'm losin' my senses on account of him. Sometimes I even think: Pajča, either you'll go to a monastery, or to the madhouse Toponica, you ain't got a third choice . . .

And it's all 'cause of that date, the fourteenth of March, nineteen and forty-five, and because of beans, like they say . . .

It all happened somehow right before the liberation (you hadn't come to our parish yet, preacher, you was still just a young squirt, stealin' your neighbor's cherries—c'mon, admit it, ain't it true?), I mean when the Russians attacked Vranovac.

Well, just then Gornjak stormed into Zjapina, with that *flyin' corps* of his, on his way back from Ozren; the communists fucked him up pretty bad, if you'll pardon me, killed all of 'em except for a few. And the few that was left—they got bloodthirsty as dogs. Their eyes was red with hate and bad blood, their beards was dirty and gray like ashes in a chimney, and their tongues hung outta their beards, black from thirst and exhaustion—a sight to make you run away and never come back. They came flyin' in sometime about noon, but the village was empty. Some of the people ran off and hid in the thickets and ravines to save themselves in case somethin' happened; and some left real early for the fields, to get all the corn brought in before the fight for the Sejmen valley began. And from Vranovac you could already hear cannons boomin' and roarin'! From the one direction, from Zaječar, the Russians was firin' with tanks and *katyusha* rockets; and from this way, Vuk Babić and his partisans were cuttin' across through Zmijanac, to hit the Krauts from behind. What was the Krauts gonna do?—If they wanted to get out alive, they had to follow the railroad tracks to Verbovača, and from Verbovača to Zjapina and through the Sejmen valley—which meant they was headin' straight for our village. Well, that's what we thought, and that's what our elders told us too, who'd lived through Jedrene and Albania and the Solun Front. But thanks be to God, it wasn't true: the Krauts took off in the other direction, towards Boljevac, and the only thing comin' our way was Gornjak—he wanted his *flyin' corps* to meet up with Djordje

Graničar's *četniks*. But as soon as the first Russian rocket hit, Graničar vanished into thin air and the next mornin' Šterbac's mill, the place where he had his headquarters, was empty. When Gornjak got back from Ozren, the bastard didn't find no one at home, and started up the hill towards our place—hungry, thirsty, and mean!

And where was he gonna go, preacher, except for to some well-to-do place? They're all like that, and so was he. And in our village the best household was my brother Jelenko's. God bless his soul, you didn't know him, preacher—God know's there ain't ever been a better man on this world than him. And so they came, Gornjak was ridin' his horse, with that shaggy hair of his—you didn't know where the hair stopped and where his fur hat started—and the others were on foot. He saw my brother's farm—the likes of which there wasn't in all of the Krajina, Saint Nikola be my witness to that—he stopped next to the hedge, took a good look, and said: "All right. Here."

When my brother saw 'em, he went out, draggin' his bad leg—he'd been crippled since he was a child, here, in his ankle: once he stepped in a trap that our uncle, dead Uncle Milija, had set in the vineyard for dogs—he hobbled across the yard and greeted 'em like the common folk did, and like Draža's men did, too. "God help you heroes," he said. And the *flyin'* men said back, "God help the master of the house!" and started millin' around the stables and cellars. Gornjak was just struttin' around, givin' orders, sendin' out patrols and puttin' sentries in the plum orchard and along the river, all the way up to Zlodol. But he never got off his horse. "Master, how about gettin' some dinner on the table?" he said, and rode off somewhere. The horse's hoofs started kickin' up dust, a lot at first, then less and less, till you couldn't see him at all.

And when he came back—midday was about over, the sun was already in the west, and from Vranovac you could hear the cannons blastin' away like the mother of all thunder—and hailstorms was movin' in our direction—there was somethin' to see: in the middle of my brother's yard there was two big pots full of beans cookin'. And Toša "the Vampire," the famous killer, had set the bench outta the guest room down between 'em, and my brother, dear preacher, was tied to it. They'd pulled his trousers down to his ankles, God forgive me, his ass was bare, and they was gettin' ready to whip him. "What's all this?" asked Gornjak (my Bosiljka told it to me later; she'd climbed up in the attic and saw the

whole thing through the roof tiles). And "Vampire," she said, just looked around with his cold eyes and walked back and forth like a mad dog, and then hissed through his thin woman's lips: "He made us beans for dinner, sir, fastin' beans, no meat, communist bandit!" "Is that so?" Gornjak asked, but didn't dismount; he didn't even look at my brother. "I guess that makes ninety-six," said "Vampire," whippin' his boot with a dogwood switch. "Untie him!" Gornjak ordered. So they did, and when my brother got his pants back up, quick as he could, Gornjak rides up to him and says: "All right, Jelenko. Do you really think you serve beans to the king's troops? Huh?" "I know, sir," my brother says to him, bowin' his head lower and lower. It seemed like it was gonna hit the ground. "I know," he says, "You're suppose' to give 'em cheese pie and roast meat, that's how we usually serve guests in my house. You know that, sir, you know it well, you've dined here more than once like the closest of friends, but now—I ain't got nothin'."

"And those oxen?" Gornjak asked and pointed with his whip at the stalls, and from the stalls you could hear Šaronja bellowin' like crazy (that's what my Bosiljka told me when I got back from the forest in the evenin'; I'd went there to chop a little wood for the winter). "I can't do that," said my brother and kept lookin' down at the ground. He kept his eyes on his shoes, shakin' all over.

"Why not?" Gornjak asked him and rode around the pots, like he was smellin' the beans.

"What'll I plow with, sir?" Jelenko asked in a whisper.

"Aha! So that's what you're worried about!" says Gornjak and starts laughin'. "To hell with that, Jelenko, don't you worry! The Russians'll make a *kolkhoz* outta your Zjapina, they'll plow your fields with tractors, and you'll just lay aroun' and twiddle your thumbs!" And all of a sudden (like my Bosiljka told me later), he went into a rage; he whipped my brother, preacher, from his horse, he whipped him across the face and started yellin': "Who the hell are we fightin' for?! Ah? Who the hell are we spillin' our blood for?! Who are my men fightin' it out with the communists for, Goddammit to hell?! For those two oxen of yours? Butcher 'em, you sonofabitch, butcher 'em! The troops gotta eat, that's for damn sure! And you, I want you to hook both these pots on that pole, and follow my troops around with 'em, and go whereever we go— until you've ate those beans, you fucking cripple bastard, all of 'em!"

That's right, sonny, that's what happened to my brother . . . They butchered the oxen, ate and drank their fill—and went off. And behind 'em, like a dog behind a gypsy wagon, my dear departed brother, my Jelenko dragged himself, staggerin', bent like a violin bow, with those two pots of beans swingin' on the pole. He went like that, eatin' those beans day after day, Monday, then Tuesday, then Wednesday, eatin', stuffin' himself with beans. Five days went by like that, passin' from village to village, from the fields to the forests. My brother made it to Gorunovac with Gornjak's *flyin'* men, he made it that far, but not an inch further: on the third day the beans was already spoilt, and his stomach already started hurtin', and then, preacher, if you'll excuse me, he was already stoppin' behind every bush he passed, until he fell down on Friday afternoon, and started squirmin' and kickin' about, all covered in his own shit. So he fell down, somewhere near Gorunovac. He buckled over in the mid-dle of the road, and the pots fell and rolled over in the ditches on either side, and my dear brother laid there vomitin', his bad leg scrapin' in the dust.

And that's when he breathed his last, my brother Jelenko, God rest his soul . . .

Later his family brought him back on a carriage and buried him, like's proper . . . I wasn't at the funeral, 'cause Vuk Babić called me up for the militia; all winter and spring we chased Draža's troops and Captain Marko. Those was bad times, but you know, when I think about it, I fared better than a lot, better than if I'd of been on the Srem front. But again, if they'd sent me to the front, preacher, I'd of never done what I did. I'd of ended up like the rest of 'em—either my bones would of rot-ted there in the flatlands, under some mulberry tree, or I'd of came home and lived in peace and quiet, without no worries . . .

But the way it is . . . The way it is, I don't sleep, don't joke, don't laugh, don't have fun, I don't even talk with people like I used to—I mean before my cow got me with her horn. Now, preacher, I just think, I think of what I did on the night of the fourteenth of March, in forty-five, and about Ljuba, who ain't here no more, except for in my head, and about this other fourteenth of March, this last spring. I think, I try to figure it out, and wonder: is there a God?

Because, if there *is* a God, then why did I *hafta* go and do what I did, preacher, huh?—and when nobody asked me to do it? You know, it's

true, I loved my brother a lot, I loved him, admired and respected him more than everybody else; when I think about him, I'd say that I loved him more than my own son; but, again, I didn't get Gornjak, I got Ljuba. Why's that?

And I wonder: if you do exist, God, who art in heaven—like I was taught to say by the dead priest Stojan Babić, the son of that same Vuk Babić of ours, who took to the woods and started the rebellion in forty-one—if you're everywhere and in every place, then why didn't you show up *then*, why didn't you finish what you started, instead of makin' the third shot go off?

It happened on that cursed day, in forty-five, around evenin' time.

We found him in a hut above Sjokovo—Ljuba, I mean. We found him in the mornin'.

We hunted Captain Marko—freedom was already blowin' through the air like the smell of spring, men and women and kids appeared on the doorsteps and intersections—the people wanted to live in peace again and to have a rest from all the fear, from requisitions and death. But Vuk Babić and two others, Blaško Jotić (the OZNA man from our village), and the other one, called Zeka, wouldn't cool down; they wanted to get Marko no matter what and clean up the area around Vranovac. Captain Djergo Graničarski was already gone—they found him dead, all stiff between his brother Prvan's beehives. But there wasn't a trace of Gornjak. We also hadn't got Marko—Babić kept sendin' us like dogs in the woods and thickets to hunt him down.

Well, on one of those patrols we broke into Gornjak's hut above Sjokovo. There was only three of us: Zeka, who died the next day at the monastery, Žuća Jotić, the OZNA major Blaško Jotić's brother, and me, the militia. "Where's your pops?" we asked him, but Gornjak's son, Ljuba, just blinked and stuttered. "I dunno," he said. He'd took his shoes off and was standin' in manure barefoot, and around him the sheep was gettin' all upset and runnin' around the pen, bleatin' and ringin' with their bells. I thought: oh, hell, what if his pops's around here somewhere, what if he hears us and comes runnin' out with a tommy gun? But nothin' happened.

"Whaddya mean, you dunno?" Žuća asked. He was a boy just like Ljuba, his beard wasn't even full yet. "You lyin' bandit!" he shouted in a squeaky voice and popped him right across the face; the boy went out

like a light and fell over in the manure. Then Zeka gave Žuća a chewin' out, and they both went off to Sjokovo and gave me orders to take Ljuba to Vranovac as soon as he came to.

And so we started off, preacher, him in front and me behind him. He had a bag over his shoulder; I had a rifle, one of those short Italian things. First, I waited for him to get his shoes on and get some cheese out of a barrel. He put the cheese in a covered wooden bowl, put the bowl and some cornbread in his bag, and we left. At first, we took the path, but later we took a shortcut through the orchards and forests. We just walked and didn't say nothin', him in front, me a few steps behind him. He didn't say nothin', and I didn't either. I kept away from the paths where everyone goes; for some reason I didn't want nobody seein' us together, I was thinkin' about his daddy, Gornjak, and my brother. I kept thinkin' and walkin', my legs was already beginnin' to ache, and we still had quite a ways to go to get to Vranovac. When we got to Babji Vis, and came to that split cliff, where that clear and cool spring is, I said to take a break. We sat down, him a little in front and me behind him. We was sittin' and not sayin' nothin', till he said:

"It's almost noon, ain't it, Uncle Pajča? I'm kinda hungry, and look, the water's clear as glass!"

"It's past noon," I told him. "Ljuba, if you're hungry, go ahead and eat, there ain't nobody stoppin' you."

So I said that to him, and we didn't say nothin' else, but I felt better: when a man hears a human voice, it warms his soul up. I thought: everything'll be fine, the war'll be over soon, and I'll go back home. That's what I thought, preacher, and I looked at Ljuba: he took out the cheese and broke the cornbread, and offered the first piece to me. "Here, take it," he said, like he knew that I hadn't put so much as a crumb down my throat for two days, then he took some himself and shoved it down like after a hard day's work. So we ate his cheese and cornbread, not sayin' a thing, and the spring was gurglin', beggin' us to take a drink. When we'd drank our fill, we set out again: him in front and me behind him. He didn't say nothin', neither did I, but then I got an itch to ask him somethin', all the sudden, right outta the blue: "So, kid, why'd you lie about where your father is?"

He stopped, like he'd tripped or somethin', and looked at me, waitin' for me to catch up. God, I thought, why do I gotta go shakin' up a hor-

nets' nest?—but now I didn't have no choice. I go up to him and stop there in front of him; he's just lookin' at me, still pale from bein' knocked out. Lookin' at me, not sayin' nothin', and then, all calm-like, he says: "I know, but what's the difference if my father ain't around here anyway?" —"Well, where is he?" I asked, all tense inside but tryin' not to make him suspicious. And he says: "My dad went off to the other end of the world, Uncle Pavle; to Australia—if you've heard of it."

"I ain't," I told him, now I was already confused. "And what's he gonna do there, in Australia?"

"He's gonna raise kangaroos, Uncle Pajča," he said and smiled. His smile was sort of crooked. I tell you: his lips were laughing, but his eyes were mockin' me. I could tell he wanted to put me down. "Well what's he gonna do with those . . . whaddya call 'em—kangaroos?" I ask him, just to be sayin' somethin', but I could feel an icy coldness growin' inside me; I'd of liked to stop the conversation. "What's he gonna do with 'em . . . ," Ljuba says, and I could tell that he was tryin' to make fun of me openly now. "You sure are dumb, Uncle Pajča. If you can't understand that, you're real stupid. I bet you can't even remember your own name!"

I shut up, rememberin' what he said, and started walkin'. The day was short, and it got dark pretty fast. Him out in front and me behind him. I kept walkin', my legs was hurtin', I had a blister on the sole of my left foot, and it stung and stung. I kept walkin' like that, watchin' his back. It was broad, still young, still like a child's, but his neck was thick, like a bull's—his father's was the same way. And above his neck he had thick, black hair, just like Gornjak. A chip off the old block, I thought, and saw my brother Jelenko again, my dear brother, my only brother, but I knew —he was gone. And so, while all those things was goin' through my head, we came out on the slope above the brick kiln, and from there you go down through a ravine and past two or three villages, and then you come to Vranovac. It was dark, there wasn't nobody nowhere. A dog barked and then quieted down again. I was cold, and I felt like there was a hundred miles between me and that kid! And so I kept goin', with him in front of me, when all of a sudden we come to the Gypsy Cemetery. And I thought to myself: If we cut through the cemetery, we'll be in Vranovac in no time, but if we go around it, we'll be wanderin' around till midnight; so I says to him: "Keep goin' straight."

He looked at me. His eyes flickered in the darkness, gleamin' suspiciously, as if he had a sort of bad feelin', and he went off down the trail. We went out in the middle of all the crosses and everything might of been all right, but then I saw a plum tree, preacher, a little to the side, in the middle of the darkness, and under the plum tree a fresh grave. They'd just dug it up—probably that evenin', 'cause there was gonna be a funeral the next day. I saw it and thought: well, that's handy. And I stopped! And he could tell I wasn't followin' him, so he stopped too. "Well now, Ljuba," I said all of a sudden and took my rifle off of my shoulder, "If you're hungry again, sit down and eat, 'cause it'll be your last meal."

He looked at me and didn't move an inch. I almost thought, preacher, that it wasn't a man in front of me, but a vampire. "C'mon, c'mon!" I told him, hurryin' him up, and pointed over with the barrel of my rifle to the pile of fresh, yellow soil that'd just been dug up. "Siddown and eat, I ain't got a lotta time."

He sat down. I saw how his fingers were stiff from the cold, like branches in wintertime; he barely could get the bag open, he could barely get the bowl open, he couldn't make himself swallow nothin'. I waited: he jabbed his fingers into the cheese, chewed on the cornbread, and the whole time he was leanin' and lookin' over his shoulder at me—I could tell: he didn't believe it.

"You done?" I asked him. He nodded and didn't take his eyes off me: he was afraid, he wanted to get up. "Well now, Ljuba, say a prayer for yourself, son," I said, and pulled back the bolt on the rifle and shut it again. "But say it for Jelenko too. He was my only brother, and your father killed him without battin' an eye, not even with a bullet—with beans." And then—I pulled the trigger! But my dear preacher, it misfired —there was only a *click,* and nothin' else. He gave a shudder, my hands was covered in sweat, all I could see was red; I loaded another bullet quick as I could, raised the rifle and took aim, but *click*—another misfire! "Oh God!" I thought, "What's this? You' surely can't be watchin' over him, you can't all the sudden be worried about justice and honor! You can't be too concerned about Ljuba's life, either, since you didn't raise a finger to help my brother, huh, God?!" And so I'd quit thinkin' and talkin' nonsense, so I could put it all behind me, so I wouldn't spend no more time daydreamin' and gettin' upset, I raised that damned rifle for a third time and took aim. And Ljuba Gornjakov, huddled there like a

swath of black grass, groaned: "I hope God lets my daddy suck the blood outta you with a straw, Uncle Pajča, like you're suckin' mine outta me right now . . ."

It was hard to listen to him, my dear preacher; that wasn't a voice I was hearin', preacher, but a curse; I pulled the trigger for a third time, and the rifle thundered . . .

All I saw was how he rolled down the pile of dirt and slid headfirst into the grave. I said at OZNA later: attempted escape. Who would of doubted it?

That night I slept like a log. But the next day, the fifteenth of March, I got some kind of sickness and started vomitin'; they sent me home to get some rest. Off in the village, I felt a little better, 'cause every day I could see my brother's empty yard, and his wife all dressed in black and shriveled like a dried apple, and his poor kids, who didn't have no father . . .

Later, times changed—nationalization, requisitionin' of food, workers' cooperatives, the split with the Russians over the IB's; new troubles and new worries. And preacher, I recovered a little, too. In the middle of all that change and commotion, I forgot about Ljuba for a while, and later, when the peasants had it a little better, I started livin' like's proper, too; that is, what respectable folk call a *normal life.*

Right up till this year. Till this damn fourteenth of March. Till my judgment day . . .

I didn't die, that's true; I just ain't got my spleen no more. But I don't thank God for that, preacher. 'Cause I don't know, preacher, whether there is one or not . . . Tell me. Help me understand what it is that happens with people. And with me. With my head and hands. Then, when I managed to load that third bullet. Tell me—I'm askin' you, prayin' to you, beggin' to you in the name of God, no matter if he exists or not. Tell an old man, Pavle Gligorijević, called Pajča "the Turkey," a peasant from Zjapina, Vranovac township, ruddy and full in the face till they took out his spleen on the fourteenth of March, but now thin. And yellow. From lack of sleep . . .

Translated by Stephen M. Dickey

Mladen Markov

Mladen Markov (born 1934) is a prolific storyteller and novelist. His stories are regularly included in anthologies of Yugoslav short stories and have been translated into several languages. His most important collections of stories are: *The Banat Train* (1973), *Frog's Leap* (1974), *The Middle Bell* (1979), *For the Leisure of Working People* (1978), and *Old People in the Country* (1986). His novels are: *The Elimination* (1972), *Moot Times* (1976), *Wringing the Soul* (1984), and *The Dog Cemetery* (1990).

Markov works and lives in Belgrade.

THE BANAT TRAIN

The Serbs from Samoš, the old-timers of Banat, had been smuggling since the first days of occupation. They carry flour and eggs to Pančevo and return with bags full of money bills.

In the evening, in the light of an oil lamp, Grandpa counts the money. In the middle of the room, on the earthen floor, a pile of money bills. Grandpa runs his bony hand through the pile, as if winnowing wheat. His eyes are beaming.

The Isakovs most often travel with their grandson who, due to his innocent looks, serves as a shield. They are cunning—they are always taking the boy to the doctor. It is easy to arouse pity with occupation authorities.

The train from Pančevo runs to Samoš, where it is switched to a siding; there it spends the night and is returned to the track in the morning.

The people from Samoš take their seats with great noise. When it is still dark, at the crack of dawn, they call to each other, trip over the rails, and fall on their bags, knitted peasant sacks over their shoulders. They stagger in the dark to take their seats on wooden benches in the cars on the siding. They quarrel with the conductor, who at first tries to stop them but then stands aside, as if faced by a torrent breaking through a dam. Anyone could get up early and take a seat before the others, but the scene blocking the steps is repeated every morning, accompanied by curses, screams, and shrieks from the same women, whom they called black marketeers.

These are women whose husbands are in German prison camps and

doing forced or voluntary labor. They have taken up trading, smuggling, and other dubious activities connected with night travel.

Going to the train station, the peasants gather in small groups, afraid of the buck sergeant, Werner, who often fires his gun without a reason.

The Samošans make themselves at home in the cars and from their bags take out their breakfast. In the yellow light, their faces look waxen, half dead. They spread a white towel over their knees, cross themselves, and place boiled eggs, bacon, and a piece of white bread on the towel. They eat noisily, swallow and choke on the half-chewed food, hiccup with wide-open and frightened eyes.

Accompanied by the whistles of the railroad workers, the shouting, and noise of the buffers, the train switches to the main track. The peasants enjoy this part of the ride. They titter like cheaters. They say they are riding for free. The locomotive comes out of the roundhouse, takes on water, hisses, gets warmed up. It lets off clouds of steam. While the train switches from the side track to the main track, the peasants in the cars tumble about. Those who are seated rock but don't stop eating. They choke and cough. They curse the conductor quietly, through their teeth.

The train leaves on time, first moving slowly, then it accelerates. Through the half-opened window, soot and cinders fly in. A signal cabin and a cemetery glide by, and the train leaves their district.

By the trees near the tracks in the plain, they know that the first stop is approaching. They are already nervous. They hurriedly swallow the last pieces of food, as if eating their last meal, stuff the towels in their bags, and squeeze closer to each other on the wooden benches, as before a storm.

Entering the station, the train releases circular clouds of steam like cigarette smoke rings, and the Isakov boy, with his face pressed against the window, barely reads the Latin characters PAAA-DIII-NAAA. Uncertain of the letters, he turns to his father and grandfather. "Is this Padina?"

"Slovaks again?"

"Totovi," the father whispers.[1]

The boy would have asked more, but the wheels begin to screech, and in the clouds of steam he sees men and women in Slovak costumes milling

1. TOT was a fascist work organization in various nations. Members wore uniforms and were for the most part the keepers of law and order. (Translator's note)

around as if emerging from a fog. More and more. They dash into the cars shouting.

"Move!"

"Move, Pavluška!"

That is Father murmuring, making fun of the Slovaks' famous soccer player, Pavluška, whom the fans cheered in those peaceful times when they still played games village against village.

The Samošans are tittering. Then suddenly they place their hands over their mouths, hiding their smiles.

The Slovaks burst into the car as if they have run two miles, panting and hysterical, without interrupting their conversations begun in the village or at the station. They push the Samošans, they grab them by their collars, push them off the wooden benches, and take their places.

The Samošans get up unwillingly, but they still get up without a word and give up their seats.

Now the Slovaks from Padina sit, and the Serbs from Samoš stand in the space between the benches. Leaning against the wooden car walls, they look with envy and hatred at those who have ousted them from their seats. The exchange takes place in silence, without a word. Only somewhere, at the end of the car, a voice of a Totovac can be heard.

"Move over, f——— your Serbian mother!"

The train travels on.

Until a short while ago, the wheels had been knocking so pleasantly, so sonorously against the rails.

The boy can no longer press his skinny pale face against the glass of the wet window and watch how the poles fly by or how a frightened hare runs diagonally across the field; he has been pushed with his father and grandfather into the passage between the cars. Grandpa's bony hand squeezes him painfully, as if someone wants to take him away and they are protecting him, holding him tight and pressing him to themselves.

At the next station, Kovačica—again, a Slovak village—the scene at Padina is repeated and the Samošans are pushed into the hall. The people from Kovačica, like those from Padina, without a word take space between benches and raise those Samošans who have kept their seats by playing dumb, push themselves by them; and the boy, with his grandpa and father, suddenly finds himself in the hall.

He is trying to crawl out from under the wide Slovak skirts, to push

away a jacket with seams of felt that is tickling his face. It stinks of moth-balls. He is pressed by a fat-ass Slovak in cotton trousers who is persistently pushing a woman from behind with his fists: he wants to force his way into the car. Even the clattering of the wheels cannot be heard anymore. Only the soft, Slovak, singsong speech. The odor of sweat.

All the way to Debeljača, the boy is trying to remove from his face the wool from the seam of a jacket, to see a strip of light through the window, but his grandpa, weaker than those standing inside, pushes him toward the door of the toilet. A stink from there. The boy is mad at Grandpa. His father has raised his head and is looking somewhere at the ceiling, at the fly-specked gas lamp; he seems to be pretending not to see anything.

In Debeljača, which the boy knows by its fairs, heart-shaped cookies, and the multitude of cars at the fairground, the Hungarians get on. Debeljača is populated only by Hungarians. The train halts in Debeljača a little longer. Through all that flesh, jackets, skirts, and the patter of rain, one can hear music from the station loudspeaker and a woman's voice singing quietly and sorrowfully in Hungarian:

> Kisètáltam nagy—körösy temeton,
> Elvesztettem piros—sárga keszeenöm.

> (I strolled through the Negkeresz Cemetery,
> I lost my red-yellow handkerchief.)

The Hungarians jump in while the train is still moving. They are merry, and most of them are drunk. They hang on the step railings. The boy hears their cursing and a sudden scream of a Samošan who has not moved away in time. The Hungarians jump on the train with less noise and more dignity, but with more blows to the ribs of the Samošans.

Now it is the Slovaks' turn to get up and give up their seats to the Hungarians.

The Hungarians sit down sluggishly, relax, shake the raindrops from their fur hats, and the Serbs crowd into the toilet and onto the iron couplings between the cars.

Someone curses in Hungarian that a Serbian swine has stepped on his foot.

"Move, Serb!" an emboldened Slovak voice is heard.

Everybody is cursing the Serbian mother.

The boy finds himself in the toilet with his grandpa. Grandpa hugs the boy tighter and tighter, covers his eyes by pretending to straighten his cap at the ears. Obviously, he does not want the boy to hear or see anything. He always regrets having taken him along, but that lasts only until time to depart, when the smuggler in him wins over. The boy complains and pushes Grandpa away, just as he does when they give him a bath on Saturday evenings and the soap begins to burn his eyes. The whites of Grandpa's eyes look like big ground glasses; frightened and tired, he sits on the toilet seat with the boy between his legs. The bag of one of the two Samošans who have also squeezed themselves into the toilet hits the boy's face. From the bag wafts the smell of lard.

The Banat train travels on.

The boy then listens to the commotion at the Crepaja station. Somebody is yelling in Serbian that there is no more room, and a Hungarian voice duly curses the Serbian mother and says they ought to be forced to go on foot. And where is that Serbian riffraff going anyway, the Hungarian voice asks again; they ought to be forbidden to go anywhere.

Grandpa looks funny. He sits with his legs spread wide on the toilet seat as though he is relieving himself. His face looks that way too.

The boy stands on tiptoe, sees through the broken window how the people from Crepaja hop onto the steps, dangling from the cars like those being hanged. The autumn rain beats into their faces.

The train rumbles on, pulls its weight with difficulty, moans. Cinders fly in through the windows, soot burns the eyes. The train breaks again, squeaks, moans, lets off steam, and the conductor yells: "Fraaaaaanz-veeeeeld!"

This word he sings in two parts. He prolongs the first part, then the second, and the boy feels Grandpa's hand clench his shoulder. Having heard German words many times during frequent smuggling trips, Grandpa suddenly gets up. The boy keeps asking where Grandma is. The old man pays no attention to the boy's questions but, trembling, with sacks in both hands, he pushes the boy ahead of him and, as if surrendering, comes out of the toilet.

From the platform he hears the German word: *"Wohin?"* Then again: "Where to?" Prolonged, persistent, as if this word is being bored into someone's head. The question remains unanswered.

Boarding the train now are the Germans, natives of Franzveld. First

to step aside are Serbs from Crepaja. They withdraw humbly and stand to one side, close to the car, looking at the ground. The Slovaks sneak through the hall hastily, like thieves, close to the car walls and into the vestibule, and the Hungarians unwillingly get up and give their seats to the Germans.

Now the Germans are sitting, and in the space between seats, bristling and angry, barely controlling their rage, stand the Hungarians, glaring at the Germans, who do not even deign to look at them. The Slovaks are in the corridor, in the toilet, and in the vestibules, and the Serbs hang like scarecrows from the car steps. The wind buffets them, the rain runs down their faces.

A general dissatisfaction reigns. Everybody curses the Serbs.

Every time the boy wonders about that, because, according to the logic of his children's games, he knows very well that those who are sitting and are forced to get up ought to be cursing.

The people of Samoš and Crepaja are hanging from the steps. Grandpa has grabbed the bar with both arms and is hugging the boy, who would like to let go, to get down and run across the Banat field, because Grandpa's coarse beard is scratching his neck and his breath stinks of home-made tobacco.

On his arm, the boy feels Father's strong hand. His soul is penetrated by Father's gentle, warm look of forbearance, trying to cheer him up and with tightly pressed lips advising him to endure just a little more, because pretty soon they'll arrive in Pančevo.

Translated by Vasa D. Mihailovich

Grozdana Olujić

Grozdana Olujić, born in 1934 in Srem, writes novels, stories, and fairy tales. Her first novel, *An Exursion to the Sky*, appeared in 1957. After that she published *I Vote for Love* (1963), *Let Sleeping Dogs Lie* (1964), and *Wild Seed* (1964). In 1985 appeared her collection of short stories, *The African Violet*. She also published three collections of fairy tales: *Mother-of-Pearl Rose* (1979), *Heavenly River* (1984) and *The Starry Wanderers* (1987).

Olujić is one of the most frequently translated writers of her generation. She lives in Belgrade.

THE AFRICAN VIOLET

Later he tried to recall who had brought the African violet into the Records Office and why. But all he could remember was how the dusky, lovely sound of its name had rung out as the greenish faces of the clerks floated behind the glass partitions, as in some huge aquarium. He remembered, too, that he had felt an involuntary pull: the African violet hinted at humid, torrid African nights, at the scented armpits of the jungle and the snakelike bodies of black women, something intoxicating and dangerous for which he had no name, had never come close to, nor ever would. Haltingly, he snapped off a leaf, cut it at the stem, took it home, and planted it in a flowerpot, vaguely aware of a strange sensation of familiarity. Marta's irritation was astonishing.

"For heaven's sake, Danilo Aracki, what do you want with that thing?" she cried, calling him by his full name, as if they had not been married for the past thirty years. He did not know what to say, so he climbed silently into bed.

In the tepid dream taking shape behind his eyelids, the succulent, fuzzy leaf of the African violet floated through the night, turning into a bird at one moment and into the black hair of a woman whose face he could not remember the next. He woke up in a sweat and looked toward the window where the flowerpot stood on the sill between two panes of glass. The sun streamed down on the drooping leaf, and it seemed to unfold under the light. Then he thought he saw it wave the green banner of its smile at him.

"Look, it's saying hello!" he remembered thinking and smiled at the strange quiver that rose from his belly.

"Ridiculous!" he whispered to himself, but he could not explain either then or later why his whole body had trembled. He had never liked flowers, he seldom even noticed their shape or color, not to mention their names. What was happening? He went to work and forgot both the quiver and the question. But as he recorded the petitions and complaints that morning, his mind kept turning to the violet: he remembered its meaty, fuzzy leaf and worried whether it would unfold, whether it would ever bring forth a plant, a flower with dark blue, mysterious petals, like the dark blue night butterfly. And then he wondered at his apprehensiveness.

"Why, it's only a flower, what's the matter with me?" He buried his head in the petitions and complaints, but somewhere behind the papers the flower was turning a darker and darker shade of blue, like the dreamy eyes of a girl. Later, he was never able to explain to himself how he had actually *seen* the flower, when only the leaf was in the flowerpot. How he had known its shape and color, sensed its character and habits? But he was sure that he *had* seen it, and so his friendship with the African violet started before it had produced even a single petal, at a time when it was still uncertain whether the leaf would ever unfold and take root at all.

Marta was convinced that nothing would come of the violet.

"Absolutely nothing," she said and smiled. He thought he saw a certain triumphant smirk in that smile and he winced.

"He probably got that flowerpot from some woman," she thought hatefully, and moved it to the hall, sure that the leaf would wilt before he got back. She was all the more surprised, therefore, when she saw it back at the window the very next day.

The African violet was moved back and forth, and so began their silent war in which neither asked himself or the other why the violet was being moved and still less why the husband took such tender care of it while the wife held it in such utter contempt.

"Why, it's me she hates," it dawned on him, when he noticed that the leaf, which by now was sizable, had drooped in the draft. She knew how he detested drafts, how they left him with a headache, and this was one of her ways of showing that she disapproved of something he had done or said.

"Now, what's bothering her?"

He was surprised to see that the violet reacted almost the same way as he did to drafts, but he paid no attention to its sagging leaf, although he did notice that the edges had curled. He was more surprised by the expression on Marta's face: it was hard, set, mean. How had he never noticed that before? How had she managed to hide it for so many years? He remembered the brief chill he had felt two years ago when, for virtually no reason at all, she had forced her own daughter to marry a man she did not love. Her face gleamed then with the same hard, mean look. Had it been like that when she had persuaded him to leave his job on the boat for one in an office, saying that she was worried about his health? He could not remember, although he did recall that when he entered the Records Office he had felt the stomach cramps of a man diving into dark, oily water with no way out.

With time, that impression only grew. Behind the glass partitions, the grayish faces of the clerks moved almost soundlessly from seven to three on Mondays, from seven to three on Tuesdays, from seven to three every day, from the beginning to the end of the world, forever. Sometimes he thought that this underwater life, dark and oppressive, would continue even when he was no more, while somewhere out there ships sailed along the Sava and Danube, past the silvery shadows of the weeping willows, where water flowers rose up past the Tisa to meet the boatmen. How had she ever managed to get him off the boat and why had he let her? He did not know. Now he was here, half-stifled, half-dead, wanting nothing, listless, the way she wanted him, if that was what she wanted.

The banks of rivers whose names he did not know slid past Danilo's closed eyes, water lilies opened their eyes, strange shiny-feathered birds flew by. The office workers whispered that Danilo was just dozing, but they did not disturb or report him. He was usually the first to finish his work, and then, out of boredom or kindness, or whatever, he would do their work too, with no thought of recognition or repayment. If Marta had known, she would have thought he was out of his mind. She had never understood him. He was still young, although graying at the temples; he could have achieved a lot, but he had achieved nothing. The lowest of the low, a pathetic little scribbler, that's what he was, and that is what he would be until the end of his days. He was so completely devoid

of any desire for success that even the smallest raise in salary or promotion surprised him, almost worried him. The books he brought home to read were alien to her. They were not books to help you advance, get ahead in life. She hated them almost as much as she hated the African violet, but she did not dare to throw them out of the house: she knew his quick temper. But she did not know about Danilo's recurring dream about crossing a ramshackle bridge.

Water rushed under the bridge that he tried so hard to cross, for on the other side stood a shining castle, translucent. Inside, a girl with dark blue eyes waited for him to come as if her life depended upon it. Then the girl would turn into a dark, mysterious African violet, the boards of the bridge would give way under his feet, and he would start tumbling down toward the dark swift-moving water, but he would wake up before he actually fell in. What did the dream mean? His was an ordinary life, gray, no ups and downs. Tired, as if he had not slept well, he shaved, shoveled breakfast and coffee into his stomach, and went to work, forgetting both the girl and the violet.

In the office it was like being under water: oppressive and dark. The dreamy, flaccid faces of the clerks wafted past the glass walls. They moved in uncoordinated slow motion, like people in a dream. The feeling of being under heavy layers of water grew until he began to suffocate, remembering someone saying long ago that the Arackis died of heart trouble. Ridiculous. As if it made any difference whether you died of heart trouble, diabetes, or your kidneys: man is swollen with his own death, he just does not know when the dam will burst.

For days afterwards, he wondered whether he had said that or something else to the doctor when he woke up after the heart attack. The doctor looked at him anxiously, wrote out a prescription, and left, surprised that the patient had asked no questions, hadn't even tried to find out how many days had elapsed between that hot July morning when they had picked him up like a sack and shoved him into a hospital and the moment he woke up in his bed and saw the flowerpot with the African violet.

The flower that had blossomed from the still tender leaves was just as he had seen it in his mind's eye, in his dreams. Even the dark blue petals, with their threads of black at the bottom and sprinkle of silvery powder,

had the same color, arrangement, and shape. For a second he thought the flower was watching him, following his eyes and movements, that it *knew* what he felt, intended, or wanted. That surprised and almost scared him. But in the coming days the impression grew that the flower was not living beside, but with him. It reached a point where its petals would droop, wilt, when he was not feeling well, or it would flutter fretfully when he was having palpitations. By now, he could tell from the way the African violet behaved when he would develop a fever or have a fainting spell or pain, and when they would pass, because the flower would cringe with him at the pain in his chest.

In the morning, when the sun skipped out and he felt better, the flower's leaves and petals would seem to come to life, straightening up spryly and fluttering in the wind and sun. Nightfall was as hard for the flower as it was for him. Danilo Aracki thought they awaited it with the same dread, that the petals even dreamed the same dream in which a dark blue butterfly circled a candle until it flew into the flame and burned. The butterfly had the face of the violet at one moment and Danilo's the next. He thought this was the fever coming on and whispered feelingly to the flower to hold on: they would cross the bridge over the rushing, dark river, reach the castle, and open the gates leading to the hall full of light. He did not know what awaited them in that hall, but he felt it was there and that they would reach it, that for some reason it was very important to do so.

It was snowing outside now, but the African violet kept blossoming, rejoicing at every drop of water he gave it, at every chance ray of sun, although it was not too fond of heat and light, just as it did not like a change of setting or a change in the weather.

"We are alike in that, too," he smiled inwardly, as Marta shook her head suspiciously.

"What girl is he secretly smiling at?" she wondered hatefully, eyeing the flower that had to be some special keepsake. She couldn't wait for spring to come so she could finally get it out of the room.

As when the children were small and did something naughty, their eyes would now cross paths over the flowerpot with extended spells of pregnant silence. Then their eyes would meet, and she would turn away her head. Danilo trembled, feeling that with that one movement she was

simply writing him off. She was in good health and would live long; she would outlive both him and the flower; she should show more patience with them. He asked her to bring the flowerpot nearer to him, to put it on the night table, but then he remembered that the flower did not like to be moved, so he changed his mind.

"Never mind, let it stay by the window," he smiled, "it's better for it there!" The tenderness in his voice made Marta furious. Who had given him that flower, whom did it make him think of? She left the room and slammed the door angrily behind her. He never worried about where *she* would feel better, why should she be so stupid to care about him and some dumb flower?

Marta would leave the house feeling worse and worse, leaving him alone, first for hours, then for whole days, wondering whether he even noticed her absence. She could not tell from his face what he felt, what he thought. That was what had first attracted her to him until it slowly, inexorably began to repel her. That shuttered, cold face lived somewhere inside itself, for itself. There was no place for her in his world. Rejected, she stood on her shore while he sailed waters known to him alone, taking root in the damp, dark soil of the jungle, surprised that the violet accepted the lean, loose, foreign earth. Marta could never forget the mountains from which she hailed.

"She never loved me," he thought and gazed gratefully at the dark blue African violet, sprinkled with silver powder.

"She was never like you," he muttered, unsurprised that the flower was looking at him trustfully, opening its eyes wide like a traveler who has finally come home after a long searching journey.

"That was me who summoned you!" he thought and smiled.

"Or, maybe, you summoned *me*?" He suddenly felt his entire being pulled toward the light, his cheeks and fingers touching the cold surface of the glass, as he bent to see the face of a man whose eyes were turned longingly to the window. He vaguely realized he was looking at himself from out of the violet, but he felt neither fear nor surprise that the memory of the willow's silvery shadows should mingle with memories of the jungle's dank darkness. Then he drew a long breath and smiled: a new, more mysterious and richer life opened up before him, slowly, serenely, happily, like the African violet when it opened its dark blue eyes at the

coming of the dawn. All he could do was accept it, happy that Marta would never learn that he now existed in a different light. With his petals, like fingers, he touched the smooth glass and smiled. A new day was dawning over the rooftops.

Translated by Christina Pribićević-Zorić

Danilo Kiš

Danilo Kiš (1935–1989) was born in Subotica, near the Hungarian border. His father, a Jew from Hungary, perished at Auschwitz, and Danilo was raised by his mother in Montenegro. After graduating from the University of Belgrade in comparative literature, he started to write early and translated French poetry into Serbo-Croatian. Kiš taught at the University of Bordeaux and at the Sorbonne and died in Paris.

His works include the novels *The Attic* (1962), *Psalm 44* (1963), *Garden, Ashes* (1965), and *Hourglass* (1972), and several collections of short stories: *Early Woes* (1970), *A Tomb for Boris Davidovich* (1976), *Encyclopedia of the Dead* (1983), and *The Lute and Scars* (1993). He also wrote several volumes of essays and a number of plays for theatre and television.

Kiš's books have appeared in major world languages. *A Tomb for Boris Davidovich*, *Hourglass*, *Garden, Ashes* and *Encyclopedia of the Dead* were published in the United States. Kiš was awarded major Yugoslavian literary awards and in 1989 received the Bruno Schulz Prize.

Kiš tells his stories in a lyrical language and in a string of dreamlike sequences. According to William Gass, "It is the consistent quality of Kiš's prose that counts. It is its nearly faultless execution that takes away the breath and produces admiration."

THE LUTE AND SCARS

Although I had sworn that I would never set foot in there again, nevertheless, one evening, after a two-year absence from Belgrade, I stopped by the Writers' Club. I had already convinced myself that associating with writers is unpleasant, full of misunderstandings, envy, and insults. But I was also aware that this type of spiritual struggle, *escrime littéraire*, bitter and sterile, is also a part of the literary craft, like writing reviews or proofreading. In addition, I recalled Chekhov's advice to a young writer, his challenge to leave the provinces and mix with the literary circles in the big city so as to lose some of his false idealism after becoming better aquainted with other writers.

It was a warm early fall, and people were still sitting in the park. A murmur was heard, the scraping of silverware, the titter of women. Entering the garden, I glanced over the crowd and discovered, to no surprise, that nothing had changed during my two-year absence: all the people were sitting in their old places, and it was as if they were still drinking the same bottle of wine they had ordered on the last evening I had been there. Only the women were a bit plumper and the men had turned a little gray at the temples and their stomachs had swelled. The circles under their eyes were even darker, their voices hoarser from drinking and smoking. I turned my back to the garden, and now in my field of vision there was just one table, beneath a gnarled tree, the one closest to the entrance. Two middle-aged men whom I didn't know sat at the table with a woman with a round face, bleached hair, and small expressive eyes.

The woman smiled at me. "You don't recognize me?"

I shook my head.

"Anjutka," she said. "We met once at Nikola's place."

Then I remembered. "Don't spit in the well from which you will drink," I said quietly. "How are you?"

"I got married," she said. "This is my husband."

She looked like a shaggy old dog. Each time she brushed back the hair that had fallen over her eyes, she tossed her head back coquettishly, causing the sagging skin on her cheeks to shake. She was one of those women who did not know how to age, who add a grotesque mask of false youth to the misfortune of aging. I easily figured how old she was. When I slept with her, she was thirty-nine and I was twenty-three. Some fifteen years had passed since then. "I could be your mother," she had said to me. "Almost." I lived close to the Danube Station then. She demanded that I address her in the formal way. "*That* doesn't give you the right to address me informally," she said; then she would begin to roll her eyes and to feign passion. In the morning, I took her to the trolley and told her that we wouldn't see each other again. She answered me with a proverb: "Don't spit in the well from which you will drink." She was right. A week later I looked for her once again!

"I was thinking about you, Anjutka." The next morning, I greeted the dawn at her maternal breast.

At that time, she was a tour guide for the Russians and engaged in black-marketeering. She managed to sell me Bulgarian rose water (tiny ampullae in a wooden box, similar to salt shakers), a bas-relief brass portrait of Pushkin on a base of Caspian marble, and the collected works of Alexander Blok in three volumes (Moscow, 1958). I knew that these were presents that she received from tourists . . .

Leaning toward the men at the table, she quietly told them something while shaking her head. I saw the treacherous efficiency of the work of time on her face.

I asked the waiter to deliver a bottle of wine to her table and left as soon as I had finished my soup. It was around three in the morning. As I passed her, she grabbed me by the sleeve.

"You weren't at Nikola's funeral," she said. "No doubt, you were abroad again."

"I was."

"There were all of four of us at his funeral. He died in his sleep. They found him a week later. I don't think he suffered. Here's my card. Please call me."

I heard her voice as if from a distance. I remember shaking hands with those two men, one of whom was her husband. I went down Francuska Street toward the Square of the Republic, then toward the Hotel Moscow. The showcases in the passage of the Zvezda movie theater were still illuminated: dirt had crept into the cloth-covered doorknobs, changing their colors; dead flies lay at the bottom of the glass, as in a dried-up aquarium. The early daybreak was violet, a distant announcement of dawn. While in the passage, I heard the ringing of an alarm clock; a light came on in a courtyard window.

The wooden porch at the back of the courtyard was rotten; rusty garbage cans were arranged in front. A cat jumped between the cans and dashed in front of me. I peeped through the rotted boards, inside it was dark and smelled musty, it seemed to me that I heard the squeak of rats. I went out to the street again. Reaching the corner, I turned down Balkan Street. Through a metal fence, in the first light of dawn, I saw a junkyard. The wall separating it from the house in which I once lived had been demolished, the windows of the house removed, the roof destroyed. In the junkyard, beside a large spool of wire cable, stood a dump truck loaded with bricks and debris. All at once, I heard the chirp of birds and I looked in that direction. A tall wilted tree, leaning toward the courtyard, shook its still-green leaves, upset by the presentiment of the sunrise rather than by the breeze that had began to blow. I recalled these words: "People can cut it down, but a shoot will sprout in another place. It will bore through rock or concrete."

In my last years at the university, I found an apartment in the center city—the dream of all students, especially those from the interior of the country. It gives you, besides a certain social prestige, the privilege of staying in the cafes until very late without fear of missing the last bus and having to wait until early morning for the next one, freezing in the winter—an experience with which I was all too familiar. The apartment was located in a passage that connected two streets. After walking through the passage—in which were located the display windows of a leather goods shop and shops for mending nylons, fountain pens, and buttons—you then came to a courtyard paved with stones. At the back

of the courtyard, to the left, was a porch from which you descended on crumbling brick steps to the lower level, to Balkan Street. The building was very old, a single floor with a Turkish porch and walls from which the plaster had fallen off, with warped window frames and shaky wooden doors. The landlords were elderly Russians, emigrants from the twenties, a married couple without children. They rented the apartment for a sum that covered only a part of the charges for electricity and water —you could say, for free. Anjutka, the tourist guide, recommended me to them. I met her on Skadarlija Street through some Russian writers whom I was supposed to take over from her and escort to the Writers' Club for an official dinner.

I slept on a metal army cot, while another one, leaning against the opposite wall of the room, was occupied by Nikola. Maria Nikolaevna spent her time in the other, smaller room that also served as a kitchen.

Since I spent much time outside the house—days in the library and evenings at the club—I was satisfied with my new apartment; it was a free place to spend the night, and in the center of the city, too. I had a bathroom with hot water, and my landlords never objected to my coming home late.

Maria Nikolaevna was a sickly, slightly sarcastic woman with a swollen face scarred on one side by traces of burns. Her hands also suffered from these burns: the contorted skin pulled back the tendons and muscles, and her fingers looked like claws. Maria Nikolaevna rarely came into the "men's room." She would knock on the door and, sticking her head in, would issue a reprimand that allowed no objection: "I know that you don't own anything besides that guitar. There's no need to lie"; or, "Somebody threw up in the bathroom last night. I hope that it wasn't Nikola. Next time it should be cleaned up better. Good night"; or, "The bathroom was full of smoke yesterday. And you weren't at home. That means that Nikola has started to smoke. It's all your influence." In a very strict voice: "He has also started drinking with you. He *never* drank earlier. He's become a bohemian because of you."

Nikolai Aleksinski was an old man of erect bearing with short gray hair and cheerful blue eyes. He was deaf as a post, but that didn't affect his spirit or his cheerfulness in the slightest. He rose early, took a cold shower all year round (then a "hu-hu-hu" and "ha-ha-ha" would be heard from the bathroom). He fasted once a week—Fridays—for health

reasons; on that day he would drink only spring water, which he brought from somewhere in a large demijohn. But all this was not that almost inappropriate warding off death typical of old people; rather, it was much more of a type of spiritual, military discipline and hedonism. I learned to communicate with him with my fingers through a kind of sign language. The alphabet consisted of a schematic survey of the old Russian Cyrillic alphabet and symbolic abbreviations: touching the hair with a finger meant the initial letter of the word or the word itself, *h* as in hair; a touch to the teeth, *t* as in teeth; the clasping of hands together *f* as in friendship, etc. It was enough to show him the first few symbols; as soon as the word was started, he would finish it aloud, looking you right in the eye.

I show him: open thumb and forefinger *(s)*, then I put the tip of these fingers together *(o)*, spread them apart *(v)* . . .

"Soviet," he says.

I show him: *l, i, t* . . .

"Literature," he finishes. "Soviet literature is still young," he says, "like young grass. One must wait for it to grow."

I tell him (showing my fingers): "They are constantly walking on that grass."

"No one can keep that grass from growing," he says. "You see that wilted tree in the courtyard. It grew from the concrete. Look."

I tell him: "People . . ."

"People can cut it down," he is reading my mind, "but a shoot will sprout in another place. It will bore through rock or concrete."

I ask him: "Did you know Prince Zhevakhov?"

He looks at me in amazement. "Where did you dig up that name?"

I tell him: "I read his book on Nilus."

He waved his hand.

"Zhevakhov lived," I say, "in Novi Sad until recently. The Russian immigrants had their headquarters in Sremska Mitrovica."

"Zhevakhov was an unlucky person. In old age his mind was almost completely gone. He had visions. Don't you have any more intelligent work to do than to be occupied with the crazy Prince Zhevakhov?"

"I'm gathering evidence," I say. "He wrote, regarding Nilus, about the *Protocols of the Elders of Zion*." What did this Zhevakhov look like?"

"In his youth, he was handsome, tall. The last time I saw him was be-

fore the war. He still wore his old-fashioned *pince-nez* and the Order of Nicholas on his threadbare jacket."

I hand him the manuscript of my first book. (That book would be published three or four years later.)

"It's as if you belonged to the Serapion brothers' circle," he says. "The same approach can be perceived. Your reality is poetic."

I tell him that poetic reality is also reality.

"Reality," he says, "is like the grass and the earth. Reality is the grass that grows and the feet that walk on it."

I tell him that that is also a poetic picture. A metaphor.

"A picture perhaps," he says. "Let's have one more. This is sour cherry brandy from the village. Some of my friends brought it to me. A writer should," he continues, "perceive life in its entirety. To point to the grand theme of dying—how man should be less arrogant, less selfish, less evil—but, on the other hand, to make sense of life. Art is the balance between these two contradictory thoughts. The duty of man, especially of the writer—and you'll say that I'm talking like an old man—is to exit this world leaving behind him not deeds, deeds are everything, but something from goodness, something from knowledge. Every written word is like a genesis." (A pause.) "Can you hear: the first birds are already singing. Let's go to sleep. Maria Nikolaevna will be angry if we continue in this way until dawn. She has had a difficult life. Very difficult."

I never dared to ask him about the fire that left those horrible traces on her body. Just as I never learned anything about his life. From that acquaintance who sent me to their apartment and who recommended me, I learned only that Maria Nikolaevna "suffered in a fire during her escape from Russia," and about Nikolai Aleksinski just that he arrived in Belgrade through Constantinople and that he was a forestry engineer (a profession that I later assigned to one of my fictional heroes in one of my stories as a remembrance of Nikolai Aleksinski, since even then he resembled fiction to me). Although I spent many nights in conversation with this fine old man with a cheerful spirit, I never heard a single confessional sentence from him. I thought that my trust would put him in the position of debtor and that at some point he would open up to me. In spite of all of my confessions, I never heard from him a single fact about his earlier life.

I tell him: "What . . . am . . . I . . . going . . . to . . . do? I . . . love . . . two . . . women."

His face immediately takes on an expression of sincere concern; his eyes, with a smile which cheers one up, show that the matter of my romantic troubles has touched his heart.

"Love is a terribly difficult thing. Don't hurt either one of them. And don't act rashly. Because of yourself. And because of them."

I tell him: "You saw one of them. I introduced you to her a month ago."

"Clytemnestra," he says. "A real Clytemnestra. She is in a state to do something evil. To me or to you. Love is a terrible thing. What can I tell you? You can't learn from someone else's romantic experience. Each encounter between men and women begins as if it were the first encounter on earth. As if there had never been from Adam and Eve till today a billion such encounters. But, you see, the experience of love cannot be transferred. That is a great misfortune. And a great happiness. God arranged it so. One more and then I will put the bottle away. Maria Nikolaevna would get angry. Be careful. Never insult anyone. Wounds from love leave the deepest impressions in the soul. And don't let literature replace love. Literature is also dangerous. Life can't be replaced by anything."

From time to time, I would ask him to play something on the lute. If he were in a good mood, he would say: "Tune it for me. You already know how to do that."

I would tune the lute and he would begin to play. He knew a few lieder and romantic gypsy songs. In his extinguished hearing, a few melodies still smoldered, like a distant memory. He emitted strange sounds, like a growl.

"I think that it is giving a good sound today," he says.

I agree with a nod of my head.

"That's because it's cloudy outside," he says. "The lute had dried out. This weather suits it. Is it tuned well?"

Bending over the instrument, as if he were trying to hear it, he strikes several chords. Then he looks me straight in the eye.

"A minor," I say.

"It is cloudy outside. The humidity suits it."

I visited him years later when I too had already turned gray. Whenever it was difficult for me, whenever I needed some advice, I would drop by his place. I knew that he followed all of my work published in journals, as well as reviews of my books.

"Talent is a curse," he told me. "Pushkin suffered because of his talent. There isn't any greater envy than that provoked by the grace of a gift. Talented people are rare, but there are millions of mediocre ones. It is an eternal struggle. And don't completely isolate yourself in books. Travel. Listen to people. And listen to your internal voice. Maria Nikolaevna is waiting for you. And don't blame her that she occasionally chides you. She is sick. And unhappy.

Maria Nikolaevna, wrapped in a worn woolen shawl, is sitting by the window. The window looks out on a dark courtyard enclosed by a crumbling wall.

"I read in the newspaper," she says, "that the theater where you work is going to Russia. Are you also traveling with them?"

"Yes," I say, "we are going on a tour for about fifteen days."

"That's what they write in the newspaper. Would you be able to do us a favor?"

"I would be pleased to."

"Here, I have written down two addresses, both in Moscow. The first one is the address of my sister, Valeria Mihailovna Shchukina. The other, Maria, like me, Yermolaevna Shishkova, that is her best friend. Mine too, once. The last time I received a letter from them was in January '56. That is, nine years ago. There is a chance that they are alive, or at least one of them. I assume that someone would have already been found to inform me if they had died. Here, just in case, is one more name, Karaeva, Natalia Viktorovna. She is the youngest. Let me write down that address also. She could, if you can't find those other two, tell you what happened to them. Would that be difficult for you to do for us?"

The second day after our arrival in Moscow, I managed to bribe the strict guard on my floor. Before the door of the hotel stood an invalid in a threadbare military overcoat who supported himself with a crutch; he stuck out his greasy cap to passers-by. I gave him some change. He thanked me as if he were reciting a passage from Dostoyevsky.

As soon as I disappeared around the corner, I found the taxi stand that

I had discovered a day earlier during our official tour of the city. The taxi took me to a large apartment building with a dark entrance and long cold corridors.

I spoke to some little girls who were playing in the entrance. They looked at me in astonishment, then left without a word. Finally, a woman appeared and I read her the names and addresses I sought. "I don't know," she says.

"Who could I ask?"

"I don't know. There are many tenants here."

I didn't want to give up. Having found myself in the building, I figured out the meaning of the numbers and the abbreviations in the address: they were entrances, floors, wings and apartments. Finally, when I had decoded the message, I knocked on a door. After a long pause, I heard a woman's voice: "Who is it?"

"I am looking for Valeria Mihailovna. Shchukina."

"She doesn't live here." The voice comes from immediately behind the door. I know that the woman is looking at me through the peep hole.

"Do you know where I would be able to find her?"

"Are you a foreigner?"

"Yes, a foreigner."

I hear her unlock the door. The woman shows her head. "Let's have a look."

I give her the address. "Do you know any of these three?" I ask.

She shakes her head. "We've been living here for three full years. Ask over there, at the end of the hall, the last door on the right. Ivanova. Varya Ivanovna Strahovska. Perhaps she knows." She then returns the piece of paper; I hear her once again lock the door.

I knock slowly, cautiously. No one answers. At once, I realize that there is no one behind this door and I push the lock. The room measures five by five meters. An electric lightbulb without a lampshade hangs from the ceiling. In the corner is a large stove, like those in a workers' cafeteria. I realize that this is a communal kitchen for the whole wing of the building. As if I've come across a secret hiding place, I quickly leave and close the door behind me. My inspection, evidently, had not gone unnoticed.

"What are you doing there? Who are you?" A woman is draped in a long knitted shawl; her hair is pulled up in a tall bun. On her feet are sturdy military boots.

"Excuse me," I say, handing her the piece of paper with the addresses as if it is an official paper. "They told me that Varya Ivanovna Strahovska lives here."

"Are you her relative?"

"You could say that."

"Foreigner?"

"Foreigner."

"Varya Ivanovna is very sick. The heart. Wait here." She knocks on the door, directly across the way from the communal kitchen. She disappears for a moment, then returns. "She says that she doesn't have anyone abroad. Nowhere."

"I am a friend of Maria Nikolaevna Aleksinska. Tell her that. She'll know." The woman once again enters without knocking. This time she stays longer. Finally she appears. "Go in for a bit. I am responsible for this building. You should have let us know ahead of time. Go in."

The room is like a cell. Bare walls. The bed is placed against the wall, alongside is a wooden stool. A glass of water and a small bottle of medicine are on it. A pale, emaciated woman is lying on a low pillow, she is covered up to her throat by a singed military blanket.

"I am Varya Ivanovna Strahovska. I heard who you are. You are asking about Natalia Viktorovna Karaeva. She died two years ago, in this same bed. She was a friend of Maria Yermolaevna, who died four years ago. No, five years ago. I also knew Maria Nikolaevna Aleksinska. And her children. They burned up in a fire. I am glad to hear that she is alive. Her sister, Valeria Mihailovna Shchukina, died first, about eight years ago. Now, you see, I am dying. I have told you everything that I know, and now, I ask you to please leave me. I don't feel like remembering or talking anymore. I am preparing for death. There are no more encounters for me on this earth."

"Excuse me, I wanted to be able to tell something more to Maria Nikolaevna about her sister. And about the rest."

"What is there to say? There are lives that never deserved to be lived. We lived like we were dead. Farewell."

She closed her eyes as a sign of her decision to speak no more. At that moment, the door opened. "There, you found her alive," says the woman with the bun. "And now go before I call the police."

For months after my return from the tour, I put off my visit to my

former landlords. Then one day, passing in front of the Zvezda movie theater, I dropped in on them. First, I went in to the room of Nikolai Aleksinski. He was reading Berdyaev. I told him my impressions of the tour, my visit to Novodevichy graveyard, the Lenin mausoleum. He served me sour cherry brandy.

Then Maria Nikolaevna appears at the door. "Excuse me," she says, "I don't want to disturb your *binge*. I just wanted to see how our traveler is. Is he still unhappily in love?"

"We're talking about Moscow," I say. "And about Leningrad."

"Ah," she says," what could you see in fifteen days. Nothing."

"I saw Dostoyevsky's grave," I say. "And Blok's."

"You see," Maria Nikolaevna says, gesturing to the old man with her fingers, "I told you that he would forget to look for my sister. He just drank vodka with actors in Russia. He is a bohemian."

"I couldn't break away from the group." I say. "That's not so easy in Russia." (Then I translate that into the alphabet of the deaf.)

"I knew it," she says and leaves.

"Don't worry about anything," says Nikolai Aleksinski. "It is better that you drank with the actors than to roam around Moscow. It's better this way. That *she* doesn't know anything."

I realized that it was clear to him that I had carried out my mission.

"Let's drink one more," he says. "Then I will have to put away the bottle. Maria Nikolaevna is very sick."

Post Scriptum:
Due to the influence of Truman Capote, I tried in this story, in my own way, to approach a narrative genre called the nonfiction short story, where the share of the imagination is reduced to a minimum while facts are everything. In the story "Jurij Golec" I did not succeed in my intention: when the characters in a story, even if they are secondary, are living and concrete individuals, the writer is sometimes compelled to make precious rearrangements and concessions because of completely understandable human sensibilities.

Translated by Paul M. Foster

Momo Kapor

Momo Kapor (born 1937) is a prolific writer of fiction, essays, plays, and travelogues. His novels are *Notes of a Certain Anna* (1972), *The Pretender* (1974), *I Didn't Tell You That* (1975), *The Provincial* (1976), *Ada* (1977), *Zoe* (1978), *Seven Till Three* (1980), *Una* (1981), *The Book of Complaints* (1984), *The Green Cloth of Montenegro* (1992), and *The Last Flight to Sarajevo* (1995). His story collections are *And Other Stories* (1973), *Last Year's Snows* (1977), *I Roam and Talk* (1979), *Off* (1983), *Hello, Belgrade* (1991), *The Blockade* (1993), and *The Chronicle of the Lost City* (1997).

THE GIFT

Having traveled from Paris to Belgrade for their Christmas vacation, they spent the first three days delivering money, medicine, and various small parcels their friends in Paris had sent to relatives back home.

On the third day, on Sunday, they found themselves in New Belgrade, in a section of the city they had never been to before—a complex of high rises known as Block 45. The immense gray defensive walls of the huge apartment buildings, resembling cement honeycombs, seemed immensely drab in comparison to the City of Light. The entire area was encircled, as if a muddy watersnake had coiled round it, by a flea market—a sodden, swarming line of despair, the black market, misery, and haphazard destinies resembling in no way or form the motley, cheerful crowds of the Clignancourt flea market, abounding in antiques and various bizarre objects. Although the woman's gray fox fur was rather conspicuous, indeed almost indecent, against the gray Belgrade landscape, and her high heels were entirely inappropriate for the thin layer of slimy, slippery mud coating the street, the two of them, completely mesmerized by the sight of it all, embarked on the vicious circle created by the dreadful blockade imposed upon their city.

People stood in the rain as it slowly turned to sleet; some were reconciled to their bad luck and worse fate, while others remained brazenly cheerful, full of optimism and a curious capacity for survival, as if defying life under the heavy leaden skies. A good many were slightly inebriated, having consumed the Russian Stolichnaya that their Slavic

black-marketeer bretheren sold for next to nothing, or a mere two and a half Deutsche marks per bottle.

"Was this what my education was for?" an elderly lady cried out, gray wisps of hair brushing across her face. "Mother must be turning in her grave!" She was selling the last remaining knicknacks from her home—a brass art deco lamp, silver dance shoes, a coffee mill, and a box full of mismatched colorful buttons.

"I used to have a fur just like the one that lady has on," she said, pointing to the former native of Belgrade, now a Parisian, who, blushing, hurriedly immersed herself in the river of buyers and idlers.

"Dear madame! A special item just for you!" A slight elderly man, hawking an old radio and a telephone with no receiver, grabbed her by the arm. "Take this Chinese vase! An original from the Ping-Pong dynasty!"

Displayed everywhere were old grandfather clocks, faucets, fur hats, and other odd and shapeless headpieces, crumbling books, tricycles, wooden headless horses, garlic, sausages, and mismatched dishes, paintings worth less than their frames—an entire former life was on sale, a life without luster, soaked, rusted, futile. One could fall no deeper than into this ubiquitous mud this side of the Sava River, the outer limit of the now dry waters of the Pannonian Sea. And yet, curiously, most of the people here were somehow desperately jubilant, partaking of that mood that descends upon a funeral party once the departed has been buried and everyone has had something to drink, when despair is forgotten and life, despite it all, simply goes on.

"We've lost everything," a middle-aged woman confided to a listener in a strong Herzegovinian accent. "They even destroyed the Old Bridge, the criminals! Look at my husband, the poor man! He still can't get over it. We lost everything—two cars, our house, our land . . ." They were selling Bulgarian sardines, American cigarettes, and Romanian honey. The man stood by timidly, unsure of what to do with his idle hands.

The sellers displayed their wares on cardboard boxes or simply on spread-out sheets of newspaper already damp from the eternal, indestructible Balkan mud that follows us, she thought, like some slimy metaphor, from infancy through the length of our lives.

"My God, what have they done to us?" the woman whispered to her

husband, who followed her closely, protecting her with his refined and dependable air, just as he had protected her in Paris over the past few years, after the termination of her first marriage, which she recovered from as if overcoming a critical and almost unbearable illness. "Just look at this!"

They made their way through the crowd step by step, without pausing to look at the faces, gazing instead at the items displayed beside the feet in muddy sneakers, rough shoes, and boots.

All at once, among the pervasive grayness and misery, the woman caught sight of a tiny shimmering oasis, a glimmering island amid a sea polluted with oil and debris. She headed toward the island and almost knelt before a cardboard box containing Christmas tree ornaments. She almost forgot New Year's! With her hands in deerskin gloves, she lifted a golden globe whose magical surface reflected her mature face, the face of a forty-year-old semi-Belgrader, semi-Parisian, and a corner of the leaden sky, which instantly turned to gold.

As if in a dream, she went through the small valuables, recognizing the silver ornament that graced the top of the tree, a colored sugar Santa, shiny ribbons and a small satin Pierrot which she had made herself from the scraps of her grandmother's living room cushion. All the ornaments from all her trees were there, from the very first tree in the room she had as a child—the remnants of a life after many moves—to the first branches of the silver tree that she and her ex-husband had carted into their rented room on Čubura—ornaments from that first heavenly New Year's night they had spent in what was finally their own tiny abode, and all the ornaments from later dwellings that reflected the usual arguments of a married couple before the arrival or departure of guests—everything, all of it, was right here, in this plain cardboard box now covered with sleet.

"Pierre! Pierre! Come here, look at this," she called out to her husband, who now approached the box with the ornaments, failing to notice anything unusual except some old and somewhat shabby Christmas decorations.

"Yes," he said, somewhat absentmindedly. "They're nice. Buy them."

She had seen nothing of the man selling the ornaments except for his worn-out sneakers and faded jeans. Finally she stood up and looked at him. Before her was her ex-husband, the ailment she had been recovering from (and believed herself cured of) for a full seven years! He stood

there, as if nothing had happened in the meantime, looking at her with his slightly tired, sad gray eyes, a week-old graying stubble covering his pale face.

In a corner of his mouth was the eternal cigarette, as if he had never even bothered to take it out. A young woman with long, straight light brown hair, bundled up in his old winter coat, which reached down to her ankles, stood beside him—she, too, smoking. Dark-eyed with high cheekbones, she had one of those thin faces that seem to despise the entire world, guarding some secret known only to itself.

Thus they stood and gazed at each other without a word, perhaps half a minute or half a century, what difference did it make, while her husband examined some ancient camera set out on the adjacent box, with the characteristic calm manner of a skilled appraiser.

"How much?" She whispered in a barely audible voice, nodding toward the box.

"It's free," replied the man with the graying hair, the cigarette still dangling from his mouth.

His companion gazed through the woman in the silver fox.

He reached over and handed her the entire box, carefully adjusting the open sides of the cover.

"Thank you," she said.

"Why did you give it to her?" the young woman asked.

He gazed after his former wife as she made her way through the flea market, arms around the box.

"It's hers," he said.

Translated by Anita Lekić

Branimir Šćepanović

Branimir Šćepanović was born in Podgorica, Montenegro, in 1937. He published two collections of short stories: *Before the Truth* (1961) and *The Death of Mr. Goluža* (1977). His novels are: *The Shameful Summer* (1965), *A Mouth Full of Earth* (1974), which was translated into eighteen languages, and *Redemption* (1980).

The themes of Šćepanović's works are universal: man's confrontation with death and the purpose of living.

THE SCREAM

I was silent for a few moments, expecting him to ask me something or to make some sort of gesture that would indicate at least a modicum of curiosity. But he didn't even look at me. He seemed to be listening to the wind howling secretly, just like that night long ago when Anton burned to death. Then suddenly his lips curled into a frozen smile that I was unable to decipher.

"Is that the only reason you came?"

"I had to come, you're the only person who can understand what happened to me."

"What is there to understand? That you took a whore to bed?"

I did not dare say anything more. I even thought I should drop the whole idea. So many years had passed; what could I ask of him? To exonerate me? Or to share, perhaps, the torment I was trying to reveal to him?

He lit a cigarette and inhaled. Reclining in his armchair, his eyes closed, he did not move. He seemed to have forgotten all about me.

"Don't tell me your conscience is bothering you."

"It is," I said.

"You're crazy!"

"But she was Anton's daughter!"

He flinched as if from an inner twinge. Then, carefully stubbing out his cigarette, his face suddenly assumed that calmness for which I had always envied him.

"Our Anton?"

"Yes," I said, standing up to turn on the light, but he stopped me with a gesture of his hand. We continued to sit in the large sumptuous drawing room, motionless, with bated breath. We remained silent. We were alone and strangers to one another, but well aware that we could not look each other in the eye at that moment. Fortunately, the darkness of night was spilling in noiselessly through the wide windows, enveloping us and our memories.

"Did she mention her father?"

"Yes, but only after it was all over, when I started dozing off."

"She didn't speak of his death, did she?"

"She even knows that he burned to death! Strangely enough, though, there wasn't a trace of either pride or grief in her voice. Nothing!"

"But she hardly knew him. She couldn't have been more than three at the time."

"Four," I said.

Groping for the lamp beside him, he stopped for a moment, as if he was of two minds about it. Then he switched on the light: his elongated face surfaced from the darkness. He was smiling, probably to conceal his feelings. But his voice trembled. "We promised each other, remember, that if we ever came out of it alive and victorious, we would look for Anton's little girl and make sure she grew up into a decent human being."

"We never looked for her," I said confrontationally.

"We forgot all about her!"

Hunching over, he had a fit of coughing that lasted so long I thought it would choke him. Then, out of the blue, it subsided and, without the slightest reproach in his voice, he said:

"Well, then, you went to look for her."

I rose to my feet and pulled back the heavy curtain. Outside the wind was still howling: bare, dark branches bowed right down to the windows.

"Didn't you?" he said with a tight, suppressed smile.

I thought he was punishing me, and it gave me a strange sense of pleasure. Perhaps I wanted him to torment me. He could do that better than anyone else: he knew what the two of us owed Anton.

"I met her by pure chance," I said. "I didn't know who she was!"

"You're lying! It's impossible that of all the girls in the world you should have run into her!"

"You're a real bastard," I said softly. "You don't really think, do you,

that I've forgotten how her father died in agony in order to save you and me?"

He inclined his head vaguely and took another drag on his cigarette, but he held it in so long that I thought his lungs would burst.

"What's the matter, don't you remember how it was?"

His lips twitched oddly, but I am sure it was not because of the cigarette clenched in his teeth, as if he was about to bite it in half before it turned completely to ash, but because he did not want to talk about the night they had offered to spare Anton's life if he would tell them where the two of us were hiding; the moment when they poured gasoline all over him and we were terrified that he would give us away; the scene when he burned to death before our very eyes! I was certain that the recollection of it was not easy for him, that it was as hard for him as it was for me.

"There was nothing we could do," he said.

"That's not true! If we had fired our guns when they started torturing him, he might still be alive today."

"Why didn't you fire yours?" he smiled, as if genuinely surprised.

I stood up again and moved toward the window. The wind was bending the branches even more violently than before. A wooden tram was gliding down the street, the muffled ring of its bell sounding in the dark night.

"I was a coward. Like you," I whispered.

He waved away my words with his hand, as if in self-defense or perhaps to say that he wasn't really interested.

"Did you tell her that too?!"

"Don't worry. She knows nothing about us!"

"Why torture yourself, then?"

"What else is there left for me to do?!" I said. "How can I forget that she's Anton's daughter? When I crawled out of bed and locked myself in the other room, she even thought I was joking around; she called out for me to come back, enticing me shamelessly. But I wanted to be alone. And I didn't confide in her simply because I was suddenly disgusted with myself. And scared! Imagine: while she was laughing, I saw her father again in that other room and heard his scream."

"What scream?" he cut in. "Anton burned to death without a sound."

"But last night, locked in that room, I heard it quite clearly."

"Maybe Anton didn't scream until last night," he said maliciously, turning suddenly toward me so that his left cheek emerged from the shadows. As he took another drag, the glow of his cigarette illuminated the other side of his face as well, and it was too grave for him to have been joking. We sat in silence for a long time, as if there was nothing more to be said. I could not tell if he had thrown the words out just like that or actually suspected what later happened.

"All night I felt ashamed," I said. A dull, undefined pain spread through my chest. I am no longer sure whether it was an ache or a feeling of emptiness, but at least it told me that I was still human and that there was still hope I might be able to redeem myself. But what happened is something I still find hard to believe to this day.

"I know," he said softly.

"You know nothing! At daybreak I entered the room where she was asleep. I was ready to tell her the truth, to offer her my help or to do whatever she wanted. I stood over her, observing her for a few moments, hesitating whether to wake her up or not. She lay there, naked and beautiful, a strange smile on her sleeping face. Suddenly she started to edge her long legs my way, as if she sensed that I was standing over her, as if she truly desired me. Her arm, its elbow crooked, rested on her belly. To me it looked as if the arm, excited by the touch of its own body, was trembling ever so slightly, and at that moment I felt myself tremble as well. I said to myself: 'For heaven's sake, man, that's Anton's daughter!' I believed that the words would stop me from doing what I wanted so desperately to do. Perhaps I would have succeeded in suppressing the desire that was burning me up as if this was my first time with a woman, because again I said: 'Anton burned to death because of you,' but just then she stretched her whole body and opened her eyes. If only she had at least said something! I stood there stockstill, helpless, speechless! She merely smiled at me, and before I could move away she reached out and drew me to her. How miserable and how elated I felt at that moment!"

"And?" he asked softly.

"I no longer felt that shame or that pain that had kept making me think of her father all night. There was only a beautiful flame dancing before my eyes and, with all thought wiped from my mind, I plunged into her body."

"And what happened afterward?"

"Nothing! She asked me to pay her and left."

He looked at me with raised eyebrows, but again did not move. I bowed my head and heard the wind howling outside as if it would never stop.

"And you? You want me to console you?"

"No! You can despise me, if you want! I keep asking myself what kind of a man am I, anyway? Do I deserve to live?"

This time he did actually move, his entire face sinking back into the shadows: in its frame of graying hair, that face had a strength and sureness about it. He looked thoughtful.

"Then go and kill yourself! But bring her to me first."

His eyes turned pale and his voice became like ice, distant somehow, as if it was not me he was addressing. "I suppose I can pay her too!"

At that moment, I again saw Anton in flames and his scream pierced my ears.

But he stood up, thrusting his face down into mine. He looked at me as if he could no longer recognize me. "Why did you scream?!"

"That wasn't me," I whispered.

He stood up straight and his face darkened. As he wiped his brow with his hand, I noticed that his fingers were trembling and in horror realized that he had heard Anton too.

"That wasn't me," I muttered once more.

Then, as if afraid of his own voice, looking at me helplessly he said, "Then it was the wind."

I opened the big window wide: there was not a breath of wind outside. Everything looked deserted and quiet. I was silent, devastated, and even more alone, understanding nothing. And in that unreal silence I wondered whether there was anything one could believe that night.

Gliding noiselessly down the street was a red tram, brightly lighted and empty. I watched its progress for a long time: it moved off as if in a hurry to be devoured by the darkness as quickly as possible.

Translated by Christina Pribićević Zorić

Mirko Kovač

Mirko Kovač was born in Petrovicí, Montenegro, in 1938. He started to publish in the 1960s in the journals *Student, Vidici,* and *Mladost.*

Kovač's most important works of fiction are *The Scaffold* (1962), *My Sister Elida* (1965), *The Life Story of Malvina Trifković* (1971), *The Wounds of Luka Meštrović* (1971), *Making Fun of the Soul* (1976), *The Door to the Womb* (1979), *Introduction into Another Life* (1983), *The European Decay* (1986), *Heavenly Betrothal* (1987), and *Crystal Bars* (1995).

His stories have been translated into many languages. *The Life Story of Melvina Trifković* has recently been published in France.

THE OTHER SIDE
OF OUR EYES

Sitting here with my friend, Dr. Frano Musić, I will tell a tale about death, the story of how I got tangled up in its strange and mystical ordeal. Although it happened recently, it all began way back at the end of September 1963. The days are beautiful at that time, the heat has ebbed and a mild period begins that is conducive to thoughts about fleeting life. After a long absence, I was visiting my hometown, without knowing why I had come. I arrived on the bus from Dubrovnik, where I was spending my vacation. The return to my hometown aroused anxious feelings, almost panic.

When I found myself in Mahala, on a steep street lined with worn cobblestones and two rows of tumbledown houses with walls eaten away by the dampness, I trembled at the thought that here I might find "the remains of my spiritual life," for I had read somewhere that such was possible and the mystic Gurdjijev had written about it. But let us return to real events.

I wandered at a leisurely pace through Mahala and stopped in front of the house where I had once lived. It was dilapidated, the roof was crooked and the walls darkened by the rain. The front door, lined with tin at the bottom, was worm-eaten and decayed. I stood in front of the house, convinced that no one lived there anymore, when the face of a young man, long and resembling my own, appeared at a small, dirty windowpane.

For a moment, I thought that it was I who had entered the house so as to invite my undecided self inside, standing there before that spiritual door, before the door of my childhood like a stranger. Some of the voices still seemed familiar, while everything else was foreign, as though coming from mythical distances.

Just as I had decided to head toward the center of the city and rest under the plane trees, the young man came out of the dilapidated house. The door didn't open, it simply fell and the hinges slid from their casings. He took my hand and led me inside. He had a kind and gentle nature, but his eyes betrayed his anxiety almost as mine did.

"Well, goodness, you're not going to pass by without visiting your childhood bedroom," he said. "If you're tired, rest here, on your bed."

He looked at me pleasantly, a gentle smile on his face, and then touched me with his fingers as though wanting to make sure I was real. There was nothing reminiscent of the room I had once lived in, and I thought that this was not the same room; I knew it so well and so often in my stories I had described every nook, every bump on the wall and dent in the floor. And the unknown youth—who was he? Wasn't he my mirrored image? But no, that face, regardless of how much it resembled mine, expressed something special. *A face is a secret*, as Berdyaev says.

"Well, what do you think of the room you spent three years in?" asked the young man, laughing. "The room of your adolescent dreams? You wrote something about it, but a lot of details originate here, from these walls. I read your book, too, the one they're hounding you for. It almost destroyed me as well. Whom do I thank for the fact that you're here now? And why are you in this cursed city, where no one wishes you well?"

"I'm wondering the same thing," I said.

"Ever since the campaign against you started, I've worried that you'd do something foolish. There was already something in the newspaper that didn't sound like you. But we'll go into that and my objections about the book another time. I have more important things to discuss with you. Are you interested in how the two of us are related? Want to hear?"

"But this is the first time we've met."

"Hmm. We don't know about that. People live in communion even if they're unaware of it. That's what I wanted to talk to you about."

The stranger gave me an inquisitive look, as though making sure I un-

derstood this strange concept. I noticed that his face showed dried flecks of blood; that happens to me, too, when shaving. I thought that it was my face and wanted to scratch one of those spots with my nail.

The young man continued guardedly, "Now I want to tell you a recurrent dream that I have, but before that, let me say a word or two about my father, with whom I live more or less under terms of war. He's a drunk and gives me a hard time. When he's had too much, he's feisty, and when he sobers up, he's remorseful. In the dream Father appears with a kitchen knife and simply cleaves my body in two as easily as cutting an apple. One part of my body is immobile, that's the dead part, and the other separates and transforms into your figure, your body. Then I live your life, I suffer your misfortunes, I undergo your hardships—which is why I know something about you. How it happened to be you who is one half of me, and how I am able to tell you about it now—well, I can't explain that. I suppose there are things that escape us, that we can't figure out. Now, if this is also a dream, if this is my cleaved part here instead of you, then I'm a split personality. And ready for the madhouse. Can you prove that you're really here?"

"I'm going to start wondering, too," I laughed.

He became disheartened for a moment—the thought troubled him— and perked up only when I said that I too could not explain this sudden return to my hometown. He urged me to stay and rest in the quiet nook of my boyhood room. I glanced out the window overlooking small plots and gardens; everything was dry and withered. The fragrance that used to assail my senses so deliciously from that direction was gone. We remain prisoners at the heart of time, I thought. As though reading my mind, the young man said, "If it wasn't so, we would climb a ladder and watch our lives from above."

I thanked him and said good-bye. We parted warmly, like close friends. Later, as I rode the bus, I didn't have the will to ask myself a single question, but it was nonetheless strange that I had decided to take a day off from my vacation and visit my hometown, almost furtively like a plague-infected visitor, like an outcast who could be stoned. Yes, yes, there's something odd there—leaving amiable company, passing the time gossiping with an unknown young man, listening to his foolishness, and, what's more, without knowing why you're there—that is truly something suggesting the paranormal, which thank heaven does not interest me.

Considerable time has passed since then, and this compels me to be cautious—the interval is long enough for many doubts to appear. If we hadn't started talking about death, who knows what might have become of that encounter in 1963, but since death has gotten mixed into the story, then that encounter from my hometown becomes something mystical, now only the introduction to the second part of the story. Taking the risk of appearing to be swayed by literature that I have almost never condoned either as a writer or as a reader, I shall begin the story and fear the judgment of my friend, not only a good interpreter of mystical happenings, but also a keen critic of all that is superficial and impulsive in that type of literature.

I woke up one morning with the foreboding that the day was off to a bad start. I was tortured by dreams and lay awake a long time in bed. I was tormented by all sorts of thoughts, including some I wanted to dispel as fast as possible, but one wouldn't leave me alone, and that was the thought that I might die that very day. Maybe those thoughts were induced by what I had written the day before, although I had read somewhere that right before his death a man is overcome by feelings of happiness and satisfaction; this is why one often sees a radiant smile on the face of a dying person. *Where the deceased is going he will be welcomed by everyone,* reads the last sentence of the book on death. But that morning there was no joy in me. I tried to read, to overcome somehow that state of depression, that melancholy Sunday, but there was absolutely no way to get into the book. I was a superficial reader who was holding a book by Dr. Andrija Puharić, *The Sacred Mushroom* (Victor Gollancz Ltd., London, 1959), but in spite of its entertaining passages about the mysteries of the mushroom and its ritual growth, in spite of the witty comparisons with a fertile phallus and its succulent cap, this book did not help me, even though I had once used such material for the sake of parody and literary games. And then the telephone rang; I grabbed it expectantly, hoping that it was a friend or dear one, someone who would cheer me up. But this was not the case. Someone spoke in a weak, hoarse voice:

"Come to the Internal Medicine Clinic today, room 4! We have to say good-bye!"

"Who's speaking?" I moaned, but the caller had hung up.

Was it a hallucination? Or just a wrong number? Perhaps it was the

cry of someone lonely who truly wanted to say good-bye to someone close, a misdirected cry. I didn't know anyone in the hospital! No, it hadn't been a call for me, but I decided to act on it, even if I ended up the victim of a hoax. That call changed the course of my thoughts and dispelled my listlessness. As secretive and disturbing as it had been, it brought me tranquility. I cut myself under the nose while shaving, tried to stop the bleeding, and when I succeeded a feeling of pleasure overcame me. Around noon I went into the city. I dined in the garden of a restaurant and then took a taxi to the clinic. I didn't buy a present, I didn't want to spend the money; in addition, I was suspicious about the call and the mysterious voice and believed that in a few minutes all of this would be cleared up at the Internal Medicine Clinic.

This is not the time to go into details, so I will leave out the conversation with one of the patients; I'm not really concerned about his derisive reaction to my story. What's more important right now is that I was told that a patient had died early that morning in room 4 and that I could see him in the mortuary. An orderly offered to show me the way. We went down in the elevator, then took a winding stairway even lower. The orderly was a happy man, and from time to time he apologized for his humor. He justified himself several times. "Don't be offended by my clowning—when you're with death on a daily basis, you have to joke around a bit."

He opened a heavy metal door and took me inside. A neon light flickered. I went up to a table covered with an oilcloth. The orderly uncovered the dead man's face, presenting him to me like some sort of macabre sight, staring at me askance with an inquisitive look. Without hesitation I easily recognized the young man from Mahala on the slab. Even though we had met only once, briefly, I remembered his face. Time had passed since then, but he hadn't aged or changed very much. They say that death distorts, but it had actually made him more handsome and bestowed on him a certain gentleness. I was struck by something else: how was it that on his face, under his nose, was a shaving cut just like mine? However, that will lead us elsewhere right now; I'd do better to give a brief description of the deceased. His lips were very, very pale, and the region around his eyes was dark red—the color of spilled blood. His face was blue, its expression tranquil and eternal.

It's not out of place to mention once again that this man had dreamed

his father halved him with a butcher knife and his halved part became *me*. Well, now everything was finished, and there I was standing over him. I hesitated a long time before making this story public, and even now I'm sorry. I have kept this story to myself until this very day.

My friend Dr. Frano Musić mumbled something about phenomena that happen on the other side of our eyes, and then he said, "Each person has his own vision of death, and the world cannot get enough stories about death. Those who tell the stories and those who listen to them are equally attentive, for there are countless variations."

Translated by Alice Copple-Tošić

Slavko Lebedinski

Slavko Lebedinski (b. 1939) is a writer of fiction and essays. He published several collections of short stories, *My Friend Isak Belj* (1971), *Baldachin* (1977), *Shirt with Addresses* (1977), and *The Sweet Turtledove* (1984). He is the author of a novel, *Late Walnuts* (1977).

Lebedinski lives and works in Belgrade.

SWEET TURTLEDOVE

On our street, the first below Dušan Street, angry knives with tin handles and dark blue bruises were held in high esteem. So were doves with metal rings on their legs. And yet, having one switchblade was not as big a deal as having two. So don't dare to ask a Dorćol guy why he carries one in each pocket when he goes out in the evening. There's nothing much to talk about—things are clear.

There's nothing to hide about this, either. In Dorćol, people would die violent deaths at the end of the day, with a dash of cheap cologne behind their ears, after an afternoon nap and a third shot of murky swill.

The police didn't like to get involved in the fights down here. Their blue uniforms just stirred up the boozers who headed off to deaden their hangovers in the first available bar.

A black flag appeared on Života Barović's house. Barović was laid out on a table, the victim of a bar fight. Who took part in it? Just ask those who stayed around till the end of the performance. Života fell, covered in blood, and there was no time even to call the priest. Father Joseph had long ago given up on the bar's patrons: let the waiters conduct their funeral services and let them place broken beer bottles on their graves— the weapons with which the dead once used to defend themselves.

But that same day, Ljubinko Karaveljić, manager of Renovation, a warehouse for various building materials, also received notice of his death. He didn't mix with the Dorćol bums; decent people had no business in the streets below Dušan Street paved with Turkish cobblestone, nor did they make any friends in the bars there. Karaveljić lived in a house with

an elevator on Rigas Ferreos Street. His wife, Marika, cooked him spicy goulash and grumbled endlessly about the neighborhood. Ljubinko knew that his wife had a kind heart, but she was born a loudmouth—and, well, that was it. He loved his daughter Cana, who always took his side and who brought him his slippers when he returned home from a business trip shivering with cold.

Having a daughter in the house need not be dangerous unless your fate was sharpening its teeth in the knife sharpener's booth in the Bajlon marketplace while you were striking business deals in Šabac. Living in Dorćol and having a daughter, did that have to be a path to an early grave in the New Cemetery?

But let's take one step at a time. The day before Ljubinko Karaveljić was lying mortally wounded on the sidewalk, someone had hung a black flag on his house. Everyone was alive and well, thank God, yet a black flag was fluttering in the wind. Cana was off primping in the corner of the room, minding her own business. Marika kept saying that the flag was a bad omen, but Ljubinko claimed it was all just female nonsense. As for him, he'd like to get hold of that idiot—the guy would be real sorry once he got his hands on him.

Marika wanted to cheer Ljubinko up a little, so why not go ahead and let the girl go out and get some air for a bit? Oh, no. Absolutely out of the question. He knew those Dorćol street punks well. Wasn't she hanging out with that Mikica Osanović? And he didn't like the guy. A pickpocket and a crook.

What could Cana do but wipe her left eye? The right one seemed completely dry. She just had to see Mikica. But her father was in the way. And he would see to it that she didn't get out.

Cana caught our attention the first time she came to visit her godfather, Desko Jončić. He lived in a building across the street from a home for the blind, his door just to the right in the hall. There was no light in the hallway, and whichever way you turned, you ran into this box with sand in it.

We all fell in love with Cana—as if it could've been any other way. She was all curves, with a thick braid that flicked merrily at her back and a nose that she wriggled whenever she was angry. God, don't ever let that nose fall off! The gap between her front teeth revealed her as a nervous high school girl. A hidden anger was concealed behind her brown eyes.

"Whoa! Man, would I like a piece of her," Mile the Greek muttered to himself.

"You think I wouldn't?"

You were considered nothing, a nobody, if you hadn't screwed a woman. In Lower Kalemegdan, under Nebojša Tower, pairs of lovers would sneak down Dušan Street. All of us would gladly have joined in that procession accompanied by Cana. There were other girls, but they couldn't hold a candle to her.

Cana could wriggle her nose in anger all she wanted, but it wouldn't help. Mika the Mast claimed first rights. He told me openly that there was nothing for me to look for there.

"Hey, come here. I want to tell you something," I said to her as she passed by, suffocating herself with a giant salty bun. That was on Jevrejska Street; the sun's rays were climbing the sides of the buildings. After yesterday's storm, everything was washed clean and calm.

"Get lost—leave me alone. Why are you so hung up on me?"

"Come here and I'll tell you. I'm not going to eat you, you know."

"Fool," she stuck out her tongue at me. In her hand she held the half-eaten bun.

"A fool is calling me a fool."

She flew at me and began hitting me before I knew what was happening. Fine. I let her. She threatened me with her godfather, she said that I was hurting her and not to squeeze her, that I should be ashamed of myself pretending to be strong. She told me that and wouldn't even look at me.

I didn't show up at the drugstore at six. Cana was there waiting, I knew that. I got the crap beaten out of me. My nose was as red as a bunch of roses. A kick in the balls really did me in. God, if only I could take a good leak. Blessed is the stream that eases the pain.

It wasn't my buddy Mikica who beat me up. He didn't have any idea who I was going to meet in front of the drugstore. He just didn't pick up on what was going on. The two of us fought against some guys from Čubura, three brothers. We ran into them at the Balkan movie theater; we knew those guys pretty well.

If you don't fight, you're just a nobody, like two zeroes on the door of the Church of Alexander Nevsky, which add up to the same as the

two on the door of the entrance to the student beach. The Dorćol specialty was to ram someone in the stomach with your head, something Toške, the pigeon keeper, tried to teach us without much success. We tasted our shame in the blood from our noses; to overcome it we had to give this magic drink to someone else. I'd begun to dish it out long ago, and all three of the Zelenac brothers were well aware of this. But the way they could sock you in the jaw was also pretty convincing. And that middle one sure could fight, the one with the drooping eyelid—like he was going right for your throat. Mikica covered my back, so we could really show those bastards what we're made of.

Women just can't appreciate a good fight, even if they are named Cana. I stayed out of the way of her dad, Ljubinko. I was sneaking around trying to see his favorite daughter somehow, but no way—it didn't work. She pouted to let me know: everything between us was finished, quits. No second chance. She'd been waiting and counting the trams as they passed in front of the drugstore. Who did I think I was?

Cana wanted to put me in my place. My buddy Mikica sat by her at the movies now. After the movie they went to take a stroll down by the Danube. He wanted to show her the smouldering slag they dumped in the yard by the power plant. Mika's the only one who could tell you what's so great about it.

I learned this later. In about a week, it came to me why she was so deadly indifferent when I asked her to come out so I could explain and we could make up. It was Mika, in fact, who told me.

"I don't like anyone to be around when I'm on the job. You got it? When I dump her, then you can do what you want."

"But you stole her from me."

"I told you: eat shit."

He turned around and left. I wanted to go after him. But I gave up. I wasn't a coward; I just put off giving him a piece of my mind until a more suitable moment. He'd be collecting his teeth before he realized what I meant.

But Cana's father chased him off before we met on the green grass in the yard of the Church of Alexander Nevsky.

Karaveljić recently moved to our part of town, got an apartment on the second floor, and looked down on the gang from above.

"What a bunch of idiots. They have nothing better to do than to pull knives on each other," he ranted about us in the offices of the local party representatives. "They don't give respectable people any peace."

"Shake them up a little," chirped the pimply party secretary. "The police can't handle them."

"Even they are afraid to come."

Manager Karaveljić believed that it was possible to solve everything at a meeting. You summoned the people, you read them the party newspaper, the *Struggle,* in which it was clearly written who the imperialist supporters were, and then, under the last item on the agenda, you simply strong-armed everyone who spread crime in Dorćol. We had to help the police, and we had to try to put an end to the heavy drinking. The ability of the worker to rebuild the destroyed homeland must not be poisoned by cheap, mass-produced alcohol. Let them realize that he was addressing politically aware comrades whom he expected to deal with these undesirable events. If anything was unclear, they knew whom to contact.

Toward the end he asked if there were any questions, and Života Barović raised his hand. He rose up just enough for his head to poke up. He preferred not to approach the podium.

"Come out so that we can see you," said Ljubinko. "Silence, please, comrades. We will listen to everyone," he blathered on.

"Who asked you to preach to us? We'll continue to live the same way that we've been living. I'll drink when I want to and I'll die when my number is up. I've never been a snitch, and as for you, I wouldn't allow people like you to run this warehouse into the ground."

Someone shouted, "That's right. You tell him, Života!"

Ljubinko himself cut in. "I'm not prepared to engage in a dialogue of equals with drunkards. As I see it, even the rest of you aren't thinking like good Communists."

Who could tell that death would load both of them up on its cart on the same day? This would never have occurred to either of them. Karaveljić could've shouted himself hoarse, or he could've received some help from his backers, and the people from Dorćol would still have gone their own way: they were stubborn and they were ready to pay for their asinine stubbornness. They married young, with the shadow of their first

mustache. They caressed their ruddy brats who from infancy learned to love the Turkish cobblestones and pigeon droppings and felt the joy that smells of graveyard mud. No one was in a hurry to step forward and try to dissuade warehouse manager Karaveljić; he obstinately believed that he knew how to deal with people.

He was not exactly showered with questions, and the meeting was brought to an end. Karaveljić told them that he expected to see some results. He took a sip of water, and that was it.

No one wanted to tell him that he was in the wrong. The janitor hastened the others out: he was only human, and he needed a wash basin full of warm water for his swollen feet. He patted Ljubinko on the shoulder and told him that the turnout was respectable. The black blotch on his face spread as he puffed out his cheeks.

People want to be in the right with every inch of their being, if not more. Can you expect any better from a party official? He took this task very seriously, like invoices at the warehouse for building materials.

Ljubinko knew how tall he was, and he figured someone would have to measure him for his length. This was not usually done without a coffin. Mika the Mast was not at the briefing. He was off studying the flora and fauna with Cana in Lower Kalemegdan. Ljubinko's daughter returned home with her cheeks flushed and her eyes shining. Only she knew why. But her father also wanted to know. She lied to him, told him he could ask her classmates—she didn't go out with street punks.

"That manager's girl is quite a little slut," my father Ivanuška once muttered. It didn't end there. When the news got around that I was going out with Cana Karaveljić, he didn't say a word. He pretended not to know anything. He gave me a whipping because my grades fell.

He beat us in turns, my mother and me—both of us. He'd usually come back from the bar pretty loaded and take his anger out on us. The rest of the night we'd spend in confidential conversation while my father lay passed out on the couch sawing wood. We used to forgive him everything, even when he sold my mother's winter boots for booze. My mother told me that there were other girls around besides that Spasenija. That's what she called the Karaveljić girl, whom she barely knew on sight.

I didn't let her know that my buddy Mika had stepped into my shoes

and that I had an appointment with him in the churchyard that day. He was a head taller than me, but what good did that do if his head was full of air? I was eager to pay him back for all the punches that I had swallowed since that first moment when I grabbed my jaw in the churchyard. In my right pocket, I had the cheap switchblade with the tin handle wrapped in a checkered scarf.

The sun's rays and the cart of the soda man woke us early, as well as the pigeons cooing from the window and the howling of a stray dog. The howl was not of hunger, but of misery. In our house we never gave anything to dogs, since we could barely make ends meet.

And yet, poverty did not affect our plates at lunch during the first week of the month. The slice of bread and pork fat sprinkled with paprika was so thick that you could barely shove it into your mouth. It satiated your hunger, and that was fine. I dressed in a hurry. I wanted to disappear before my mother woke up with all her questions and before my father took a blurry-eyed swig of cold water from the pitcher. I started toward Rigas Ferreos Street where Toške had his pigeon coop.

A flag fluttered on the house of Života Barović. It was a matter of time before they would pour his last glass of booze. Tall of stature and woolly-haired, he drank with a persistence that made him a troublemaker. It broke up his family. He sent his wife Stefka back to Umka with the three kids, and he had no intention of returning to work at the tool factory—let those nuts work if they wanted. I wondered what happened to his tumbler pigeons, since not a single one was perched on the flagpole. I wanted one of those myself, one of those acrobats whose heads they used to tear off as if punishing them for all their skillful airborne maneuvers. I thought of stuffing one under my shirt and taking it with me until Mikica showed up. Then I could throw it up and let it fly.

Maybe I was expecting to run into Cana. She hadn't been coming to school for the last few days. Her father wanted to cut her off from the others, to pull her out of her surroundings. He was going to send her to a school in Tašmajdan where there are decent kids. "I don't want to see a single tear," he said. He also used his belt when he found out that she was messing around with Mika Osanović, the crook. "Argh, I'll take some precautionary measures and lock him up in jail, so that he won't come sneaking around this house."

The black death-banner still fluttered in the wind. I stayed for half an hour at Toške's. Pigeons, like women, fly wherever they want to. Was I hungry? he asked. Then I could go to the pigeon coop.

When I saw the flag on the three-story apartment building with the elevator, where the Karaveljić family lived, an irrational fear suddenly overtook me. What was the meaning of that rag if all of them were alive? I could've wracked my brains for three hours and I wouldn't have been able to figure it out.

I perched comfortably on the fence in front of the Church of Alexander Nevsky and waited for some of the guys to come by. Maybe Jole the Greek had returned from Juvenile Hall. He had crippled Perkan with the chain from a broken Rog bicycle; and he hadn't forgiven Perkan's sister for being a girl either. Trifke moved to Karaburma. With him I had some unsettled accounts, but I let them go for now. Under my shirt I could distinctly feel the tumbling pigeon that I took from Toške's pigeon coop. If people don't give you something on their own, you have to find some other way of getting it.

When I got bored, I took a stroll to the barber shop, the one by the power plant. Displayed proudly in the shop window were a shiny trophy and a photograph of the prewar soccer team Slavija. The goalie was sitting on the ball. I hung around there for a while before returning to my post in front of the church. My right pocket felt heavy, and every now and then I would check to make sure that the switchblade was still in place.

I spotted Mika coming. Strictly speaking, he dragged along Dušan Street and stopped at the tobacco shop. He had a dark blue jacket on, as if he were going to a wedding. He was walking on the opposite side of the street and didn't give a damn that I was waiting for him. Maybe he forgot entirely that today I wanted to rough him up a little. The rags fluttered like soccer team banners.

I could've let him pass. It was obvious that he was in a hurry. But I didn't have time to waste hanging around either.

"Here I am, you jerk!" I shouted.

But he didn't pay any attention to me. With his head thrust forward, he continued to walk toward the Bajlon marketplace. I made my way though a line of trucks filled with rubble rolling down the street. He was

mine now. He could feel me breathing down his neck. I stared at his back. We could start right there if he preferred.

"Here I am, you jerk!" I howled.

He didn't hear me. I stopped in amazement—I had to fix him good then and there. I stuck my arm up my shirt, pulled out the pigeon and threw it up as high as I could. I felt the switchblade burning in my pocket. I'd never used it before.

Right in front of my eyes, Mikica stabbed the father of our plump Cana with the full length of the blade and then took off across the small field and into the first yard he came to. All of this happened in silence.

The linden trees were in bloom, the day was clear, the paint on the park benches was flaking off. Should I even bother to mention the fine gravel that didn't quite cover the entire path?

Mika ran like mad, I saw that. He turned toward me and looked at me as if he'd never seen me before. He'd ducked into the nearest gate before I knew what was going on. A single moment was all that he needed; everyone was astounded by the realization of what had happened and the cold-bloodedness of the steel blade.

Ljubinko Karaveljić lay spread out on the ground on his stomach, then tried to rise and flipped over. An issue of the *Struggle* fell from his side pocket. Then he began to twitch like a slaughtered turkey.

No one approached him. The grass in the churchyard shone and the cross on the top of the church surged upwards, as if it were chasing the pigeon. The rectory was in the churchyard. At the window the priest's wife was airing the bedding and sunning her wrinkled face.

"Hey, kid," Ljubinko addressed me.

My legs felt as heavy as molten lead and as soft as pigeon feathers. At that point, I should've gone up to him and taken hold of him around the waist.

"Get him! He'll run away!" a tall, skinny old man with a hunter's cap on his head shouted with a groan. A carp wrapped in thick newspapers stuck out from his shopping bag. The dead, round eye of the fish grew as if it would swallow us all into its deadly indifference.

"Men, what are you waiting for?" the old man sighed, almost tearfully.

I wasn't waiting for anything. I was standing motionless. I could've gone my own way. I could've rushed after Mikica so as not to watch

Karaveljić rise, shifting his gaze back and forth indifferently above my head.

Was this death? How could I know it? The blood streamed on the Turkish cobblestones and I tried to decipher its illegible message. The pigeon was like a receding black dot in the middle of the blue void. The fallen man pressed his wound with his hands, and the blood gushed profusely over his green shirt. As if he wanted to direct the red stream at me.

"He killed him, the poor man!" wailed a beggar woman from the church stairs.

"Ooooh!" I heard a painful sob from the opposite direction. I turned toward the priest's wife at her window.

Cana's father stood up and began to tear at his shirt. Then he started toward me as if he were learning to walk. I jumped away instinctively, although we were some five or six yards apart. He walked with a limp, bending to the side where his wound was. He was stooped over as if he were trying to catch turtledoves. The cross on the church frowned silently.

"The police are never around when you need them."

"You don't need the police to die in this country," said a man in a forester's uniform. His hat sat cocked to one side on his head.

My eyes fell on the carts overloaded with bed frames, stove parts, cast-iron sinks, sooty stovepipes, and radiator ribs. The overloaded cart jolted along Francuska Street. An emaciated old man of about fifty pushed it before him like his own destiny and muttered something incomprehensible. Nothing of what was going on bothered him; he was singing. He was too far away for me to catch the unintelligible words, entangled in a wise skein like human life and sorrow.

He was bald as a prophet, and his shoes were full of holes that peered out curiously on all sides. The protuberances of his toes stuck out from under the shoe leather. There was not a single button on his jacket. He used a thick rope as a belt. A golden coin shone like an enormous bug on his lapel.

It was too late when I turned around. Cana's father reached out and embraced me, collapsing on me with dead weight and deadly fear.

I nearly fell down. I lost my balance, but somehow I stayed on my feet. I felt sticky blood on me. I smelled the odor of someone else's death.

I felt like the worst coward—and I took off running. The houses pressed after me.

"Get him!" I heard the squeaky old man.

I flew into the gate of Sofronije's bakery. I was met by the peace of soaking-wet bed sheets spread there a moment before by his busy wife. My tears mixed with the wetness of the white sheets and I knew that I had no place to go. The stump on which they cut firewood stood covered in blood by the cellar door.

Translated by Amanda Blasko

Filip David

Filip David (born 1940) writes modern fantastic prose. His first collection of stories, entitled *The Well in a Dark Forest,* appeared in 1964. His other works are: *Notes on the Real and the Unreal* (1969), *The Prince of Fire,* (1987), *Pilgrims of the Heaven and the Earth* (1995), and *Fragments from Dark Times* (1995).

The major themes of David's works are death and the fantastic or a magic reality that can be realized only in dreams. A number of his stories have been translated and published abroad. David also writes theater and television plays. He lives in Belgrade.

THE PRINCE OF FIRE

The inn stood where several roads crossed. Jews from the north, south, east, and west stopped there for the night and then journeyed on. At Beneventa, Aron ben Sh'muel Hanasi was at the center of the events recounted here. But, as sometimes occurs, from one tale, another issues, and from that, another. The tale from which the others here emerge and into which they flow is recorded, in part, in the Chronicles of Ahimaazo, in Hebrew and rhymed prose.

We learn from the Ahimaazo manuscript that it all began like this: Hanasi, a miracle worker and mystic, highly educated and from a prominent family, stopped late one afternoon at the inn at that large crossroads. A sudden rain had drenched him, so the weary and chilled traveler was glad and grateful for the hospitality.

There were already some ten travelers, on the floor and on two benches, in the long, low, dark main room. The bad weather had made them unexpected overnight guests at this station along their way. They were silent men, each turned in on himself, most of them praying in a barely audible mutter, explaining to or debating with himself the trials and errors of this world. The new arrival chose a place in a corner. The innkeeper had just lit a candle, and the faces of the travelers were less invisible in the flickering light.

Close by the wandering mystic, a youth sat, turned toward the gray, cracked eastern wall, and rocked. He recited the words of a prayer with rare feeling. But suddenly his lips would twist, his voice would be lost and the prayer interrupted. His face would go white, as though drained

of its last drop of blood. But after this terrible and inexplicable silence, the words would begin to flow until they stopped again, blocked by an invisible barrier that arose between the speaker and his words. The mystic listened carefully. The praying sounded more like wheezing. His dark penetrating eyes caught each movement of the youth's lips. A great disquiet overtook Aron ben Sh'muel Hanasi. He got to his feet behind the youth. "Stop!" he cried, "Turn and look at me!" The youth gave no sign of moving; though his shoulders shook. "You have no right to pray; you are dead!" The room fell silent. Everyone hung on the words of the mystic. "Not once have you been able to speak His name!"

The youth suddenly turned and fell full-length at the older man's feet. The mystic placed a hand on the youth's head. "Do not fear. Speak, here, before all these men, the truth about yourself!"

All were now staring at the two. The rain, driven by the wind, struck the wooden shutters covering the window. The breath of the storm and smell of dampness penetrated the inn. "Listen, all!" cried the youth, "This man is right. I will tell you my tale, and then you may judge me!" A circle quickly formed around the speaker. At the center stood a menorah with lighted candles. The youth's pale face appeared even paler in the candlelight. The elongated shadows of men unknown to one another played on the walls. The men were brought close at this moment in anticipation of the strange tale of the unhappy youth. And here is what he told them.

Although my mother died very young and I cannot really remember her face, she left planted in me what would become the distinguishing feature of my person: a dreamer's imagination. From what I heard from others and from my vague remembrances, she was delicate as a flower and light of step, as if spun from dreams, and always had a trace of sorrow in her large blue eyes. She was a wonderful storyteller. Many of her tales I have forgotten, some I remember only in part. Sometimes I think I have spent my entire youth searching for those forgotten tales. It is as though I could bring my mother back to life if only I could put the tales I heard from her together again. My father was strict, a conscientious Jew. He knew the Talmud well and observed the Torah in detail. He taught me our laws. By my early youth, I could hold my own with my elders and scholars. My misfortune was an imagination that would not

be satisfied with rules and canons, so like the poor lad in the well-known tale "Loyal to the End," I had a question to add to every answer, and each question opened ten more. And I began saying out loud that the worst ignorance was to believe that all questions had answers. My father suffered greatly when I said things like this.

One night a rabbi passing through stopped at our home. He was a man of great learning and wisdom. He talked at great length with my father about everything, and then my father confided to him his fears for my future. "Allow me to take him with me," the rabbi said. "I have for some time now been looking for somebody to accompany me on my travels and to help me." My father could not bring himself to place me in the hands of an unknown, even if clearly learned, man. Still, he knew deep down that I would have to go on such a journey if I were to be freed from my dangerous thoughts and separated from the books that had begun to sow doubts in me instead of knowledge. He answered that I was his only son and he would never recover if anything were to happen to me. "You need not fear, as long as he is with me. I swear here before you that he will soon return safe and sound, that he will see and learn a great deal."

He later came to my room and said, "I know what is happening to you, because it happened to me and to many others who lived before you and before me. You started with a question and received an answer. You passed the first gate, and there a new question was waiting for you; you answered it and passed through the second gate, and a new question was opened. You will keep walking on and on like that until the fiftieth gate. The final question is there, to which no man has yet found the answer. If you step through that gate, you will go plunging into the abyss!"

"You mean I will then have to turn back," I cried, a great, undefined danger making me feel anguish.

"There is no turning back, because the gate you pass through disappears. It is time you set out and traveled, left your father and your home; you must no longer wait here for your future, but go forth instead to meet it."

After great hesitation, my father finally decided to place me in the care and charge of our guest. At our parting, he mentioned once again how much I reminded him, in looks and in manner, of my mother, how

this brought him sad memories for a moment, but that he at last understood, as he himself put it, that "learning is perhaps not the shortest way to understanding, that the main source of understanding is the heart." I embraced him tightly; I felt his tears upon my cheek. I had never in my life felt so distressed, nor do I believe that I ever shall. It is written: when a father came to the rabbi and asked what he should do with a son who had started down the wrong path, the rabbi answered, "Love him more than ever!" But what good are tears when each must go his own way? We held each other by the hand, not wanting to part. This was our last time together; it was time now for us to part. He lived in one world and I in another, and those worlds had parted precisely at the moment of our embrace, had parted never to come together again.

Thus I left the house where I had grown up and through whose chambers my mother's soul still walked. I left behind the house of my childhood where I had become a stranger. I now walked the earth with my new teacher. The moon crossed the sky many times; my clothes became those of a beggar; we lived on what we were given by the merciful; the days rose out of murky dawns and sank into cold and damp nights. One cloudy day, we arrived at a village where a crowd had gathered in front of a house. The rabbi inquired as to the occasion. He learned that a dybbuk demon was present in the house and had entered the body of the owner's son. We went in, and inside we saw the weeping parents and the one possessed. The young boy's eyes shone with a brightness they certainly could not have had normally. His entire body was in a strange tension, and his every movement spoke of a great restlessness. The boy, Haim Gaon, we were later told, had from birth been different from other children. He was weak and delicate and seemed to live in dreams. He was surrounded by special care because of the dangers known to threaten the weak. When he woke from his reveries, he spoke about faraway countries and places nobody had ever been able to prove actually existed. He was frequently absent, although his body remained in this very same room. It is possible that in one of those moments the dybbuk had found a haven there.

Learning that their unexpected guest was a rabbi, Haim's parents begged my teacher to expel the dybbuk. In a strong voice and calling on the good angels, the rabbi bade the accursed spirit leave the body that

was not his. The dybbuk quieted down but would answer no questions. Pressed from all sides by words that were in themselves vehicles of great power, he nevertheless revealed his name and recounted his calamity.

"My name is Nathan. I am a Jew, as are you. In life I sinned no more and no less than any other wandering minstrel. I played at births and weddings, for those who reveled and those who mourned, while never giving a thought to death myself. And then death took me by surprise, while I was distracted by the celebration of a wedding. I did not feel death take me because I was engrossed in music. Wrapped like that in a melody, I somehow passed between worlds; I neither went to where all souls go after death, nor was I allowed to return to earth. Clearly, there is only one moment for the soul when the way is open to the world of peace. I missed that moment and have continued wandering with my melody. But I too have wanted rest. I have been forced to enter plants, and finally a stone. And Sefer ha-Bahir says that this wandering and hither and fro can last a thousand generations. Why, Rabbi, do you call up all of God's angels and threaten me with lengthy passages from holy books? Why don't you help me? I am more to be pitied than any of you, because there is no end in sight to my wandering."

Everybody listened in amazement to these words, which sounded more as though they came from a living and unhappy Jew than from an accursed dybbuk. The doors and windows were full of pious Jews, curious to hear what severe words would drive a demon to obedience.

"If it was just a misunderstanding, and it must have been, because that wedding was the wedding of the daughter of a distinguished rabbi, why must there be such a terrible price to pay for an ordinary human moment of distraction?" the dybbuk continued. "Let each of you imagine what it is to live a life of neither this world nor the other, in a world where you are always a stranger and cannot even for a moment feel at peace! Is it possible, I ask you, for a human spirit to live and prevail in a dumb blade of grass, shaking leaf, or cold rock? Was it not said: *It is a greater duty to show mercy than to sing psalms!*"

A muttering ran through those inside the room and those outside. The unhappy dybbuk was drawing pity.

"*Mercy is greater than a sacrifice at the altar!*" my teacher cried, "*but suffering is greater than any mercy! And further, My love is greater for the sinner aware of his sins than for the good man aware of his goodness!*"

"If we are quoting the words of others," said the dybbuk, raising his voice in agitation, "have you forgotten these? *Care for your soul and the body of others, and not for your body and the soul of others!*"

To this the rabbi answered: "*Banishment carries in it salvation, as does the seed contain in it the fruit!*"

This sharp exchange, in which each side scored points, had all those present following the unexpected duel with bated breath. Even I felt a certain sympathy for the Spirit Denied Rest.

The rabbi, as though he too felt the pain and injustice of the minstrel's suffering, addressed them all somewhat distractedly: "*Everything in the world constantly changes form, dropping to the lowest and climbing to the highest. The gilgul, or migration of the soul, is a passage through space that we can never follow or understand entirely.*"

The dybbuk made no comment. He had withdrawn into silence. He wanted peace, and yet they insisted. The spirit was only asking for a little peace but was condemned to have none. The rabbi put on his prayer shawl and took three steps, coming right up to the body the dybbuk had entered. "Unclean spirit of Nathan," he called in a strong voice, "I order you in the name of the God of Israel to get out, to depart this Jewish body that Satan helped you enter, leave it to him to whom it belongs, to Haim Gaon, son of Abraham!"

"And where am I to go?" asked the dybbuk in a voice so miserable it brought tears to the eyes of many.

"Your fate is to wander through nameless space until you have earned mercy!"

Silence descended on these words. Everybody waited to see what would happen. Suddenly, a strange music was heard, like the music played by wandering minstrels at weddings. Except this music bore no joy with it; it bore only a terrible sorrow that went straight to the heart. The rabbi's hand trembled as he removed his prayer shawl. Haim Gaon breathed heavily, as though waking from a deep sleep. At last he opened his eyes. Seeing the deep emotion on his parent's faces and his home full of people, he was unable to say anything for some time.

When he realized they were all there because of him, he answered to the many questions being asked, "I have had a long and unpleasant dream. I passed through harshly lit rooms, pulled forward by the power of a melody. In the last room, whose walls were covered with frighteningly

real pictures, stood a Jewish musician in a long robe. He held out his violin to me. I took it and then found myself alone in the room. The pictures around me showed the end of time, the terrors of the final hour, the hidden world of Gehin, faces of evil spirits and the fate of souls in the hidden world, the burning river, with the chamber of the 'seven houses of sin' that opens across from it. The pictures were all so real and powerful, they blurred my mind. I dropped the violin and sank into a deep darkness from which, you can see, I have just wakened here."

"Beware of such dreams," the rabbi said, "that suck the whole of you into them. There are many worlds, and the paths leading to them cross and recross many times; once you go astray, it is difficult to find the world from which you started out; what at one place is the sky above you in another land is the earth beneath your feet; the heavens you look up at today are tomorrow the bottomless pit into which you fall."

We left that house unable to convince ourselves there was salvation for the young man; we do not rule our dreams, our dreams are masters of our souls and bodies.

Not long after this (I still dwelled on the music pervading different worlds and the misfortunes of two persons whose destinies came to touch in those worlds), as we continued our travels, we came upon a scene that would pull us into a new tale. Men and women armed with sticks were chasing two ragged paupers. The poor things sought refuge in the woods. Since our path also led through those woods, we soon caught up with them. They tried to run from us, believing we were among those who had been chasing them. But my teacher explained that we too were vagrants and, as a token of our friendship and good intentions, offered them bread from our common sack. They did not hesitate to accept this gift. Only then did we notice that the older of the two was a mute; his lips would move as though speaking, but words did not pass between them. He had to use his hands when he wanted to be heard.

A little later we stopped in a clearing and built a fire to warm ourselves. The night carried a chill. Our new acquaintance gently and most respectfully wrapped his mute friend in a tattered cape and then said, "Do not judge us by what you have seen. I tried to steal a hen because for too long our begging has failed to win us alms. This old man was once, before he forgot how to speak, a greatly respected personage." The

old man clearly was not interested in our talk. He had closed his eyes and was off somewhere in his thoughts. The younger man continued:

In his youth, he was the best student at the Yeshiva of the Eastern Lands. The Great Teacher, just before dying, spoke apart to him, saying: "Of all my students, I have chosen you because the tales you tell are the loveliest. I myself have felt deep satisfaction listening to them. The other students will continue interpreting and copying the holy books. But you must go forth into the world and stop wherever there are people desirous of hearing a story about our yeshiva, about what has been and about what has never been. If you keep in mind all that we have talked about over all these years, you will never lack bread or high repute. But beware: words are the most powerful force of this and all other worlds!"

Thus it was that after the death of the teacher, he went out into the world. Many of his tales became famous, and people were glad when he came. Surely you have heard of such beautiful and moving tales as *The Prince of Fire, The Bird Language, With No Return*. It is said: speech is man's greatest gift—the mother of reason and discovery. The Great Teacher taught: speech that goes unheard and catches no attention does not exist! But, as I have said, he also warned that words are more terrible than the high winds of a storm. No hand can strike as powerfully as words. Once upon a time, there was a wise man who was begged time and again to go on and on speaking because his words were as intoxicating and moving as a wonderful poem. Finally, he raised his arms high and cried out in extreme despair: "May I be stricken deaf and dumb if I speak as beautifully as you say!"

It is in man's nature to enjoy listening, because words spin tales much as dreams open doors of new worlds. Human life is obscure and mysterious, and there is nothing in life either simple or easily understood. Every, even the simplest word, hides something of a great secret; ordinary speech has its deep, hidden meaning, while the words of the storyteller seeking beauty and perfection of expression are like a deep and infinite sea that can never be completely studied or understood. And the words of one and the same tale can be various, and a word given a different place in a sentence can make a new, unexpected meaning. By his storytelling my friend spread his learning from the yeshiva, but this learning in a new, slightly altered tale would take on dangerous and dark meanings, so that the poor man, as he advanced in years, tried

to grasp what was beyond a tale, in the distant ultimate sense, but contained in its telling in a highly complex manner. In the years when most men seek peace, a fire erupted in him. Once his storytelling had come easy and had given him pleasure, now he began to fear his own words. One day, somewhere far away, he met an old kabbalist who introduced him to the *Sefer yetzira*, the Book of Creation. "*All things derive from the twenty-two letters of our alphabet. Every being who has ever been or shall ever be is composed of these twenty-two letters. Spoken, they are engraved in the air and their abode is in the throat, mouth, on the tongue, between the teeth, on the lips. Interlocked, these letters make up the two hundred and thirty-one gates of knowledge.*" He studied the six chapters of this book that he might reach the greatest secret. He forgot that only satisfaction with the world brings peace; restiveness is the harbinger of catastrophe!

Whenever he came to a country where he had not been before, he would bend in prayer and pick up a piece of earth. He would put the earth in a sack he carried slung over his shoulder. He cared for the heavy sack (already full of earth) as he would for his most precious belongings. He decided he would, with the help of the letters, make a living being—a golem. The earth he would use was from all over the world—so it contained the whole world! Waiting for sleep under the open sky, he looked at the stars and mused: "At some moment, everything came from nothing, from dust the earth, from earth, life." But what of his tales? People listened to them and wept, sighed, laughed, mourned, rejoiced—but all of this was short-lived illusion, a deceptive substitute for the real miracle, which remained unrealized.

One evening, when the moon had just appeared above the hills, he stopped on a desolate plateau, opened his sack, and poured out the earth he had been gathering for so long and with such patience. With the help of the four elements, air, water, fire, and earth, he molded the body of the golem, remembering carefully what was written about how Rabbi Levy, in the Jewish year 5340, in the month of Adar, had breathed life into earthly dust. Reciting the creation formula, he stood first at the feet of the weird effigy, then turned his face toward the face of the golem, still no more than crudely suggested in the pile of wet earth being licked by the flames of a crackling fire. He circled the motionless, ugly-looking thing seven times, from its right side to its head, from its head to its left side, and back to its feet. The fire rose higher. The golem's face became red. Steam rose from the earthen body and everything became wrapped in mist. From thoughts of creation and words of creation

emerged what might be called an actual creation. Just before dawn, as the sun rose, the golem moved. It lifted itself on its heavy arms and got to its feet, a huge hunk of earth with its square face turned toward the sun. And its maker, instead of satisfaction and release, felt fear. The earthen thing had turned, arms raised, toward him to crush him. For some reason it wanted to destroy its maker. But words stopped him. Words had created him, they now ruled him.

The unfortunate old man then continued on his way. The thing walked along with him, as obedient as a slave. People locked themselves in their homes. Nobody came out to greet them. Their travels became a nightmare. The golem's term is forty days, and no more. For forty days the expressionless, mute monster, containing a bare spark of life within him, went along like a sleepwalker in a world that had no place for him. Its only show of anything had come together with life, and had been the attempt to destroy the one who had breathed life into it. On the fortieth day, the golem crumbled in dust, turning back into the earth from which it was made.

The whole episode was swept away by the wind. The old man sat down again among people who looked forward to hearing one of his enchanting tales. Words were born deep within him, quivered in his throat, set his tongue and lips in motion. But they froze on his lips; he spoke, but no one was able to hear even one word. In his mind he saw everything about which he wanted to speak: his youth, the yeshiva, his teacher, the stars and sky, the roads and people who lived along them, but the pictures were not transformed into words. Indeed, he then realized he would never again be able to speak. He had not found satisfaction in illusion, yet when he lost illusion he found he had actually lost reality. And instead of words, tears began to flow down his wrinkled face, and he wept because of his fate.

There, that's the story of the old man who forgot how to speak.

Then the rabbi, my teacher and guardian, said: "The tale you tell is extraordinary. I will not ask how you can so faithfully recount what can only have been the secret thoughts of a wretched man. I will not ask, either, when it was you came to join him. Life is complex and involved, and this case, I am sure, being no exception, has no simple explanation. Perhaps this was just one of your tales. And then again, perhaps it wasn't. But tell us, where are you now going, what are you seeking?"

"I will answer: we are seeking the gates of Paradise. In several tales, which could be true stories, such gates are mentioned. This wretched man

and I go, one with the other, just as the sun goes with the moon, light goes with shadow, one side always with another. We have long been wandering, and perhaps we have reached the end of the world. That gate might perhaps be in these woods."

At this, the rabbi again spoke: "Here is what happened once to a coachman. He had lived his entire life with his coach and horses. One day, in a terrible accident, he lost his coach and horses. He could not imagine life without them. He died of sorrow. He went to heaven, but when he got there he continued to mourn. He found neither peace nor satisfaction. So he was sent to an imaginary world where a coach and four magnificent horses were waiting for him. And there were wondrous roads for the coach to fly over day and night. This good man could find rest only in a false paradise and not in the real one. That is the case with you."

The rest of the night passed in silence, and the next day we parted, going in different directions, they to seek what wasn't there and we to continue on our way.

After traveling for some time, we reached a small hamlet and stopped in front of a house hidden among high trees. It was a beautiful spring day. We saw a garden with lovely greenery filled with many paths, along which young people my age walked, talking or deep in thought. My teacher confessed that we had reached the end of our way. The great Rabbi Mendel Baer lived here, and it was into his care and concern that he wanted to recommend me.

We were soon sitting in a large chamber with a long table. Rabbi Mendel listened to our story, his eyes closed. "I have passed through the fiftieth gate," he said, "but great knowledge has a great price." He raised his head, opened his eyes, and we looked into two completely white orbs, as if they had been burned by a great fire. "I have become blind that I might see what others cannot."

After a short silence, he continued. "Many, many years ago, having read all the books I could find, I was the best-educated man in Lublin. Then I came into possession of a note which, I have no idea how, had come to be placed between two pages of the Talmud commentaries on life and death. I began reading it in my room by candlelight. Suddenly a thousand suns blazed, and I lost consciousness. When I came to, I was in total darkness; my outstretched hands were seared by the flames of the

still burning candles. Horrified, I cried for help. My elderly teacher hurried to my aid, but when he heard what had happened, he said, 'Nobody can help you. You have looked at Original Light, the light of the first days of the Creation. Whosoever looks at it remains in the dark forever.' It took me a long time to discover that a blind man sees much more and much better."

He called his students. They surrounded us on all sides. The blind man started to ask me questions, and I answered in exaltation. I wanted to convince him that my place was among his students. He listened to me carefully. Suddenly he began to shake, and tears started running down his face. His students ran to him, asking why he wept. "This youth will soon die," he cried. "And this has made me terribly sad." Hearing this, my teacher fell into despair. "I promised his father I would return him safe and sound. If anything should happen to him, I myself cannot survive."

The blind man grasped the true despair of my teacher. And I was taken by such fear that I could not speak a word. "I can work miracles and give you eternal life," said the blind man, after a long silence. "But," he said, "I must warn you: because man's life is short, his dream is to reach, as quickly as possible, the ultimate mystery and attain absolute knowledge; and he will draw closer and closer to such knowledge. Eternal life is without this hope, even the possibility, because it is not for man to be equal to the Greatest Power. Do you want an eternal life in which you will forget all that you know and where the doors to new knowledge will be forever locked to you?"

At that moment, imminent death so frightened me, I simply did not think. I wanted to live.

The rabbi ordered a knife brought to him and cut four letters into my right arm: YHWH. "Now you may go home or wherever you like. You will live as long as these letters remain on your arm."

I took my leave that same day of the blind rabbi and my teacher. But, instead of going home as I had promised, I began going aimlessly from country to country . . .

A voice called out from the dark: "Why do you reveal your secret when you have been given the chance to live eternally?" The youth raised his head and stared into the shadows with his empty, cold look. "Eternal life such as I have been given is nothing more than eternal wandering." He

rolled up his right sleeve and showed where the holy letters were carved into his arm.

The host brought a funeral shroud. He held the candle high. In the silence, the youth put on the shroud. Aron ben Sh'muel Hanasi took the young man's right arm and, with a knife heated to glowing, touched the letters. The youth made no sound. He did not feel pain. His body had long been dead, ever since the day he left the house of the blind miracle worker. When the last letter had been erased, the youth's body crumbled into dust before the eyes of the deeply moved men. Hanasi said: "It is written on the first day of the year who is to go and who is to come, who shall live and who shall die. Some will be taken by fire, others will be victims of wild beasts, hunger, thirst, earthquake, or plague. It is written that this one shall rest and that one shall wander. For one, everything will be easy, for another, troubles will pursue him throughout his life. Some will become rich, others poor. It is written who shall keep silent and who shall speak."

When it was all over, the only sound to be heard in the inn was that of the raging storm. And the name of the one whose ashes the men stood over remained unknown.

Translated by Karolina Udovički

Vida Ognjenović

Vida Ognjenović, born in 1941, is best known as a playwright. She also writes short stories and essays and translates works from other languages into Serbian. She is the author of two collections of stories entitled *The Poisonous Milk of Dandelions* (1995), and *The Old Watch* (1996), and the novel *The House of Dead Smells* (1996).

Her plays are *My Name Is Mitar* (1983), *How to Make the Master Laugh* (1985), and *Did the Prince's Dinner Ever Occur?* (1990), among others.

THE DUEL

Walking is a very important part of family and social life in this town. There are many serious people who, every day at a set time, proceed along the same path. There are those who do this only as guides for their distinguished guests. Most common are those who fulfill this obligation on holidays or Sunday evenings when the weather is nice. Then, dressed in their best clothes, they pass by the Patriarchate several times, stop on the square by the fountain, look to see who is there, chat with neighbors, and then home. Every now and then, young people stroll down to the Danube. Idly and aimlessly. They have the time. Otherwise, the inherited belief holds that the man who is seen on the street on a working day is to be greatly pitied. He is surely in trouble, otherwise he would be at work. Therefore, the residents almost always rush when they are going somewhere, except when they are out walking, and some even do this briskly. They greet one another quietly and quickly, according to the time of day, their age, calling each other by name, when appropriate, but without much formality or making a fuss. They don't stray from their path, they only speak to those they encounter directly, to others at a distance they simply nod their heads, there is no shouting or noise. All rush to complete the task for which they left the house, then return to what they do for a living. Here, haste is really a national custom.

Those who take a walk every day, under normal circumstances do not change their route, nor their conversation; even when there is a larger group of strollers, there is little variation. Hosts who show the town to visitors talk to them about something else along the way, but it can't be

said that this place buzzes with human voices. They are almost inaudible, except when the students scatter in groups as they leave school.

The local resident is honestly proud of everything there is to show to a curious guest. And he himself likes to peek inside here and there.

There is even a kind of customary, necessary direction of movement on the pilgrimage to the town's sights. It begins with a visit to the marble fountain of sculpted lions' heads that face toward the four directions of the compass. It is in the very heart of town. The fountain is very beautiful. It weakly fizzles as a stream of water gurgles from the lions' jaws; these kings of the beasts, so wet and somber, seem to shed endless tears that roll down their stone faces. Then a guest might cup his hands under the stream to catch a little water, just to taste it, believing it could be therapeutic (rarely does one skip this gesture, even in winter); a visit to the three churches might follow: the cathedral and the lower and upper churches. If permitted, they might gaze for a while at the iconostasis in the cathedral, the works of the great masters, from Zaharija Orfelin to Uroš Predić, and if they cannot go inside, they might circle the building a bit, gaze at the height of the spire, feel the walls, and wonder at the beauty of the carvings on the heavy doors. They could also look at the majestic bishop's residence, then be slowly directed to the lower church, which is, one might say, in the neighborhood.

There it would be mandatory to speculate a bit on the deeply moving ordination ceremony, performed there sometime in the distant past, of one of the Montenegrin bishops. Usually, no one knows which bishop or when. They might sigh and thoughtfully nod their heads, complaining that time really flows downstream. The ages pass so quickly, brother!

On the way to the upper church, they might stop several times to view one of the old houses, or wrought-iron decorations on the windows, a well-built gate, or a preserved facade. A little further down, everyone stops in front of the building in which Baron Rajačić once lived and slowly reads the inscription on the wall plaque.

In the upper church, the visitors usually light candles, even those who immediately protest that they do so not for religious reasons, but because of custom or for cultural reasons. Thanks to the good sexton Bajić, the church is usually open. He also happily starts a conversation. As thanks for the offerings, he immediately volunteers the fact (always the same story) that people are always cold in this church, whereas miracu-

lously he is never cold. Not even during the bitterest St. John's Day frost. Yes, he does wear a wool robe, winter and summer, but it is never buttoned. When he sees people bundled up to the last button, and even how those ties are knotted, he pities them. He would choke, he says. He wouldn't be able to breathe, wrapped up like that. A man couldn't freeze in a church, he claims. It is heated from the flames of the candles, and how! And it holds the heat, even though it is so high. If they would allow him to, he would even sleep in the church—God forgive me, he says.

But don't ask him if he knows when the church was built. He doesn't. He is astonished that you even ask something like that. My goodness, how should I know? A long time ago, that's for sure; when, I don't know.

Although he lives close by the sights that he respects, the local resident (as long as we are not talking about an expert or a specialist) is usually unable to cite the origin of a certain structure, an important date in the life of a hero whose portrait bust is displayed, or the fate of the owner of a beautiful ancient house you are standing in front of. It is useless to ask the name of the builder or the sculptor. Even an educated and reasonable man will answer: *it was a long time ago*—but those who are careful about how they speak of every artifact from the past use the word *ancient*.

This detail should not be too quickly judged a spiritual laziness, since that would not be quite exact. It is more a particular relationship to time that is common among the inhabitants of old towns, where the past is not so strictly separated from the present. In such places, scarcely anything that existed at one time has disappeared without a trace, so that it can be said with certainty: there you have it, that is the past. The inhabitants, it seems, also lack a completely sharpened sense of the distinction between the present and the past. They live in that general time. From birth, they have encountered an order of extremely old buildings and a collection of already ordered historical facts. They grow up alongside them, live and grow old with them, and get accustomed to all that. They don't notice that something in their surroundings is extremely old. And when they return after being gone for a time—long or short—no visible changes in the surroundings await them. Everything is there, in place, just as they left it. They are simply used to time being wide open here, and the duration of things continues, sometimes as far as the eye can see. In this place, years, decades, and centuries move along the same circle.

All of this is merged into one goal, by which both the place of occurrence and the temporal intervals are marked, but it says: *here*. What happened *here* was long ago, sometime, from time immemorial, but also now, nowadays, soon. For this reason, natives of such towns see no particular reason to state the precise temporal details in connection with their surroundings. All that was around them still continues. For them, that unity of the past and the present seems completely natural.

Anyone who stubbornly clings to the noble goal of being an industrious guest, an explorer, determined to learn more and more, let him give up on time. It is only an illusion that the day is without order. Let him marvel and be amazed, in that everything for him will be generous in his hands and he will have much to be amazed at. Up to that point at least, and after that, what more do you want?

Although natives of the town do not recite them like the alphabet at every opportunity, historical facts are not lost and scattered, but studied and arranged in thick books and articles, as they deserve to be. This town has the fortune of being a favorite of historians. The facts are known, but the real story is avoided. Nowhere are to be found those unusual people, or the one-time exploits, ideas, and discoveries made right here. Their conflicts, poetic flights, departures from the community, travels abroad and return are no longer remembered. There is no one to recount them. Ask about them and people will respond with trifles and nonsense.

The local storyteller is capricious, too cautious, difficult. He prevaricates, hesitates, and avoids the real theme. Most of all he would prefer to say something that would, as it were, relax you. Allegedly, what he tells are true anecdotes. Grief and sorrow. But about the important things, he is silent or diffident: that is not known for certain; they who would shut up the crowd, they will say anything; maybe that really happened, or maybe it didn't. He can hardly wait to move to the firm ground of jokes.

Just as a certain high school student excused himself to the catechist Mikić during theology class: Excuse me, I can't answer today, I drank the whole night by my sick grandfather! The poor kid wanted to say that he *spent* the whole night by his sick grandfather. The teacher Mikić says: Well, my son, I hope you ate something too, instead of doing that all night on an empty stomach. That's a joke for us. And he will feel very offended if you don't laugh heartily. They wonder how anyone could not take pleasure in such comical slip-ups. Or they begin to explain, with many

tedious asides, but all the while laughing, how during a harvest long ago at a rich man's place, the grape pickers once amused themselves by diverting the tub of too hot must not into the cask but into the trough, and how the pigs got totally drunk. The whole village echoed with the squeal of the pigs, and their overseer, fuming with rage, cursed out the drunken pigs.

And when they finally come to stories about Djena, the hero of various local events, there is no end. They can keep going all night. For instance, Djena, otherwise a very reputable man and a member of the church choir, once drank so much that he answered the *synapte* in a loud voice: To Madagascaaaar! To Madagascaaaar! He had a deep baritone— his voice was heard even in the churchyard. The priest grew so angry that in the middle of the service, he thundered: what kind of Africans are howling there? To that Djena shouts an answer: Oh, they will pay for this.

It is hard to find on earth a more pitiful work than the lively, humorous small-town tale, nor a more crude storyteller, with less talent, than their local yarn spinner. But there is nothing more pitiful than those who take delight in them. Everything goes around in the same circle. If these miserable storytellers did not weave, like spiders, wonderful events and characters, generally made to look like simpletons, they would do little harm. But in this way they are dangerous. The poor teachers and former clerks, leeches, slanderous chroniclers, high school dropouts, poor, dusty, industrious ants. The blessed futile toil of these pests and their foolish belief that they are providing a cultural foundation for the people by collecting and noting these barn-floor gleanings. It is pitiful that they never realize how much harm they cause to real events and real human motives by their own narrow-mindedness and occasionally refined evasions of the truth.

Let's just take that Djena, about whom there are so many jokes. He is the well-known wine magnate Evgenije Maširević, a fact you would never learn from a single yarn about him. One of those amazing individuals who made the whole turn-of-the-century epoch seem like a time of daring, but enthralled people and unusual events. For them, nothing was out of bounds. Mocking the bad singing in church and the teasing of priests, these are jokes for the village dandies and libertines.

According to the family tradition, one late fall, on the eve of St. Arandjel's Day, on the way back from his studies in Pest, Evgenije-Djena

Maširević stopped in Kovilj, at the estate of the landowner Todor Sekicki, abducted his daughter, Persida, who was betrothed to someone else, and swam across the Danube, carrying his future wife, who did not know how to swim, on his back. The posse almost caught them. Her angry father borrowed boats and pursued them, but Djena and the girl hid in a marsh. The posse were behind him, but their rowboats got caught in the reeds. They trudged through the marsh, but miraculously the kidnapper was nowhere to be seen. Djena, with his Sida, spent the night in the reeds, the slime coming up to just below his neck, but his beloved Persida did not even get a foot wet. I won't tell you how I crawled through the mud, he said.

In the morning, the reed cutters found them, as they sat on Jović's sandbank sucking fresh duck eggs, which Djena had collected from the nests in the swamps. And those poor devils from the posse were floating in their boats along the river. At that time, that little mound along the Danube was not yet called Jović's, just the sandbank. It could also have been named after Evgenije. He deserved it.

Of course, it wasn't so easy to discover who this Jović was and why that knoll was so called. Some remembered that a Dr. Jović lived there, an eccentric, a well-known lawyer. His house is the one with the wrought iron on the windows. Now the family Dejanović live in it. Many immediately said that it was surely that Jović who invented the mechanical potato peeler, and then turned to praising that invention. Great savings were realized by that little machine. A housewife with a knife cuts off half the potato, apple, or cucumber. This way, only the outer peel is removed. It was if we had concluded that Dr. Jović was an idle, self-taught inventor of kitchen gadgets so that housewives, out of gratitude, awarded him a sandbank along the river.

Most of all, that infuriates Professor Petrović, who is hesitant to tell us about him. What machine and what nonsense! he shouts—an otherwise quiet and reserved gentleman. People will say anything. The world attributes its own nonsense to its greatest offspring. He made that gadget for his maid Evica for her birthday, almost as a joke. She sang his praises and then others took it up. There you have it, Kosta Jović is a master; the professor is infuriated. I can imagine how the poor man would complain if he could hear what he is remembered for here.

That Jović was a rare individual, Professor Petrović explains to us in

great detail, saddened almost to tears that we remember such a man for meaningless trifles. An old local family, from the very first migration. He was of the third generation of great lawyers. His father Miloš was the legal representative of the Serbian ecclesiastical council, author of the first legal draft for Vojvodina, and the Miletić's defender at the first trial in the 1870s. Konstantin Jović, after whom the sandbank is named (his grandfather also had the same name), received his Doctorate of Law degree in Vienna and was a philosopher, linguist, poet, translator, metaphysician, and a bit of an eccentric. He returned here as an accomplished jurist, inherited the family office, brought with him his young wife, who was born somewhere in Galicia. She died in childbirth and left him a son Miloš, to whom he was, by necessity, both father and mother. He lived his life reading. He studied languages. He had taken an oath that he would read every book that came into his hands in the language in which it was written. And he was very good at that. And what wasn't he good at? He wasn't a common man. There was nothing he didn't know. I looked at his novel—well, it was like Balzac. It is a pity that he did not complete it. It would have been a good book. Jović went on walks while reading. He carried his son, Miloš, on his shoulders, who would play with his hair, and he would read and walk slowly.

A fine attorney, he defended only the most difficult cases. It is not remembered here that he lost a single case. And when some client came to thank him or to bring him gifts, he locked himself in the house and allowed no one inside. He displayed a note on the window: "I'm not at home, I've left and won't return soon." But it could be easily seen that the paper was supported from inside by a hand.

Besides this novel, he wrote, together with Professor Kolarović, a book entitled *Benjamin Franklin* and also a great number of legal, linguistic, and historical articles. He was a passionate historian. He researched in detail the revolution of 1848 and Kossuth's revolution. He translated the *History of Hungarian Law* in two volumes and some of Schiller's longer poems, Tennyson's "Enoch Arden," and almost the complete works of a young Hungarian poet, a friend from the university by the name of Djula Dolnaji, whose suicide he mourned with a moving epitaph in the journal *Branko's Kolo,* sometime in the spring of 1903, if I am not mistaken.

And that novel—imagine, the manuscript through some strange cir-

cumstance came into my possession, Professor Petrović says confidentially. I am sure that that is a youthful work. Perhaps he started it while he was still studying and then put it aside because of other interests. I believe he would have finished it eventually. It is a historical study of a certain Jozef Bem, a Polish nobleman, an officer to whom Jović was related by marriage. Jozef Bem was, like Jana Pachova-Jović, born somewhere in Galicia. As a sixteen-year-old boy, but already an officer, he marched with Napoleon's regiments to Russia. He became a hero only when he arrived in this area, in order to join Louis Kossuth. Evidently, this unusual life attracted Jović. Jozef Bem is one of the brave military leaders who ran the Austrian army out of the Banat. Only when he had run them off from that side of the river Tamiš did he pull out to Transylvania, Jović tells us. The advance of Russian troops surprised him there. He barely had time to collect his troops, but everything was already crushed and broken. He survived by blending in with the corpses and spent two nights and a day buried under dead soldiers. Finally, when he somehow got out of that hell, he escaped to Turkey, since for him no one remained in this region. You only have to see these descriptions of the escape, details of his wandering from village to village, meeting with gypsies, deserters, and thieves. I tell you, a real writer. Jozef Bem died as Murat Pasha, in the town of Alep, in the embrace of a swarthy Moldavian woman who secretly stabbed him with a knife for a bit of money. A romantic story, full of historical facts and studiously researched details. I tell you, it is a shame the novel is unfinished. In the subsequent chapters, it probably would have been explained why he was killed and what he experienced on his difficult journey from fugitive to pasha.

Professor Petrović did not allow us to take the manuscript from his house. We could leaf through the beautifully penned calligraphy of the text only in his presence. That is a fond memory for me; I apologize, but I came to it through a real fluke of providence. When I founded the museum, more than twenty years ago, I stipulated that all the old papers purchased by the museum should be brought to me first, so I could choose what should be saved. And what do you think, one day from a great pile, this one stuck out. If my health holds up, maybe I will prepare it for publication. This would be the least that this town could do to honor its one-time leading citizens—the family Jović.

And I too have digressed, he added bitterly, after a short pause. Who

is interested in such things today? They wouldn't print that, even if it were finished and the novel complete. What does the sparrow know about Beethoven?.

If Kosta Jović had lived long enough (but he didn't) to realize his wonderful innovative conception of multilingual dictionaries, an idea that had already been advanced in scientific circles, then for that alone his name would appear in all the world's encyclopedias and he would have spent his last days as a valued emeritus of who knows what well-known university department. And not have simpletons cite him as the inventor of a little machine for peeling potatoes. But what can you expect when nice things don't happen to us? Good things happen only to the rabble.

It was precisely during those days, before what seemed inexorable had finally occurred, that a group of prominent linguists were supposed to meet here, at our high school, to begin negotiations for preparing the first edition of that new dictionary, according to Kosta Jović's conception. I remember how much was written about this in our newspapers. He passionately defended and explained his idea of multilingualism as an important factor of human freedom. Man is closed in only by his mother tongue, he wrote, as though in a language preserve limited by origin, family relationships, and conspiracies, while exposed to permanent blackmail, and he himself constantly suspicious and doubting everything expressed in another language. We students applauded him enthusiastically. Dual-language dictionaries to a certain degree aid in escaping that claustrophobia, he maintained in his papers. They are constructed to bring two different forms of the same substance face to face so that one excludes the other. *Either-or,* that is their principle. If you say it this way, you can't say it the other way. Real dictionaries must be parallel, an omnilinguistic picture of a concept. A good dictionary should be examined like a well-conceived atlas, to encompass multiple living and classical languages, to offer the opportunity for comparison and investigation, to promote a free inspection of different forms. Such parallel understanding of words should free people of the fear of an unknown language, from other kinds of meaning . . . But, well, all this ended that day when he fell head-first to the grass on that sandbank by the Danube.

Professor Torer tried to continue the project, but nothing came of it. The war quickly broke out, and then he died—too soon. I don't know whether such an idea appeared elsewhere. If only. It still hasn't arrived

here, and why do we really need it? We have our little machine for shaving the skin from the potato.

We, all the same, return to Jović's sandbank. Why is it really Jović's, we ask? Did it perhaps belong to the family, like property? In his lifetime, besides books, he did not own anything, not even that little bit of earth. Then how did he get it for himself? we ask. By death, Professor Petrović answers resignedly, that's how.

When was that? Well, somewhere on the eve of the First World War. A few months earlier. Through one good soul we paid the entrance fee to that bloodletting, in which we later died in vain, like wild animals.

Well, then, not to prolong the story (this is usually not his favorite saying), a German by the name of Schnabl, a wine merchant, suddenly arrived here that fall. He was not very well received. The local suppliers had their own dealers whom they trusted and with whom they had long done business. Among them was Herr Lenis, whom they considered almost one of our own. But although they waited for him, Gustav Lenis did not appear. This Schnabl burst in instead. How, now, all of a sudden, could an unknown man buy the wine in bulk? That was not at all usual. The fairies brought him, that's where he came from. He arrived before the others and paid a good price—and well, really, he did a good job. At the beginning, they did not want to sell to him, but, little by little, well, it started. That was after the tariff war, so wine here was at a low price.

One evening a large group of friends gathered at Dišinica's café. Mr. Schnabl was very sociable and even spoke a bit of broken Serbian. He gladly went wherever they invited him: to dinner at the winemakers' homes, to weddings, to drinking bouts. He loved to sit and talk in the evenings with our people.

A choice group of gentlemen gathered at Dišinica's that evening. They tasted the new vintage, but also drank an old wine. People were enjoying themselves. Dr. Jović came in late. Once in a while he would dine at Dišinica's. The conversation began. About the European crisis, what else? Someone said if the Russians didn't jump in now and save the world, no one would.

All at once, Jović, out of nowhere, began to revile the Russians. Heaping insults on them, as if he wanted to avenge his hero Jozef Bem right then and there, that very evening, in Dišinica's café. "What kind of help can anyone expect from them?" he yelled. "The world has had enough

of their Scythian tactics. For once, let them go toe to toe like a real army. And their military strategy! They wander across the steppes, they kill whoever they meet, and when their butts are set alight, they run all the way to Siberia." People were laughing, but Schnabl most of all and most happily. A certain Berdić translated everything for him. "They have betrayed the republicans, wrecked the Duma. They have shot all the educated people. All those with a scrap of morality have turned their backs and left, regardless of the consequences. Russia is today, my brothers, in all the European spas, she is suffering in rented apartments in the cheapest quarters of the capitals. What kind of Russia is that to save the world? Let her heal her wounds, it is better for her." Schnabl applauded. *"Ich danke Ihnen,"* he thanked Jović, bowing. The one who declared that Russians would save the world was now silent, but that same Berdić, who was translating for Schnabl, snapped at Jović: "Doctor, haven't you exaggerated a bit? One cannot talk about a great power in such a way, regardless of our personal idiosyncracies . . ." He hadn't even finished his sentence when Jović began again: "A whip, a whip for their sanctity, for that great power! She is used to suffering and being small. She hauls the boat along the Volga and sings—well, where else do you have that? Who else can do that! They also don't know that man can live and that his back doesn't always have to be raw with wounds from beatings."

Now Schnabl could no longer restrain himself. He jumped to his feet and took over the conversation from Jović. "The slobbering pigs," he yelled, "and their pig revolution!" He sipped a bit of wine and continued still louder: "They are all dying from hunger. Their nobility is eating hay. Orphans grind dried cow dung, that is their only flour! And that's why they're doing that!" Then he bought a round of drinks for the whole café. Some accepted, but others didn't. Jović ate in silence. He hadn't taken part. "I don't drink," he said shortly. "Thanks." Schnabl screamed and enjoyed himself: "Riffraff, baggage! It's finished, you don't have the Russians any longer! *Ende gut alles gut! Genug, Russen kaput. Haben Sie die Russen wo gesehen? Nein!* There aren't any Russians, they're all dead!" Then all of a sudden he began to dance a parody of a *kazachok* across the café and shrieked: *"Russen tot! Russen tot!"* It was a bit much for everyone. The scene was unreasonable, even for a café. And why did this German get so infuriated? Except for himself, almost everyone was silent. Drinks somehow didn't go with all this.

Suddenly, Jović stood up, approached Schnabl, and then delivered a slap across the face, and then another, and another. "Don't dump on the Russians, you are a pig!"—and then again, a slap across his face. Schnabl was so stupefied that he didn't defend himself. He was barely able to stammer: *"Was ist los? Ich bitte Ihnen, Herr Doctor . . . warten Sie mahl!* Didn't the Herr Doctor curse them a bit ago, here, in front of us all, didn't you?" Jović shouted in reply: "I can curse them! They are my people! I am family with them, do you understand? But you shut your muzzle, you Bavarian prankster!" And his voice all of a sudden swelled, became somehow resolute, powerful. In the meantime, Schnabl composed himself a bit, grew bold, and began to threaten: "You will pay for this! I know where I will go for this!" People calmed Kosta, fearing that he would attack the poor devil. Everyone began to bustle around. He broke free. He stood in the middle of the café and addressed Schnabl: "You still don't know where you will have to go for this, but now you will realize immediately, you nobody, you spy! Come tomorrow at one o'clock to that flat by the embankment below. I will wait for you exactly on that level sandbank. I challenge you to a duel!" Since he didn't have a glove and he wanted everything to be exactly as it was in his novel, he once again struck Schnabl on the snout: a slap. Some held Schnabl and others pulled Kosta toward the exit. He freed himself, ran out on the street and then home.

Many hoped that nothing would come of this. First, they were certain that Jović didn't have a pistol, which was the truth. Second, they hoped that Schnabl was a chicken, which was also true, and that he would run away in fear to Novi Sad that very night, which didn't happen.

The next day at exactly one o'clock, two very nearsighted men stood on the sandbank along the Danube, dressed in black tails and top hats, like two strict school monitors at a high school graduation exam. One was the duelist, Dr. Jović, and the other his second, Professor Torer. They stomped along the sandbank a bit, but there was no Schnabl anywhere. They were almost ready to head home when there he was, with the police.

When Jović saw the time, he spread his arms and started off toward them, but a bullet came from that direction; it was never determined publicly who fired it, but Torer suspected one of the policemen. Schnabl did not shoot, that is clear. But someone did. The shot passed through

the coat and poor Kosta's thick layer of shirt and sank into his wonderful and innocent heart. He collapsed, rather astonished, without the slightest sound. Torer tried in vain to pick him up. Then the police also came. They completed the investigation. They sent for a doctor and declared publicly a day later that Dr. Jović had committed suicide.

Torer tried to give a statement in front of witnesses at the police. He claimed, completely contradicting the police report, that Kosta had been murdered. The police rejected his version as an overly passionate defense of a dead friend. He initiated a lawsuit. He even found Schnabl's address and asked him to testify. But the war broke out, and everything went to the devil.

Kosta left behind only his mentally retarded son, the poor little Miloš. He was then about ten years old but behaved like a five-year-old. He did not know exactly what had happened. He just repeated: "Father has gone far away, Father has gone far away." Probably the maid Evica told him this. She took care of him, since there were no closer relatives and Professor Torer had been named guardian. And the orphan boy himself did not live long. He died from a cold, several years after his father, somewhere around Christmas. They could not bury him until the third day because the ground was frozen solid. Evica said that she wasn't afraid of having a dead person in the house. It was as if he fell asleep, my little child. He was such a pleasant child.

What had really happened? Why did Dr. Jović die? We tried to bring in Professor Petrović to tell us more. He shook his head, stood up to get a drink of water, talked about the weather, hesitating. Obviously, he would gladly steer clear of this topic. And what he had told us up to this point was without his famous *élan* and witty wordplay. He—whose eloquence was greater than his?—noticed even what God's own eyes would miss; this time he only arranged the information, almost as if he were testifying at a trial. When the main current of the story carried him away, then he had to make an effort to shove off from it and get into its flow; clearly he was struggling. He was rushing to the end, which is not his style of narration. On the contrary, his stories have everything except endings, since the listener can't wait for it.

Although almost sixty years have passed since those events (the professor was a student when it had happened), he told us in a whisper the remainder of the story.

I think that Kosta Jović was killed on someone's orders. No one can convince me that Schnabl was not sent here with a list, to help the police. He was simply a common provocateur. Now, whether Kosta himself challenged fate and ran to meet his misfortune, I cannot figure out. Berdić, who had befriended Schnabl quite well in a businesslike way, later claimed that he was surprised by how much that same Schnabl knew about the leading people of our town, which he at the time attributed to his merchant's skill. The man had inquired thoroughly about those from whom he planned to buy. That wasn't a small job. Berdić had described in detail to Professor Petrović the evening at the Dišinica's café. Perhaps he always had the habit of giving exact information. In this way, Schnabl had made inquiries before his arrival.

That Kosta Jović was on Schnabl's list, there seems no doubt. Why, I never found out. Which of his numerous occupations most bothered the state, by then tottering, and became the reasons for an order of execution, it is hard to figure out. Perhaps it was enough that he was just so smart.

That tall thin gentleman, who up until recently went for a walk to Jović's sandbank every day around five in the evening, was Professor Petrović. He never found a publisher for the novel about Jozef Bem.

Years later, among Professor Torer's papers a letter was found in which the young lawyer Jović informs his friend of the date of his arrival in Vienna. At the very beginning he tells him: "I can't describe how happy I am to see the faces of my friends once again, and I long for the hours we spent exploring each other's souls and sharing deep personal revelations—for which, here in my own small birthplace, I am eternally hungry and thirsty." Later, he asks his friend (whom he addresses as Leo) to buy for him the books listed at the end of the letter, before his arrival, as many as he could, since he would be stopping only briefly in Vienna; "because of this I have missed the visionary meetings and lectures." First on the list in the postcript was Ludwig Anzengruber, *The Raising of Human Souls*. At the bottom was only the signature: *dein* Kossta.

We wonder today whether if at one of those apparently frequent visionary meetings Konstantin Jović was able to see a vision of his own tortured path toward destruction. Perhaps he did. What if it really was a suicide? What if Jović had intentionally challenged Schnabl's senseless absurdities uttered that evening in the café and the next day arrived

empty-handed at the duel? In that case, neither Schnabl nor his controller ever realized why they killed Dr. Kosta Jović, linguist and lawyer, writer of historical novels and translator of Djula Dolnaji. One of his poems that Jović translated begins with this line: *For three days now, in my breast, I have been carrying a dead bird.*

Translated by Paul M. Foster

Vidosav Stevanović

Vidosav Stevanović, born in 1942, writes poetry, short stories, plays, novels, and literary criticism. He has published several collections of short stories: *Refuz the Dead Man* (1969), *Suburban Dragons* (1978), *The Caesarian* (1984), *The Balkan Island* (1993), and *Christ and Dogs* (1993). His novels are: *The Humble Ones* (1971), *Konstantin Gorča* (1975), *Testament* (1986), *Love Circle* (1988), and *The Snow of Athens* (1992).

Stevanović has received a number of distinguished literary awards, and his works have been translated into many languages. *Suburban Dragons* was published in French in 1971, and a Greek translation of *The Snows of Athens* was published in 1992.

D. S.

D. S. is (or was) my father. A few random photographs are all that is
left of him, the only heirlooms I have—tangible, yet stiff and unconvincing. All who once knew him have forgotten him completely; but
memories of the dead are forgeries anyway—people only tell you what
they think you want to hear. His parents are no longer alive, either. They
have been dead and buried for a long time: thus vanished the last of those
for whom he was precious and important. D. S. has disappeared; he is an
empty void.

He was killed at a young age (twenty-three) and left few traces behind; at present I am twenty-four years older than my own father. I did
not know him; in fact, I never even saw him, but I find myself thinking
of him more and more often; I remember him even when I try to think
of more cheerful things, of life and my future. I dream of the empty void
called D. S. I cannot see anything, I cannot make out his features, but I
know it's him. Will my sons one day have the same kind of dream, without knowing what (or who) it is—a head without a face and a face without features, a mask made of dreams and nothingness?

Maybe in this way (with or without my help) D. S. is slowly returning to life, reincarnating himself psychologically, in secret, struggling to
acquire a form that he will inhabit for a while. Or is it only that I remind
myself of my indebtedness and am repenting in my dreams, but refusing
to admit it while I am awake? The dead remind us of nothing; it is we
who remind ourselves of them. Intuition is really the sole human trait
that makes our acuity possible: it finds something even where we search

for nothing, it turns the past into the world that is yet to come, it discovers and revives.

I am describing D. S.'s death as I would describe my own. Somewhere within me I have inherited the hidden genetic makeup of his destruction, and it is only fitting that I try to discover and decode it. Art is presentiment and, sometimes, the revelation of a secret.

A few years ago I was driving past a remote town that is cut in two by a river polluted with crude oil and heavy industrial waste. Any conscientious ecologist would include it on his list. It was a damp November night; something between fog and rain moistened the patched pavement of the road. A thin, barren forest glided by on both sides, and the trees bent over me like phantoms hovering over a solitary traveler. A local ghost story could have been conceived at that very place and time, but another, a different one, created itself.[1]

A dull feeling of fear and nausea (similar to that left by the foregoing footnote) took hold of my bowels, my hands trembled as they held the steering wheel, and I knew that I had to resist or I would swerve off the road. What was happening to me? Why did I want to go in another direction, to be someone else? Maybe I *was* someone else? But why? I pulled over to the side of the road but did not turn off the engine or headlights; my cigarette tasted as bitter as ashes.

"Go to sleep!" I told myself, as I might have told a sick man that I had found by the side of the road and put into my car. "If you don't go to sleep, if you don't get some rest, you might never see your family again. Death is not in the car or on the road. It is within you. It lures, provokes, and attracts you. You must resist it somehow!"

Memory is a tortured feeling; only occasionally does it bring any relief. A cryptic, opaque name floated at the edges of my consciousness,

1. I put down a period at the end of that sentence and paused to rest. My wife, Maria, interrupted me. "Go outside!" she said. "Help them carry out our neighbor." A blonde girl with a frozen face was at the door. The door of the apartment below us was open. Three people bent over a man who was lying on the floor, between the bathroom and the coat rack. His face was darkly pale, his skin yellow. A small woman held his head and cried. "My love," she said. A boy called out, "Help!" Later I realized that he was a young man, delicate and frightened. "The ambulance is on its way!" said an old woman standing in the next door. I heard myself barely managing to say: "Don't touch him. Maybe it's a heart attack." Ten minutes later, the ambulance crew declared him dead; he had been electrocuted while mending an old boiler. I have written down everything the way it happened. I cannot fathom the meaning of that episode.

touching it, disturbing it, without revealing itself in letters. The invisible landscape all around oppressed me with its barrenness and the foggy rain. In the yellow beams of my headlights I could make out a young, suffering face that I had seen occasionally in my dreams. And I recognized it; I was overcome with a painful happiness. Not far from the town was the village where my father, D. S., had once been fatally wounded. Maybe I was also in that village, sitting and waiting for something, listening for the whistling of shells? But I would definitely not hear the one that hit me. We are deaf only to the mysterious sound of our own deaths.[2]

For several years I collected the traces that D. S. had left behind. I talked with members of his unit who had survived the war, with his superiors, and with doctors and political commissars; I read everything I could find concerning the campaign that was later called the Srem Front. I did not miss a single detail; the next day it might turn out to be something important, decisive, and fateful. Hunched over maps, I followed the movements of armies, their clashes and retreats, trying to imagine myself a strategist who sent hundreds of thousands of people into battle with a wave of his hand, aware that a considerable number of them would die. I imagined the military, political, and other aims that had been the cause of such butchery. During that time I met all kinds of people—lunatics, liars, dreamers, icy cynics, taciturn men livid with hate, as well as those who had tried to forget everything. I placed their vivid characters around the black silhouette that was D. S., arranging them like sinful saints on an

2. Here I had to stop writing again, to pack up and leave for Germany. I was going to a Buchmesse in Frankfurt-on-Main. I was sick and tired, apathetic like a man who has just lost hope and who has difficulty getting used to life without illusions. The dark shadow of a new war had been hanging over my sons and the country that I was leaving, but I could not do or say anything. I thought, "If you don't come back, everything will still be the same. So go and don't turn back!"

Twice I drove by the place that I have been describing—on the way there and on the way back. The first time I felt nothing, nothing moved inside me—neither presentment nor fear. On the way back (ten days later), I was so tired that I fell asleep. The jostling of the car kept me barely awake, barely conscious. It seems that I was dreaming and seeing at the same time; those two states were mingled and interwoven like patterns in a carpet.

I dreamed that I was driving the car myself and that I felt like sleeping; at the same time, I knew that a healthy young man was driving. A bulky freight truck with a TIR sign, which resembled a wild beast, had crossed into my lane and was flying toward me like a monster; I heard the deafening impact of the collision, the scream of crushed metal. I suddenly found myself wide awake. In a split second I passed into a state of clear consciousness: the driver was just braking to avoid a collision with the very same truck in reality.

indifferent iconostasis. And I did not ask myself: "Were all those sacrifices inevitable?" but rather: "Who they were for?"[3]

In a remote village in Šumadija I met a serene red-haired man with gleaming teeth who told me that he had been wounded by the same shell as D. S. He showed me the scar on his strong, muscular thigh. His fair-skinned daughter-in-law offered us water and fruit preserves on the terrace of their new house at a table covered with a green plastic sheet. She smiled at me intimately, as if she recognized me, and a smoky flame of desire leaped out of her blue eyes. The spring sun shined down warmly upon us: when he finished his story we sat for a long time, silent like two men who had waited to meet for many years and who understood each other. I left, and he saw me to the gate; for a moment he kept my hand between his hard farmer's palms and looked into my eyes as if he wanted to see what kind of man I was. Then he kissed me on the cheek in a fatherly way.

D. S. was wounded at the break of dawn, as fog rolled past the barn they were sleeping behind. One piece of shrapnel hit him in the right shoulder blade, another in the left hip. He was lying on the ground, covered with blood, yet conscious. He did not scream, but looked at them astonished, his eyes wide open. Maybe he did not believe it had happened to him, and at the very end of the war, when he was already daydreaming

---

3. The Srem Front was "a section of the general strategic front in Yugoslavia, which was established on the eve of the final operations of the Yugoslav Army for the liberation of the country. It stretched between the Danube, the Bosut forests, and the Sava River in Srem, where it stabilized by the end of January 1945, after fierce fighting between the First Army and the German XXXIV Army Corps. The front stretched along a line to the east of Mohovo and to the east of Tovarnik and the village of Lipovac on the Bosut. It remained static until 12 April 1945, when the First Army broke through the German positions. The Germans had established this line to prevent the westward onslaught of the First Army (in Srem) and the Third Army (in Baranja) between the Sava and the Drava, and thus to protect the Army Group "E," which was withdrawing toward the northwest through the Bosna River valley. . . . In the morning on 12 April 1945, after a brief artillery and air preparation, the North Group of the First Army broke through the main defense lines of the Srem Front and on the same day quickly crushed the German resistance on the second line of defense, capturing Vukovar and liberating Vinkovci as early as 13 April . . . The importance of the breakthrough on the Srem Front lies in the fact that it enabled a quick westward advance of the First and Third Armies between the Sava and the Drava Rivers, which in coordination with operations of the Second and the Fourth Armies hastened the defeat of the German and Quisling troops in the Yugoslav area of operations" (from the *Small Prosveta Encyclopedia*).

of his return home. Maybe he had just discerned the pale, blurred face of death standing behind the backs of those who had run up to help him.[4]

Either they did not have a doctor, or he was busy with other casualties; the unseen German artillery had bombarded them all night long. A stout, rough nurse, with her hair cut short like a man's, bandaged his wounds. He did not scream, he did not complain. He appeared absentminded, remote, drowsy. He only said: "Mother, will they cut off my leg? I'm a farmer." She answered him with a smile: "Everything will be okay, comrade. Victory is ours!" They put him on a creaking cart. The man who sat behind the mud-covered oxen was gaunt and stooped. No one remembered his face. The red-haired man could not tell me anything else; through the thinning fog they soon rushed the unseen enemy. D. S. disappeared from the sight and lives of his friends, never to return again except as a part of a story.

The descent into hell is a symbolic image of death, as is the Christian representation of soul ascending to heaven; D. S. experienced his agony during his journey across the plain. Instead of returning home, he was leaving, going farther away, disappearing slowly. He was (and he still is) a vanishing shadow, a traveler disappearing without a trace. If the imagination of an artist, a writer, cannot picture this and show it to others, then it is not capable of anything. A reliable test of artistic expression and style is the description of someone else's—one's own—death.

A fertile plain is a Pantagruelian image of abundance, succulent fruits, rich soil that bears one crop after another, drunken harvests, carnival feasts. On the other hand, a plain also represents something sad, depressing, oppressed by thoughts of suicide—in the middle of an endless, monotonous void man is tiny and insignificant, as worthless as grass that

4. D. S.'s last letter was somehow preserved. It was found at the bottom of the wooden chest which his grandfather (my great-grandfather) had once carried off to the Balkan wars. The pencil handwriting has faded, and at some places it is completely illegible. I copy only the legible parts: "Friday, April 2, 1945. Ase, a village near Beljina. My dear parents, today I have time to let you know that I am well and in good health, which I wish to you as well. May God give you good health . . . When you receive this letter, answer me and tell me what the news is. It is too far for you to come here, but if you still decide to come, you will find us near Beljina or in the town, because we expect to enter it any moment . . . If you still decide to come, bring me some underwear, because here I have not received . . . You do not have to worry too much. It is not easy for us, but it has to be that way . . . I send my love to all of you. First to little Vida, then to my father, mother, and Olga, then to all of our relatives and neighbors. I send my love to all of you . . . My address is as follows, First Artillery Brigade, Fourth Mortar Battalion."

rots and turns into compost. But D. S. could not see any of this, because his vision had been narrowed and stupidly limited. The cart in which he was lying had sideboards, and whenever he opened his eyes he saw only the enormous, deep blue sky.[5] Soon he ceased paying any attention to the stooping back of the silent, nameless driver.

That sky is the same today; maybe it can be changed by some possible ecological cataclysm, but then we will not be here to witness or describe it. Several times I have tried to look at it with the same eyes as D. S., but daydreaming is possible only with one's eyes closed. Psychological identification is impossible. Anything else is incomplete, a more or less incorrect projection, an indefinite fantasy. Are we left with nothing but the imagination? And when we try to imagine things, are we therefore not violating the fundamental postulate of truth—its ability to be tested and proven?

D. S. will not succeed in becoming someone else, not even posthumously. I will never be him, I will not even resemble him; the wine of his blood dripped onto someone else's lips, while mine are chapped and dry, as if I had a fever. Death is the lifelong (as I see it) difference between us, tomorrow and forever; we have taken different paths, which will never cross, not anywhere. However, there is no point in thinking about death; death itself is pointless, although each and every second of our lives seems valuable and unique. Death's pathos is grotesque and horrible, while its romantic side reeks of a gangrenous wound.

A profound, terrible pain slowly breaches the border between the spirit and consciousness and becomes its own antidote. The void filled with painlessness echoes the announcements of the end, of the last breath, of silent death. In an infinitesimally short, sweet moment D. S. realized that he no longer felt any pain, that he was floating like a dandelion in the soft breeze; he could not feel his shattered body or his festering wounds—he only felt himself (his own loosened, disintegrating self),

---

5. . . . . Above him there was nothing but the sky—the lofty sky, not clear yet still immeasurably lofty, with gray clouds gliding slowly across it. "How quiet, peaceful, and solemn, not at all as I ran," thought Prince Andrew, "—not as we ran, shouting and fighting . . . How was it I did not see that lofty sky before? And how happy I am to have found it at last! Yes! All is vanity, all falsehood, except that infinite sky. There is nothing, nothing, but that. But even it does not exist, there is nothing but quiet and peace. Thank God!" (Leo Tolstoy, *War and Peace*, vol. 1, translated by Louise and Aylmer Maude, edited by Henry Gifford [Oxford, New York: Oxford University Press, 1983]: 294).

as something undefined, waving, shimmering—transient. Suddenly he ceased to feel fear, anxiety, discomfort. Everything moved away somehow and became tiny, invisible. It was night, the twinkling stars were gliding slowly backward, the heavy odor of mud drifted in from every direction, the ungreased cart wheels were creaking and groaning, the driver's back straightened and grew taller, blocking his view to the north and east . . .

Solitary between the sky and earth, D. S. realized that he was not alone, that he was only a single star among millions, the reddish light of a tiny, lost joy amid a cold, endless expanse; and his kin (all except me, his only son) were also warm, pleasant stars, humming softly, dimming and vanishing, losing their brilliant features . . . Excluded from this harmony, forgotten, I am compelled to put on paper these few disconnected, painful images.

Translated by Bogdan Rakić

Ratko Adamović

Ratko Adamović, novelist and short story writer, was born in 1942. His collections of short stories are *The Yellow Submarine* (1972) and *Everybody Dies* (1979). His novels are *The Rope* (1977), *The Naked Guard* (1982), *The Workshop for Madness* (1986), *The Sacred Oak* (1990), and *The Caravansary* (1993).

The theme of isolation of the individual from the outside world serves as the foundation for Adamović's metaphorical prose, in which the absence of a sense of time prevails.

Ratko Adamović works and lives in Belgrade. His works have been translated into many foreign languages and his stories included in world anthologies of short stories.

SOULS OF STONE

As he made his way toward the path that was marked through the undergrowth, he didn't think he had passed that way earlier and he wondered how anyone could pass that way at all. However, it was not energy he lacked, for the very thought that the next day he could start working on that stretch of stone with his easel, under the sun, on the comfortable carpet of moss, made every new thorn that pricked or branch that lashed him in the face seem less hostile and painful.

He finally reached the large iron gate. It looked so mighty, framed by the enormous stone wall, with wrought-iron decorations he had not seen in a long time, that he decided at once it would be the trademark of his new cycle and the major exhibition he had announced.

Fortunately, coming his way was an old man with a heavy, clumsy gait. His every step seemed to cause him pain. He was gray-haired, wearing the clothes of a pauper, but his worn-out clothing was gloriously clean. Unusual. If there was anything that inspired Valdeg's immediate liking, it was a neat and clean man, regardless of the clothes he wore, even rags as long as they were clean.

"I wish you well. Are you the watchman here?"

"No. No. Where did you pop out of?"

"The north. Valdeg. I'm a painter. Can I come in?"

"Well, brother, woe to those who enter here. Why do you want in? Don't you have anything better to do today?"

"A painter's curiosity, nothing more. I'd just like to take a little look

around this old building and, if you don't mind, draw this magnificent old gate."

"Well, sonny, you're the first person in my lifetime who's found it beautiful." The old man motioned to Valdeg to continue on his way.

"You're not the watchman here?"

"You again. No, I'm not, brother. Would you like a cup of coffee? Come on over to my place."

The old man led him into a modest room of the former admissions building. "Shall I put on the coffee? What did you say? Where is it you're from?"

"The north."

"Well, can you people up there talk without coffee? Shall I put it on?"

"Put it on. But I won't stay long. I just wanted to take a little look, do a bit of drawing and, if possible, come back again. If you don't mind. Or tell me where I should go to get permission."

"Just you go ahead and come. What nonsense, permission."

"Do you work here?"

"It's like this: before that big war, sonny, I was a guard right here, in the prison of these here barracks. Yep. Damn it all, who asks a poor man what he wants to do? And I got the job because my pop served one of the officers well, and so he got them to give me a job. My old man almost went crazy with joy when I came home after my first day of work wearing a uniform.

"Every spring he'd bring out a hidden bottle of good brandy and ask, as though asking to enter the king's palace, all important and sweaty from the expectation, whether this spring I wouldn't be promoted to a new rank. And what was I? A prison guard. For all time. Poor Pop. When he walked through town by my side, God forgive me, he was just like a peacock. He didn't even walk like a man, he seemed to flutter along next to such a regal officer. And he died, poor soul, and I never told him what I actually did up here in the army.

"Everyone else in town knew perfectly well, but whenever any relative, or someone who had just arrived, asked him where his son worked, he would go to the gate and point proudly toward the barracks. Where did you say you were from?"

"The north."

"That's fine, buddy. Better than being from these parts. Damn these parts."

"Tell me, old man, that wall down there that leans against the bluff, on the rock . . ."

"Wait, poor soul. We'll get around to the wall, too. Don't rush it, heaven forbid. It's all for the wall. We're next to a wall here, too. Some see and some don't. Why, when my old man died . . ."

"Gramps! Don't tell me the story of your life now. Say, what are you doing here alone? What's the reason for living in this abandoned barracks? And please, tell me, what is that down there, I mean, when did that water on the wall begin to . . ."

"Conversation with you is hopeless, brother. Where'd you ever learn how to talk to people, anyway? I talk about people, and you about the wall. Let's take a seat, if that's the way it has to be. Ah! Do you have anything to drink in that huge bag? I've never seen anyone but a plumber with one like that. Is there some little bottle left over?"

"No, but there will be tomorrow. I'll come again tomorrow, if I can— if—if it doesn't interfere with your work, because . . ."

"You really will have to. I can see that."

The next morning, for the first time since he had reached the caravansary, his customary ceremonious first cup of coffee in the old part of "Europe" failed to hit the spot. Everything bothered him that morning, even the amiable waiters who had been informed from the very first day about the artist Valdeg; they seemed to have conspired to be slow and inconsiderate.

He climbed up toward the barracks, checking whether he had brought all the equipment he would need.

The old man was waiting for him. He raised his hand in greeting, and when he saw Valdeg take a bottle out of his bag, he smiled and pushed an old Austro-Hungarian armchair toward him, the kind that men once grabbed and risked their careers for, offering him a seat.

"I'd rather go to the gate first. I'll start with it."

"You're really serious about drawing all this. My, but you find the strangest things worthwhile."

"You didn't even tell me your name yesterday."

"What's in a name? My father gave me the name Harun, after some

Harun al-Rashid, the caliph of Baghdad. I even know his title today, they made me say it over and over again. The Baghdad caliph of Abasović."

"The Abbasid caliph?"

"No, brother, Abasović. A poor father is always a fool. Just listen, Harun. Prison guard and emperor of Baghdad. And I won't know what the men I guarded called me until we stand up there before His righteous face. Come on, let's have a shot. But please, let's not start the conversation the wrong way this morning. Let old Harun teach you. First you sit here in silence a bit, then you pour the drinks and take a little sip, then you sigh for all your troubles and for all those who aren't with you at that happy moment, then you take another little sip, and then sit in silence again. Now, that's a conversation. After the second or third sip, you start slowly, as though coming in from some field, you say a few words, then a question, but not a serious one, and then you're quiet again, then you take another sip and . . . Dear brother. You have to take it step by step. And you, before you even entered the house, yelled, 'Tell me Everything!' When Everything is said straightaway, then you've got nothing straightaway. A bag of garbage. You take it out and empty it. Who would go around carrying Everything all day long? And when you talk to a man slowly, and even draw a few words out of him, then in the excitement of the conversation, even what has been thrown out long ago, can be gilded as it slowly emerges. Something exists only when it unfolds slowly. There, I've begun as though giving you religious instruction. Sit down, pitiful soul."

"Mr. Harun, sir, if it's permitted, I'd like to go and work a little."

"Well, now you've paid my way into heaven with that 'sir' of yours. Sonny, I stopped being 'sir' the day they gave me that guard's uniform. And I really think I stopped the day my mother gave birth to me. Go on, now. I'm just ragging you a bit. How could I ever change those habits of yours?"

After he'd finished drawing the gate, he felt perturbed as he headed up toward old Harun, expecting to find him, old and alone as he was, completely drunk and incapacitated by the liquor that he himself had brought.

He felt ashamed when he entered the old man's room. Harun was sitting there holding that very first glass, almost full, staring somewhere out

the large window that looked onto the entire misty top of the strange caravansary.

He went up to the old man and began to leaf through his drawing tablet, showing Harun what he had just sketched as though he were a close friend and colleague of the same standing, something that artists do rarely and with difficulty.

Harun took the drawing tablet without a word and began to leaf through it once again, causing Peter to smile briefly, for he suddenly resembled his old professor from the Academy of Art in Paris.

The old man took a sip, then offered Valdeg a glass, keeping his eyes on the artist's face: "You're not from where you think you are, sonny. You originate in someplace special. God has blessed your hands. Who'd ever say that my suffering and atonement could look like that? If a person didn't know better, and saw this, he'd like to come here, expecting to find some kind of palace. Peter, dear Peter. What you have done here is dangerous. Dangerous.

"When you transform that damned gate into something so beautiful, imagine what you'd do with something really beautiful."

Valdeg accepted the glass and drained it.

"Just look. Not even five or six sips. Straight down the hatch. Is that what you do up there in that north of yours?"

"Grandpa Harun, are there any pipes down there by that southern wall over the bluff?"

"Yes, yes. There used to be big, dangerous barrels there."

"I was thinking of water pipes."

"How could a water pipe be a gun barrel? I don't understand a thing you say."

"Grandpa Harun, down there along that wall over the bluff, are there any pipes there, for water, some old bathhouse, or a fountain?"

"Fountain?! Oh, yes. There used to be one down there. They'd shove you against the wall, open that enormous fountain as big as the sky, and then start to spray. That there water you're asking about would carry you away forever, into the mud and some excrement that no one has seen as yet. Woe to whoever comes across that fountain.

"But, sonny boy, let me ask you something. What did you really come for? We've been beating about the bush for two days, and neither of us

understands the other. Is that north of yours so complicated? What do I look like to you, anyway, when you won't ask plainly, talk plainly? Speak openly, damn it to hell, even if everything goes to ruin. What you've got to say isn't something wondrous that can't be swallowed. And even if it were, forget it, we'll roll it down there over the bluff, and let anyone who wants to figure it out. Come on, let's hear it. It's leaked out. Don't high-step around anymore, for goodness sake. You've tired me out, and you're going to ruin my simple pleasure with this bottle. Did you say Peter? Well, out with it, and let the devil be damned. Whoever carried off everything from this place, let him now take what you've got under your tongue, and whatever comes of it, if you say so. Let's hear it."

"I don't know how to even start, Harun. You've spent your whole life here inside, understand, inside these walls, along the corridors and around the cells. I'm only inside when I draw. Otherwise, whenever possible, I'm outside. I go around, I follow every path that can be taken. But down there, out there, on that wall raised above the bluff, there above that beautiful little stone plateau covered with moss, I've been looking at something since I arrived in the caravansary . . . It's a natural wonder, if that is nature, if that down there isn't . . ."

"Oh, poor Peter. Get it out. Say it. You can't? Of course, you can't. What you want to say now, the reason you came to see me, can't be said.

"Sit down, poor thing, you're shaking all over. You're certainly thinking of that female wonder, down there on the wall? That's what you saw, Valdeg. A door?! That female doorway enticed you up here? Oooh, poor Harun, I've spent the past two days and nights all flustered and full of questions, wondering what it could be. Well, son, now we can speak plainly.

"I go down that way, too. That little path along the wall is my path, Peter. What I really think is that some woman from heaven happened to be here when her labor pains began. She got caught here and stayed like that, open, over that chasm. She was petrified by some kind of fear. She started to give birth on that wall, and then the dawn caught her. When she saw where she was and what lay under her, nothing but that gray bluff, she became terrified and stuck right there to the wall in horror. That's how it was, and no other way. That's why it's so wet there, on that reddishness. On this side the wall's as dry as gunpowder, and on that side

it's always damp. And where else is it always cool and damp except at a woman's door? It only heats up when you bring it the key. But, sonny boy, there is no key for that door there.

"Dear Peter, we're here in this barracks almost for the same reason: you find it strange, and to me it's been a millstone my whole life.

"So listen to me well. You asked about the fountain. The water. The pipe down next to the wall. For two centuries, down there along the lower wall above the bluff, that was where they executed those who were sentenced to death. There. They washed them of their lives at that damned fountain. For two centuries.

"And you know, Valdeg, it's one thing when a man dies peacefully, and his soul is released slowly, like a breeze, and rises up to where they're waiting for it. But everything's different when it's forced out by a bullet. And I've seen both one and the other, so I can talk about it for some time to come.

"It's even more trouble when there's no desire to go. I've seen the men being taken away. Some go like sleepwalkers. They don't even have to be led. They look at that wall as though it makes them happy. When the firing squad shoots, they fall down peacefully, and their souls almost take wing, poor things, as though they could barely wait.

"But, son, when they drag them along, wrestle with them, and they yell and clutch at the morning, it makes your heart break. They call each person by name. They yell so much that a man really thinks—just who said that tomorrow would be a better day if they execute the poor wretch that morning?

"Well, when the souls of men like that are forced out, they simply gush. They're so terrified of the bullet that they explode like the cork on a bottle of champagne. Where's the poor soul to go, forced out as it is; it rushes to that wall, then goes right through the stone. It doesn't form a little cloud, it goes through the stone. It escapes through that door you saw, it wants to escape through the opening of that woman from heaven. It gushes so much you can't ever forget it. Such poor souls, forced out by bullets onto that wall for two centuries, finally broke through that door. They had to go somewhere, if only through the stone. Well, that's the door you saw . . .

"And, my child, if someone was to draw that door for me so that I

could put it on the wall in this room, I'd kneel more obediently before that picture than before any other god. Every single day, until I pass on. My religion forbids me from praying before any picture, but if I had that . . . Maybe then I'd fulfil my promise and somehow do what I'm here to do until I go. But who would tempt fate because of a crazy old man and copy down something whose master and purpose are not known?

"Now, come along with your Harun."

With slow steps, almost stealthily, the old man led him down along the edge of the wall whose other side held the unusual fresco. Valdeg noticed that Harun was now walking differently and had lost the sluggishness and impression of crippled legs that he had when he came out of the underground corridors of the barracks.

Helping each other, they climbed to the very edge of the wide wall.

Both of them trembled before the abyss. The river was so far below them that no babbling could be heard.

Old Harun sat on the edge of the wall with his legs dangling. He helped Valdeg sit next to him. Peter liked nothing better than heights, particularly when they were within touching distance, like that edge where nothing would prevent him from falling.

"You're not afraid, you northerner?"

"I love it."

"You see that little island there in the middle of the river—that sandbank?"

Valdeg nodded.

"Well, you're in luck, that's where they are. Each of those little pebbles down there is one of the souls that a bullet forced out from men who were executed down here, behind our backs, for two whole centuries. Dear brother, no one in the world is as ready as a river to receive and console. The poor things came gushing out, there below us, expelled, and when they found themselves above this void where nothing awaited them, they turned to stone. They fell down to the river like pebbles. That's how it went, from life to life, from cursed dawn to yet another dawn—the whole sandbank. I wouldn't even set foot in that water down there, particularly not me with these big lame, plaguy feet. Those down there always heard my footsteps in fear. That water is holy, honest it is.

"One year, a man started to build a house, and he pestered me about taking the sand from that very island. He said it was just what he needed. Dear brother.

"First I tried to talk him out of it. I tried everything. I took him to another place, trying to convince him I knew where the best gravel could be found. I lied and told him that the military experts had shown me a secret place. Nothing worked. You can't deal with a fool, and that's it. I gave up and let him take it away.

"I spent that whole summer sitting there right where you are, watching him take that petrified misery up the mountain, suffocating them in cement and building them into a house. And nothing happened.

"Well, when he had put on the roof tiles and invited people to celebrate, I wasn't here on the wall, but I heard their songs echo through the night.

"When they went home, having eaten and drunk their fill, and after the household had gone to bed to spend their first night under that spacious roof, they had just gone to sleep when some sort of commotion and yelling could be heard along the walls. They say that everyone in the house could plainly hear the walls.

"They all barely had time to escape when the house began to tremble like some sort of huge bird whose wings have been glued together. It wanted to fly, but couldn't. There was a little more flapping and jerking, and then all of a sudden everything crumbled. Absolutely everything!

"That man came to see me, his eyes as big as saucers, terrified. He came to ask me what to do, since I had told him long before what he should not do.

"I told him, give the river back what belongs to it, and you'll atone for everything. If you do that, there will be no more solid house than the one you build.

"Well, he followed my advice. He started to bring it back. People crossed themselves and were amazed, but he just loaded it up and took it back. He returned every single pebble. Brother, I never told him, or anyone else, why his house collapsed.

"The man would have died on the spot out of fear if he found out he'd used petrified human souls to build his house.

"So you see. Now the time has finally come to tell you what I'm doing here. And you asked me from the gate, without even entering, am I the

watchman, am I the watchman or not? Let's go back up so I can give you an answer. Some kind of chill's come over me, God forbid. It's like someone is listening to us. And, the bottle is up there, too."

They walked at a funereal pace, dragging themselves along. Valdeg was briefly obsessed with a vision of the mosaic formed by the gravel down below, some enormous composition from old Harun's story. A mosaic of petrified souls. But he was not skilled at making mosaics, and then the very idea of moving those stones once again, gluing them close together, forcing them into an unnatural form, almost made him ashamed of his thoughts.

When they entered the room, old Harun sat down and started to unbutton his shirt. "Pour the drinks, Peter. Now we're the same, there's no more host and guest here. And I suppose in this house there never really was. Where did you ever see a prison guard be a host? Dear brother, as though I'd been here all alone for years and become the host."

"Mr. Harun, sir . . ."

"Please, for heaven's sake, don't call me 'sir.' No one who has sat with me on that wall can call me 'sir.' I'm speaking to you like I've spent my whole life with you, and you call me 'sir' again. You northern jackass, you and your manners. Out with it."

"I didn't expect any of this. I just wanted to visit the barracks a little, to ask in particular whether I could leave my bag here, and then disappear after a few days. But since we've already gotten into all of this, I'd like to ask you, sir . . ."

"There you go again with that 'sir.'"

"All right, all right. What does a prison guard feel when he takes a prisoner down there to be executed? This sounds really awful. But, after days and days, sometimes months of some sort of acquaintance, some sort of companionship . . ."

"Dear son, a prison guard is the least talkative person in the world. Where did you ever see a doctor going around the house talking about what happened at work that day, who he had to cut and what, and who died and how? Come on.

"If I wasn't here for the reason I am, you would only have gotten a 'hello,' 'you can,' 'you can't,' 'after you,' 'good-bye.'

"Ah, but when you sketched the gate the way you did, when I saw

what all you could do, then I opened this lock a little that wakes up every morning amazed that it can still open and that everything inside hasn't broken and stopped.

"Now you're going to laugh, but I'll tell you all the same, you've got a nice name, brother—Peter! Like a king. And, my northern king, when a man spends forty years in those corridors and bars, he rusts just like that iron. I'll have a hard time admitting this to Him, but I've seen all kinds of things, I sure have.

"When they take some beast down there to the wall, you don't really care. You won't go or watch. You let someone younger go who can barely wait, since the fools have made it into—God forbid—some sort of ceremony. They all get gussied up, serious, important, some important people push their way past you, when in normal circumstances they wouldn't even dare pass in front of your house, and so a young guard feels that he's participating in something important, and they're all the worst shits. They shoot and you think, thank God. And then there were those that make your heart break. Brother. You're disgusted with yourself for days, you don't eat, you shower twice a day, as if you . . ."

"But once . . ."

Harun paused. He lifted the corner of his untucked shirt and wiped his sweaty face. He motioned to Valdeg to pour him a drink, and he looked at that moment like a man whose words and throat had been closed by an iron door that had not even given him time to take a last breath. He took a little sip, stood up, walked slowly around the room, and as he stood silently facing the window, it seemed to Valdeg that he had trouble stopping his moaning. When he calmed down, he took a chair and brought it a bit closer to Valdeg.

"Once I guarded a child. They told him he had killed someone. That's about all they told him. They hushed up everything else about life. Well, now, if they'd at least executed him right away, while he was still dazed, there'd have been no grief. He wouldn't have even understood. But for some reason they were determined to wait and wait. Oh, dear God, help me, I've never told anyone this before.

"I took the kid under my wing. I started to teach him all sorts of things. Like I knew things; well, just what I knew then. And he was as pure as driven snow. Wherever you stepped, his gracious soul peeped out. Wretched Peter, how did you get me to say this?

"That morning finally came. Damn them to hell, ever since then I've begun to do some serious praying.

"I saw with my own eyes that the day was crying for the lad. A feeling of horror came over the entire barracks, the garrison, all the regiment, the guards, the prison—everyone. Nature wanted to explode in the rush to get out of this place. Strange.

"The fat henchmen stood there in their uniforms, decorated with all the garbage they could find. They asked the young man if he had a last wish.

"The boy was weeping through that rarified silence, and the whole barracks was, too.

"The child asked if I could go down there with him, to the wall. Could I stand next to him during the execution. He took hold of my hand while he asked them, as though I was going to take him for a walk. Poor child, he didn't even know that you have to go to that water all alone.

"That was the first time I went down there, to that sandbank, and looked for his pebble. I recognized him right away by his dappled eyes. They were all white, and he was dappled. And you could see he had just arrived, he hadn't gotten used to the water yet. Whenever he got wet, he dried real fast.

"He wasn't used to either this side or that."

The old man stopped talking. He pushed his glass away and slowly took the bottle in his open hand. As he drank, it seemed that his bare chest, weighted down by the drops of painful sweat, would explode.

Night was drawing nigh, when old Harun started to speak again. "So, that's what I'm doing here. As soon as the barracks was emptied and stopped being that, I decided to come back here and move into this big admissions building. And it was late in my life, too.

"Harun, whose crazy father named him after Harun al-Rashid, the caliph of Baghdad, decided to live here alone, atone for his loathsome life, and pray for all those in the cells, those down on the sandbank, for these walls, locks, rust, to pray and pray and pray, whether anyone was listening or not. And don't ask me another thing. Nothing."

Valdeg heaved his equipment bag over his shoulder, went up to old Harun, bowed deeply, and kissed his hand.

Translated by Alice Copple-Tošić

Moma Dimić

Born in 1944, Moma Dimić is a professional writer who shares his residence between Sweden and Belgrade. Dimić is a poet, an essayist, a playwright, and a travel writer. His works have been translated abroad and awarded prestigious literary awards in Yugoslavia.

His most important novels and collections of short stories are: *The Long Life of Tola Manojlović* (1966), *The Antichrist* (1970), *Maxim of Serbia from the Home of the Aged* (1971), *The Citizen of the Forest* (1982), *The Bump Who Likes to Take Risks* (1985), and *The Little Bird* (1989).

He also published three collections of poetry and several travelogues that rank among the best in Serbian literature.

NIGHT UNDER
THE KOSMAJ

"He is like you, same features, a little less rounded in the face. And the hair too, everything; only he doesn't have a beard. I don't know how you haven't met him; at every wedding or dance party he stays till dawn. He's never sad, always cheerful, with a smile on his face. I should say, like you, in fact."

With a hospitable smile, my host points to the picture on the wall of the son who is in Germany. I notice only that all things in the room—two beds, stove, table, bench—are pushed in one corner, against the white walls.

"So, fine," he continues, with the same melancholy smile, "he fancied to go out into the world and make money, but doesn't he care for his child!? His wife and child are in Lajkovac, at her mother's; he is over there, and the two of us, the old folks, live here in Bukvanja, even though he built a huge house in yet another area. I never thought he would stay in Germany so long. A year or two, I thought, but he keeps lying to me, saying he will come in the spring to work the land. You see, it's almost exactly ten years now since one night like this one he stormed into the house and threw his passport and papers on the bed and said he was going abroad for a while. 'I will tear all this to pieces,' I yelled at him right there, forbidding him to go. 'No, sir,' he said, 'I'll get new documents in three days if you tear these up.' He had just come out of military service

and had gotten a job as a metal painter. His pay was low . . . Tell me, where are you from? From what family, son?"

Every now and then, the wife comes into the kitchen, preparing food or collecting firewood and bedding for the sudden guest. She secretly listens to our conversation. The dry, red skin of her wrinkled face smells of milk, the stable, and the cold. As she leaves the room to continue with her chores, she stares pointedly at her husband and grumbles: "Why don't you forget about those stories of yours? Let him be, son! Can't you see, he's an older man. He's got his own farm work. Don't make a fool of yourself in front of people. Why would anyone care how you live—you live like every other creature!"

"What? You are not used to bacon?" says the host kindly, offering me food, filling up my glass. As soon as she goes away, with sparkling eyes and a wide grin, he comes back to his son. "You are just like my Negosav. He also eats poorly, like a baby. He adores only dairy products. But for him even to come near the stable or to chop wood, God forbid! When he was leaving, I told him: 'Listen to me, you will never get used to living there, they eat only potatoes.' He only waved his hand, as if he would get used to it somehow. Those potatoes. I remember when I was taken prisoner there. Kamp Sigenheim, Stalag 90. When they finally brought me home, after twenty-one months, it was in an ambulance. And now, my son Negosav drives a car there, a Mercedes. He says he's bought skis, too. He's even spent some time in Iraq. He's had several employers and got along well with all of them. The last one trusted him so well that he let his youngest son go with him to Yugoslavia; a fifteen, sixteen-year-old boy. The only thing I don't like is that some of our Kosmaj loafers he's grown up with have gotten hooked on him. That's no good. They keep visiting him, bringing various kinds of merchandise, machine parts, cars, and who knows what else. Before he went to Germany, they wouldn't even greet him on the street. Now, he's next to God to them! While they seem to be as timid as rabbits, he's got strong nerves; he's as cool as a cucumber when crossing the border. He can, as they say, smuggle a camel across, right in front of the custom officials' eyes and they wouldn't even notice. Because, you see, the Kosmaj is not a big mountain, but people here are sharp and resourceful. A rare animal, as someone wrote. He even speaks the language perfectly. But when he comes back for good,

you'll see, those same people will turn their backs on him! I didn't ask—do you smoke, son?"

Bent, with a crooked spine, the old man stands on his feet, like a roadside tombstone.

"And listen to this," he continues, aided by his weakened arms, "Last year, that Nega of mine used an entire wagon to deliver agricultural machinery: combines, tractors, planting machines. I got ready, took with me four million dinars, as he told me to do, and headed straight for Belgrade. Just the cost of transporting this was two and a half million. To pay the tariff, they told me to come back tomorrow. So, the next day, I went there again, lowered my head, and proceeded straight in that direction. When some officials saw me, as I was dressed in peasant clothes, they yelled at me: 'Hey, old man, you're making a mistake, the customs are there!' As if they were puzzled why I was there at all. I replied, 'I know,' and proceeded in the same direction, all the while thinking how I was going to pay for all this. And, suddenly, just in front of the building, there he was, Nega, with his open arms and laughing: 'You thought I wouldn't come. Don't worry, old man, the money is right here!' and he pointed to a loaded bag. Later we transported all that to a village and quickly sold it all, because here, at our place, there are no people who can work!"

The first snow has melted and the plowed fields appear black. The dusk slowly begins to encircle the purple-gray peaks of the Kosmaj. By the front steps, just as in an ancient mythical scene, the host's wife sifts flour into a wooden bowl. In the bare hedges along the road, one can see only red rose hips.

"In spite of all my troubles, I'm doing all right," spoke up Uncle Borisav again (that's his name), lighting up a cheap-brand cigarette. "There's enough bread, and taxes aren't too high. Milk is our main produce. My wife sells it to private homes in Sopot because a few policemen live there. But she has also injured her spine. Once she used her back to hold up the cart so I could change a wheel, and something just snapped in her spine. I have a pinched cartilage there between the fourth and the fifth vertebrae. I suggested to the doctor: 'Tie me up at top and at bottom and stretch that thing.' He said: 'You must have lifted something heavy.' I kept quiet; I knew what I had lifted—a tree log! Since then, I live as if under a glass; I mustn't get wet, and I must avoid strong wind, nor should

I be in the hot sun. I am writing myself off, slowly getting into old age. Life is long if it's in the cards!

"When Kale Lekić, a guy from our village, received his first pension check, the mailman said to him: 'May you enjoy it for the next fifty-two months!' He thought a little, calculated, and when he realized this amounted to only four years, he cursed the mailman and gave him a good slap across the face: 'Who do you think you are, to be telling me how long I will be using my pension?!'"

By the table, behind a pile of dry bread, there is an attractive miniature ivory-coloured Philips radio. Uncle Borisav, who seldom misses anything, immediately catches my eye. "It doesn't work; it's not registered. Nega left it here five years ago, when he was building his house. Next time, when we meet in Sopot, I will show it to you; everything is finished, windows, plastering inside and out, pantry, bathroom, sewers, running water. Only, he says, he did not have panelings installed in the attic. The rooms have sparkling parquet floors, so beautifully laid in, just like ribs. We were standing at the entrance and I kidded him a little: 'When I get inside I will slip and fall!' Because, I said, I was not used to that. As you can see, I've got concrete floor everywhere. That house is perfect, but what's the use if everything is kept locked?"

His wife comes in again, looking somewhat more compact, shorter, and more robust. She appears relieved and more assured because her daily chores are done. Nevertheless, she continues to grumble a while longer over a burnt-out bulb in the stable. While she stokes the fire and puts a pan of bread dough in the oven for tomorrow, it seems that our "tiresome" conversation still appeals to her. In any case, perhaps only out of habit, once in a while her face assumes its former expression of caution and hides unspoken thoughts of her own.

"The other day, in the evening, we finished taking care of the stable as we usually do," my host, Uncle Borisav, begins again, scratching his head a little under his cap: "Everything was taken care of. We have a small calf; it was born on St. Demetrius's Day. The old woman and I went into the house and had dinner. We were sitting alone, not speaking to each other. I was killing time reading a newspaper, a book, whatever. For instance, I can't stand for an instant having a neighbor touch anything of mine, that is, take things without my knowledge. Nevertheless, I don't lock anything up. Everything is kept unlocked—although, as I grow older, I will

have to start changing my ways! Then, suddenly, without a knock, the door opens and an unknown young man came in. He was wearing a yellow windbreaker and some kind of a light-colored hat. It was unsettling: here it was late in the evening, quiet, and somebody just walks calmly into the house! I didn't even hear the gates open. The dogs were on a leash a little way away from the house. And this fellow comes through the door, without knocking, and enters freely and suddenly. When he took his hat off and smiled, I recognized him and said, "You rascal, why didn't you call first? Instead, you come in like that and frighten me!" He sat down next to me, gave me a hug, and continued to laugh: 'Listen, Dad, I can come whenever I want!' His mother began to hug him, crying a little and wiping her tears: "Nega, son, my precious, you really frightened us!" At this moment, I tried to remind her: 'Be quiet, don't cry in front of him!' Now and then, even I am moved, but I don't like anyone to see it. And when a tear appears, I go behind the house or a haystack, outside, alone. A man's soul is tough . . .

"A little later, he pulled out a pack of cigarettes and offered me one. I told him I smoke only my kind of cigarettes because they are plain and cheap. I am afraid to get used to the expensive ones. In response, he took out of his pocket a big carton and gave it to me. 'Here it is for you to smoke; I brought you the kind you like.' 'I know,' I said to him, 'you brought me so many cigarettes because you want me to croak as soon as possible so you can get your inheritance!' You see, when it's free, I smoke a lot. This way, one pack lasts me two to three days! That night we continued talking till twelve-thirty. Already that morning, he had gone to Lajkovac to see his wife and daughter. He gave me his firm word that in the spring, by June, he would come back for good. He stayed here only for two days and then went back to Germany. What can I say, our people are scattered all over the world . . ."

"And what do you do? Are you a priest by any chance? Oh, you aren't . . . If you come to live in our village, perhaps you will be at my burial and give a little speech . . . Now, let's have a toast!"

Translated by Robert Gakovich

Milisav Savić

One of the leading Serbian authors, Milisav Savić was born in 1945. He is a novelist, short story writer, and editor of numerous anthologies. He also translates into Serbian from Italian and English. He taught at several universities in the United States and Europe.

He is the author of several collections of short stories: *The Bulgarian Barracks* (1969), *The Uncle of Our Town* (1977), *The Boys from Raška* (1977), and novels: *The Loves of Andrija Kurandić* (1972), *The Poplar on the Terrace* (1985), *The Jug of the Guerrilla Leader* (1990), the highly acclaimed *Bread and Fear* (1991), *The Footnote* (1995), and *Scars of the Silence* (1997). Savić writes stories in strikingly different modes, from chronicles recording real-life events to fantastic stories.

THE LOCKSMITH
WAS BETTER

Jorge Luis Borges, the greatest storyteller of this century, most probably was not awarded the Nobel Prize for literature because of his deep
hatred of communism, which, according to the blind writer, was the unfortunate offspring of Western liberalism. For Borges there was no better
remedy for communism than a right-wing military dictatorship similar
to the one that overthrew the left wing–disposed President Allende of
Chile.

Members of the Nobel Committee would not have objected so much
to a hatred of communism (and they did not, if it came from a communist-
country writer), but they also did not like open praise for a military junta.

As an example of Borges's hatred of communism, there remains his
ironic commentary on the funeral of Yugoslavia's President Josip Broz
Tito, which Borges watched almost in its entirety for two whole hours
on television. Yes, he watched it through the eyes of his long-standing
companion and (toward the end of his life) his wife, Maria Kodoma,
who not only read him books and newspapers but also retold or described the events of various television broadcasts. "Such a pompous funeral was not held for even the most illustrious Caesars," said Borges,
according to his young friend Osvaldo Ferrari in his book, *Libro de di-
alogos* (1990).

One year before his death, Borges (again, according his friend Ferrari)
came across an article in a tabloid newspaper—as is well known, Borges's

occasional favorite reading—and, no doubt aided by Maria Kodoma, learned from it something that upset his balance, that typically Borgesian kind of balance. A Slovenian journalist had published unconfirmed rumours to the effect that Tito watched his own funeral on TV. The great communist patriarch, already in the autumn years of his life, was aware that he was suffering from a galloping incurable disease that was swallowing up his last days. So, aided by the chief of the secret police, one of the most powerful and most effective in the world, he arranged to have his death announced somewhat earlier, at least ten days before death's bony finger knocked inexorably on the door of his well-guarded room. In his long, stormy life, in which he traversed the path from being a poor locksmith to the absolute possessor of a whole country, from a small-time communist prison inmate to pitiless master of the lives and deaths of over twenty million subjects, he experienced nearly everything a mortal man could wish for; so that this last wish—we may call it his predeath wish—seemed a trifle compared to all the previous ones, most of which had been fulfilled. Among other things, Tito wanted to see whether his latest wife, from whom he was estranged some ten years before (she suddenly disappeared from all the photos in new editions of his biography), would appear before his coffin. He also wanted to see his old wartime and party friends (whom he had eliminated from his closest circle simply because he did not want to share power with anyone) at the funeral and to observe how they behaved. He also wanted to see what the poets would write and whether the funeral would be attended by the world's most eminent politicians—those whom he had often duped by a deft tightrope walk between West and East, between the Americans and the Russians . . .

According to the above-mentioned journalist, Tito was on the whole satisfied with his own death and funeral. At the news that the "greatest heart" in the history of the Yugoslav peoples had ceased beating, the soccer players of the Serbian Red Star club and the Croatian Hajduk team interrupted their match and, embracing each other, sniveled and sobbed; the first and most prominent Yugoslav dissident, Milovan Djilas, who because of his obstinacy and love of power had spent some ten years in "Titoist" incarceration, declared that one of the great political figures of the twentieth century had left the international scene; the poets also did not lag far behind the party poltroons with sycophantic praises, and in

fact tried to outdo each other with phrases such as "A man like him will never again be born of woman," or "After Tito—Tito"; leading world statesmen watched the funeral procession from a grandstand opposite the National Assembly building where the coffin with his nonexistent body (that is, with a bag filled with sand) was displayed: Margaret Thatcher stood next to Leonid Brezhnev, Indira Gandhi was next to Sandro Pertini, Jimmy Carter's mother Lillian Carter stood beside François Mitterrand; Tito's wife showed signs of deep bereavement and sorrow; a tall adjutant, without a spasm of pain on his face and performing an irreproachable goosestep, traversed the long road to the gravesite on Mount Topčider, behind the coffin mounted on the gun carriage; the populace, closely packing the pavements, sighed and wiped their tears as the cortège went slowly past, in disbelief (which proved to be justified) that the man who had behaved like an immortal being during his lifetime could really have died.

Several days after the funeral, Tito died. According to the same newspaper article, he was buried secretly in the courtyard of his residence at Belo Brdo in Slovenia. His grave was deftly camouflaged with clumps of grass and fir trees, and bore no inscription. Earth was returned to earth, in keeping with the law of dialectical materialism on the basis of which Broz had ruled happily for so many years.

Borges the great mystifier was not stunned or dizzied by this death game—one of his central themes anyway is death, that is, the attempt by means of mirrors and labyrinths to trick it—but rather by the fact that the communists tried to fulfill his basic idea (if they had not done so already, for at that time they were celebrating more than six decades of rule over a not inconsiderable portion of the globe and that without any signs of weakness or impotence), the idea, then, that this world is the illusion of an illusion or an illusion of words, of books. Although they invoked materialistic philosophy, they in fact firmly believed that reality is only what is written in books (the daily press, radio or television, or whatever) and that there could be no misfortune, no misery, no hunger, no death unless officially stated and written down, in printed or broadcast form. And that there was happiness, there was love, there was wellbeing, there was a paradise—if this was confirmed in words, in political speeches or reportage, in poetry and in the novel, in studies and feature stories. And if found in neatly arranged and richly bound books in libraries.

Thus paradox, so dear to the great Argentine writer, played a trick on Borges himself. He did not receive the most illustrious literary award because of his immoderate outbursts of gall against a system that tried to materialize his basic philosophy and literary idea (regardless of the monstrosity of such an attempt), which was to subject reality to the printed word, the book and the library.

After following Tito's pompous funeral on television, in the company and listening to the comments of his wife, Maria Komoda, and friend Osvaldo Ferrari, Borges did not immediately or without reservation arrive at the conclusion that the communist countries represented the monstrous embodiment of his idea that this world is the reflection, or image, of what is written or spoken. A tiny seed of doubt leading to such a conclusion had been created by the dissident writers whom Borges admired for their courage, if for no other reason. Their books undermined the world of communist orthodoxy, just as heretical books in the Middle Ages jeopardized the closed and divine circle of Christian doctrine. (Anyhow, Borges's undivided sympathy for the apocryphal, for the occult, for forbidden literature, is well known). Nor is it any wonder that the communists persecuted writers more often and more relentlessly than the gravest criminals: they deprived them of jobs, threw them out of their homes, dispatched them to insane asylums and prisons, and even killed them. In the long history of dishonor, writers as victims deserve a special and honorable place.

According to the testimony of his friend Osvaldo Ferrari, Borges foretold the early beginnings of disintegration of the huge communist empire, for, unlike the Christian theologians, the communists did not know how to revitalize their book and to endow it with the semblance of everlasting originality and freshness. As Borges insisted would happen, communism would be overthrown by heretical books—that is, by the banned books and secret libraries. Borges, however, did not live to see the beginning of the fall of communism. Death, which no labyrinth can resist, not even the Borgesian one, deprived him of that satisfaction by only a couple of years.

According to Ferrari's statements, published in the *Book of Dialogues* (1993) and enlarged in a special chapter entitled "Conversations in a Mirror," Borges, the deceased Borges, inhabitant of the realm of mirrors and shadows, was not astonished by the course of events: everything fell out exactly as he had expected.

During one of the regular spiritualistic seances held in Ferrari's study every Thursday at midnight, Ferrari drew Borges's attention, or rather that of his blurred image in a dimly lighted mirror, to the fact that communism still stubbornly persisted in Yugoslavia, in the dismembered Yugoslavia or what was left of that beautiful and fairly rich country—even though this Balkan nation did not lack vociferous dissidents, from philosophers to poets, from filmmakers to painters, who, like their colleagues in Eastern Europe, bravely stood at the helm of all the main opposition movements and parties.

Wherein then was the mistake? asked the celebrated writer in his nocturnal colloquy. Was the communist regime in Yugoslavia more rigid than the others? Was the Yugoslav dissident literature weaker than other such literatures?

To both these questions Ferrari answered what Borges probably suspected anyway: It was not!

As concerns the first question, a confirmation for such an answer was proffered by the fact that Borges's *Fictions* had been translated and published in Serbo-Croatian for the first time in Yugoslavia, in Belgrade, as early as 1962, before it appeared in many other Western or East European countries. As to the second question, Yugoslav dissident literature, to judge by the few works that had been translated into the principal world languages—was at least a shade better than its Russian, Czech, or Polish cousins, insofar as it contained less about day-to-day politics, which Borges undoubtedly hated from the bottom of his heart.

During that time, Ferrari read in the London *Times* a commentary by Desa Trevizan, in his opinion one of the best-informed Western journalists on the entangled Balkan situation. The commentary was a lamentation over former dissidents who overnight became fiery advocates of precisely the regime that had persecuted them, even though in the meantime it had concealed its face with cosmetics. The great writer asked his friend to bring to their next midnight meeting a handful of pages written by the converted dissidents.

Ferrari did so. He chose for the man who wrote in short literary forms a dozen or so aphorisms by some of the most persecuted and (judging by their biographical notes) most talented writers.

"A perfectly filled order!"—Borges interrupted his friend after hearing several sentences read aloud to him. This comment was not clear to

Ferrari: for whom did these poisonous stings represent a "perfectly filled order"? Departing from his usual procedure, Borges tried to explain what he customarily left in hints or ambiguities.

He who had watched his own death and funeral on television once again demonstrated that he was a great and unparalleled mystifier in producing literary and ideological reality. In contrast to his moustachioed Georgian teacher, he did not even try to create "engineers of the soul." Having had scant schooling (he was a locksmith by profession), Josip Broz Tito basically despised writers, even when they were his faithful subjects. (Borges reminded his friend, referring to a bit of Tito's biography, that he had held one of his wartime comrades, a poet who had dedicated a beautiful poem to him, under house arrest for a dozen years.) Whenever writers were in his presence, most often as guests on the luxury yacht *Galeb* during long cruises, the greatest honor Tito accorded them would be a game of chess (primarily because they were poor players of that game). Tito decided to create dissident writers without their realizing it, unless they were the guinea pigs of the all-powerful secret police. The unwritten agreement between Tito and dissident writers was (regarded a posteriori) quite fair. Only talented writers were taken into consideration, or at least those who cleverly pretended they were gifted; as to genres, priority was given to humorists and satirists, principally because of the popularity and affection they enjoyed. But chances were also offered to writers of historical novels and dramas, to critics and philosophers. It was made very clear to the writers that they would be excluded from public political life, that they would appear on television, on the radio, or in the leading dailies and weeklies, that they would be general targets of attack and criticism in political reports, that all state awards would be denied them, that from time to time their books would be banned and occasionally they would spend a month or a year in jail—although care would be taken to apply this last-named measure only in the direst need, because Tito was anxious that the world PEN Organization, Amnesty International, and other human rights organizations should not have a bad opinion of his rule. In return, writers could expect the following: their books produced by the smaller publishers would have a broad readership; they would be given important literary prizes; their earnings would be considerable; they could, if they so wanted, obtain sinecures, travel freely abroad, give lectures at prestigious universities

and in literary circles, at home and abroad; they would enjoy warm sympathy and admiration; from time to time they would take part in secret dinners or play a game of cards with selected high party officials who, surrounded by the grayness of the poltroon one-party system, would genuinely enjoy the writers' sparkling and brittle anecdotes, even at the expense of their boss, and even if such anecdotes had caused others to be imprisoned for much less offensive stories.

Anyway, these aphorisms, although they seemed highly spiced at first glance, were the best possible directives for Tito and his retinue, indicating to them how best to organize their lives and consolidate their rule. This meant how to live in luxurious villas, drive the latest-model Mercedes cars, and bejewel their wives and mistresses in gold and diamonds; how to surround themselves with fools; how to set up a powerful police force able to be everywhere and at all times a huge eye and ear; how to give parties where champagne poured like water; how to make everything, even their own system, into an operetta.

"Man's life has value and meaning only if others, especially those who are wiser, can envy us such a life," said Ferrari.

"And who could believe," the deceased writer concluded, that such writers with such a literature attempted (if they really did) to demolish communism?"

"If, in your opinion, Tito created those who composed odes to him and those who wrote squibs about him in equal measure, then the former are closer to me. A clear-cut order is more honest than a masked one," remarked Ferrari.

"Do you mean to say that the real communists are more highly valued than the masked, false dissidents—although, to be frank, we can never know which of them really wears a mask?" asked the blind writer.

"It would seem so," agreed Ferrari.

"But you don't seem to realize that this was precisely what the great master of mystification wanted; I would not be surprised if someone in Zagreb or in Belgrade at this moment is writing graffiti on a wall: *The Locksmith Was Better*," said the great writer, smiling, directing his empty gaze toward the flame of a candle that flickered in front of the mirror before him.

Translated by Vidosava Janković

Miroslav Josić Višnjić

Miroslav Josić Višnjić was born in 1946 in the region of Vojvodina and studied at the University of Belgrade. A versatile writer, he has produced plays, poems, short stories, children's stories, and novels. He established the first privately owned publishing house in post–World War II Yugoslavia.

His works have been translated into Polish, Dutch, Hungarian, French, and German. They include two collections of short stories, *Beautiful Helen* (1969) and *Twelve Rings* (1977). His novels are *The Czech School* (1971), *Novel About an Art Gallery's Death* (1970), *TBC, the First Joint: Access to the Light* (1980), and *Defense and Fall of the Town of Bodrog During Seven Turbulent Seasons* (1990).

An unusual combination of lyrical and epic elements characterizes Josić Višnjić's prose. He lives and works in Belgrade.

THE FOREST OF
PERPETUAL DARKNESS

We did not know which way to turn.

It was night. Refugia stumbled. Then she fell. To the right and to the left of where she lay stretched out on the ground, I saw two bright points. I was not certain people were living there, but I so wanted to hear people's voices.

I begged Refugia to get up somehow, to look, to listen. She breathed heavily, but said nothing.

I took out my last cigarette and lit it. Then I went into the bushes. I was looking for blackberries. I felt thorns; warm blood covered my hands.

Refugia ate all the blackberries and, grabbing hold of my neck, began to get up. She too looked at the bright points on both our left and our right.

We turned left.

We tripped on stones, stumps, and roots. It might have been better if we had turned right. We fell into holes, into mud, as if our bodies were hovering between the black forests and the dark earth. We were wet from the mud, but no one could see that. Refugia could not go any farther. She gently wrapped herself about me. She wanted me to carry her in my arms.

Perhaps she also wanted to sleep, to dream.

Perhaps also for me to whisper that I love her.

I no longer saw the light. I sensed only its existence, somewhere deep in front of us, somewhere deep in my vision. With one arm I took Refugia about the waist, the other was under her weak, folded knees. I carried her and stumbled. I tried to call for people.

Then everything began to rock. I felt the surrounding oak trees start to shake; the stones moved. Only occasionally I would hear the incomprehensible sounds of the birds, the water, and the leaves. It looked to me as if Refugia were hovering over my arms, and I believed that at least they were free. I barely lifted my feet. They were peeling and the soles were sore.

Suddenly the light became more powerful. We ran toward it. I held Refugia firmly by the hand, actually by the elbow, and constantly spoke her name.

We tripped, fell, got up, ran, tripped. And the light disappeared and grew by turns. We descended lower and lower, the darkness got thicker and thicker. I held on tight to Refugia.

And then before me, beneath a large green rock, I caught sight of a huge palace lit by torches. On a broad table lay food and drink. Above golden towers shimmered silver roofs. But not a soul.

I stretched out my hand and the place disappeared. The darkness carried off the entire left-hand side of my body, and I trembled. Refugia said we were in the vicinity of the light. I saw nothing.

We moved on stone. Behind us was the abyss. Dizziness seized me and I did not know where I was going. I found a huge, knotty staff and, leaning on it a bit, cleared the way. Just a bit more, just a little bit more. There was not one bone that did not hurt me.

I caught sight of the light and instantly told Refugia. Then I also heard a man's voice. It was calling someone to come back into the cottage.

We were on a small plateau. I saw a large cottage, and in front of it a fire.

A little girl sat on a stump by the fire, breaking twigs.

A bit farther was a pen full of sheep.

"Grandfather," she said, "someone is coming." And she got up.

A bearded, hairy man came out of the cottage. Only later did I learn that this was the awesome Makavej, and the pale little girl was his granddaughter.

I looked about and saw that I was lying on an enormous heap of fern.

My feet and hands were wrapped all in rags. On my right, the little girl lay asleep. Grandfather was stoking the fire. I did not see Refugia anywhere.

I got up and went outside. The cottage looked even larger and wider.

Grandfather told me that I had slept two days and a night. And said also that Refugia was here, in the forest. She woke up before noon on the second day after our arrival, sat for a while on a large stump, ate smoked meat and cheese, and spoke with grandfather and granddaughter about the other side of the forest.

Grandfather Makavej also said that it was good that we had turned in this direction. The forest to the right was impassable.

It is fenced in by a great wall, he said, and it is not for nothing that people call it the Forest of Perpetual Darkness. Certainly you have never come to this part of the world, he asked.

I forgot for a moment about Refugia. I looked somewhere through the darkness and heard Grandfather's voice.

Once, in my own grandfather's account, on a wall, in some incomprehensible language that was later translated, the following was written: *Each one carries within himself a Forest of Perpetual Darkness, and this is the one forest that no one will ever be able to conquer. For he who enters it will die, and he who does not enter will die slowly. And so it is to the present day. And will always be.*

The fire sputtered.

Refugia did not return, so I went out into the meadow.

I called out to her.

The echo returned to me, broad and dark.

I went into the cottage.

Next to the heap of fern on which I had slept, I caught sight of a piece of paper. I picked it up and looked at it. The letters danced before my eyes. I looked at the sky, then at the soft and shimmering edge of the forest, and moaned.

But Refugia did not come.

It appeared to me that everything was falling apart and that I was falling into a deep pit. Grandfather Makavej looked now at me, now at the Forest. Thick oaks were tearing at each other and falling to pieces. The noise was intolerable.

I told Grandfather we must immediately set out to find Refugia. His

granddaughter could wait at the entrance, while we, constantly calling to her, would certainly find Refugia and the exit.

Grandfather was silent and stared at the fire.

And then together we began to call out to Refugia. We heard even the echoes of our voices. I even believed that we could still catch up to *her* at the entrance to the huge Forest, full of swamps and snakes.

I raised the little girl to my shoulders and hastened off. In the darkness I felt terror. I said nothing either to the little girl or to Grandfather, who was thrashing behind us. I was more terrified for Refugia than for myself.

What is she looking for there?

What are you looking for, Refugia?

"Daylight has never penetrated there," said Grandfather, as we stopped to listen. "The swamps are deep there, the trees thick and large, and the stones slippery."

"We must find her, we must lead her out and save her," I said to Grandfather. I looked at the frightened little girl.

Then we started uphill. Crying, the granddaughter kept repeating that we dare not go *there*, that we must return to the cottage and wait.

I only repeated: "We must lead her out."

The Forest was black, wrapped in a thick mist. Its quivering wall undulated gently downward, toward us. The little girl clung firmly to my neck and wept quietly. She murmured something about a one-armed fiery ogre who burns up children. Then about a man with a hundred heads who plucks up oaks and boxwood trees and throws them over the mountain.

Grandfather walked silently ahead, with a sure step. His granddaughter squeezed my neck tighter and tighter, so that I wanted to throw her off and run downhill. Nevertheless I walked peacefully along in Grandfather's footsteps. Later she admitted that she had wanted to suffocate me and thus turn Grandfather back.

We walked for a long time, bent over, across roots and stumps, across sharp stones and thick layers of damp rotten leaves.

We stood before a high wall. It was covered with rambling bushes and green slime. It was as if the black stone had been put together deliberately. The upper edge of the wall disappeared in warm layers of mist and

darkness. It appeared to me that the wall rose toward heaven for at least seven times my height.

To the right the wall was broken down, so that anyone might immediately imagine that once upon a time here stood a wide and heavy door. Decorated in metal and merely ajar.

Grandfather said: "This is the only entrance, the only gate to the Forest of Perpetual Darkness. There are people who in making their way along the wall have turned left, toward the east, and after seven months returned to this gate again."

I stood without understanding anything.

Blocking the entrance, the bearded ramblers said, as it were, that they were the true witness to the fact that none had entered or exited for a long time.

The liitle girl squeezed my neck and spoke loudly of stones that could howl and kill.

Grandfather cupped his hands around his mouth and uttered a drawn-out shout for Refugia. Everything in me began to tremble. His granddaughter was as heavy as the stone on which I was standing.

Grandfather called out ceaselessly to Refugia. The wall began, as it were, to rock even more, and the little girl slipped down from my shoulders. Grandfather's deep and powerful voice resounded from the stones and ancient trees.

I entered, and immediately I felt I was sinking in a thick, overgrown swamp. Grandfather started off after me. We took each other's hand so as not to get separated, not to get lost, not to drown. I feared that the little girl would also start out after us.

I listened.

I heard only her thin, piercing voice.

We sank in the mud up to our waists. I wanted to return and tell the little girl to remain at the entrance and to call out to us constantly, but Grandfather held me back.

Birds flew around us, I thought, but we did not see them. I no longer saw even Grandfather, and he was somewhere next to me. I held on to his hand.

I don't know how long that lasted. A dry branch hit me in the middle of my face.

We were in mud up to our knees and could barely move. I no longer

saw either the wall or the gate or myself. But it must have been that we were moving. The little girl's voice was becoming weaker and weaker, fainter and fainter.

I think some bird flew at me. I don't know. After that, I felt firm ground under my feet. We stopped, I know, and began to shout at the top of our voices. Once again, our words disappeared without an echo.

No one called back. And I was no longer certain whether we were moving forward, to the left, to the right, in a circle or uphill. I still heard the little girl.

When once again we began to slip into the mud, I thought we were going back. Something in me said that we were lost in an enchanted forest and wandering along unimaginable precipices. I no longer felt even fear. On the contrary: a pleasant warmth coursed through me. Somehow I was happy that I had entered this pit. And I said to myself: we must find her. We must, we must.

Grandfather called out to Refugia ceaselessly.

I no longer felt even the mud under my feet. I broke off a branch and began to knock off thick layers of mud. The voice from the entrance was merely a gentle noise in the ears. And when I could no longer walk, I lay on the ground and began to crawl.

Grandfather took a loaf of bread and a large wheel of salty cheese out of his bag and said: "It's time for us to rest. To think. Our road is unknowingly long and distant."

And it was as if we had disturbed a flock. The noises of the wings of enormous nocturnal birds came at us from every side. I said we did not have a lot of time, that if we wanted to find Refugia alive, we had to get going at once.

I do not know how long we walked! From time to time, it seemed that we heard a sound that most of all resembled calling. From which side, I do not know. Simultaneously from all sides, I believe. And I knew only that one little girl, certainly crying and trembling, was standing at our entrance and saying something.

At that moment, Grandfather fell before my feet. Then I fell over him. I began to shake him and tried to pick him up.

He was immobile. Mute.

I pressed my ear to his chest. His heart beat weakly and irregularly.

Frightened and crawling, I began to drag him over the rocks. I won-

dered only whether I would be able to pull him all the way to the wall. He gave no signs of life. I knew that the same fate awaited me. I grasped that at once. And I began to tremble.

The darkness thickened everywhere about me. I was tired from the crawling and from Grandfather's weight. I sensed the presence of snakes crawling in the same direction.

In a fatigued voice, I called out to Grandfather's little girl. I no longer heard her voice.

Grandfather was becoming heavier and heavier. I spoke, whispered, mumbled: "You must, you must, you must . . ."

To continue looking for Refugia, to save Grandfather; to save Grandfather, if that were at all possible, and leave off the hunt for Refugia; to save myself and Grandfather and at the same time continue the pursuit of Refugia.

Though I listened carefully for a long time, as I leaned against a thick, damp tree, I could no longer even detect the voice of Grandfather's little girl. I decided to do the third thing. I was no longer capable of even thinking.

I crawled, dragged myself, crept, called, thinking only that the little girl was standing at the gate, calling, and that I would at some point suddenly hear her voice. Would hear it, especially when I had found Refugia. When I had caught sight of the wall.

The wall!

In the darkness I perceived the wall.

I flew, I know.

I embraced its slippery stones. I even began to cry. Then, from somewhere above me, I heard a moaning. I squeezed Grandfather's arms tight and then leaned against the wall. I think I wanted to fly upward. "She is crying," I whispered, "she is crying."

I do not know how long I dragged myself. Everything went dark in my head. I caught sight of a bit of the sky, I remember that. And then the gate.

On a great overturned stump sat the little girl in a kind of moldy, milky haze, whimpering quietly, with her head in her lap. I approached her in silence: if only I don't fall now, if only I don't fall.

Slowly she raised her head.

She is . . .

"Refugia," I screamed. "Oh, Refugia!"

It was Refugia. As if made of mud and grass. I could not pull myself together.

"Refugia," I said more quietly, so quietly that I could not even hear myself. Everything began to turn within me.

Suddenly I realized that this was not that gate. The one through which I had entered with Grandfather, where the little girl was waiting for us now. I grabbed Grandfather by the arm and Refugia by the waist. I knew we had to go because of the little girl: she was waiting for us and crying.

I set off with them, along the wall, supporting myself against the protruding roots of oaks and chestnuts. I do not know myself where I got such strength at that moment.

Refugia held me with one arm around the neck; with the other, she reached for support against stones and trees. I had to drag Grandfather again. Beneath us was a bottomless abyss. We could have plunged into it at any moment. We moved away slowly, more slowly than I could feel. The stones were sharp and dark.

I sensed the nearness of light and placed my feet more cautiously: Refugia's hold on me now weakened, now strengthened. And then I saw the little girl, squatting against an old pine tree near the entrance, sleeping and weeping.

At almost the same moment, everything began to rock. The tall wall began to shake and, with a crack, collapse into the Forest. Oaks exploded and fell. I heard all sorts of animals racing from every side. The stones rumbled. Refugia pressed my neck harder and harder. I heard the little girl howl and saw her disappear, with hands and legs outstretched, into the sheered-off mountain.

The morning with its freshness pushed in on me. Some unknown people were conversing animatedly about something that I could not immediately understand. You were holding a chipped little mirror in your hand and arranging your hair. I looked through the window and lit my last cigarette.

"Hey," I said, "we get out at the next station. If no one is waiting for us, that means your father and our daughter are surely up on the mountain, with the sheep."

Translated by Henry R. Cooper Jr. and Gordana B. Todorović

Milica Mićić Dimovska

Milica Mićić Dimovska, born in 1947, is a well-known writer of fiction. Her story collections are *Stories About a Woman* (1972), *Acquaintances* (1980), *Thaw* (1991), and *The Last Rapture of Milica Stojadinović Srpkinja* (1997). She is the author of the novel *Ghosts* (1987).

SMILES

His widow stood there, looking at the bust tightly wrapped in a red scarf. He should be facing the passing trains, she thought, instead of turning his back to the railroad tracks. She smiled sarcastically, because bitterness alone was not enough to satisfy her anymore. It was too soothing for her state of mind, too full of self-pity, and who really deserves self-pity? The living don't; that was her old conviction, and now, suddenly, she could afford to be not only bitter but also sarcastic at his expense, and even more so at her own. Her lips kept twitching, as if she were about to burst into tears, very old-ladyish ones, easily triggered and physiological, in that they could start coming even at the slightest thought of the injustices she had suffered throughout her life. In spite of everything, she had accepted the invitation to participate in this festive event. When she saw the black limousine, as it glided along smoothly and stopped in front of her home, she felt a touch of vanity. It was the first time a limousine had ever come to pick her up, and she did not fail to notice that some of her neighbors were impressed. An instant later, she felt ashamed, not because she was riding in a limousine, but because the limousine had arrived for her at a time when privileges for politicians had become disgusting—not only to her, but to everybody else. To a certain extent, limousines are almost *passé,* she thought, like something that somehow still clings to life even though totally rotten, just like the two old cocky veteran partisans sitting in the limousine who looked even more decrepit than she, a stroke lurking behind their pudgy red cheeks. . . . That, too, was ironic, the fact that they had remembered her now, when she could

only be ashamed of their attention. Even though she had first wanted to reject this invitation out of wounded vanity (where were they earlier, these so-called war heroes, before the earth began to shake under their feet?), she had forced herself to swallow her disgust and contempt because of him, who was not at fault, yet was not a hundred percent innocent, either.

Oh, yes, she still carries deep inside her some of his words, now maybe a little more condensed and a bit better chiseled, thanks to the passage of time, but their meaning has not changed. He said to her: you must be merciless toward yourself for the benefit of the future generations or future society—he could have used both these words. It was not really important whether he said *generations* or *society*—that was not important at all—but it was important that he asked her to be merciless toward herself because of him, because of the others, even though those others—and she knew quite few of them—had never been merciless toward themselves. On the contrary! . . . How could he leave her alone with a child, without any means of support (she was almost imprisoned, almost ended up in the Banjica concentration camp), just so he could accomplish that subversive mission, obey an order from who knows whom? She remembered that she told him, "May God make your mission a disaster!" He came back out of darkness, out of the reddish darkness of the summer dawn . . . in her bare feet she felt few drops as she stood at the bottom of the stairs in a clump of wet grass, incapable of subduing the sweet pleasure she felt from her curse. He came back and slapped her across the face. The communist. Good heavens, and now they had decided to erect a monument to him, right there at the place where he had accomplished that mission. By this tiny railroad station, in this godforsaken town. A train thundered by as they led her to her seat in the front row, together with the two former partisans from the limousine. According to the schedule, there would be no more trains until the afternoon—that's what a man from the town office said . . . She could remember even the most insignificant details: for example, how she felt the urge to collect a few white plums lying in the grass and eat them. Then she returned to bed, rejoicing somewhat that he had hit her, and in this elated state she kissed the child who had fallen asleep on the straw mattress and almost forgot that it was fear, fear for survival, and not defiance that had caused their quarrel. Then she spat out a plum that had been penetrated by the

thread of a worm, resembling rust. I should have realized then that survival is not for everyone. Neither is death, which by-passes old people—she thought to herself, sitting down on the chair facing the small podium and the bust by the tracks. Mostly people of her own age were seated to her left and right—she noticed that—and also filled the rows of chairs behind her. Not more than a hundred people! Several girl students, who had recited revolutionary poems during the ceremony, still milled around, and she caught the eyes of one of the girls as she passed by—eyes filled with contempt and disgust. Not only for old age, she thought, conscious of her deep wrinkles and spots, and her lips that sagged at the corners; this was not the only cause of the girl's disgust, it was the expression on my face. Every day she had to face that expression herself, which was sort of caked on her face. An expression of disgust for life and for her fellow men. She was even disgusted with herself. What was the purpose of her being here, what purpose did that past have? She felt an urge to tell the organizers that she was dressed in black not in mourning for her husband but for her son, who had been killed in a car accident four years ago. When she recalled the years since her son's death, she could not help but compare those four years with the forty-eight or forty-nine years since her husband had perished in the war, and she was unable to feel any difference in the depth of the time gone by, in the distance between the two events. Time seemed squeezed between those two deaths. For a moment it seemed to her that she had lost even her orientation in the very space around her; she became almost afraid of her surroundings, which suddenly seemed so unreal. Another glance at the wrapped bust caused her to feel a tremendous pain in her mouth, as if a tooth ached under the cap, and she felt an urge to pull off that cap, that cocoon in which the pain was concentrated. It seemed to her that his eyes under the red scarf followed her, reproaching her, even though she had never run away from death . . . She had even learned how to talk to death, trying to persuade it, in simple words, to take her with it, since she had not been able to forbid it to take her son away.

The bust was supposed to be finished two years ago, a veteran from the limousine whispered to her furtively. This was a small town. He knew many dirty details about the officials in the town that were not for public knowledge. He was born near Kraljevo and came to Belgrade after the war, just as she had, but she did not know him personally, she had only

heard of him, he used to appear at the meetings of the war veterans. His nose was crooked, she thought . . . every one of them, these old goats, had a nose and a mouth crooked from envy. She, too, was now nasty. She asked, "Will there at least be something good to stuff ourselves with after all these dull speeches?"—but that sounded undignified, she realized that. She shouldn't have debased her pain with such a question. On the other hand, all of these people were only "small fry," there was no reason she should prove herself to them! None of the famous ones had come. She was bitter again, the bitterness rising to the surface like mildew. Even her brother-in-law had not come, an official who had adapted to the new circumstances like a merchant at an open market. Brothers . . . Her husband risked his life many times, even though she often questioned his motives. It seemed to her that he had to be in places exposed to the winds of the war not because there was any real need for it, but because he himself had the urge to prove himself a hero in front of others. His brother, on the other hand, remained a quartermaster either of a detachment or a brigade throughout the war, always close to the cauldron. But still she had expected her brother-in-law to be here, although she was not surprised by his absence. She only regretted not having the opportunity to tell him that she knew very well who he was and what kind of a man he had been. She smiled without realizing that she was smiling. An unaccustomed twitch of her lips was the only thing that bothered her for a moment . . . Her brother-in-law probably had figured out that this event, this gala-gathering of vampires, this memorial service held at an inopportune time, would not advance his career one bit. Her hardened heart could not forgive anyone. She could feel the dregs of injustice settled in her heart. She thought: death has bypassed my brother-in-law's family. Perhaps that pleases the Lord. Her lips tightened stoically. The speaker also mentioned death several times, as if collecting points. He mentioned that three followers of Ljotić died in the explosion. For the first time it occurred to her that those followers of Ljotić were also Serbs. That fact changed everything: the heroism of her husband was slightly tainted. But she still felt sorry for him, even more so because he was guilty for the death of those followers of Ljotić . . . Had he been alive, he would have been here, an old man, resentful and full of spite, or . . . full of kindness. She now felt pangs of bitterness, now kindness, softheartedness, engulf her, and she suddenly felt sorry for everybody. His death

was for her something completely esoteric, she thought, something like air, because she never saw his dead body. It remained somewhere far, far away—in some forest, on some mountain. On the other hand, she touched her son's death, on his bluish, earth-colored face, which felt so brittle while she wiped off the traces of blood around his open mouth. Both his eyes and his mouth were open, oh, Lord, and there was no answer in them, nothing, absolutely nothing. Her daughter-in-law and her grandson were afraid to touch him, but she wanted to grab him, to shake him well, not realizing that she was holding just a body, just a cocoon, while covering with kisses everything that she could recognize, like his nose, slightly bent from a blow in childhood, or his moustache, or the clean-shaven chin.

And now, suddenly, all that became fused together: the image of kissing her son's face and the image of the bust, which appeared in front of her in all its angelic whiteness and purity, having almost blinded her when the red scarf slid down the pedestal like the skin of a snake. It was the face of a smiling young man. Her legs almost gave out in front of the bust, when she incidentally touched the smooth marble which was not a bit cold. It was even pleasant to the touch, she thought, not like a dead body. They moved her slightly away from the monument, and some of the war veterans from the Organizational Committee held her for a moment, so that she regained her composure quickly and was even able to accept the large bouquet wrapped in cellophane and place it at the base of the pedestal on which the bust stood.

She had to face it, it was clear that the bust resembled her grandson. He often smiled at people the same way, trustingly, with only the slightest touch of disdain. A smile twinkled also under the white marble membrane covering the eyes. She could not look into that face, into those smiles. She backed away two or three steps, staggering, catching the end of the prickly boxwood wreath held by one of the war veterans. The whistle of a locomotive announced that a train was approaching, and soon, behind the bust, a train, pulling several cars, thundered through the station. We planned it this way, to have the train salute him when the festivities ended . . . he, like us, was a railroad man—said a man from the Organizational Committee. Taking her by the arm, he led her to the station restaurant in which the luncheon was to be served.

Through the window of the station restaurant she could see the black

limousine, standing there as if on duty. Like a hearse at the cemetery, she thought, as they set before her a plate of roast suckling pig. She was at the funeral feast, she muttered; that was her punishment, to be at the funeral feast. She kept muttering that between bites, occasionally lifting her glass of wine. She could even see the multitude of people who over the years had poured through that station. They kept silently passing through the walls, as if the walls were no barrier to them, as if the time of a universal movement had begun, a procession of the dead and the living on the day of the Last Judgment, still undivided, not separated into those who would be resurrected and those destined for destruction.

Translated by Biljana Šljivić-Šimšić

Radoslav Bratić

One of the most prominent writers of Serbia today, Radoslav Bratić was born in Herzegovina in 1948. He started to write as a student and was one of the founders of the avant-garde literary journals *Znak* i *Književna reč*. He is on the editorial board of the journal *Književnost*.

Bratić writes novels, stories, and plays. Each of his books has been awarded a prestigious literary prize and his stories have been included in world anthologies. His works include *Death of the Savior* (1973), *Doubts about Biography* (1980), *A Picture Without Father* (1985), *Fear from Bells* (1992), *Winter in Herzegovina* (1995), and *Scheherezade's Lover* (1996).

Bratić bases his narrative on his childhood memories, which are filled with legends and superstitions of his native land.

A PICTURE
WITHOUT FATHER

We all stare at the lump on Father's throat, as it saps and drains his body, shriveling it before our very eyes—and no one knows what to say to him. The wound has torn open and turned outward. Inside, there's a gaping black hole. It presses on his windpipe and releases fiendish pain. It makes a caricature of him. You only have to look at the nerve strapping his face—throbbing and stabbing as if it were full of poison and venom. It warns him that life is short. We all stand there, as if we've forgotten how to talk, and he stares straight through us, out at the orchard. Who knows what pictures he sees out there amid the trees? It's as if he's praying for salvation, but we don't hear it. He got that wound in the last war, and now it has jettisoned him back into the trenches, to remember all the suffering and pain. Life weaves its circle. You can see him clench his sweaty fists and in his mind he's charging. (Do his ears ring with the order: "Full attack on the enemy—fire!"?) But the muscle in his neck tightens; he flinches, grits his teeth, and lifts himself up against the headboard of the bed as if he were surrounded by layers of darkness, and calls for surrender. Then he turns to look at the photographs on the wall, to grab some last vestiges of life from them. That's why they were made. One shows his father standing among the children, his hand raised in a victorious salute, strong and healthy. It's as if that picture has long since become phony to him. What a gulf between what he sees and what he feels! Father's face is moist, but it isn't from tears, it's from sweat and

pain. Perhaps he's just remembered something. A shadow of bitterness creeps across his lips. They are dry and hard. Swollen both inside and out. Like a bomb about to explode in everyone's face. It reminds me of the time when he scolded us and told us not to poke around the walls of the house and fence because bombs and munitions from two wars still lay hidden there: who knows who planted them? We laughed at these stories until one day a bomb claimed both hands of Djordjije's son. Lame and crippled though he is, he still waves around what's left of his arms. But Gospava says it was meant to be and that she saw the signs before the child was even born.

"Where are you, son?" Father keeps calling to me, staring at me and sizing me up to see whether I look like him. I see his lips move, he's whispering something. Outside, we hear voices saying the disease is incurable. But who can believe that? I lean my face close to his, but my father-creator doesn't see me, his eyes are glazed. And like the *karst* caves, they send out a whirl of smoke and mist. It envelops everyone, making everything hazy. We must look like ghosts to him. And yet there was such goodness in that man.

No one looks in on the house, the pain is not theirs. They're afraid of sudden illness; they're all up on the mountain looking for grapevines to plant as borders for their animal stalls and houses. There's no one to scream and drive away the illness, which can spread. Life accumulates, is torn asunder by some inner force, and then suddenly collapses. It is with this fear that one should embark on life's journey.

There's no Mijat to come and swear like a madman at his creator, then clap himself over the mouth in horror and remorse. There's no Bosiljka to beg Father to burn the droppings in the beehive while she takes out the honey. She loved Father's hand, which had touched her breasts, too. There's no Kosa to tell us about what's going on in nearby Italy, who's fighting with whom, how the horse trading with them is flourishing. She knows yesterday's news as well as tomorrow's.

Father holds on to the doorpost, fingering it: a picture of collision between everything and its creator. It's as if he isn't standing on his legs, as if there's a rupture somewhere inside him, a chasm making him crazy and shaky. As if there's an ambush lying in wait behind the walls and trees, as if everything has conspired together and is waiting for the sound of the cowbells and sheep bells to herald death. That's the sign for Uglješa

to take out the yellow boards and start making a good coffin. Whispers mold Father into a hero of the first order, and then into a doubtful character in the Curd Cooperative fraud. But we know all he did was finger the crooks and that he was opposed to creating a lake in the middle of the village and flooding the area for the sake of the future dam.

Mother rushed around, she sapped her strength digging up the garden, planting the vegetable bed with onions and beets. She labored under a load that was more than she could or should carry. She would burst into the house, grasp the medicine bottle, and thrust it into Father's mouth. This was some sign of hope, especially when that gentle smile appeared on his face as the pain receded! Then she would spray into his mouth a yellowish liquid with a pungent and unpleasant smell. It drugged and numbed him to both pain and life, which still assaulted him from all sides.

And here, within reach, is the unfinished water barrel. It still needs to be shaved down and have the hoops drawn over it. The sight of it pains his eyes (and his liver). He had laid out the tools neatly with his own hands, so that he could always find what he needed. But there is always something hidden or missing. You can feel the sweat from Father's hands in the wood and metal of the adz and cutting tools hanging above the door. Even Špiro Mastilović didn't know how to fix the mill dike or get the right stroke on the water wheel, until Father showed him. Here, too, is the *rakija* barrel that he had started to make, with its nine big hoops. We're going to fill it with the Konavlje *rakija* bought for Patron Saint's Day and for all the other saints in the year. At least then you can be sure people will make the sign of the cross. Everything torments and taunts him, but we don't see it.

Maybe he wanted to tell us something important. A secret from the war, from the prison camp. He pursed his lips and grimaced, but only a soft moan came out.

Mother rushed to repair the worn fence, to weed the dandelions around the spring lettuce and pull up the nettles. Instead of opening her mouth, listening and remembering. All that work in vain, because the weeds only grow again, inundating everything.

The smell of new grass in want of a good mowing comes through the windows. Nature is cruel, spitting on everyone and humiliating the help-

less. The shed in front of the house looks ramshackle and angry to his eyes. It's probably mad at him for having done the wall so badly. It's crooked and yellow. His army boots hang from a thick cord held up by a nail on the wall above his bed. Hanging next to them are his World War I cartridge belt and knapsack, full of living memories. All the things he smuggled in it through Herzegovina and Dalmatia, from tobacco to dried figs and all kinds of medicinal herbs. The gold-plated chain watch lies there on the chest. It worked on its own, showing nothing to anyone. It ticked without winding. Grandfather was the only one who ever wore it. He would pull it out from the depths of his pocket to see how far the day had progressed and stand in awe of those strange moving hands. In the evening, he would look mistrustfully at the numbers, feel the pulselike ticking, until sleep got the better of him. As if he couldn't understand how the day had passed so quickly!

Does no one remember the sermon given by our dear and slightly inebriated priest Zimonjić, who forever called on the people to do good, because you only get as good as you give. But who can believe in that? Tanasije, sitting under the pear tree (he spent his entire boyhood in its shade) tosses pebbles into the chimney stack of Poparina's house, but only as long as no one sees him. And here's Dimitrije, soaked in sweat and sorry that he hadn't come much earlier so that he could put his own two cents in and relate what he had seen and heard since this morning. But it's never too late. Even the rain can't fall unless he announces it first. I know, he'll start off by grumbling and complaining about his brother, with whom he hasn't been on speaking terms for well onto twenty years. Two brothers nursed at the same breast. It's enough to strike fear in your heart; who'd ever believe it?

The drought was getting worse as we waited and Father's torment grew. Dry blades of grass jutted from the cracked, thirsty soil. The torrid wind was as parching in the shade as the sun. As if this summer had escaped all control and everything was again plunging into chaos. The seared wooden trough has become deformed, and you no longer know what to use it for. The bees alight languidly on what was once a pool; we see it in our mind's eye and just for a second live in our imagination. Lizards and frogs mingle together in this hell on earth, they touch and drool over each other. If Tanasije looks a little closer, he'll realize that he

has already seen this picture. And that means having spent his whole life in one spot. If he looks up at the treetops, he'll see Nikodije stuck between the branches. As if he were somewhat mad.

"There's so much water in the sea and we're going thirsty . . . this place is burning as if we've committed some terrible sin!" says a voice from the trees.

Tanasije talks about the great flood he dreamed of the night before. He dreamed how the water had rolled away the trees and stones. And then some reptiles had appeared. And then desolation everywhere. In the evening a flood, next morning parched land!

"Can we expect rain again?" asks someone we can't see. A young girl runs down the road and off to Stamena. She holds out her white breast and shows it to the woman, whose hands are deep in dough, kneading bread.

"This mole appears in two days . . . I dreamt that it gushed blood . . . What can that mean? Then light issued forth from the wound and illuminated us all! There's a deafening in my ears."

Maybe she caught fire and is looking for the touch of a man's hand.

The lizards and dying bumblebees are the best proof of this story. You can't help feeling sorry for them. The cattle are dying, they are herded down to the river to water. By the time they come back, they're thirsty again. What a pointless exercise! The common water pails stand forlornly, eaten away by rust; they're afraid that the disease will spread. And no one asks us anymore for the brandy container that the settlers had brought from Banat, the one we use for roasting coffee. At the crack of dawn, there's the sound of song from the road in front of the house. Someone is bursting with health and joy.

The smell of tobacco from the coffin makes you want to smoke. Father's pipe is lying there on the table: inside it are ashes and poison. Surely he remembers Stojan, who brought it to him from Dubrovnik.

Father flinches and looks at Mother. "Could you find some snow for me to put on my wound . . . to cool the burning heat . . ." The words come out with difficulty. Mother slips off her *opanke*[1] so she can run faster. She runs off to the mountains with a wooden trough on her back. This is a battle for life, for everything that gives her a reason to live. She

---

1. *Opanke:* a type of peasant footwear. (Translator's note)

Radoslav Bratić

manages to descend into a cave and bring out a handful of snow. She comes racing back. Father reaches for the ball of snow as if it were a life-saver. He opens his mouth to let out the fire, swallows the snow, and presses it against his wound. As if his intestines are tied in a knot and sinking. Oh, martyr! The pain starts again and tears at his throat. Mother hovers over him. She'd give him her life if she could. She pulls out her left breast and milks the wound as if it were a child. The pus-laced blood of the wound mixes with the white liquid of Mother's breast. She puts a mixture of honey, wormwood, and shallots on it and finally an herb sent by an herbalist named Salatić from Bogdašić. He brought it back with him from America.

But there was no cure. In the secrets he left and placed in the chests and boxes around the house, Father found peace without a word or a sound. Who could put those two different pictures together: Father getting up from bed, so tall and strong, as things were moved out of his way, and now, lying there so still, his face distorted and sickly yellow. Now I understand why Šakot says that "life is a dream."

Jelisaveta mourns and wails, she evokes the dead (whose names she sometimes gets wrong) and warns them to take care of themselves in the other world. Then she sends them a message: to her Djuradj that she has been faithful to him, to Grandma Ješna that she still has the blouse and a vest with the gold plates and to somebody named Grković that she loved him more than anybody else in the world. She stands at the front door, all in black, and won't let anyone pass.

It is only after they bathe Father, wrap him in a sheet, and lower him into Uglješa's coffin (Uglješa is already drunk and doesn't understand what's going on), that the women start rummaging through the old chests and drawers, looking for Father's picture. Gospava takes a box from under the bed and starts rummaging through it. (So many people together in a split second. There are some to whom Father never even said "God be with you." They hide in the crowd.) Everyone could have sworn that Father was there in the family picture hanging above the bed. Now, they cross themselves in astonishment, because his face isn't in the photograph anymore. Others say, "Maybe the picture has faded and his face disappeared when he passed away." It followed him into nothingness. It's as if he'd never had his picture taken, even for his army ID.

How can we mourn him, how can the dirges be sung when there's no

picture? The mourners have nothing to look at. In these parts, a dead man is immediately nailed down in his coffin and forgotten. Out of fear the disease may spread.

In the middle of all this chaos, turning the house upside down, Baldy lets out a bellow, as if to say even a cow can feel pain. Once again they dig through the chests and boxes stowed away from the human eye, and once again they see there is no picture. After they've gone through everything and found no photograph, Gospava (pointing straight at my forehead) cries, "We'll put Jakov next to the coffin—it's his father, and he's his spitting image! They can look at him while they lament the dead man . . ."

Everyone breathes a sigh of relief. These words seem to still the panic. They grab me, dirty and tear-stained as I am, and start undressing me. Gospava yanks the sweater off me; she doesn't care that my head won't go through and that the collar cuts like a knife. They pull at me from all sides, as if they want to crucify me. I know what it is. Gospava is paying me back for that window of hers I broke. They strip me naked as the day I was born, and Gospava looks as if this is the moment she's been waiting for. They take my things out of the house and throw them in a heap where they can't be seen. Then they grab me and hoist me into a tub of hot water, the same one they just bathed my father in. I can feel the cold of the metal, it feels as if death had touched it just a few minutes before. My cries are drowned in all the sobbing and crying. They scrub me down with a hard brush and wash me as if I haven't had a bath since the day I was born. Jelisaveta grabs me between the legs and washes me there, too. "At least he'll be clean for the other world!"—says Gospava with fervor, as if I'm the one who's dead. Jelisaveta rubs me down with alcohol, "to keep the worms away."

Velizar's mouth droops open; he must be worried about his potato patch needing water. Or else his mind is off somewhere, thinking about how he'll gather snails as soon as the rain falls and earn more money than anyone's ever seen. Further off, some unknown people are talking, as if they've forgotten why they came here in the first place.

Once I'm properly bathed and scented, they start dressing me. They try not to touch my body. First they pull Father's big white shirt over my head. It's so big my whole body could fit in just the sleeve. They dress me in his trousers, in the shoes Father had bought in Dubrovnik

after he sold the tea. Last of all comes Father's coat, which covers me up, protecting me from evil eyes. They turn up the sleeves and pull out my arms and neck so that at least some of me can be seen. They start raking at my hair with a wooden comb, as if they're stacking hay. Mother is overcome with grief, she can't tell who is who anymore.

Somebody says the body is ready. Three women dressed in black immediately kneel by the coffin, their kerchiefs slipping from their heads, as if they longed for the sound of crying and wailing.

Someone named Kosara wails that the spirit of the deceased will live on in the masterpieces he has left behind. She describes his build, his face, his hands, and his feet, as if she had been in love with him. (Mother would die of jealousy if she were in a normal state of mind. Maybe she would push her away from the coffin.) She extols him, but she can't think of anything to improve on the picture of the dead man. Somebody named Latinka, who had fallen into a trance at the very beginning, says that it is a terrible pity such a young person should be going to his grave. She beats her chest, wailing, "Oh, pain, what about your books, your friends and teachers . . ." She collapses in despair and loses consciousness. The crying and wailing gets louder, as the people prepare to mourn me. And again, it's as if many of them are putting on a show, as if there is a kind of furor to their voices. Latinka tears her hair, but her voice loses its melody. It's as if this is just a trial run for the real dirge (which turns into song) at countless funerals across Herzegovina.

The loudest sobs come from Mitar (who would have thought he had such a tender heart?) when Latinka starts sending greetings to the dead.

"Say hello to Stanoje for me and tell him that his two kids are alive and well . . . Give a kiss to Staka and tell her that Momir has remained a bachelor." Some of the words get lost in the open hole of Gospava's mouth. The wailing gets louder, everyone cries and wails for their dead ones. A woman embraces her daughter's grave, kissing the cold stone. People collect around a fresh mound of earth, wailing. The men's voices are too harsh and hard for lamentation.

Tomislav comes up behind me and slaps me on the shoulder. He's checking to see whether I'm alive and whether he'll have someone to play with tomorrow. My legs are stiff and cold with fear. A crow flaps its wings nearby, its joy is so far removed from everything!

Kosara wails that the effigy is as handsome as a god. That's the first time I've heard a compliment come my way. It sounds damned unconvincing to my ears.

As they mourn Father one minute and me the next, you can hear the shriek of the lambs. Nebojša is slaughtering them for the meal that follows the funeral. Brandishing his knife, he plunges it through their necks. It's terrifying to watch. Where does he get all that steely courage and skill?

The next to speak is Špiro, the cooperative manager. His eyes look out at a point somewhere above us. His bulging neck is fat from eating so much cooperative curd. He says a few passing words of eulogy about the deceased and then starts talking about how the lake has to be created and repairs done on the school. Špiro holds forth, saliva spewing from his mouth, as if he were addressing some public rally. He talks about construction and progress, about the new road over the hayfields and meadows. And he'll screw anyone who dares say differently. Here he's referring a little angrily to Father, but he's well into his speech and doesn't mention him by name. His deputy pokes him from behind: it's time to bury the deceased. But Špiro goes on and on, he's delivering a big speech about the country's construction and renewal. It's his thing.

Nikodije, who's standing right next to me, lifts me up when the wailing stops, wanting to toss me into the hole. When he comes to his senses, he bursts into tears. I see Metodije swing his shovel and strike at the earth, covering up Father. He looks as if he's digging a well. He's suddenly become enterprising and hardworking. He's cool and collected, although there's always something a little spiteful and vengeful about him. Men and women come up and toss clods of dirt on the deceased. There are all kinds of faces and mugs. But the earth is not choosy.

We're girdled by the cemetery on all sides and it's a good thing the gates are open. In just a moment, many people will even forget where they've been.

We go home, and my thoughts are morbid. I can't think of anything but Father's picture. Everything taunts me, I see his spirit everywhere.

Just before nightfall, Metodije runs over to take Father's scythe, the sharpest in seven villages, and along with it he asks for the anvil, the water horn, and the marker. As if he had been waiting for this very moment. Then the miller comes along asking for seven sacks woven of the finest

wool, with special markings in the middle. And in the evening Kruna drops in, her pointed nose piercing the air as if the world has never seen anything as smart as she. She asks for the Hungarian wool-combing machine—the first one to be brought to these parts by Father when he was released from the prison camp. Mother gives everyone a shake of her head, at which Kruna, raising her pointed nose like a blade of grass, takes off through the plum orchard. The next day, Mojsije puts in an appearance. He, too, wants something, and I don't even know whether he was at the funeral or not. He asks for the four wagon wheels made out of special wood and iron, and brought from Vojvodina. He leaves empty-handed. Overnight, the wheels disappear. We don't know who stole them, but we do know that no one would dare use them on his wagon, because Mother would immediately say, "They're mine!"

But you can still feel Father's eye watching over all these things, controlling and running everything. He taught Jelisaveta a lot of things. The loom Father made out of maple wood, with the light reeds for pressing the yarn, is with Dmitrije. Dočjin was given the packsaddle; Bosiljka, her legs spread, would ride on it. She liked being close to Ognjen, touching him inadvertently with her hot thigh.

Father's clothes, the bed mattress, and the comforter full of chicken feathers, piled up near the house, waiting to rot, are all reminders of him. All night long, Kruna rummaged around the mattress in the hope of finding any gold coins Father may have forgotten to take out in his illness. (They say the late Šćepan left her a jar full of gold buried on their property, but she can't figure out where it is or how to dig it up. That's all she can think of, she can't get her mind off it.)

The children run away from me, as if they're afraid to touch me. Velizar shouts, "Beat it, there he is, the dead man rises again!" And Kosara shouts, "The devil's luck, look, he's like a vampire! We've already mourned him once and here he is resurrected . . . that's not him, it's his ghost . . . And he'll toss horsefeed into the vat again and he won't even be able to drink the water!"

Before I fall asleep, I always hear Father's reproachful and angry whisper. I see his face fade, vanishing somewhere behind the stable.

For days we gather up the summer crop, the little that is left from the drought. Gospava crosses herself as soon as she sees me, as if she wishes they really had buried me. We tie up the rye in sheafs and arrange them

crisscross in blocks, the way Father used to do. We put dry grass on top to keep the kernels from rotting. At night Mother jumps in her sleep, shouting something, but you can't decipher what. When she wakes up, she says, "I dreamed of your father, he said we have to restack the grain, it'll rot and go dank as never before." We immediately start rearranging the sheaves, changing everything.

Everything we do seems to ask: how would Father have done it?

Everything is a frightening warning.

One moment it's as if it were long ago, the next as if it were now.

Translated by Christina Pribićević Zorić

David Albahari

David Albahari, born in 1948, is one of the leading postmodernist authors in Belgrade. He writes short stories and novels and translates works of English, American, and Australian literature.

His collections of stories are: *Family Time* (1973), *Ordinary Stories* (1978), *A Description of Death* (1982), *Fit in the Shed* (1984), *Simplicity* (1988), and *Cloak* (1993). A collection of Albahari's stories, *Words Are Something Else,* was published in 1996. His novels are: *Judge Dimitrijević* (1978), *Zinc* (1988), *Short Book* (1993), *The Man of Snow* (1995), *The Bait* (1996), and *Darkness* (1997).

Albahari's works have been translated into Hebrew, Hungarian, Italian, and other languages. He is a noted stylist who strives to compress his stories into minimalist structures.

THE GREAT REBELLION
AT THE STULN
NAZI CAMP

I. My father's hair turned gray on March 18, 1961.

2. Two large, clear teardrops welled in his eyes.

3. "Not from unexpected self-pity," he protested later, "but because of the change. A change which demanded that I understand time, that I notice its passage and admit to its implacability. That I obey it more diligently."

4. Until then, therefore, my father did not acknowledge the implacability of time or its necessity.

5. In this, my father was similar to the heroes of antiquity.

6. Or were the heroes of antiquity aware of time after all?

7. (Did the heroes of antiquity fully possess their own timelessness? Their out-of-time-ness?)

8. Unlike the heroes of antiquity, my father often, before and after the stated date, in conversation or during his afternoon monologues, compared time with money. "Time is like money," my father would say, "the older it is, the more it's worth. The rarer it is, the more significant."

9. My father, as an amateur of course, dabbled in numismatics. He had over four hundred different coins. He had no idea what at least half of them represented.

10. He had about fifty monetary bills, mostly from the Independent State of Croatia and prewar Yugoslavia.

11. It is crucial to state that my father developed and perfected a longish list of terms and concepts closely aligned to his favorite topic of

conversation: time and money. Unfortunately, it is impossible in this limited space to even list them, let alone go into any detailed description. But from the initial logical postulate, i.e., that time is money, it is obvious that for every situation known to the monetary and the financial world, my father had a corresponding temporal counterpart. (And vice versa.)

12. Inflation of time, for instance.

13. Or the time market. A dropping time rate. The second-world dollar. The Middle Ages of money. A deficit of time. A temporal crisis.

14. Revaluation of time, as well.

15. His favorite term, however, was *mechanical time*. He maintained that with the industrial production of watches, alarm clocks, even church towers, time had gotten nothing. Quite the contrary, it could only lose. The fact that time is always within reach, claimed my father, only creates an irreparable multidimensionality and distortion of real time. That and nothing more. And since, fortunately, mechanical time is based on the principle of the spring, a product of a given technological process, and since technology has no place in determining time, my father simply did not acknowledge any mechanical and electronic manipulation when calculating time. Without blinking, of course, he was happy to accept any hourglass or, in his opinion, the most ideal of all: sundials in gardens and on the walls of houses.

16. He was most indifferent to nuclear timepieces.

17. What happened, in the meanwhile, to the heroes of antiquity?

18. The heroes of antiquity would disappear the moment they grasped the transitory nature of time.

19. Here is one more difference between the heroes of antiquity and my father: my father, on March 19, 1961, understood time, but he did not disappear.

20. Quite the contrary. His overall physical condition improved visibly.

21. But, alas! The consequences for him of his participation in the Second World War were indelible.

22. In the year 1941, in the spring, my father—as the reserve sanitation officer in the prewar Yugoslav army—was wading up to his knees in the Timok River, but his heroism reached its apogee only after blowing up the Bor Copper Mine.

23. The military command issued the following decree: "We are retreating, but we will not leave anything for the enemy! In the name of the king and our Fatherland!"

24. They laid out explosives up in the Bor Copper Mine.

25. BOOM!!!

26. The Bor Copper Mine blew up. (The enemy was advancing on all sides.)

27. My father—a young reserve sanitation officer of the prewar Yugoslav army in collapse—was present at that event in an unusually vital capacity. He was in charge of caring for anyone injured during the blast.

28. Indeed, my father vividly recalls, rocks spewed out for a distance of up to 320 meters from the mine entrance.

29. It is believed, however, that there were rocks that hurtled even further.

30. A soldier, jerking back at the moment of the blast, injured his finger which was hooked into his gunbelt buckle.

31. The bang was enormous.

32. Horses neighed.

33. The Bor Copper Mine ceased to exist.

34. My father was of the opinion that the soldier's finger should be amputated. He proposed total anesthesia and ordered that all the instruments be boiled.

35. Then a medic noticed that the soldier had, in his opinion, merely sprained his finger.

36. The soldier was sitting on a tree stump, smoking.

37. My father said that he would only know for certain once the patient was on the table. Until then, he emphasized, the outcome was entirely unknown. The enemy was advancing on all sides and every pair of hands was needed. If he were to hesitate, my father thought, human loss would be inevitable.

38. My father went into the tent.

39. The medic went over to the soldier and with a few deft movements returned the dislocated joint to its place.

40. The soldier thanked him. He said that it hurt much less, but he would like to know how much longer the finger would be this swollen.

41. The medic said that it would last a day or two. He washed the hand and went off with the cured soldier to eat.

42. The afternoon bugles sounded.

43. At that moment, my father came out of the tent all in white, a surgical apron around his waist and warm surgical gloves on his hands.

44. In front of the sanitation tent, there was nobody at all.

45. The soldier's cigarette butt was distinctly visible in the green grass.

46. As a well-trained reserve officer of the prewar Yugoslav army and an exemplary student of the Zagreb University School of Medicine, my father stood, so to speak, at attention, waiting for events to take their course.

47. Two weeks later, at dawn, the entire regiment surrendered to the Germans. A certain number of soldiers were executed on the spot.

48. The enemy had been quite far from the site of the explosion at the time when the Bor Copper Mine was blown up. When the enemy saw the destroyed equipment, the enemy was quite surprised.

49. Some German officers, my father recalls vividly, were extremely angry. They raged and howled out curt, harsh sentences in German.

50. All the German officers shouted in German.

51. The translator asked, "Where are the French engineers who were in charge of exploiting the Bor Copper Mine?"

52. The answer was: "The French engineers who were in charge of exploiting the Bor Copper Mine ran away."

53. The translator translated this response into German.

54. "*Was?*" said one German officer. He was wearing glasses.

55. Then the translator asked, "Did the French engineers participate in blowing up the Bor Copper Mine?"

56. "Yes, they did," was the answer.

57. The translator translated the response into German.

58. "*Was?*" said a second German officer. He was not wearing glasses.

59. The first German officer didn't say anything.

60. And so it was that my father and his entire regiment became prisoners of war of the Wehrmacht. On slow trains, through the Vojvodina, Croatia, and Austria, they were transported to officers' and other camps throughout Germany. Soldiers and officers, ordinary troops and colonels, they stood by the little windows and bade farewell to their native land. Some of them cried. Some were unshaven. A choking smell rose from the corners of the wagon.

61. Lübeck.

62. Nürnberg.

63. Stuln.

64. Four years later, in late winter, my father returned home. He was wearing an American sweater and American pants and an American shirt and American shoes. On his head he had an old hat, dusky in color, which came to his ears and slid down his forehead. In his right hand he held a peeling army box in which he had: a shaving kit and 712 letters and postcards—*correspondance des prisonniers de guerre.*

65. At the time, my father was not my father.

66. All in all, and in comparison with some other officers, war prisoners, my father had exceptionally poor luck—he gained only four pounds.

67. There were Englishmen, my father vividly recalls, who had to let out the seams on their trousers each month. Or they walked around on green meadows, constantly patting their bellies.

68. (History soon showed whose suffering was worth more: my father's or that of the Englishmen who patted themselves on the belly.)

69. The English ate chocolate every day, my father went on to recall vividly. Maybe that is what influenced the inevitable loosening of their stomach muscles?

70. In any case, this was quite a nasty picture: all those Englishmen, officers, mostly soldiers, with sagging bellies, who were no longer able to snap to salute sharply at the command: "Attention!"

71. Quite a nasty picture.

72. The Germans also ate chocolate every day, but they were so slender, so erect.

73. How their heels clicked!

74. My father was the first to suspect that girdles might be playing a key role in the German case.

75. "During a group outing," my father vividly recalls, "in the immediate vicinity of the camp, I spotted a textiles factory."

76. What could a textiles factory in the immediate proximity of a German camp for imprisoned officers in the heart of Nazi Germany be producing?

77. "Girdles," said my father.

78. "Girdles," concurred several Polish prisoners.

79. English officers held a two-day hunger strike. They demanded emergency approval for the use of girdles among the prisoners.

80. The German Command ordered that three Yugoslav and seven Russian majors should be summarily shot.

81. So that is how the great rebellion in the Nazi camp in Stuln was repressed.

82. The Stuln Nazi Camp was an international camp which the Americans liberated shortly before the end of the war.

83. This explains why my father returned dressed in an American sweater and American pants and an American shirt and American shoes.

84. This, of course, does not explain how my father came wearing the old hat, dusky in color, which reached his ears and slid down his forehead.

85. The old hat, dusky in color, is another story.

86. My father has never told me that story.

87. The hat sits, even today, in the closet. Mother says sometimes that the time has come to get rid of all unpleasant mementos. She suggests that we throw out the hat. Or, better yet, give it to the Red Cross.

88. "What use can the Red Cross have for one old hat, dusky in color, which I have had since the Second World War?" asks my father. "The Red Cross is a massive humanitarian organization that collects tens of thousands of blankets and tents, and sends them to Nicaragua, Guatemala, Palestine, Pakistan . . . wherever they are needed."

89. "Thank God we don't need anything," says Mother.

90. So the hat stays in the closet. It smells of lavender and tobacco leaves, which Mother slips into closed places against moths. Now and then, however, and particularly on March 18, 1961 (when his hair first turned gray), my father takes it from the closet, and with the hat on his head, stands in front of the mirror.

91. Two big, clear tears welled, then, in his eyes

92. He slowly took off the hat and ran trembling fingers through his white hair.

93. The streets at that moment were full of evening strollers.

94. There is no chronicle that records the heroic role my father played in blowing up the Bor Copper Mine.

95. (After the Second World War, with the transition to national ownership, the renovated Bor Copper Mine suddenly began to flourish. In 1958, it produced 2,268,000 tons of copper ore.)

96. But there are chronicles that record less valiant roles of heroes who

were less significant than my father. These are what we call "subjective chronicles."

97. According to my father's opinion: "objective history" does not yet exist. An awareness of the historical role of individuals makes the existence of objective history impossible.

98. "In a certain way," my father admits, "I, too, am one of those individuals. I obstruct history."

99. At that moment, two big, clear teardrops welled in the eyes of my father. He left the hat in its place, went into the living room, and switched on the television.

100. Cowboys and fearless champions of law and order flitted across the screen.

101. My father cried long into the night.

Translated by Ellen Elias-Bursać

Saša Hadži-Tančić

Saša Hadži-Tančić, born in 1948, writes poetry, novels, short stories and essays. He has published eleven collections of short stories: *Jeremiah in the Throes of Death* (1976), *A Perfect Form* (1984), *Descent into Time* (1987), *Linked by Stars* (1990), *Galloping Soldier* (1990), *On the Edge Is the Best Path* (1990), *Removal of the Armor* (1993), *The Key for a Strange Lock* (1994), *The Temple in a Suitcase* (1995), *The Return to Nais* (1997), and *The Heaven Gubernya* (1997).

His novels are: *A Holy Place* (1993) and *The Color Red* (1995). His stories have appeared in English, Polish, Spanish, Macedonian, and Italian translations.

SKULL TOWER

An unhealthy sense of relief. Momentary oblivion achieved by writing down a small sign of the cross, making it possible for them not to think about the world; they could focus on themselves alone. They were at the end of their rope, and they wrote without thinking. From the heart to the pen. Perhaps by placing these crosses on the paper they would be able to peer into the murky depths of their being; it was time to take stock of everything in their lives. Their ears buzzed and their chests hurt. As if they were listening to the incessant tolling of the bells in all the churches.

It is true that all was hopeless. That they admitted defeat by placing little crosses under their names, as their captain suggested.

There was no more dilemma: would they retreat or would they stay to the end?

They would stay to the end!

With heads held high, pale, they knew what this meant. What more did they have to lose? They had already lost the only thing they had left to gamble with: life.

The Turks were already attacking from all sides.

They surrounded the trenches.

They surged into the trenches.

The circle was slowly closing: the darkness of the heavens descended upon the powder chamber. At the most critical moment, the captain, preoccupied with measuring the quantity of his last breath, raised his pistol in a split second and fired. Instead of sound or smell or light, the rose of

his shot bloomed upward in the last moment of their consciousness (before it was extinguished forever). Around that rose shimmered a bright aura; it trembled slightly, like a messenger from the next world.

The young visitor thinks: who, looking today at these skulls built into the walls of the tower, would assume any fundamental link between the historically recorded event on the hill of Čegar[1] and the moment when, propping their heads with their hands, they directed their eyes as one person through the narrow opening of the tent into the unseen?

Many skulls are missing, fallen long ago from the walls of the tower and lost forever.

With time, they have changed entirely, their constant presence a reminder of this fatal battle. That is perhaps why, even today when the first sun of spring shines on them from Čegar, the skulls grow darker instead of glowing. And in the winter when the unbroken snow begins to sparkle, they gleam with cold whiteness.

The young visitor looks at them as an astronomer would observe celestial bodies.

All those skulls once belonged to entirely ordinary people like himself, he thinks.

Dry, petrified behind the calm, gray surface of the protective glass, they live in ethereal eternity.

And it is as if each of those four rectangular glass surfaces extends past the small, narrow windows and the entrance door into the dense currents of the busy everyday life that is reflected and mirrored in them. But only for a moment; then they become again the quiet envelopes of these walls of bones. Those glass walls hover like mirrors in which faces long gone are reflected, but only the underlying bones can be seen.

Each of these skulls, the young visitor thinks, longs today for its own lost face. One of them longs for a big, motionless face with elongated wrinkles and black, ugly, protruding bags under the eyes. Another for a well-proportioned oval face with delicate and tender rosy skin. This man surely slicked his hair back, parting it on the left side; instead of a

1. On May 31, 1890, in the battle of Čegar hill, near the city of Niš, the Serbian commander Stevan Sindjelić fired into the powder chamber, choosing death for himself and his men rather than surrender to the overpowering Turks. To strike fear into the hearts of the local Serbian population, the Turkish commandant ordered that the skulls of the slain Serbian insurgents be used to build a tower. Of some 3,000 Serbs killed, the skulls of 952 of them were built into its walls. (Translator's note)

nose, he now has a small rounded blotch like a nose flattened against the glass. Opposite him, there is a skull with sharp features, slightly tilted to one side; once it had a finely sculpted nose and between the nostrils and the upper lip there was probably a dark mustache. The smooth surface of another skull most likely corresponds to the smooth surface of the former face and each of its parts.

With each new group of guests, the young visitor repeatedly listens to the guide's story of the unprecedented heroism of the insurgents from Resava and about their captain who led them into the fateful battle. And up until the last moment, it was uncertain whether other commanders with soldiers from the southeastern front would come to their rescue.

"The well-known Serbian rivalries!" pronounces the guide emphatically, arousing the appropriate psychological tension in the visitors.

Did everything necessarily have to be that way? they wonder, contemplating the consequences of the battle.

If we don't assume that everything could be different, we will accept the inevitable, thinks the young visitor. Or better yet, the predetermined, he corrects himself. An epoch barely comes to a close, and we have already begun to scrutinize certain events from its life and history. I am bringing up new details that shed light on the old details. If this or that had been done, or if something else had not been done, then neither the following event nor the subsequent experience would have had such an outcome. It would have been different. Many fateful moments have already been reconsidered and reexamined. Some were overestimated and others were underestimated (then the first underestimated again and the latter overestimated); they were viewed from different angles, from which the same moments are seen in a different light. One can always find reasons to look for new facts in light of old circumstances. It seems that the latest facts are decisive. But in general, all things considered, it is still not by coincidence that all of those facts were interpreted as they were and not in some other way. In moments like this, every single case is reexamined (just as he is doing now): hasn't consideration of some element that affected the course of the events been forgotten?

Aware of this, the young visitor tries to go back to the facts he learned from archives and books. But all those facts are fading away, faced with the meaning and the riddle of life and death experienced in the whirlwind of time.

All those heroes, it now seems to him, had to remain on that strange, hellish stage. They had to play every scene according to fate's preconceived plan; it was fate that pulled the strings. In the service of immediate interests, they were lifted upward into the tranquil sky by that shot into the powder chamber. Death was their only and last support. The thought that as yet not everything was lost, that there was still a way out that was not horribly shameful, offered them much less joy than the bitterness with which they prepared for their departure. They would have taken their farewell more calmly and with clearer conscience if they had not felt so helpless and useless. The distant landscape began to disappear in the sorrowful twilight, and the brave men continued to fight up to the last moment, until the fateful shot. Nature was still, as if nothing had happened. But above, the sky was a monotonous gray and a pattern of gray clouds spread over the mountains as the only distinct shape, covering the entire sky. Above Čegar, the young visitor envisions the shining and almost weightless head of the captain hanging as if suspended from the sky on threadlike wisps of clouds. It looks as though it has just separated from its body and taken off, flown up above the hills into the domed vastness of the sky. And it is impossible to discern whether the copper-red face is noble or vicious, good or evil. On that face, as calm as all dead faces, flickers a barely perceptible ironic smile.

Only the young visitor can see that smile. This is the captain mocking the new rivalries, he thinks.

Time is wearing away at Skull Tower. There are disputes concerning the protection of the tower. Some support plans for restoring the exterior and interior of the chapel, while others insist that to prevent further deterioration, restoration of the bones must not be postponed. Since the building is in poor condition, they argue, a new building should be erected around the existing chapel, in which there will be more air and space with controlled humidity and temperature. This would protect the skulls from further deterioration. Fearing that all preservation efforts would stop here, still others support using the latest scientific methods to preserve and restore the bones.

The ironic smile from the sky is directed at these disagreements as well.

Deep in thought, reflecting on the incorporeal presence of those whose skulls are embedded in these fragile, deteriorating walls, the young visi-

tor is trying to imagine how the Resava heroes felt in their last hours: happy indifference before the fiery flood of death.

The young visitor sees the bony walls of the Skull Tower everywhere around him.

At home, countless times in the half-light of his room he discerns a figure. Since it always has its back to him, he wants it to turn toward him, to see its face. The figure actually begins to move, then suddenly disappears into the darkness.

The young visitor sees some special warning in this.

Long afterward, he feels as if his own head were built into a wall. The invisible but ever present wall of his room is studded with skulls, and he examines each of them one by one, searching for his own.

Translated by Amanda Blasko

Tiodor Rosić

Tiodor Rosić, poet, literary theorist, and writer of short stories, was born in 1950. He has published several collections of poetry and fairy tales for children. His collections of short-short stories are *A Goat Who Wouldn't Be Mounted* (1987) and *Twelfthtide Days* (1995). His novel is *The Dog's Skin* (1990).

In his stories, everyday realities turn into bizarre happenings that cannot be explained in a usual manner.

Rosić is an editor of BIGZ, a publishing house in Belgrade.

THE YELLOW DOG

Angelina and her husband, Vasilije Obradović, lived on the ground floor at 31 Deligradska Street, next to a coppersmith, near the Prokupac bar. Angelina was a housewife, she bore three children, she knitted, cooked, and cleaned the house. At the age of eighteen months, each child dried up, withered, and died of some strange illness.

The children died, Angelina's sight deteriorated, she lost her desire for knitting, for further births, she didn't even keep house the way she should. She complained that her hands were growing, they were changing into paws, everything has stopped, people and automobiles no longer move. When there was a full moon she would go out on the veranda and raise her hands above her head to warm them in the moonlight.

Vasilije had a small business building houses and digging tunnels. He remodeled many apartments; only for his own did he have no time. He left it for better times, but when his children died, he stopped building even for others. He sold his business and became a day laborer. I'll turn over the money today, I'll turn it over tomorrow, he said to Angelina, but he didn't turn it over either today or tomorrow. When he returned from his day labor—bricklaying, painting, or carpentry work, depending on what he was offered—he stopped in at the Prokupac, drank brandy, rooted for the Red Star team, sang to himself in his beard, and sometimes, for no reason, he laughed. When he ran out of money for brandy, he bought miniatures, loaded his pockets with them, and, sitting at the bar, secretly poured them into his glass.

"With Vasilije," they said, "it never goes dry."

Angelina sold the living room set. "It is made out of wood cut in the first quarter of the moon," she said. At length and in detail she explained how, in wood cut during the days of the first and second quarters (the first and second half-moons), a weevil lays eggs, how out of them, in time, a weevil develops. "We have to sell the furniture. I can't sleep because of the weevil," she explained to herself and to her husband. After that, she sold the jewelry that had been left to her by her mother; and, at the end, for Saint Nicholas's Day (the day of her husband's and her deceased childrens' patron saint), her wedding ring. "I had to do it," she informed her husband, "the ring had already grown into my finger, I hardly got it off."

For the saint's feast day she prepared carp, radishes, potato and cabbage salad, wheat cake, and plain apple pastry; she cut the sacramental bread in church; and, sitting by the tall candle burning for the saint, she waited for her husband to arrive for dinner. When Vasilije finally appeared, he went straight to bed and fell asleep. He slept uneasily, twitching and groaning. "I won't!" he repeated, turning himself over. The empty miniature bottles fell out of his pockets onto the bed, rolled about, and fell on the floor.

Angelina ate alone. She collected the scraps, threw them into the trash pail. She picked up the miniature bottles and moved toward the door. At the door she stopped, turned toward her husband, waving her hand dismissively. She went out into the courtyard, by the street, and threw the trash into the container, but returned without the trash or the pail. She flew into the house, breathless, disheveled. "Vasilije, Vasilije!" She shook her husband by the shoulder.

"What is it, for God's sake?" he asked, not opening his eyes.

"I almost lost my head," she said.

"Who?" he replied.

"Me!" she answered.

"How?" he asked, raising himself on his elbows.

"When I threw out the trash, a dog was waiting for me behind the container! He was yellow. He had shiny eyes . . . Probably he was rabid."

"It's always something with you," her husband replied.

"What do you mean, always something, by God," she protested. "He tore at my clothes, I almost lost my head!"

"Women," said Vasilije. "You could have done the same thing to him. That would be entertaining!" he added, laughing.

At first, he laughed unobtrusively; in fact, he just smirked; but then, being drunk, he began to belch and giggle. As he giggled, Angelina noticed shreds of fabric and threads from her house dress between his teeth.

Translated by Veselin M. Šćekić

Radosav Stojanović

A poet, prose fiction writer, and critic, Radosav Stojanović was born in 1950 in the region of Kosovo. He studied at the University of Priština. He still works and lives in the city of Priština. He has published three collections of poetry: *The Allegory* (1979), *The Manuscript from Čemer* (1982), and *Devil's School* (1988). His two books of short stories are *The Death of Ariton* (1984) and *Apocryphal Stories* (1988). In 1993 he published a novel, *The End of the World.*

THE CLOCK IN THE
ROOFBEAM OF HVOSNO

Even now, from time to time, when I shut my eyes and plunge myself into darkness, I hear the clock from the old house beating its own time serenely. Yet as the years pass, I feel less and less its soothing pulses and I have become ever more lonely, sad, and nervous. Sometimes months pass during which I neither remember the clock nor hear its clear, tranquil progress through time. As though the time in which now I live and the pulses that the clock measures do not have anything in common. My own time became crushed into small change, cheap coins, pulled apart like my own life, while its time remained part of eternity, part of an inexhaustible ocean of tranquility and warmth. Today things look more and more that way.

No, I am not talking of an antique family clock. We didn't have a clock to tell the time in Hvosno. We never needed one. We mostly measured the time by sun and daylight. For us, there was dawn, morning, evening, and midnight. The smaller and more precise hours we used to estimate roughly by how long it would be until sundown, or by the length of a man's shadow, which we measured with our feet. There was never any problem with time; we always agreed easily and always arrived at the meeting place on time, at the right hour.

Perhaps the invisible clock had existed in our old house even before I discovered it, when I was in the sixth grade of elementary school. It's hard to say whether it happened by chance or not, but I was first expelled from school and then transferred instead to another class where I really didn't want to go. On the day I was expelled, I came home de-

pressed and gloomy and immediately went to lie down on my wooden bed. I felt like crying aloud, but only choked on my tears. Now that the school was set against me, nothing mattered any longer, friends or games, school or studies. I felt completely alone, without any support, as helpless as a baby.

I didn't have a father. Mother worked as a sharecropper. My two brothers and sister were gone. Who could I confide in? Who would understand me? No one! Who was there to lend me a helping hand, to support me? True, I had punched the principal's son right in the eye. (A bruise the size of a plum immediately appeared on the spot.) No one wanted to hear why I did it, or that he had called me a *shkiya*, what they all call us, the Serbs, at Hvosno. I didn't resist and I smacked him. I wouldn't allow him to insult me. The school administration tried to hide it and I was kicked out, while the principal's brat got a warning: "One more offense and you will be expelled."

I was lying flat on my bed, sad and immersed in my thoughts; then, looking at the sooty beams of the ceiling, all of a sudden I started to feel how somewhere in the beams, silently like a good antique clock, time was ticking. At first I thought it might be a real clock, even though I knew we didn't have one. But after convincing myself that we hadn't anything of the kind, I returned to the bed and remained there for a long time staring at the ceiling, from which low but perceptible pulsations reached me. The clock was beating serenely, as though nothing else moved except its calm, simple sail through time. As though nothing else existed but its tranquil pace. I couldn't help myself; I went again to check, climbed to the attic, listened around, but I could not find out the cause of this strange phenomenon. I went outside repeatedly and returned to the house, checking to see whether the clock could still be heard. I changed my angle and position in the shanty, but it kept on ticking patiently and persistently, as though on some see-saw of time. I completely forgot the misfortune that had befallen me that day and fixed my eyes instead on the ceiling, listening to the ticking of the invisible clock hidden somewhere in the sooty rafters.

I started to believe that the house itself was measuring its own—or perhaps our family's—time. After that I understood that most probably our old house breathes in that way. Since that time, I've tried to pay attention to the invisible clock. Its regular beating would soothe me, mak-

ing me concentrate on my own self, returning my self-confidence. It would speak to me: "What are all the pains and problems that now torture you, compared to the endless sea of time that flows on for centuries, and into which we all flow at the end?" The invisible clock became a measure of my life. I turned to it whenever I didn't have a solution for a real-life situation. Whenever I felt like sobbing, I listened to its calm pulsations, finding in them peace and support. When I lacked force and will, I felt its calm thrust through space, its beating in my veins. There were days when its stifled sound was the only thing I had left, when all I wanted was to hear its pulse once more, and then I could accept whatever was coming to me.

Soon I was back in school, in a different class, though. They couldn't forget my dead father's merits. He had been the commander of a brigade during the resistance. I didn't ascribe my return to school to that mysterious and calming sound coming from the sooty ceiling, which I listened to more and more often during sad nights. This was more like the justice one tastes after some personal misfortune. I finished grade school, it seemed to me, thanks to the clock, which taught me patience and the wisdom that everything passes. Indeed, it was true. There were many changes in my family. I was studying in town. Mother was getting old; my brothers and my sister got married and were scattered around. Only the invisible clock, like a good spirit of our house, continued to tick patiently in the ceiling beams, as though it were in a vein of our general transiency. Coming home for school breaks and official holidays, I looked forward to its silent ticking. It always gave me the strength to withstand pressure, to finish up things that I had started, to overcome obstacles that life put before me.

Then Marika came into my life, and then children and a job in the city. At the end, our mother, after having borne four children, remained alone in Hvosno. Life took its own course. With time, we all drifted apart and started to forget our common nest. Only mother's letters arrived, from time to time, in cyrillic and written with peasant's hand, and then they too became all the more rare. We all continued to invite her to move in with us. Surely there was room for her in any of her children's homes, but she wouldn't accept. At times, after seeing my wife and children off to the seashore, I would go to Metohija to spend a few days there in the shade of the old orchard and the shelter of old memories. I would

help around the house, fix the fence around the yard, repair the thresher and the barn, or paint the house. And then, as in my youth, I would listen to the ticking of the old clock. I had the feeling that I was living in a world entirely different and, for me, almost forgotten and lost forever. This listening, I felt, restored my strength, and I would return rested and more self-confident. However, I was not able to go to the old clock whenever I needed it. Life develops its own demands independent of our own.

Then Marika went her own way and the children with her. Mother died while I was on a business trip, and only the oldest brother attended the funeral. The others, just like myself, were busy with important affairs. When I came back, forty days had already passed since her death. One day I was invited to my oldest brother's house. This was the first time we would all be together since we had left Hvosno. We were joined by a stout older man with a twisted moustache. I didn't know him. My oldest brother introduced him. He was our mother's neighbor. He had come to Hvosno some six years ago. He had helped mother a lot. He had also assisted with the funeral. While mother was alive, he and she had made a deal whereby he would buy the house and the three hectares of land near the river and give the money to us. The little fellow kept nodding his head, trying to say something about how good our mother was, but he had difficulty with the language. My brothers and sister said that they agreed with the plan, since nobody came to Hvosno anymore. The man had already got the money and was ready to pay. He told us that he would pay in German marks, which was the way real estate deals were transacted at the time in Metohija; he would even raise the sale price because we had come to an understanding so easily and because we honored the agreement he had made with our mother. It was her will, he repeated. Just at that moment, I felt the old clock start to tick desperately inside me.

"No, I don't want to give up the house!" I said, amazing them all.

"What? Didn't we all agree to this?" my oldest brother asked.

"We did, but I don't want to give up the house. You can do with the land whatever you wish."

"We all agreed that no one will return to Hvosno. Even you said so. What do you want now?"

"I don't know whether I'll come back or not, but I don't want to give up the house. Our clock is still ticking there . . ."

"What clock? Don't talk nonsense!" they said in one voice.

"I'll add one thousand more for the house," said the sinewy old man, "even though it is not worth it," he added more for himself than for us.

"What are you going to do with this rotten shack? It will surely collapse under the next winter's snow!" said my sister excitedly.

"This man is going to build a bigger house out of bricks. For him too this one is too small. He has a big family. He is even giving us more money," added my middle brother.

"I could not give up the house even if it were wormeaten. I simply cannot," I repeated.

"You take for yourself the extra thousand he is giving us. With your share of the money, you can buy a summer cottage in Grocka," my oldest brother said.

"I don't want money," I said.

"What exactly do you want? You neither want to live there nor to sell it?" asked my sister.

"I want to know my birthplace. I wasn't brought to this world out of nowhere. My heart still beats in those roofbeams."

"If you didn't find that out until now, you never will!" said my middle brother.

"Don't you see that everybody is moving away from here? I don't have to tell you that, you know it all. If you don't sell the house now, in a few years you'll have to give it away. After all, wasn't that our mother's will? If no one wants to return to the house, we ought to sell it to this man, or else all will go to ruin. You can see this man is honest," said my oldest brother.

"I am not saying anything bad about this man. I am not going to part with the house; you can sell your own parts. I cannot sell what I didn't earn. As far as I am concerned, Mother cannot do so either. The house is older than all of us."

After this, we parted without closing the deal. They were all angry with me. I myself felt full of some emptiness, which like an echo multiplied a certain muffled fear. A few weeks later, they called me again to come and meet at my oldest brother's place. I told them that I would come over my dead body, and that I wasn't going to give up the house in which I was born and where my heart was still beating. What happened after that I do not know.

Many years have passed. I never went to Hvosno again.

I'm sure that whenever they remember this, my brothers curse me. Yet I couldn't do it any other way. In that house remained the only clock I cared for.

For some time now I have not been able to hear the clock from the old house. It doesn't help even when I bury my head in my palms. I have a harder and harder time recalling it. For whom is the invisible clock now ticking, in the roofbeams of the old house, if it still exists? Our time has already run out. As for myself, I am constantly running after that beat, as though I am following the lost sound of my name.

Translated by Radmila Gorup and Hallie Stein

Jovan Radulović

Jovan Radulović, born in 1951 near Knin, is a story writer, novelist, and playwright. He published three collections of stories: *The Month of July* (1978), *The Pigeon's Abyss* (1980), and *Far from the Altar* (1988). His novels are *Half Brothers* (1986) and *The Life Has Gone* (1997).

His stories have been translated into many languages and his works have been awarded prestigious literary awards, including the Andrić Prize for *Far from the Altar*.

Radulović's stories are historically defined and evoke tragic experiences from his own childhood.

Radulović works and lives in Belgrade.

LINEA GRIMANI

> And as it is appointed unto men once to die, but after this the judgment . . .
>
> The Epistle of Paul the Apostle to the Hebrews 9:27

Of the former Glišan's inn, which later became an Italian border watchtower, now only ruins remain—gray, full of lichen—and there are fewer of those every day. The dried-out lime mixed with sand is crumbling and stones barely hold together; during the autumn rains even these start sliding, causing whole corners of the building to fall. First, one can hear creaking, squeaking, and then resounding thunder—one feels guilty without reason, searches for something within oneself, although one doesn't know what that might be.

There is no real road to Glišan's ruins. It did exist once, but it is now all worn away and has turned into a ditch. The cobblestones have been pulled out and taken somewhere else. Only around the edges can there be seen a forgotten and smoothed-out tile or two. Blackberries weave wreaths along both sides of the road. Lizards of all kinds, and sometimes even a viper, rustle in the weeds. Sparse foliage has grown up. Wild grapes have wrapped the tree trunks. By midsummer they are totally dried out by the sun. The red berries turn rock hard—because of the local name, "snake's grape," children rarely pick them. Even though they are touched by chance, a child will run home and wash his hands, rubbing them with soap for a long time.

Although it is difficult to climb up to Glišan's ruins, there are those

who spare no effort when they need well-cut stones. Thus the building's thresholds and cornerstones were first to go. Today the smaller stones are hauled away by teamsters. The inn went out of business and was ruined at the same time that ruin came to its owner. According to gossip, this happened more than a hundred years ago. It was restored not as an inn but as a border watchtower, when the Italians took over the border with Bosnia after World War I, following the frontier line just below the Dinaric Range established by maps over two hundred years old. The line was labeled *Linea Grimani,* named for a Venetian official, Giovanni Grimani, who once marked the border between the Ottoman Empire and the Republic of Saint Mark. The Italians were angry with the local population, who every so often crossed from one side to the other and who did not recognize their maps and borders.

Why is it that the wild nut trees, stinking and empty-shelled, not even good for firewood, like to grow in such places? Next to these, growing right out of the building's foundations, are ivy, dog rose, traveler's joy, and nettle burst. Thus both the former Glišan's inn and the Italian watchtower became haunted. People stopped by rarely during the day. Even the tobacco black marketeers ran away from the ruins, fearing they would bring them bad luck or might be a trap set by the tax collectors. Yet sometimes someone stops by on the road to town to relieve himself, hidden by the ruins.

In the past, the military used to come to the hill—one can see the tracks of maneuvers, of bunkers, half-filled trenches overgrown with blackberries. Local boys turned over every stone searching for empty ammunition shells, delighted by their yellow brass color.

An archeological team arrived at the ruins of Glišan's inn and the Italian watchtower. They brought workers along and put up a tent. They cut down the foliage, cleared it out, and cleaned away the excrement. The custodian of the local museum, a professor, and a few students eagerly await what will be unearthed by their explorations. Every lump of soil is crumbled and set through the sifter. So far nothing has been found, although they have even dug under the foundations.

Would anyone have thought of searching for anything here, if someone, while deep-plowing a vineyard with a tractor, had not dug out heaps of bones and skulls under the hill on which the ruins stand? The mystery was solved quickly: exactly on that spot, about a hundred years ago, a

group of Bosnian paupers were buried after they rose up against the Turks and fled to Dalmatia before the Turkish terror.

People quickly forgot the wretched Bosnians and their deaths from typhus and hunger. The unmarked and untended graves fell in and disappeared. The land, neglected for so long, was again cultivated. It was plowed, fertilized, dug. Crops were changed annually. After a hundred years, it was time for a vineyard. The field had to be deeply plowed. The tractor's plow cut the sandy soil, crumbled chunks of earth, and look—it turned up the bones hidden so long ago. They were gathered into a heap. Whoever passed by would stop and take a look, especially children. Messages were sent to Bosnia—to Mračaj, Crni Lug, Peulje, Obljaj. It was known approximately to which villages and families the remains might belong, but nobody arrived to claim them. Nobody even pronounced the words: "We don't care whether they lie here or there." The curious followed the plow, they crumbled the soil with their fingers hoping to find something of value: a ring, a wedding ring, a knife, even a simple hook or a chain link. The wretched Bosnians went to their graves with nothing of any value. If they had anything, it quickly turned into dust.

Both Glišan's and Guiseppe's graves were opened. The teacher rolled a big stone downhill, and sure enough, just three feet below the surface, two skeletons were discovered. The older skull was empty but had all its teeth. He decided to take it and keep it in the classroom. Ten days later, the archeologists arrived. The stories of Glišan's inn and the Italian watchtower were resurrected—the ones about the accursed owner and the commander, about the destiny that joined them in a common grave.

2

Nobody remembered Glišan's surname.

He was an orphan when he came down from the mountain Dinara. Only rags hung from his body and he was totally penniless. At the first inn he stopped at, he got a job roasting lambs and suckling pigs. Although he was young and untried, he became good at the job. He could cut the thickest wood and remove the hardest stump. For all his work, he received only a miserable wage from the innkeeper, and a special re-

ward was bread to dip in the fat that dripped into the dish beneath the lamb as it cooked. The innkeeper never left him alone—when there was no roasting to be done, he made Glišan collect two buckets of dung along the road where cows and horses trod for his garden. It was not so easy. Other kids collected the dung as well. Often there were quarrels and fights: who will first catch the animals' droppings? Most often, it was Glišan who came out the winner. Because of his obedience and hard work, the innkeeper took him on permanently a few years later and paid him a monthly salary. Glišan never spent a penny on himself. He listened to the innkeeper's advice—money should be saved for tough times—and, just as the innkeeper did, he began to lend his money at high rates of interest.

After he amassed enough money, and after being exempted from military service by the draft commission, Glišan bought land on a hill just outside the town and opened an inn, from which few left sober. By skillfully managing his accounts, according to which everyone owed more than they borrowed, Glišan acquired a large number of debtors. He also acquired friends; refugees from the law who escaped into Bosnia found refuge with him. The police needed him as well. Skillfully and without anyone noticing it, he reported robbers, cattle thieves, and criminals. After completing their sentences, doubting nothing, their first stop would be Glišan's. At his inn, forged receipts were drawn up, false last testaments were written, horses were stolen from their owners, and gold coins disappeared even from people's wallets. Glišan would wander between tables, his right arm always behind his back, and repeat the well-known wise words of the innkeeper: "Do not drink and eat on credit—for credit is a bad companion." Then: "Don't ask me to give you something I can't." Glišan became powerful and started repossessing the houses and property of his debtors, selling them at a profit. The once filthy inn soon grew into a stone building with rooms for rent, an attic, a cellar, stables, and a tall fence around the compound. Many had forgotten that he had come down the mountain and his low beginnings. They were ready to give their daughters to him, but Glišan would frown at the very mention of women and marriage and change the subject to other matters. Glišan had no hired help, no servants. The townspeople understandably wondered if he ever slept.

There was an insurrection in Bosnia. In and around Grahovo, the

Turkish towers were burning, but the paupers' huts were on fire as well. Refugees crossed the Drina and found shelter in caves and holes in the ground near Glišan's inn, ready to do anything for a piece of bread. As much as they were able, they paid by working in the fields. Prominent rich men came from Bosnia to secure their wealth with friends, trusting them to save their sacks of gold coins, then return to take up arms to fight for the liberation of their homeland. Many stopped by Glišan's with this request. They remembered that he had helped them before, even though he demanded a high rate of interest. For such cases, Glišan devised a plan that he executed carefully. He would take a Bosnian into a room and, first in a whisper and then in a louder voice, would set about convincing him not to leave his treasure with anyone, not even with him. One never knows when one will need to take another's property and spend it, he would say. Who knows if one could ever repay it?

Yet he would advise a confused and hesitant Bosnian friend, "My sweet brother, here are my attic, my cellar, my yard, stable . . . Hide it wherever you want . . . So that I don't see it. Only God and you will know where you hid it. Take a mallet, a shovel, dig up a stone, hide it, put the stone back, I will have nothing to do with it . . . When the insurrection is over, if you survive you will find it where you left it . . . My red apple, go kill the Turks . . . If I had someone to leave this work to, I would go with you so that I might chop off a few heads myself."

And suddenly Glišan would grab the Bosnian by his shoulders and, although weak, he would give him a good shake, kissing him like a child a couple of times.

The Bosnian would listen to this friendly advice and conclude that this was the best and safest way to hide his money. For security reasons, he would choose the attic, stable, or cellar over the yard. He would climb up to the stone roof and push the gold coin sack behind some high beam. Glišan would sneak in behind him unnoticed, like a cat. The walls and floorboards had holes known only to him. He would see approximately where the Bosnian had hidden the gold. As they said farewell, the Bosnian would embrace his friend Glišan, saying, "My brother, save this little bit of wretchedness for me. This is all I have. If the Turks kill me, give it to my wife, she will need it to feed the children."

"I know nothing," Glišan would respond. "Did I take the gold from

you? No . . . Then I cannot save it for you . . . God Himself will save it for you, your wife and children . . . Tell your wife where you hid it."

As soon as the darkness fell, Glišan would chase all the guests out of the inn, lock the gate, take candles, go down into the cellar or climb up to the attic, and easily find the hidden treasure. By the following day, he would be lending the money to someone or buying new properties. Nobody suspected anything. They knew him as a thrifty and stingy inn-keeper whose business was doing well.

One evening three Italians, two men and a woman, burst into Glišan's inn. Tired, carrying heavy bags, they explained what their goal was— they wished to cross over to Bosnia and join a fighting unit of rebels as volunteers. The woman took off her shoes, touching her ankles without shame. A twisted muscle caused her to weep long into the night. Glišan was surprised and enchanted as much by her face as by her sudden cries. As if summoned, the police knocked on Glišan's door. The Italians rushed to conceal themselves, looking around helplessly for a hiding place. Glišan was the first to collect himself. He pushed the woman, together with her luggage, under the bed, pulling the covers to the floor. The police burst in, guns cocked, requesting to see all foreign passports. The two men looked at each other in confusion and showed their papers. Their luggage was taken away, and they were tied up and led to jail. Glišan's room wasn't searched further. Thus the pretty Italian woman, Giannetta, remained in Glišan's house and inn, grieving for her companions, who, as it was said, were deported and sent back to where they came from. How much of this was Glišan's doing remains a guess. By money and bribes he did everything to separate Giannetta from her comrades. He managed to convince her to stay with him, that it wasn't time yet for her trip to Bosnia.

Gossip circulated that Giannetta was of noble family and strong blood. Her distant ancestor was a doge of Venice. Now her only goal was to help Bosnian refugees. Mayor Katić offered her accommodations at his house, but she refused. Glišan gave her a whole flat. He chased away the drunks and totally closed the inn. Together they visited the Bosnian refugees in their huts in the fields, brought them supplies, grain, and other food. Other ladies of the town, wives of merchants and military officers, began to emulate the pretty Giannetta, starting a real competi-

tion in patriotism and in good-heartedness. Old chests were opened and brought down from attics, and new goods were ordered from the coastal cities. During these months many a poor soul shed tears of gratitude.

The ugly, rough Glišan and the pretty Italian, Giannetta, started living together, but few believed that she could manage to change his stinginess. People were saying that he would soon rob even her and kick her out on the street. Time passed. Dr. Vujatović confirmed the town gossip—Giannetta was in his office, complaining of morning sickness and vomiting. She was pregnant, and the father was no one else but the ugly Glišan. After such news, the town ladies started avoiding Giannetta, making up horrible stories about her liaison with Glišan. So their patriotism suddenly dwindled; also it didn't make sense anymore—the insurrection was over, the rebel units were dismissed, and the survivors, leaving the graves of their loved ones behind, moved back to their homes over the Dinaric Range.

Of those who left their treasures with Glišan, a few survived; but when they returned to take what was theirs, they left Glišan's inn empty-handed. Glišan would kiss and hug his blood brother, so "happy" that he was alive. He would offer him wine or brandy, and tell him: "There they are, my blood brother, the attic, the cellar, the yard, the stable . . . Seek your treasure . . . You didn't give it to me in my hands. I didn't touch it. I didn't see it . . . What isn't mine I will not even look at."

In vain, the Bosnian searched the attic or the cellar. Silently staring at the walls, bathed in sweat, he would wonder—how could I have forgotten where I pushed the sack? It is not Glišan's fault. The inn and the other buildings are the same as always. Speechless, angry with himself, he would return to Bosnia penniless, where a destroyed and empty hearth and the cries of hungry children awaited him.

Glišan was rough with the widows of Bosnians killed in battle. He wouldn't even allow them to start the story about the hidden gold coins, wouldn't let them sit down. He would chase them away, kicking them in the back and the stomach, threatening them with libel suits. Their husbands spent the gold coins on ladies in brothels. The poor widows, believing their husbands had lied to them, returned across the Dinaric Range into Bosnia, cursing not Glišan but their dead husbands.

One morning, the pretty Giannetta disappeared, heading for the sea. She stormed away in a carriage like the wind. All green and hunched,

Glišan reported her flight to the police, crying that she had robbed him, that she had taken all his gold. The police and their commander laughed, telling him that the person who could fool him hadn't been born yet, and they refused to pursue her. Glišan took off toward Zadar by himself, hoping that Giannetta hadn't yet had time to board a steamer. A week later he returned. Beaten, dusty, a loaf of bread under his arm, he was a carbon copy of the Glišan who had come down from the mountain so long ago.

Glišan fell ill, locked himself in the attic, refused to see anyone. Wounds opened on his body. The few gold coins that remained he pushed into the mattress and lay on them. Guests stopped coming to the inn. The stories made up earlier and now remembered had new elements added to them. All that had happened could have been foreseen since the days of Glišan's first job. The town's street urchins felt a surge of freedom knowing that he was now helpless. They climbed over the wall and broke into the cellar. They used sticks with protruding nails to pierce the wall, even the mattress he slept on. Gold coins fell out. The ruffians irritated and teased Glišan, but he could not defend himself. No matter what side he turned to, it hurt him even more. Fever, thirst, weakness tormented him. Feverishly, he would cry: "Get him! . . . He pointed a gun at me! . . . I did not steal that much! I love Bosnians like brothers . . . I'll return the treasure! . . . Giannetta, the whore, she stole everything!"

Without a doctor's care, food, or help, Glišan decided his own fate. With much difficulty, in the middle of the night he lifted himself out of bed, opened a chest, loaded a pistol, and shot himself in the head. The following morning, when the intruders heard no cries from his bed, the rumor began to circulate that he was dead. A court official, police officers, and a doctor arrived, opened the room, and indeed found the body. As they were discussing what to do with him, where and how to bury him, searching for even distant in-laws, night arrived and the first strange event occurred: around the inn there gathered a few old men and women from Bosnia, together with children, singing songs, celebrating Glišan's death. No one could chase them away. The priest and his parishioners would not consider burying a suicide, especially Glišan, in the cemetery. Therefore, he was lowered into the ground, without a coffin, in his own yard. Not even a wooden cross was erected over his grave.

Glišan's coins and furniture were looted by his distant relatives, who

quickly sold everything, spending the money without concern, telling everybody: "It came with the devil, may it depart with the devil."

Nobody wanted to buy or rent the inn or anything around it that could be used. It was left for time to be the judge.

3

All eyes and ears were turned toward the Dinaric Range.

From that direction, down the slopes, between the pines and beech trees, the Serbian army was supposed to gush out, victorious. That was all anyone talked about. It was December. Nothing came down the Dinaric Range but the cold wind and light snow.

With great enthusiasm, a People's Committee and a People's Guard of about 300 young men were formed overnight. Poorly armed, but orderly and disciplined, they set out on the road to Drvar to prevent the German colonists from the Stammbeis Settlement from destroying the narrow-gauge railroad that was to be used by the Serbian forces on their way to the sea. The Green Cadre members joined them, happy that they no longer had to hide in caves, rotting in the cold and damp.

On December tenth, suddenly, not intending to remain in the town long, Lieutenant Colonel Jeselinković arrived with a small unit. He was not in the mood for celebration. He had no time for toasts, drinking, flowers, and ox roasts. No one knew how events would turn out in this region. He was on his way to Split, following orders. It was clear to everyone that the Italian troops would soon be approaching.

The Italians arrived in ceremonious formation, in large numbers. After the infantry and artillery came the liaison, gendarmerie, and auxiliary units. With unhurried deliberation, they took over the government buildings as if they had left the area yesterday. They behaved as if they knew every citizen. They took the reins of government into their hands. Many spoke the local language.

As the year came to an end, Todor the Guerrilla (who fought in Old Serbia long ago) gathered a group of drunken peasants under cover of darkness, encouraged them, and launched a surprise attack on a column of Italian soldiers. Shooting was heard all night. At dawn on the following day, seven corpses of Italian soldiers lay in front of the city hall. War-

rants were posted offering rewards for the capture of Todor the Guerrilla. In the afternoon, the entire People's Committee was arrested and
taken toward Zadar.

Sergeant Giuseppe Turco—who spoke the language of the people—
was ordered to repair the former Glišan's inn and convert it into a border watchtower, of which he would be the commander. (On that spot, at
the top of the hill, lies the border between Bosnia and Dalmatia, between
Italy and the Kingdom of Serbia, the former so-called Linea Grimani.)

With the help of the local builders and with materials quickly provided from somewhere, Glišan's inn got a new roof. Glass windows were
installed. Freshly painted woodwork dried in the winter sun. The ground
floor was turned into a warehouse and the upper floor became the dor-
mitory. Soon, songs and outbursts of excitement were heard.

The lane that led from the town to Glišan's inn, now the Italian watchtower, was always neglected. This was where, hidden behind the stone
walls along the path and by the blackberry bushes, people relieved themselves during fairs on church holidays. That was how it got the name
Shit Street. Giuseppe Turco decided to stop it. His soldiers cleaned the
street, repaired the ruined walls, cut away the blackberry bushes, and
put up street signs at both ends of the street, naming it: Viuzza Roveto—
or Blackberry Lane. Prevented from using it during the day, people
started using the street at night even more often than before. Giuseppe
was furious. He ordered a guard to be placed in the street. Yet every ten
steps or so, inexplicably, there was excrement or a dirty trace of some
other sort.

When reporting to him, the soldiers defended themselves: "It is impossible. These aren't humans but devils . . . They bring shit in their
pockets, in their hands, and drop it . . . Don't we know how people shit?
. . . They couldn't do it so quickly and standing up."

Every day at a different hour, Giuseppe inspected the border, survey-
ing the Dinaric Range through his binoculars. The soldiers built stone
towers and painted them white. But when they returned the next day,
the towers were down. In vain, they angrily cursed and threatened the
shepherds. The shepherds kept silent. Giuseppe liked to go into peasants' houses and sit next to the hearth, offering candy to the children, tobacco to the elders. Thus he was sometimes invited for lunch and offered
a glass of sour wine or grape brandy.

Along the way, during daily border rounds, Giuseppe couldn't avoid the house of the fugitive Todor the Guerrilla. His wife, the famous weaver Andjelija, and their four little children lived in a low, sooty ground-level hut. The eldest boy had died recently from Spanish fever. Italian headquarters assumed that Todor's heart wouldn't resist and that he would at least visit the cemetery to say good-bye to his son. They prepared an ambush and staked it out for a couple of days and nights, but Todor didn't show up.

In every corner Andjelija had a loom, and colorful yarns hung from hooks in the ceiling beams. When she grew bored with a design, she would abandon it, moving on to the next loom. Her children helped her to spin the yarn. She was still young and pretty, but since her son's death she hadn't put up her hair. Quietly, she wailed and sighed as she worked at her weaving. She thought the Italian sergeant came to find from her where Todor was hiding, so she regarded him with hostility, ready to lie, to fight for her husband and children. Giuseppe asked no more questions. He laughed, drank water from a jug, invited the children to come out of hiding, threw pieces of bread to the cat and the chickens, amusing himself by watching them as they struggled to swallow them.

Giuseppe's visits to Todor's house became more frequent. No longer did he stay only a couple of minutes, just for a drink of water. He would make himself comfortable and start telling stories. The children got to like him. He would take an axe and cut firewood and bring it to the hearth. He was no longer a bother. He didn't ask Andjelija about her husband any more. Did Todor say anything to Andjelija about how she should behave toward the assertive Italian? Did he eavesdrop from some hiding place? No one knows. However it happened, Giuseppe began to greet the dawn in Andjelija's house.

One stormy night, while Giuseppe was taking Todor's place in bed, and while it thundered outside and rain poured down the stone tiles, Todor banged on the door, soaked as a cork, demanding that his wife open up. Giuseppe jumped out of bed. The hearth was still smoking. His pistol didn't come to mind. He was trembling. He held his pants, shirt, boots, military straps. It felt as if these did not belong to him but to someone else. Andjelija hid him behind a loom and, holding a candle, calmly approached the door. Giuseppe, not satisfied with his hiding place, dropped his clothes on the floor and got into the children's bed,

pressing against their warm, sleepy bodies while saying good-bye to his life. The children didn't move. Andjelija opened the door. In the candlelight Giuseppe saw a tall and bearded man, his gun pointed at the ground. Andjelija didn't let him cross the threshold. Whispering, she hissed in his face, "What in the devil's name are you doing here?"

"See for yourself. I have to change and warm up."

"The Italian was looking for you a while ago . . . He will return . . . Do you want them to kill me and the kids because of you? To burn the house? . . . Go away!"

Todor cursed the Italians, put a curse on his guerrilla life, and still drenched, disappeared again into the night to continue getting wet and ruined.

Andjelija locked the door. Giuseppe sighed with relief, got out of the children's bed, and sat next to the hearth in his underwear. With his bare feet he pushed through the embers, stepping on them, torturing the soles of his feet. What was that pain, compared with what this woman's husband had to endure? And she was a real martyr as well, not a whore, in spite of the fact that she chased away her husband from his own door. What right did he, Giuseppe, have to this woman and to this house instead of their rightful husband and owner?

Giuseppe continued to inspect the border, but he firmly decided never to enter Andjelija's house again. From the low hut could be heard the sound of a loom: three quick thuds, then silence, and then three more. It was their prearranged signal that the house was clear. Fighting himself, Giuseppe would hasten his steps. As soon as he couldn't hear the thuds any more, it would be easier for him.

Suddenly, amid the new spring foliage, Giuseppe and Todor ran into each other. They stopped, looked at each other eye-to-eye. Both had guns in their hands. Then, as if they had agreed previously, each broke away from the other and almost simultaneously shot their pistols into the air.

By the beginning of April 1921, the Italians knew that the Grimani border was no longer valid, that it would not exist for long. They would have to move. One unit after another was leaving the town. The people again rejoiced, hoping that the time had finally come for the Serbian army to spill down the Dinaric slopes with flags and songs. So, Giuseppe Turco went on his last inspection tour along the border. It will never be

known whether he intended to visit Andjelija for the last time. In the ravine made by the stream, overflowing and loud at that time of year, near a small forest of beeches, he set a bottle on a high rock and shot at it from twenty paces. He missed three times, but stubbornly continued to try to hit it. After cocking the pistol for the fourth time, he heard a shotgun blast. The bottle burst into pieces, which landed in the water. In disbelief, Giuseppe turned toward the direction of the blast. Slowly, his gun raised, Andjelija's husband, Todor, approached. He looked straight into the Italian's eyes, and when he was just a step or two away, he shot at his chest as if it were an immovable target.

Giuseppe's body was found two days later, its head in the water. The watchtower contingent was all set to move. Glišan's inn was again hauntingly empty, without furniture, woodwork, or roof. The death caused little excitement among the people and Giuseppe's comrades and superiors. Nobody mentioned or looked for the murderer. Todor escaped to Bosnia with Andjelija and the children. The Italians had been there two years, imposing their rule; at least at their departure they should be punished. A soldier said, "Lord, if only it might end with this!"

Giuseppe's body was brought down on horseback. The most convenient solution was to open Glišan's grave. Thus, if his relatives wanted to find him, it would be easier for them. He was lowered without a funeral speech or gunfire salute. Fifteen minutes later, the last Italian soldier left the watchtower on the Linea Grimani.

Translated by Višeslav Simić

Dragan Velikić

Dragan Velikić is a prose writer and essayist. His collection of short stories, *The Erroneous Movement,* was published in 1983. His novels are: *The Greenhouse* (1985), *Via Pula* (1988), *Astrakhan Fur* (1991), *Hamsin 51* (1993), *The Northern Wall* (1995), and *Dante's Square* (1997).

In his postmodern fiction, Velikić patiently and masterfully assembles a literary mosaic out of decomposed fragments of reality. Characteristic of the author's poetics is an emphasis on paranormal phenomena.

A WOMAN FROM
A CATALOGUE

Janko Belog tore the yellow wrapping off the parcel as he stood in the doorway of his apartment. He looked carefully at the thin elongated hard-cover notebook as if he were searching for some hidden sign. The mailman kept coughing impatiently, waiting for the signature, but only when he stamped his right foot on the cement floor did Janko raise his head; mumbling some words of apology, he signed the blank.

After one year of patient waiting, here finally was the first response. He was so excited that he stood indecisively for a full five minutes before the door until he heard steps on the staircase. Then he entered the apartment, locked the door, and stared through the peephole. The bright blond hair of the subtenant from upstairs blocked his entire view for a second. The door on the other side of the porch opened and swallowed the slender blonde. Janko's neighbor, a retired major with thick eyebrows and a deep cracked voice, entertained the subtenant from upstairs every Saturday early in the afternoon. Janko could only suppose what went on behind the closed door. The girl came only on Saturdays, and that fact was for Janko sufficient proof that her visits, never longer than an hour, were well rewarded with rustling bank notes. He was carried away for a long time with the idea that he himself should set a day for a visit from the beautiful subtenant—let us say Sunday, when he is most rested. But he was too shy to get to know the girl without an intermediary, and the idea of the major performing this role was humiliating. His biggest concern was, however, the limited time of the visit. With his modest teacher's salary, he could never afford a whole afternoon. Finally, from all this re-

mained a strange habit. During their meetings he would sip his liqueur and daydream about the day when the major would run out of strength or money and the girl would look for the closest source of supplementary income and knock on the door of Janko's apartment. So on that Saturday, with the parcel under his arm, he walked to the kitchen cabinet and poured dark walnut liqueur into a long thin glass on the low table. He raised it high, as if toasting an invisible guest or examining the color of the fluid, and drank it in one swallow. But this time he held in his hands a parcel, the long-awaited dossier, and the strange couple, separated from him only by a thick wall, quickly disappeared from his thoughts.

Janko Belog, professor of chemistry in the nursing school, accurate and orderly as only bachelors can be, dreamed for years about the catalogue in which he could record important events, memories, and dreams, everything that leaves a trace in life. The law of order, Belog thought, represented the fundamental natural law. When one was introduced to someone new, it would be necessary only to exchange dossiers and to surrender oneself to an interesting journey. The advantage of such a transaction was indisputable, even if one acknowledges that the author of the dossier presenting himself would be giving an embellished image of his inner world.

The idea of the dossier appeared to him in a dream. Many years ago, his Russian colleague Dmitri Ivanovich Mendeleyev caught the inspiration for his unique periodic table in the darkness of a dream. The blanks that tortured him for years stopped being a riddle. Mendeleyev quickly composed the periodic system of elements. With its help, scientists could predict the characteristics of still undiscovered elements. The periodic system became the basis of modern scientific knowledge about the structure of matter. Belog's dossier would offer completely new relations between people. It would free them from loneliness, from unbridgeable divisions, and would make possible easy togetherness and a higher degree of communication.

Janko found predictions of many events in his dreams, although he did not believe in the mystical meaning of nightmares. A dream is only a catalyst, an optimal condition that facilitates the appearance of the essence of future events. Like most shy men, he daydreamed about the magical ways of approaching a woman. The winged, invisible voyeur who first

materialized in his daydreams as a boy did not change very much over the course of years. He entered the bedrooms of women, made love to them, and fled the love nests. With these daydreams he would fall asleep.

He walked through an unknown city on a humid afternoon with nobody in sight. The sky was gray and it was about to rain. He hurried toward an enormous building on the square. When he felt the first drops of rain, he was already ascending the wide steps up to the building. Next to the entrance, adorned with carved wood bas-relief, he saw a marble plate on which were four words in big letters: The Museum of Women.

A custodian offered him a catalogue in the cold anteroom. There were two photographs on every page: a portrait and a nude statue of a woman, and below them was recorded the year of her birth, where she was born, her weight, breast size, hip size, eye color, a description of her character, and a large number of important facts. A visitor could buy what was displayed either with credit or cash. With his right hand, Janko groped for his wallet in the inside pocket of his jacket.

He was walking through the empty corridor, carefully viewing the exhibits in imaginatively decorated compartments. He saw a cave and a woman covered in a wolf's hide. She was strong with long black hair, and the whites of her eyes were as big as an animal's. One exposed breast was round and full, with a nipple the size of a walnut that trembled at the slightest motion. In the next compartment, on an easy chair next to the burned remnants of a temple, reclined a woman in a purple dress with a dreamy look. With a dappled fan she cooled her pale bosom and her narrow face framed with black hair. Further there were several empty and half-furnished exhibits, although they were advertised in the catalogue. The museum probably does a good business, Janko thought; it is no wonder that the catalogues soon become obsolete. In the last compartment on the ground floor, adjacent to a brick wall, there was a miniature courtyard decorated with large flowerpots. A woman in a sheer yellow dress sat in a swing holding a glass in her hand. She sang softly a tune that seemed very familiar to Janko. She smiled and with her free hand raised her hair seductively from her shoulder. Janko circled the number of the woman in the catalogue (it listed numbers, not names), deeply convinced that he would not find a better exhibit even on the next floor. But while he was climbing the marble staircase, he suddenly slipped and fell.

He woke up in a dark room, sweating from the dream. Through the half-open window, he felt the evening freshness.

He thought about the museum of women for several days afterward. The chosen exhibit appeared to him as a momentary vision as he explained chemical processes to students in the laboratory. One late afternoon, after a long walk, he started to write a dossier. He wrote for days the most intimate facts about himself, attempting to create as true an image of himself as possible. He completed the definitive version in two months and searched for marriage ads in order to check the efficacy of the dossier. The experience was devastating; he sent more than twenty typewritten copies of the dossier without receiving a single answer for almost a year. Women whose self-described principal qualifications were that they did not smoke or drink, or feel a need for adventure, and were divorced (never by their own fault), were, to put it mildly, confused by Janko Belog's biography.

Janko's surprise was therefore understandable when the mailman brought a parcel that day: thirty neatly photocopied pages bound in a hard cover. On the first page was the name of the author: Zora Petrović. Inside the wrapping he found a short letter. A middle-aged woman, whose ad had attracted his attention eight days ago, invited him to visit her on Saturday after five o'clock. He carefully examined the postmark, surpised at the post office's carelessness. The registered parcel had taken a full three days to travel from one part of the city to another. Only two hours remained before the time of the visit.

He finished his lunch, swallowing pieces of meat whole. He was too excited to taste anything. Anxiety in his chest threatened to restrain every movement. Before reading Zora Petrović's dossier, he tried to create an image of a well-bred woman as she bent over the densely typewritten text. She raises her head often toward the ceiling and squints. It is not difficult to see the excitement on her face as she catches sight of a pale-looking boy who unsuccessfully tries to slip a transparent condom on his ever softening member, to be transformed on one of the following pages into a calm university lecturer who, with a measured voice, explains to his students the process of crystallization. He fills in the small squares with manicured fingers (at the beginning of each school year he composes a perfect class schedule, which is his modest contribution to

the idea of universal order). An unknown reader, a middle-aged woman, enters the darkness of the laboratory where female students jostle each other to observe the birth of photographs in shallow dishes under a red light. Separated from the group, not interested in the images swimming at the bottom, stands a stocky girl with an ugly freckled face. She will reveal her sturdy body to the professor without passion when they are alone in the photo lab. Janko hid nothing in his confession and used dark tones mercilessly. This was a part of a thought-out gambit: to reveal himself before an unknown woman to forestall failure, since the person who had decided to meet him, after everything he had written about himself, would be different from all those other disappointed spinsters and lascivious divorcées.

Janko did not open the dossier during his lunch or as he took his bath. He kept postponing the moment as he carefully arranged things in their proper places. He stood for a long time in front of the wide open closet choosing a necktie for the forthcoming visit. His anxiety visibly grew, and he opened the notebook only at half past four. At first he read slowly, without missing a single paragraph. Then he started skimming whole pages, and after fifteen minutes he put away the dossier.

II

1. My name is Zora Petrović. To relate facts in an administrative way is to create a false image of oneself. A photograph also lies. It is often a fraction of a second, unreachable to the human eye, a nonexistent instant.

2. Zora, the name I carry and love, not only marks the time of my birth but also my most beloved time of the day.* Sometimes I meet the dawn awake and exhausted by insomnia. Before its arrival, I become restless like the birds in the treetops who suddenly start singing like a well-trained choir. Although the body may be tired, hearing precisely registers the breathing of matter, the streams of air, noises, as if every thought resounds. My breast swells as I look at the widening of the bright lines of the day in the east.

*Zora means dawn in Serbian.

3. I love the pink color of a morning that announces coming rain, glowing colors of summer roses, and the misty blue of the iris. White color disturbs me, a trace remains on it, this the color of betrayal.

4. The smell of the quince brings me back to the enchanting darkness of childhood, to the time when things were enormous and mysterious. The quinces in the cupboard have long since lost their smell, and now they are only yellow balls, plastic fruit in baskets, a kitchen embellishment from the sixties.

5. Thick vapors from the coffee pot (bought during my first trip to Trieste in August 1966) have deposited in time invisible layers on the yellowed kitchen plates, into the pores of the dried-up cabinet, and on the unwhitewashed walls. And I am afraid to cover the dirty walls with soft wallpaper and to surround myself with new, unfamiliar smells.

6. In the winter I timidly turn on the light in the kitchen. The movement of my finger shatters the membrane of the night. The hour before going to work I want to be as conscious as possible. My muscles are tense. I listen to morning sounds. The first bright ray of the winter sun makes me happy as does a cloudy summer morning. I love sea storms, cool August days; the tanned skin shivers under the touch of the soft fabric. I have been trying for years to discover the morning, long extinguished, and I have not found it yet.

7. The man I am looking for, the actor who will revive dead scenes for me, will be not only a doll but a spectator. I will be the heroine of his memories. I will move through the paths of his stories. We will enjoy joint performances alone on stage, actors and spectators at the same time.

10. Since childhood I have been a passionate reader. When I reflect that marriage might have forever stopped this habit, I feel boundless satisfaction that I am without husband, children, and daily domestic obligations. I read a lot, mostly Turgenev, Mann, Tolstoy, and Proust. I am in love with Madame Shosha from Mann's *The Magic Mountain*. Her dialogue with Hans Kastorp I know by heart. Perhaps I only want to live through the sentences and the whole chapters of my most beloved books.

11. An ordinary tablecloth drenched with copper light scattered with oranges is a sight worthy of Cézanne. I want an educated and sensitive man, susceptible to changes in the weather. Our nude bodies on a warm rug bring us the memory of D. H. Lawrence. His *Fox* I read every winter. A lonely woman becomes sensitive, a precise seismological instru-

ment registering the trembling of a man's body. In the morning, in the cold kitchen we sit at the table silently next to each other, each with a glass, as in Dégas's painting "The Absinthe Drinkers." Numerous possibilities are before us, we don't know what memory will record.

18. I have never left the improvised stage of my grandmother's house. Several of us, we grandchildren and children from the neighborhood, used to gather every Sunday to stage theatrical performances, improvising, wearing masks, surrounded by sets that only we could see. I went three times a week to ballet class. I was not talented, but such are the ones who love art with greatest enthusiasm. They don't give up like rejected children who court their parents their entire lives.

19. My first kiss happened in the darkness of a theater box during a matinee performance of *Carmen*. Even today, after so many years, I feel pleasant cramps in the lower part of my body, the swelling of nipples when darkness descends on the spectators at the opera and the tones of the overture illuminate the decorated stage.

20. I walk between the stage curtains, I shyly peep out from behind them—a secondary face that will be already forgotten on the next page. Nevertheless I don't give up, willing to be a part of the background, a stilted photograph, conscious of living an irrevocable instant that is mine only once and never again. "Nevermore," as Edgar Allan Poe would say.

25. It seems to me that time does not flow when one travels. Days on a train, on a boat, in an unfamiliar city, stop the aging process or slow it down. Perhaps they hold back the hands on invisible clocks. When traveling, I am somebody else in a new performance that will never be repeated. Everything is left to improvisation, as it was once long ago in my grandmother's house. There is neither a scenario nor a well-known cast. There are new faces around me. I can have a new name, a new past, a new play every day.

26. While the train pants through nameless cities, an illusionist, a magician, appears at night under the violet light of the sleeping car. When the third dove has flown out of his sleeve, I appear, through the din of applause, ready to bare my body in a ritual practiced who knows how many times before. I have arrived at a point that demands further explanation.

27. I work as a bank employee. I have a well-paid job and I can use the phrase "well taken care of" as regards my finances and residence. I com-

pleted a university degree in economics, and I was a virgin until my twenty-third year. Then I made a fateful decision: I used an acquaintance to leave Belgrade. He was a traveling magician whose troupe appeared in the bigger cities. After two weeks, he began to allow me to take other lovers. He was generous. Over a two-year period, by a good margin, I reached a number that ordinary women could never achieve: a hundred and twenty-four men. I retreated quietly from the scene when he found a new striptease artist. My parents never found out about their daughter's stage career. They thought I was living in Rijeka and that I was always on the road because of the nature of my business.

28. I went the inevitable way of actresses. Everything fades but the record of your career. The experience of the two years helped me to ease the sadness that would come over me later as I drowned my passions in a book. I got to meet many men, and I composed a short note about each one (I always kept all kinds of card files). Even a gentle, sensitive woman sometimes longs for an uneducated boor, just as she likes simple peasant dishes as a change from elegant cuisine.

36. I love strong drinks: cognac, whiskey, and calvados, and of the domestic beverages grape brandy. I am a passionate smoker. I drink white wine every day after lunch and in the evening. About one hundred wineglasses shine in my glass-fronted cabinets. I have a separate glass for each kind of wine. I am tireless when it comes to this: to discover a form for each content. The possibilites are as unlimited as those presented by love. It is enough only to change the lighting and the pose is different. My work on the stage taught me all these skills. A painter has a limited number of primary colors, but he creates thousands of shades. A musician does the same with twelve tones. Art is always a choice, a discovery of combinations. Lovers have an advantage, so the possible combinations line up to infinity.

44. My favorite flowers are irises. I also love roses, hyacinths, and their enchanting smell. My whole apartment is filled in the summer with the smell of flowers. Twenty flowerpots in the anteroom offer an immense pleasure to each flower lover.

46. I love fruit. There are always full baskets on little tables and tripod stands in my living room. The sight of abundant food next to my bed excites me. Whenever I make love I become hungry. Wine in a crystal glass disturbs my senses.

47. It is easy for me to find partners. I am still a beautiful and well-groomed woman. I send my dossier after I have carefully read a personal ad. Performances start in the evening, and when the night is over, tired from the play, I enjoy the dawn's freshness.

52. I love Bach, Vivaldi, and Mahler. I have a big record collection. Classical music enchants the body. Music is only a part of a performance. Actors are the most responsible ones. After a successful premiere, jazz pleases me, the long, drawn-out tones of Miles Davis's trumpet.

57. I don't have the vision of the ideal man, the blond prince from the dreams of immature girls and aged spinsters. Any man can be a good partner. My experience with women is modest. There was no response in my body to the kisses of the beautiful chosen ones.

Janko stopped reading ten minutes before five. The fear of the unknown woman filled him like smoke and choked all thought. After spending two, three minutes in front of a mirror, he put on his jacket, straightened his necktie, and left the apartment. He bought a bouquet of irises at the flower shop on the corner and, after pondering for a long time, hailed a taxi.

He stopped in front of a one-story house with a courtyard encircled by a low brick fence. A well-trod, sparsely graveled path led him to an old-fashioned door of long, opaque glass, protected from the outside by a wrought-iron gate. After a touch to the bell, a voice from the corridor's depths invited him to come inside. With his sweaty hand, he reached for the brass doorknob and turned it slowly.

III

Before the darkened corridor, lined on both sides by flowerpots of different shapes and sizes, stands a woman in a full white skirt and yellow blouse with thin shoulder straps. High-heeled sandals make her muscular, tanned legs seem even longer. Long straight hair, falling about her face, glows with reddish shades from the shaft of light coming from beneath the door to the anteroom. The woman leans her shoulders against the wall.

Her pose is a part of a thought-out game. She sees the glaring spotlight, the multicolored glass filters, the blinds distributing the necessary

quantity of light every hour. She hears the director's voice from the high scaffolding. She waits for her guest to pass through the entire corridor before gracefully turning her small head at a precisely defined moment and pronouncing his name in a solemn voice, as if announcing him to an invisible gathering in the room. Then she takes a few steps toward her guest and extends her pale hand. Whether because she has raised her hand too high, or because of her age, Janko, with a deep bow, kisses the tips of her thin fingers. Zora raises the bouquet of irises to her face. Janko carefully examines the wrinkled face, dark eyelids, and the long, slender powdered neck. It seems to him that the woman before him is on the threshold of fifty with a girl's body.

"I expected an older person and you a younger one, but clever actors easily find their way in any situation," she says.

Janko hides his apprehension with a smile. Her movements are measured and her voice solemn. She addresses him as if they are not alone, as though they are waiting for the reactions of invisible spectators. The living room is crowded with massive furniture and many little tables, stools, and bookshelves. It reminds Janko of a store displaying valuable things.

"Sit down," she says, pointing to one of the two leather armchairs crowded between a dining table set for two and the wide open balcony door. As she bends to put the irises into a ceramic vase, surprisingly already filled with water, she reveals her breasts all the way to the dark circles. Flowers are the best gift.

"There are all kinds of flowers in the flower shop on the corner across from my house. Do you like irises, or is that because of the dossier?"

"I received your parcel only a few hours ago, and I only skimmed through the dossier and the part about the irises."

"Do you drink?" interrupts Zora, and without waiting for his reply goes to the china cabinet. "Vodka or cognac?"

"I prefer cognac."

Zora carefully selects glasses from the cabinet. When she sits again, she reveals round knees and a part of a thigh in the shadow of the fold of her broad skirt. "For our première," she says and raises a glass.

"I am a beginner."

"Have you not acted before now?" Her smile encourages Janko.

"No, but I go to the theater regularly."

"Are you trying to discover the elixir of youth," she asks, continuing

the cross-examination and offering him a cigarette, although he has already refused once. "For me this is the biggest charm of chemistry."

"This is alchemy," Janko says, pleased that the conversation is touching on his field. He still does not understand the strange mind-set of the hostess or her bewildered glances around the room, as if following the movements of invisible guests.

The aging process cannot be stopped; it can only be slowed, but it is tragic to remain young in an aging world.

"What kind of role did you plan to play?"

Janko spreads his hands helplessly. "I am leaving the performance to you."

"To you, Janko. Don't get angry, but it is already time. I would say you are talented. There is something in your appearance that is indispensable for an actor."

Janko doubts no longer that his hostess is deranged.

She mentions some strange ancestors as if in a delirium. She is convinced that she, herself, at birth, had absorbed the entire accumulated artististic talent of her family. She reminds Janko of an actress from old movies. He had seen them as a boy but does not remember the actress's name.

"I like your dream," says Zora, changing the subject, "the dream that preceded the dossier. I forget my dreams. I wrote the dossier to avoid misunderstandings. I always say something else because in the presence of the persons I love, whether they are my lovers or not, I am not natural and incapable of saying the right word at the right time." She glances at her watch. "The performance starts at half past seven. Where do you want it, in which city?"

"I like Italy."

"Wonderful. I have visited many cities, and I always envy rich Americans who live for months in Florence, Pisa, or Rome. I will be a rich American in Capri or . . . it does not matter. I am a seducer."

After the third glass of cognac, Janko feels flooded with warmth, while the strange woman becomes close and dear.

"I am going to the dressing room now. We'll see each other in an hour. Find a city in the meantime—nothing can prevent us from being anywhere or anybody."

When he timidly touches her powdered cheek, Zora clasps her hands

around his neck and presses her mouth to his. This is only an announcement of the evening's performance. She turns her head to one side and asks an invisible spectator, "Shall we go to Capri?"

"I love Neapolitan music," Janko whispers, straining his eyes and searching the room for invisible spectators. Zora is waving her hands and giving some signs.

"I care very much for the stage; the set is most important for the atmosphere. A good stage producer is half of a performance."

She goes to the record player and picks a record from a pile. After ten seconds the sound of a mandolin begins to tremble in the loudspeaker. She blows a kiss to Janko from the door and disappears into the other room. Left alone, Janko pours his fourth glass of cognac.

IV

He walks around the room with a sure step as if at a reception, looks at the massive furniture, peeps into the china cabinets, and touches the ornamental figures on the shelves. The dark sunlight glows on the apricot treetops in the courtyard. The singer's voice, trembling and soft, keeps repeating the word *amore*. Perhaps I am in Capri or somewhere in Tuscany, it occurs to Janko, and he feels gooseflesh down to the tips of his toes. It seems to him that obstacles don't even exist and that he is unnecessarily cautious. Immediately after draining his fifth glass, he can already see the dark slopes of the vineyards and the lonely cypresses from the balcony door. He closes his eyes, leaning against the door. When he opens them again, there is a completely different landscape in front of him. He has not heard her steps. He feels only the touch of her palm and the smell of her perfume. He turns around. She stands like a statue in a pale yellow dress, the tops of her breasts bare and a violet brooch beneath the dark line of her cleavage, her hair smoothed into a bun behind her head.

She lights the candles with long matches. They sit at a table and eat cold cuts. The record player plays the same song who knows how many times. After dinner Janko invites Zora to the middle of the room. They dance for a long time and drink more wine. Zora suggests a walk in the warm night. It seems to Janko that somewhere near the fence he hears

laughter. They walk among tree branches. Zora mixes Italian and English, hopping among the branches, hugging him, and falling with her whole body into his embrace. She mentions that life in New York is monotonous and inhales greedily a lungful of the smell of the sea.

Blank areas in the periodic table of elements are filled up with pictures he saw long ago. Once discovered, the law of a series promises new discoveries. Like his colleague Mendeleyev, Janko Belog can predict with amazing precision the qualities and appearance of future exhibits. He gives himself up to Zora's scenario without any confusion.

It is becoming light. They are lying naked in bed. She sees a fire in the fireplace and the squinting eyes of a male fox in the snow near the courtyard fence. He does not understand the allusion to Lawrence's novel. He strokes her neck and nods his head obediently.

Zora suspects that the morning blueness will reveal everything that had been hidden by the night, that her loose flesh will melt away the illusion, and they must leave Capri soon. Performances cannot be repeated forever. Real stars leave their careers when they are at the peak of their glory. After that, only their myth remains.

She closes the curtains and goes into the bathroom. Janko dozes in bed, enjoying for the first time the nudity of his own body. Zora returns in a transparent veil with a long slender pewter glass in her right hand. "Now I want to sleep," she says, getting into bed. She drains the glass and stretches out on the sheets. "Kiss me everywhere. I like to fall asleep this way. Come on Saturday if you want." She utters the last words in a hardly audible, broken voice and immediately falls asleep. Janko dresses, fixes his tie, and leaves the house without a sound. The suburban street is empty on Sunday morning. He returns home by streetcar, lowers the wooden blinds, and falls asleep.

V

When he wakes up, late in the afternoon, Zora Petrović is far away, somewhere in the region where dream and reality mix. He looks with concern at the blotches on his flesh, teeth marks. He goes to an ice cream parlor. He returns home after a short walk, almost colliding with the major at the elevator. The sudden appearance of the major does not surpise him as

much as the presence of the young subtenant. She holds the major's arm lightly, without trying to hide their mysterious connection. She even boldly brushes the major's shoulder with her cheek. Both greet him kindly; the major even holds open the elevator door for him.

He leafs through the Sunday newspaper until late at night, looking at the personal ads. He knows that he will visit Zora Petrović on Saturday, but without flowers and certainly by streetcar.

In the morning he attended a boring conference. The whole day he spent at school and the next day he visited a relative in a neighboring town. He had to teach and attend the last conference of the school year. He leafed through a newspaper during the meeting, shielded by the large bodies of two female schoolteachers in the row in front of him. He read carefully even the pages that he used to skip. There was no telling when the meeting would come to an end, and Janko idly scanned the obituaries. And then, his sight dimmed, his hand started to tremble, and his breath stopped in his chest. Perhaps it was an accident, because the name Zora Petrović is not uncommon. But the photograph confirmed the identity of the person whom he had come to know only four days earlier. The death was tragic and there were few bereaved relatives.

Immediately after returning from school in the early afternoon, he began to read the catalogue carefully, page by page. Under the number 72 he recognized Zora's studio, the enormous courtyards that created an illusion of Tuscan gardens and the wilderness of rocky ocean shores; then he read about her impressions of a trip to Italy; and then he came to the last paragraph marked with a three-digit number.

100. Death. I want it to take place at dawn announcing a sunny day, to accept me as a dream, a liberating dream after a stormy night. I want to fall asleep nude like the Hollywood stars, with kisses of a young lover on my body and his sigh in my ear. Life exists only in a performance. The real actor dies in the last act.

Translated by Dragan Milivojević

Radoslav Petković

Radoslav Petković (born in 1953) writes short stories, novels, and essays. In 1989, Petković published a collection of short stories, entitled *Report on the Plague*. His novels are: *Journey to Dvigrad* (1973), *Notes from the Year of Strawberries* (1983), *Shadows on the Wall* (1985), and the highly acclaimed *Destiny and Comments* (1993). His collection of essays, *On Cat,* was published in 1995.

Petković lives and works in Belgrade.

THE PLAGUE REPORT

I loved people, but now I live far from them. My cell is carved high in the cliffs, far from the monastery; the wooden bridge that leads up to it is mostly rickety and worm-eaten—sometimes I look with satisfaction at the dark unhealthy color of its decay, which turns away those who come here merely out of curiosity. And there are always many of those pitiful ones who would compensate for their own emptiness by looking at suffering of others. When it rains outside, below the walls of the cell, already worn smooth by countless downpours, the water becomes a cascade; then in this little unevenly shaped window, carved in the stone, something like a curtain appears, something reminiscent of a different time, something that doesn't belong here. If it is night, the sound of the water disturbs my prayers.

I have swum in many seas and crossed many rivers. I studied at the university where the great Harvey taught and where he published his discovery of the circulatory system in the book *De motu cordi*. I remember the auditorium of the university. I also remember myself and other medical students, colorfully dressed, cheerful, full of self-confidence, determined to confront every evil and every pain with a bright smile. I remember the quiet hall of the library, its windows framed by finely sculpted arches behind which could be seen the foliage of the garden, the fine lines of the pines and cypresses. I remember the rows of books bound in brown or dark red leather, rows that covered the walls like cascades. I remember the robust color and perfectly harmonious shape of the orange that rested on my table beside the pages of engravings: a skele-

ton in motion, and behind him a wall with stone lions and the outline of a palace at the back. The quiet voices on the other side of the library door and scratching of the pen of the person next to me.

But even then—or from the very beginning, from the point at which I became conscious of myself—I also recall the empty squares where fires burned day and night, consuming various herbs and incense, those games of the city doctors who—not believing it themselves—maintained that this was the way to prevent the spread of disease. I recall the deadly quiet of the streets in which there were only armed guards keeping vigil in front of the marked houses, from which the cries of the sick and desperate occasionally reverberated. I recall the thin sound of the little bells on the trousers of the two men who, armed with long hooks, would walk before their cart laden with a horrible weight, stop in front of one of the guarded houses to wait for a body to be dumped on the ground with a thud, throw it carelessly into the cart with their long hooks, and then carefully pack their load so that it would not spill into the street. I recall the doctors with long cloaks and protective masks—which looked irresistibly like parrots' beaks—doctors who, by announcing the appearance of these carts, acted as if they were heralds of death instead of messengers of healing. I recall the graveyards for plague victims with deep, yet always full pits, from which neither laments nor complaints could be heard, where there was no other voice than the monotonous and languid mumblings of the resident priest. I recall all of this, just as I recall the brilliance of the orange on the desk in the library.

And what can a boy of twenty and some-odd years hope for when grappling with such an enemy? To stand like a knight on the square before the terrible rider, force him from his horse, and break his fateful scythe? And at the beginning, he daydreams about that, raising his gaze occasionally from the book and staring at the cypresses in the garden; then he once again returns to the pages that describe the epidemics of the past, from Tukidide to Sezara Morena; and then, mumbling softly, he reviews the symptoms of plague: constant trembling, a weak pulse—slow, quick, unequal—a heavy head that the patient holds up with pain, in front of his eyes everything as foggy as if he were drunk, his gaze expressing terror and horror . . . Like some perverse prayer, my mumbling is lost before the windows of the garden. And sometimes I go to the university chapel, in whose corner is a picture of Death, a smirking skele-

ton, similar to yet different from the skeleton in the textbook, trampling on the corpses while aiming his arrows at those still alive, still carefree.

I believed that I was ready for the battle. I repeated the words from those books with the engravings, suspecting that the world was a dark abyss in which all knowledge was just a kernel of bright sand; but I believed that even a kernel of sand could sometimes work miracles. I believed in my own strength to endure the fight, including that which every fight inevitably carries with it: the necessity of sometimes temporary defeat, a fall. And now I listen to the bells that echo in the monastery bell tower in the valley below, and I love that clean sound that rises to the stones of my cell and breaks against it, upsetting the birds that have built a nest there and who answer it with an inharmonious screech. When colors and forms disappear, sound remains.

Having finished school, I chased after the plague like a hunting dog. I persistently sniffed out its trail, I entered already closed towns, penetrating the cordon of astonished soldiers, pestering well-intentioned officers who persistently repeated, as if I were deaf and dumb, that I could in fact enter the town but would not be permitted to leave until the end of the outbreak—assuming I was lucky enough not to meet my own end before the end of the epidemic. There I cut open and burned countless boils, I listened to the difficult breathing and groaning of many victims, I investigated the surroundings, searching for sources of the pestilence in nearby drained swamps, in the dirty water that flows down the narrow stone streets. I spent nights debating with local astrologers about their theories on the present conjunctions of planets and stars. All of this was in vain, however; everything was superfluous.

Somewhere in Germany, during one of the larger epidemics, I made the acquaintance of a Frenchman, the famous Dr. Rue. We were returning from a meeting in the town hall. Because it is in the nature of man to never be satisfied with a little unhappiness—rather, when it does occur, he tries to increase it—the town, besides the plague, was afflicted by madness. A great persecution of witches and sorcerers began, and the number of those discovered grew with the number of those infected; therefore, in addition to the fires set in the streets to burn the infectious fumes, other fires were lit from which spread—besides the screams of the doomed being burned at the stake—the fumes of desperate madness.

It was night, and we were completely alone on the streets, which were empty even in the day. The fact that we were both doctors protected us from the suspicion of the town sentries, who patroled eagerly, looking for necromancers accused of casting spells on the houses of yet uninfected citizens. All the shutters on all the windows were tightly closed, and, save for an occasional moan, the silence was shattered only by the bells announcing the approach of the cart.

"And you," Dr. Rue said to me, "are working on what I have worked on my whole life; you are running after the plague, as you yourself said, like a bloodhound. I experienced my first plague in Algiers, where I served as the personal doctor of our emissary to the Algerian bey; from that point on—the horror of that outbreak was increased by the horrors of the eastern indifference to brutality—I resolved to dedicate my entire life to the fight against the plague. But now that I am old, it seems that I have been mistaken, in that it is somehow necessary to anticipate the plague to have any hope of fighting it. Mainly, it seems to me—although I haven't investigated the whole thing to the end—that the plague moves according to a distinct principle: it appears at certain temporal intervals in certain places. The plague is a restless traveler, but a certain amount of time is needed even for the unseen traveler to move from place to place. You are still young enough to have time to think about this supposition."

Then Dr. Rue stopped. In the midst of the barren and abandoned square on whose corner we had managed to arrive, a huge pyre burned. In the flicker of the flames, I caught a glance of his face, with its sad and gentle smile. "I said that I am old and I think I've made a mistake during my whole life. Perhaps this is what all contemplative people think at the end of their lives."

But I paid no attention to his last words; maybe I was just too young, too caught up in the mistakes that make up life. I was obsessed by his earlier words. For the next six months, I found myself once again in the library looking out on the garden with the pines and cypresses; the brilliance of the orange rested at the edge of my books. For the first time, I had become interested in something other than the symptoms of the sick: numbers. Codes and formulas became more important than difficult breathing. Soon numerous maps appeared on the library desk. I drew, extrapolated strange geometrical designs—fantastic polygons on whose

edges I wrote out dates and years. After several months, I knew that Rue's hypothesis was not entirely senseless, and after five months I was certain that I had found the formula.

The naive—or the arrogant—imagine that God created the world according to mathematical principles; this too was my sin. I believed that I had reached the path of salvation: how often does that path lead to final ruin? I do not want to entrust this formula to paper; I do not want to entrust it to anyone; everyone has his own path that leads to the darkness, and it isn't up to me to help him. I don't know according to what principle God created the world, or whether he did it randomly, like a thoughtless child; for me the world is a dark forest in which I am lost.

I was, however, elated and impatient to test the validity of my discovery. And, after my first precise calculations, I traveled to a town where I suspected the plague would break out. I met the town doctor, who looked at me with astonishment when I asked him whether he had noticed any sign of the coming outbreak; with even greater astonishment, he called me aside two weeks later to tell me that in the outskirts of the town two cases had already been discovered with the characteristic boils, but the government's position was to guard against panic. Therefore—because rumors had begun to circulate about the appearance of the plague—they would announce officially that the sickness in question was easily treated, although one of the victims had died twenty hours after the appearance of the first symptoms.

Thus my mathematical work was awarded in many ways. The next week, like a fire, one of the worst outbreaks I had ever seen broke out. As if it wished to ridicule the authorities' announcement, death came even more swiftly on this occasion than on many earlier ones, so that the jobs for doctors—whose help in such situations is otherwise doubtful— in fact did not exist. A man would be walking spryly down the street, then he would fall sick, he would break down, and it would remain only for the collector of bodies with his long hooks to pick him up and place him in his cart. The poor died, like the rich, caught so quickly that they had no time to escape. The weak died, the strong died, all the monks from the nearby monastery died, all who tried in some way to ease the sufferings of the unfortunate. All the doctors died—most of them just broke down at the end of their last patient's illness—all but one: me.

That I survived was already by that time some kind of sign to me; I

was just not able to correctly explain it. I was a bit surprised that it was I who had been spared by the plague, whose game I had correctly seen through, or so at least I believed, in my arrogance. Perhaps that awareness gave me some special power before it; nor was there in the corner of my mind any presumption that I had joined the plague in a secret union. What is the benefit of foreseeing that which we can neither prevent nor diminish? What is the benefit of knowing that one has calculated the degree of misfortune in the world more precisely than others, while anyone, without calculation, can feel it on his own shoulders? For years I arrived before the plague, correctly guessing the date and place of its outbreak. People around me were cut down like sheaves, while I was spared to such a degree that I stopped using a cloak and that silly mask that looked like a parrot's beak, which otherwise failed to help so many others. I stepped quietly among the dead and dying, untouched, even believing—oh, damnation!—that my wisdom, my idiotic calculations, protected me from death. I believed that I had discovered the principles by which God had created the world and that I could turn these principles into a stupid mathematical formula, more or less. I believed that with my calculation I had encompassed at least a part of God's work— the one connected to evil and punishment—and that my knowledge helped me to rise above it. Nor did I think that this knowledge really— I truly don't know which words to use now—moved me from that barely visible serpentine path on which man—sometimes—fights his way through the world. And I lost my way in that dark forest into which we are all born, once and forever.

Before I understood, others understood. When I entered a town, more and more often they would look at me with terror and suspicion—I had become a sign of the evil against which I had fought. In the beginning, they hoped for something, it's true. Soon they saw that my arrival reliably announced the plague but that it didn't soften its impact even a little; on the contrary, it seemed that the worst devastation broke out exactly wherever I appeared, and then they began to doubt even more.

Beneath a hail of rocks, I barely saved my scalp by running to the town hall. I had unbelievable luck—if luck always keeps death away— that I was attacked right in front of the town hall and that I could find shelter behind the solid, tightly closed black wooden door, behind the backs of the guards who pointed their swords at the mob. For hours,

shouts of "Witch!" "Sorcerer!" and "You brought us the plague!" reverberated around the square. The royal governor who ruled the town was —so I still thought—a reasonable, enlightened man who himself believed in the principles of mathematics, according to which the world is designed. "You see," he said to me, "how awfully dull and stupid people are; they need a witch who poisons them and whom they can burn on the square so they can at least sleep soundly at night—until the fingers of the plague awaken them once again. If you remain, the town will go into an uproar, and the government these days is so weak that you would be a victim and many others with you. Therefore the least I can do is to help you break the law—in the evening you will leave town. I know that you are not infected and that you don't pose a danger to anyone."

Oh, the majestic stupidity of the wise! This wise man was correct regarding only one thing: I really wasn't infected—at least not in that anything could happen to me. I spent several months in a monastery hidden in the mountains, collecting my strength, collecting my thoughts. I tried to laugh at human superstitions, but my laughter didn't come from the heart—it isn't hard to overcome others' doubts with laughter, but it is impossible to overcome one's own. There remained one way to find out—my spirit was still fond of experiments, regardless of the price. I still believed we must follow things to the very end, to lift every veil and to penetrate the bloody core of reality—regardless of whatever demons await us there. I made up my mind. I spent several days lost in calculations and then immediately set off in the direction opposite to the one that my calculations pointed me in, where—according to the formula— the plague was not supposed to be.

As long as I live, I will not forget the morning when, dressed as a merchant, I entered the town on the seacoast. I passed through an orange grove and went on toward the sea—unbelievably quiet, calm, and radiant as it embraced me with its scents. The town was still sleepy in its soft morning colors, but two old fishermen were already mending their nets standing next to the post to which their boats were tied. A child cried somewhere, the sea slowly moved, and the boats silently creaked. It was like a picture of Paradise. It seemed unbelievable that any type of evil could threaten this kind of place; my heart raced and I wanted to run away from an attack of appalling horror, more horrible than any man could feel: fear of oneself. But I stayed, and the only thing that I can say

in my defense is that I was afraid of the truth, although I still did not believe in it.

Two weeks later, the town government announced that rumors of the appearance of the plague in the town were untrue and malicious. I froze, I knew that game all too well; nonetheless, I stayed . . . and I won't go into details. The scenes that followed went according to a determined order: hope, horror, despair. I searched for death, I tried to get infected in any way. I begged for suffering and death—the heavier, the better—but nothing touched me; I could have kissed the dead, but the plague laughed at me.

He who confronts evil too often becomes first its sign, then evil itself. There could no longer be any doubt, the mob that drove me out was right: the world is not created on mathematical principles, rather on secrets that swallow whoever tries to delve into them. For my arrogance, I was sentenced to ignorance, I became a part of that which I feared, against which I had fought my whole life. I escaped here, to this cell carved in the rocks, to listen to the bells from the valley, hoping that it will not be long until the hour when I will cease to hear anything. Sometimes, through the hole that serves me as a window, I feel the scent of ripe oranges—a memory of lost Paradise—and I wonder if that is God's last mercy or the merry laughter of demons. But that's not important. I often think of that Frenchman who, having given me his fateful advice, suspected that his whole life had been a mistake, as life is generally.

Translated by Paul M. Foster

Svetislav Basara

One of the most talented Serbian younger writers, Svetislav Basara was born in 1953. He writes stories, novels, and essays. In 1982 he published a collection of short stories entitled *Stories in the Making*, followed by *Beijing by Night* (1985) and *Phenomena* (1989). He is the author of the novels *The Chinese Letter* (1985), *The Cracked Mirror* (1986), *The Tale of Cyclists* (1988), *In Quest of the Grail* (1990), *Mongolian Guidebook* (1992), *The Dark Side of the Moon* (1992), and *Looney Tunes* (1997).

Svetislav Basara works and lives in Užice.

A LETTER FROM HELL

My Dear Pavlović,

Dying was bad enough, but then I suffered another shock: I had been condemned to hell. Quite unjustly, to my mind, but here, they say, that's the way everyone takes it. You may well be marveling: How could someone dead be writing a letter? I admit this is not conventional. But one must consider things from a pragmatic point of view. These days, apparently, hell is not as far from the world as it used to be. The more experienced convicts claim that hell and the world touch, overlap . . . Moreover, though this may be difficult to believe, Hades has its outposts in the wastelands of Siberia. So a little news leaks, now and then, in both directions. I am taking this opportunity to draw your attention to some things that may come in handy when you are dying.

As you know, hell has nine circles. I am in the first, along with outcast sinners, paltry wrongdoers, useless souls. Famous sinners are further below, in realms of which we know nothing. Evil spirits don't torture us; we are forced to torment each other at temperatures of roughly 2,300 degrees. That is beside the point. Heat aside, there is no difference between Paris and the first circle of hell. My principal form of atonement consists of writing a confession as many times as it takes to comprehend my sin. This may not sound like much of a punishment. But it is impossible here to tell lies, to whitewash guilt with silence. For example, in the cell next to mine is a Moslem who, despite prohibitions to the contrary, drew human figures. His punishment is to draw the human figure until he

achieves a perfect likeness with the original and then to bring what he has drawn to life. He claims he has been here nearly 450 years; in that time, he has achieved an enviable degree of virtuosity; in the world, he would no doubt have surpassed Leonardo. But what is valued in the world is worth nothing in hell. There is some fellow here who used sorcery to ship his wife off into the astral realms. Then there's a member of an Indian sect who crushed thirty-four ants in his lifetime. He committed no other sin, but he had sworn never to destroy any living creature, and now he is in torment. There is a single hell for all of us. In it, as you can see, souls of all faiths dwell. It is that equality which makes hell so horrible, and the cosmopolitanism only makes it more awful. One can frequently come upon a scene such as this: Christian, Jewish, and Moslem theologians sitting around and debating. "This is hell," says the Christian. The Jew gainsays him: "No, no, this is gehenna; you are intruding." Then the Moslem interrupts with the claim that they are not in hell, or in gehenna, but rather in *djahannam*. One assertion leads to another, they quarrel, others join the fray; the upshot you can guess . . .

As for me, my nihilism landed me here. Don't be surprised that I am confessing this; here, one thinks of nothing but sin; aside from sin, nothing else exists. As you know, I embraced the view rather early that the world around me is not real. In doing so, they say, I diminished God's glory. A decisive event that reinforced me in this conviction was an illness that afflicted me suddenly, which (because I am a fool) I did not die of in time, before the vice had really taken hold. I was even clinically dead for several minutes—my ailment was that serious. As I whiled away the hours before my anticipated demise, I discovered several things: for one, that pain slows, even halts, time; that memory, hope—all those things that comprise the phrase *my life*—are mere fabrications. That's fine. Those wishing to prove the emptiness of the world must start with themselves. Painlessly, I made peace with my own illusions and accepted the fact that only the illness and the pain it caused were real . . . that they were the cylinder around which that mass of illusions was wound. But here I made the mistake for which I keep on burning and burning, never to be consumed. Among those illusions I counted my wife and my father. I watched them, somewhere from above, as they stood by my 80 percent corpse, pretending to grieve. It was a galling sight. They, not the corpse.

I watched them more attentively, as I thought at the time, because I was not burdened by the prejudice of a body and I could see that the two of them were pretending (and that they did exist, my wife more, because woman has no soul) forced to do so by a panicked fear of death that made them participate in this performance, shedding bitter tears.

How could I feel anything, upon my recovery, for those sold-out souls? What delusion of kinship could trick me and lure me onto a path of false happiness? You may certainly note that my tone is biased, that I have not repented, though I see I should. This is what hell is all about: to know you are suffering torment for a reason, yet to prefer not to repent.

"A miracle!" they said when I rose from my bed after the worst crisis, as if I had never been ill. They were disappointed that I had not died. I understood. Their behavior was human. They had been through so much, they had spent so many nights at my bedside, yet still I recovered and thwarted their expectations. I longed to tell them: you do not exist. Wake up, fools. I was resolved to shake them free of their illusions, but I had to employ tactics. This deepened the lawlessness. No one shakes free of grave delusions without terrible agony. It is not in vain that five thousand years ago, while people still had a sense of some kind of order, Lao-Tzu wrote: "Beautiful words are not the truth." If you go as a hermit and preach that nothing endures, at best you will be proclaimed a fool. But let some maniac mimic wisdom and rant and rave about great deceptions while pounding his fist on the table, and it won't be long before millions rise to waste their lives in misplaced investments.

After my illness I moved up to the attic to think in peace and quiet. I hired three little Africans—Domdo, Simbo, and Ngombo, to whip me from time to time, so I wouldn't lose my sense of purpose or grow arrogant. This saved me from ending up in one of those lower circles of hell. I revised my views. I shed my fanticism. My doctrine, in its altered form, claimed: Man is nothing, he is well on the way to becoming precisely that. However, by abusing the blowup technique he presents himself incomparably larger, more appealing, and more significant than he truly is. The real size of an average human being is one cubic inch; all the rest is exaggeration. And so it was that, shaping this doctrine, I had decided to stand in the way of this mockery, at least among my next of kin. First I took care of Marija. "Listen," I said to her once, "stop strutting around

so full of yourself. Come over here!" She did. I sketched her true dimensions on a sheet of paper, and her appearance. "You are crazy," she said. With one blow I knocked her to the floor, I sat on her stomach and began burning her with a cigarette. What a metamorphosis. Subjected to the purifying influence of pain, in a flash she had wrinkled up, deflated, shrunk to her true size—a helpless, lost creature. In that state I began to feel sorry for her. Maybe I even understood her. For strictly speaking a person is honest only when he suffers and only then should he be pitied; in moderation, of course. In all other situations, one must do what one can to humiliate, denigrate and—if possible—destroy. But in this I was absolutely wrong. Torment purifies, but only when self-inflicted.

Mr. Šalamov has quite a different opinion on the subject. Like me, he is new here. He had a chance to have his fill of sufferings in the earthly outposts of Hades, but all those years he never once embraced the torment, he never voluntarily and joyfully submitted to the agonies, so— contrary to expectation—he ended up here. This gentleman met my father in Kolimsk. "An odd man," he often says. "He never complained." Naturally, that increases my atonement. Hell works in such a way that all conversations, all thoughts, all events take you back to the sin committed and they revive it. Šalamov met my father so that he could bully me. You see, this is what I did to my father. Since I couldn't abuse him openly, I sent him as a tourist to the Soviet Union. I slipped compromising material into his suitcase. And, of course, I betrayed him to the secret police over the phone. He was sentenced to ten years. I figured he'd have the time, while cutting lumber in temperatures down to thirty degrees below zero, to contemplate the vagaries of Fortune and pick up a little Russian along the way. He had always wanted to read Dostoevsky in the original. I was not bothered by moral considerations. It is quite one thing to abuse someone for the hell of it, I thought, and quite another to do so for that person's salvation. I believed blindly in torment and this is what has avenged itself upon me. Here is what happens when barbarians take the noble truths too literally.

Rumors of my infamy spread like the plague. Even that did not teach me a lesson. Once some activists from a local charitable organization came up to my attic to visit. They protested my torture of my wife, my betrayal of my father, and said I was abusing the Africans. Tyrant, father-

slayer, slavemonger. They practically shook this in my face. Doesn't a man have the right to beat his wife? Doesn't he have the right to tend to the soul of his father? I didn't say these things to them.

I summoned the Africans with dignity: "Dombo, Simbo, Ngombo, come here!" They hurried over and started whipping me.

"Not now, you ruffians," I shouted. "These gentlemen consider me a racist. They object to slave labor. Do not the facts speak to the contrary? Did I not free you from poverty?"

"Yes, Bwana," they shouted, lucratively.

"Would you not have ended up retailing drugs if I hadn't hired you to beat me?"

"We would, Bwana."

"Do you complain about the working conditions: 450 grams of rice per day, tea, milk, meat twice a week?"

"No, Bwana." This unsettled the charitable missionaries. Even here, in hell, I cannot shake my contempt for those creatures, so certain they are of securing for themselves everlasting mercy if they offer some poor soul a crust of bread and a spot of soup. This place is crammed with people like that. They sizzle in the flames and moan. They cannot figure out what they were condemned to hell for. Their unbearable racket is my sole consolation, if such a thing as consolation exists in hell.

I won't trouble you any further with my sins. You have plenty of your own. Better that I give you instructions on how you should behave while you're dying. Keep firmly in mind that the first moments after death are the worst. That makes sense. Some countries have textbooks for such things (the Tibetan Book of the Dead, for instance): there are guidebooks for leading the unfortunate through hell. You won't have anything like that. They will dump you into a hole dug in the ground, they'll fill it in, and wash their hands of it. Don't allow positivistic nonsense to let you get carried away. I guarantee that Death is precisely as it was portrayed in medieval engravings: a skeleton in rags with a sickle in one hand and an hourglass in the other. See to it that you don't resist too much—that only increases your dose of torment. Read Origen in time; he is our only hope. If it turns out, at the Final Universal Assembly, that he was right, that God forgives everyone in the end, our torments will be over. But better not hope in vain. The keepers here say that the gates of

Paradise closed in 1320, and that they are waiting for the unoccupied places in hell to be filled.

As far as the morphology of the inferno is concerned, one might say that it depends on the personal affinities of the soul. The Moslem painter, my neighbor I wrote you about, claims that hell is an endless desert; Mr. Šalamov, on the other hand, says that it is a frozen *taiga* scattered with bundles of barbed wire; the inept theologian, the one wracked by constant debate, thinks it is one vast classroom. The eyes of my soul see it like this: an empty city with gray buildings decorated with countless posters and banners proclaiming: ONWARD TO NEW WORKERS' VICTORIES!

Translated by Ellen Elias-Bursać

Mihajlo Pantić

Mihajlo Pantić, born in 1957, writes prose, literary criticism, and essays. In 1985 he published *Temptations of Conciseness,* a collection of essays dedicated to the genre of the short story.

His prose works include: *Chronicle of the Room* (1984), *Wonder in Berlin* (1987), *Alexandrian Syndrome* (1987), *Murmur in Babylon* (1988), *Poets, Writers, and the Rest of the Menagerie* (1992), and *I Cannot Remember a Sentence* (1993).

Pantić is an editor of the literary journal *Književne novine*. He lives in Belgrade.

THE MORNING AFTER
(REMAKE)

Here's what—as A. D. would say. I don't like winter. I don't like summer either. I don't like anything. I even don't like the transition between the seasons, although, I admit, in all of that there is a certain dynamic, a certain (even if false) change. But, all the same, I don't like them. I barely live through the winter, hardly manage to get to the summer, and then it seems to me that it will never pass . . .

On one such controversial summer August evening (I don't remember the day, I lost count, for there was nothing happening to me, but let's assume that evening might have been called Saturday, as the late M. M. says somewhere), I was roaming around the city by myself, just like that, without any plans, any meaningful sentence in my head. The city was deserted, as usually happens in summer; I hadn't written anything for days and was even disgusted by the thought of doing something like that —but there is nothing worse than the certainty of knowing that eventually I would have to sit at my desk again. Rare passers-by, each of them without exception, looked as if they had waked up that instant from a long, intoxicating sleep . . . as if they were wandering around in the prolonged amnesia of waking.

I stopped in front of a movie theater, looked at a poster. *The Morning After* was playing, with Jane Fonda and Jeff Bridges, director Sidney Lumet . . . While I was making up my mind whether to go in, I turned and caught sight of the wall on my right, next to the entrance, on which was written in big letters in shiny black paint:

ŠTUKELJA IS MY BOYFRIEND

Ceca

Azemina

Sofija

For a moment I did not understand, but then it clicked in my head and, as I was buying a ticket, I burst into laughter, rather loudly. The drowsy ticket seller looked at me in amazement.

The movie had already started, the credits just over, and the first thing I saw on the screen was the huge, long white wall of some windowless building (an abandoned factory or something like that) and the daughter of the old Fonda, staggering. I stood to one side. At first, the eyes of the moviegoer who enters a theater late are not used to the darkness, and it takes some time to get accustomed. (In the theater people were already breathing calmly, evenly, and slowly sinking into the light.) When I finally began to distinguish contours, I saw that the auditorium was half empty. I found a seat in the middle section and sat down. On my left (they are always on the left side, even in the stalls), a group of Russian tourists were whispering:

—Галя, это не эротический фильм.

—Наша ошибка.

—Друзья, подождите минуточку — может быть фильм хороший.

—Нет. Нет. Я хочу посмотреть *Царство чувства.* Мы прочитали в сегодняшней газете что в кино этот идет фильм. Зал не правый. Пошли.

And then the whole group, about five or six of them, obviously disappointed because they had wasted their money, quietly got up and, on tiptoe so as not to disturb the silence, left the auditorium. On leaving, one of them shyly spoke through clenched teeth:

—Какой ты дурак, Костя.

But the movie was not really that bad. In the well-constructed story, everything fell into place. The threads of the plot were tangled and untangled at the right time, always somewhat earlier than my slow expectations, and everything else was well put together, the music, the photography, but above all, her—a perfect, cuddly, fifty-year-old girl, Jane, one you

can only dream about in this shithouse. If you ever come across the film called *The Morning After,* I suggest you see it; you won't be bored, as you are this moment, although M. S. has just the worst opinion of it . . .

It seemed to me that a few rows in front of me I glimpsed a familiar profile. Yes or no, I hesitated a little, and then the movie swallowed me, Jane was simply dragging us into illusion; Jeff also had a likeable mug, and I felt a little shitty Balkan longing for the world waking up inside me. What can I do, everything somehow changes in the summer, as if the body melts, and words, touch, and-I-don't-know-what-all flow through the skin in a different, tangible way, as if you acquire a new kinship with your own self, as if you are diving up from a dark, fresh sea; your ego is no longer a small, cramped-up slimy ball deep inside your entrails, but somehow larger, capable of talking and forgiving, and at that time there is usually no one to talk to, the city is deserted in the summer. In winter it is completely different, dull and constricted, although then too, in your sluggishness, you are somehow your own self, somewhat distant and insensitive, there are many people around you and you want your daily meal of solitude, then is the best time to work and drink. To conclude, I like neither summer nor winter. As things are right now, he's got it pretty much made, Ceca, Azemina, and Sofija are after him, and there I was, sitting in the half-empty theater, drowning in melancholy . . .

The lights came on; I looked in front of me, it really was she; I was deliberating whether to say hello, we knew each other only slightly, and I presumed that we were not on the best of terms—you will see why—so I decided not to. I moved toward the opposite exit, but it was closed, a doorman probably could not be bothered to open it.

And so I started back the other way. Darkness was streaming in from outside. Admit it, it is a strange feeling. You enter the cinema in daylight, and then, at the end of a performance, you go straight out into the night, somewhat disjointed, especially if the film is worth anything. I hope you recognize what I am talking about. She stood close to the door, the last of the patrons except for myself, lighting a cigarette. I had no choice; at that moment she noticed me, so I said, "Hello."

"Hello."

"I thought that women poets don't go to the movies."

"You thought wrong."

"It's better to think wrong than to think nothing." I tried to be caus-

tic. God, how much artificiality and stupidity there was in that sentence; I was never good at movie dialogue.

We went out into a dimly lit street, strewn with lead dust, close to each other, and, to our left, I immediately recognized on the wall the inscription about the incredible Štukelja. We were presumably to go our own ways, but I did not feel like going anywhere at all; in my empty room there was not much waiting for me, a lousy TV program, a night shower, a broken fridge . . . the day was lost forever for everything, even for writing. And generally, the whole summer was hopeless, the desolation of the long-awaited afternoons, writing fees that didn't arrive, and I felt like doing nothing anyway. And so we stood, undecided; she must have had similar thoughts. I didn't know how to break the silence, so I kept quiet until she suggested that we stop somewhere just for one drink.

You must know very well the expression "one drink." Actually, it conceals a troublesome, desperate message by which we indirectly announce our desire to someone to postpone, even for a short time, our unhurried, wearisome, slow dying.

"I don't mind," I said, so we sat down near a stand selling hamburgers and other fast food and ordered two beers. They were warm enough to make us feel dazed. We finished our beers, then had another one and another, talked idly. I paid and finally we got up, again lethargic, and then she, as you might imagine, invited me to her place. I accepted, although I had not one good reason under the heavens either for or against it, but isn't everything relative under these heavens anyway, as A. A. would say? We left.

Finally, it is proper that I introduce her. The name means nothing to you, for you (tell me if I'm wrong) don't read poetry anyway, especially our native contemporary poetry, and she was exactly that, a contemporary native poet, neither better nor worse ("a hundred better, a hundred worse," S. G. says, when rejecting a manuscript) than so many other minor, unnoticed women poets whom you meet every day, at work, in a supermarket, on a bus, at the movies, at a tenants' council meeting, without even suspecting that the person in question is someone writing verse, reading Sappho, Emily Dickinson, Sylvia Plath, Vesna Parun, and I-don't-know-who-else (feel free to extend the list), disgusted by the world and imagining secretly that she is a new Hypatia, whom young, fanatical Christians will lynch, once, somewhere and sometime, charged with every

type of heresy, maybe as soon as tomorrow, at the central city square, by tearing her flesh off with blades made of carved shells. Ah, let me not forget the reason for my hesitation to approach her. Several months before that, I had published a more sarcastic than negative review of her latest book in *Književne novine;* I admit, it wasn't that brilliant, but, I had to do some work, so I was fooling around with female writing. Luckily, out of some inexplicable courtesy, we did not mention that fact, though I knew that there was a time for everything. But it had not arrived yet, the night was slipping away before us like a staggering, drunken ship lost on the high seas.

Her flat was not far, six or seven streets away, in a quiet area, we walked slowly, it crossed my mind that we were actually playing in a bad film we had both seen before, having no will to stop it because we did not know what to do with ourselves. We surrendered to a predictable story—as it was unfolding, let it unfold to the end. The elevator slid up toward the top of the building, she unlocked the door and, turning on the light, let me in; a large, white painted odorless room (the smell of flats horrifies me) suddenly shone brightly in front of me. The attic was arranged in its own way; although there were no walls, they were somehow assumed, library, desk next to the window, large bed and so on, everything was as it should be. I sat and took the drink I was offered.

"Nice flat," I said, just to make conversation.

"Not bad."

"You got it through the writer's association?"

"Oh, no," she laughed. "My former husband left it to me."

"I see. Any children?"

"A son. Seven years old. He is on vacation with his father now. Are you hungry?"

"Not really. But I wouldn't say no."

She brought sandwiches. We sat there, eating and watching the late news. Those faces made me feel like vomiting.

"Are you writing?"

"Mainly not," I retorted. "And you?"

"The same."

"Working on a new book?"

"I am messing around with something, and I should have finished it a long time ago. When is yours coming out?"

"For the Book Fair, so they told me, but whom can you trust these days? Which publishing house, Prosveta? Nolit? BIGZ? They are all the same."

"The Yugoslav knitwear market is oversaturated with poor-quality products," a bald announcer with a little Hitler-like moustache was saying, and I did not know what to do with myself. I was sitting in that flat utterly by chance—though, let's not fool ourselves, chance is just another name for inevitability—with a woman poet at least ten years older than myself, about whom, moreover, I hardly knew anything; I was drinking, uttering meaningless sentences, and listening to nonsense about a cattle epidemic, the expansion of nationalism, nonaligned fraternal delegations, changing the distance for a three-point shot from 6.24 meters to 7.50 meters, and so on . . .

"I read your book," she said suddenly.

"Yeah," I grumbled; without asking which book, I knew what she was talking about. "And?"

"I think it's nasty."

"Nasty?"

"Disgusting. Hollow. Intolerant. Malicious. Use whatever similar adjective you want, adjectives are the worst possible words anyway."

"*Worst* is also an adjective."

"I am not denying it. But the book is certainly ugly."

"All right. Again an adjective. But, all right."

"With no understanding at all, vain, superficial, without any feeling for someone else's view . . ."

I was silent.

"You have nothing to say to me?"

"Nothing at all. I wrote what I thought at that moment." The space between us was brimming with anger.

"Don't tell me that everything you think is worth mentioning, or" (oh, foolishness!) "worth so much that it should be published."

"Of course not. But I do think that it is honorable to write only what we really think, even if we are wrong."

She gave me another drink, without forgetting one for herself. That made me conclude that our conversation was becoming friendlier. We relaxed somehow. Finally, both she and I had someone to talk to (I almost said we had each other); and outside a sultry August night was growing

late, one in which you feel that you are getting old and in which loneliness gapes at you like an animal's muzzle.

"Suppose I agree," she continued. "But I don't understand why you are turning your limitations, ignorance, and vanity into aggressiveness. What gives you the right to adjudicate things for which there is no judge, even though it be the Lord Himself?"

Or P. P., I thought to myself, but I did not say anything.

"Well?" she repeated.

I tried to defend myself. "Don't we all have that right? And aren't we all convinced that it is our natural calling, even that we are the chosen ones; don't we believe in the fact that our very own damned ego is uniquely and exclusively right? I have nothing to add to this, except perhaps that the only opinion I know is my own opinion, and I do not trust it much either. As for the rest, I am not sure."

"That's such shit."

"Ha! We are becoming more intimate."

"Any male writer would shoot you or pour shit all over you were he by any chance to be in my place."

"I do not classify writers into male and female."

"Oh, yes, you do. Allow me to read you just one sentence." She rose and went toward the table.

"I do not allow you."

"Why not? Are you afraid that I'll catch you in a lie?"

"Nonsense. After all, which text is not a lie? And, finally, I know nothing duller than my own writing." (I seemed to have hit the target. She stopped, and then we laughed at the same time.)

"Allow me to call this match a draw. Or, better, unnecessary."

"I allow you," she said, and poured us new drinks. Only then did I take a better look at her. I swear to you, she was not Jane Fonda, but she was all her own, well into her forties, without signs of aging, slim, with a slender waist, a somewhat rasping voice; in a way she was intimate. Yes, intimate. I think I found a good adjective, if good adjectives exist at all. Our film was nearing its end, the time after midnight began to roll downward, and we could not talk about anything else but writing, texts, publishers, literary gossip, while down there, outside, some other quiet life was passing that had never heard that something as superfluous as writing existed. And they were happy, those anonymous people, unlike

us who were also anonymous, but who imagined that we were somebody and needed each other only to maintain the illusion.

Then I felt a need for sympathy and solemn, difficult words; I am always like that after a few drinks. "I am telling you, these are the leaden times, especially for writers."

She said nothing. I inhaled with the intention of continuing this perfect essay, but it did not work, she was not interested in finding out what M. P.'s opinion about all that was, and she was nervously putting away empty bottles. I knew it was time to leave. The story could have continued in several directions simultaneously, we could have done perhaps the same as Jane and Jeff, but this simply was not the same film, not even a pale *remake* of that film. We were . . . to hell with it, who is asking me at all what we were? Finally, only the story remains, and in it the course of things can be the way I want it and not as it really happened. You are mistaken, I replied to myself, neither one of those two things is right. Things always happen the way the story itself wants them to happen. Here you are a more or less wrongly chosen mediator, moulding the story.

"I know a great trick," she said. "I count to three and you disappear." I recognized the sentence from the movie and smiled.

"One: Finish your drink." I emptied the glass.

"Two: We conquered another day. I hope you'll forget all this as soon as possible."

"I don't know. In any case, it was my pleasure."

"Three: Good-bye."

"Good-bye," I said, and got up as if to leave. Then I remembered the final line from the movie and repeated it—knowing, though, that the second time around everything is a farce—as, after all, K. M. thinks too.

"I haven't heard of this rule ever working for anyone." Now she smiled. She stood motionless in the middle of the room. I watched her, trying to remember anything that made sense, but in these things nothing is clever, we are programmed not to think at all, I came closer and touched her gently with my lips, she kept standing there, looking at me without blinking, I lowered my hand to her shoulder, embraced her, she let my hands slip down, I placed my knee between hers, and so, we were looking at each other, it seemed an eternity, I was hellishly turned on, but then I decided to leave anyway. I regret it even today, she was perfect

although four thousand days older than I, and I was of Christ's or Danton's age, as B. M. M. would say—and in vain was I their age, for I am still an ordinary unenterprising literary fool influenced by the seasons. That is why I don't like them. We said farewell to each other, and I descended to the desolate, squalid street, oppressed by a sticky summer that had lasted too long. I swear I shall never again write a single word about female writing.

It was *the morning after*. A little sickening, but with no dilemmas, except, maybe, for one. Whose boyfriend is Štukelja—Ceca's, Azemina's, or Sofija's? But, why the hell should I worry about it! It only matters to Štukelja, anyway.

Translated by Snežana Dabić

Mileta Prodanović

Mileta Prodanović is a painter, art critic, and prose writer. His collections of stories are: *Dinner at Saint Apollonia* (1984), *New Cliny* (1989), *Traveling Through Pictures and Labels* (1993), and *Opera of the Heavens* (1996). He is also the author of a prose work that falls between genres, *Dog with a Broken Spine* (1993).

DEGLI' IMPICCATI

At moments of leisure, in a room facing the narrow San Zachario Canal, he remembered that he needed to answer Ursini. He could write him a short essay on how bad the insects were there, paying special attention to mosquitoes, which secretly ruled that watery wet feminine rich and so on city (see the story "Regina Maris e Mosquito," author unknown). He could write him about the evening walk he had been planning and his reflections on the same. There were fish living in the canal below his room. He thought how mosquitoes probably do not present any kind of danger underwater.

But in the end he decided to write him about his last job in Florence, about the fresco he had finished immediately before his arrival in Venice. It was a public municipal painting on the facade of the Palazzo del Podestà, the palace of the magistrate, and it portrayed rebels from the noble families of Albizi and Peruzzi hanging by their feet.

And he would give him, of course, a detailed schedule of the jobs he had planned for the forseeable future—say, for the upcoming season. That way, they would be able to determine together the best time for him to go to Capodistria.

They had, in fact, been trying for a long time to arrange his trip there. He was supposed to paint some decorations in the house chapel of the Ursini palace in Capodistria. On a previous visit to Venice, he had met Nino Ursini, the celebrated poet and humanist (a poet of fiery passion), lover of painting, and occasional patron of the arts. Since then, they had corresponded from time to time.

The space to be covered with frescoes comprised a smallish semicircular niche situated under a stairway. Also to be included was the coffered ceiling of a vaulted room where one sat and listened to poems about views of the sea. Other rooms were provided for other kinds of poems.

Although Ursini had given no precise requirements concerning the iconographic content of the frescoes, the basic themes, as well as the arrangement of the desired paintings, had somehow crystallized during the course of their correspondence. The Angel of Postponement, Ursini's guardian angel, would occupy the central, dominant position. He reflected for a long time about how to do that best. Most effectively. He had even begun to make some sketches. After a two or three tries, he seemed to have come up with the right face for that rarely painted angel. The right expression. As far as the body was concerned, things were much clearer. It would be leaning slightly to one side, an inner, static movement, nothing more than the usual *contrapposto* shrouded in drapery. One hand would be raised, holding a ribbon inscribed with the motto:

ET IN ARCADIA EGO*

From the beginning, he thought the angel needed to be shown in relation to death. With an open hand (the ribbon could perhaps be left to fall freely), the Angel of Postponement would be more prominent than the clepsydra, shifting it into the background. Or maybe he should be shown suspended in the gesture of covering the clepsydra with the edge of his gown. The inclusion of death in the whole affair, its discreet entrance onto the scene, its hovering around objects such as the clepsydra, reminded him for a moment of Torquemada, a personage whom he and Ursini had often mentioned in their correspondence.

Cardinal João (or Euzebio or Anastácio) Torquemada was a slightly bizarre cleric, a Portuguese who, upon arriving in the city to which all paths lead, demonstrated a surprising inability to adapt. The cardinal's

---

*Even in Arcadia, I am there. Many years later we see the same words on the edge of a sarcophagus in one of Guercino's paintings, as well as in Poussin's canvases bearing that title (the versions from 1630 and 1642, the latter of which is known as *The Shepherds of Arcadia*). This interesting coincidence speaks more about Ursini's affiliation with certain esoteric circles and the elite of European underground spirituality than about a possible connection of Guercino and Poussin with Castagna.

legendary phlegm, combined with a bit of paranoia, had little in common with his Mediterranean origins; rather, one might be inclined to say that he came from the North, from one of those lands where prolonged rains leave an indelible trace on a person's character. One of Ursini's ancestors had received the cardinal and his retinue as guests upon their return from visiting a remote province called Bosnia. The Holy Father had sent him on that expedition after frequent reports that schismatic sects were coming to that inaccessible mountainous region, full of forests and wolves, from the other side of the sea, sects involved in matters unworthy of Christian civilization, or any civilization at all. As those savage teachings could easily spread into neighboring regions (their spread was in many ways encouraged by a lack of faith and apathy in the people, as well as by general political chaos), it was necessary to investigate thoroughly the doctrine and extent of this overzealous pseudo-religion. Torquemada was the right man for such an endeavor; his Dominican erudition (regardless of the fact that he was a Franciscan), in conjunction with his sharp eye, which he actually owed in some sense to his long ecclesiastical career, resulted in the summa *Fifty Objections to the Heretics of Bosnia,* later to become very popular reading.

One day, in one of the leatherbound folio volumes in his large home library, Ursini accidentally found a note that read HIC FVIT IOHANNES TORQVEMADA CARD. PORT., without a date or any other comment. This was the only evidence of the cardinal's visit to the house of Ursini, and one of the rare testimonies of his travel.

But more than the cardinal's grandiose name, which—if one really thinks about it—has certain poetic characteristics, more than his origins (the beautiful and mysterious Porto, where the ocean's enormous waves, formed on the very edge of the universe, break against rocky shores), and more than his dangerous excursion, it was his obsessive fear of being poisoned that attracted them to each other.

Although the cardinal was linked by his name to John, the apostle and holy chronicler of aquiline inspiration; regardless of the fact that he, like most people—especially most people who think they have devoted themselves to matters of the spirit—still believed in moments of cathartic remorse because within him, beneath a wall of impious vanity, there was a thin layer of material that might possibly produce a saint, if only one of the lowest rank, if only one of the Blessed; and regardless of the fact that he was firmly convinced that there is a fissure in the earth

through which man can see an enormous region inhabited by the Miracle (he did not have precise ideas about this region), a fissure through which the miraculous pours back out like some fluid over the heads of the irreproachable and didactically chosen—in spite of all of these things, when his pursuers caught up with him and offered him a goblet of some poisoned drink (say, wine), it was not very likely that the fatal substance dissolved in the Savior's blood would separate all on its own, take the form of a snake, and slither meekly down his arm. One needed to protect oneself against poisoners.

It is not entirely clear how the cardinal acquired the goblet that ensured his tranquility. It was a simple, yet unique object made from a unicorn's horn. At the beginning of Torquemada's career, the last, decisive wave of the reconquest, which was marked by cruelty on both sides, was in progress. However, Iberia was still not yet completely cleared of the Moors. The markets in Granada, Saragossa, Toledo, or Illescas overflowed with swarthy merchants and all kinds of wares brought in from the Levant and Africa. For more than three years, Torquemada's agents had discreetly inquired about the possibility of procuring such a goblet.

That object, which according to his wish had been immediately covered with enamel and gold, was now on the table. It looked like a normal horn cup. While the red muslin of his overly wide sleeve draped into folds that created intricate, twisting reflections, Torquemada sat with his head propped in his hands, thinking about the possible effects of that salutary goblet, which would simply destroy any poison poured into it.

Unicorns were now almost completely extinct; the only place they still lived was the tropical sub-Saharan region. Outside of Africa they survived only in dusty libraries, which was where Torquemada encountered them. He gathered a great quantity of literature about unicorns. The cardinal's collection numbered an unbelievable (for that time) 313 volumes. With the exception of two or three compilations of dubious value, the cardinal owned everything written on the subject. Although he knew about their life in great detail, nowhere did Torquemada find a precise explanation of the critical effect of the unicorn's horn on poison. The fact, presented as an axiom, was always quoted that it destroyed poison. For this reason, to get to the bottom of the matter, Torquemada was forced to invent an explanation himself, to construct a sufficiently convincing analogy.

It is generally known that unicorns were, above all, ill-tempered ani-

mals. Their cruelty was completely hidden by the beautiful contours of their bodies. With their horns, which according to some authors were the materialized, ossified—or more exactly cornified—extension of their souls (like Moses' horns), they could cut open in a moment the stomachs of victims they had hypnotized with their innocent and warm cervine-equine gazes. This had been so until the day the Blessed Virgin entered a clearing where the unicorn leader often appeared. The unicorn came to the edge of the forest and stopped for a moment, sniffing the wind. It started toward the Virgin with a step that was, for the first time, unsure. At first it bowed its head slowly, touching the ground before the Virgin's feet with the tip of its horn, and then it climbed nimbly into her lap. She blessed it. At that moment, ten blazing stars descended into the clearing and formed an aureole around that *pietà* of happiness.

A kind of circular analogy could now be successfully made. Just as the fierce and dangerous unicorn was transformed into an obedient doe in the Virgin's arms, a destructive poison is transformed into a harmless substance when it comes into contact with particles of a horn that is in a certain sense a fossil of the unicorn's wisdom.

He had the impression that a unicorn's horn—and by the same token his exquisite goblet—had, in some mysterious way that he could not explain, been imparted with the memory of that charming encounter between someone who was more than a woman and something that was more than an animal.

Poison is a truly terrible thing, Torquemada said as he fed the peafowl in the lower cloister. They were large blue hens rewarded with eternal life because of their beauty.

The cardinal often saw victims of poisoning. They appeared when he least expected it. In the sacristy, in the hallway of his residence. He frequently escaped a plot against his life by inches. His disgust for this type of death grew spontaneously from day to day, so that upon an unexpected encounter with a corpse it would reach the point of delirium. Regardless of the wide variety of poison used, the victims were always in a similar pose. Their gazes were frozen and pointed in some indefinite direction, their lips blue. Usually they had disgorged the remains of their excoriated intestines around themselves.

Initially you do not notice anything. A person who drinks poison (a powdered poison can be sprinkled into a vessel from a hollow ring, while

serious, friendly, yet somewhat cold eyes stare at you from the other side of a table—what a cliché!) coughs a little at first. Afterward, the poison burns the esophagus and stomach and enters the blood. This is already the moment when the conscience, in the form of some insect of small dimensions, usually leaves the body and, from a height of about two meters, observes the room as well as its former shell, which has become subjected to furious changes. The first (and maybe only) thing noticed by a confused bystander and the discreetly satisfied executioner is a fever-ish trembling of the victim's body, a trembling which, as the agony reaches its climax, becomes a horrible thrashing about on the floor. But the real sequence of transformations occurs inside the abandoned body. Its bones become completely soft and twist according to its convulsive move-ments, acquiring unbelievable forms; the heart lengthens and the blood undergoes a series of colorful changes, beginning with green and ending in a shade of blue, lapis-lazuli blue. The eyes of a poisoning victim are likewise necessarily blue, but somewhat lighter.

All of this takes place in a heightened, almost audible silence, because the victim's burned throat cannot scream. His spirit, transformed into an insect, then descends into the hot, fiery depths of hell, where it takes part in complex rituals of the torture of other sinners, most often alcoholics.

This type of death differed in many ways from death by hanging. Hang-ing is somehow more extroverted. Andrea had thought about this as he painted the fresco on the facade of the Palazzo del Podestà.

He was sure that Ursini had already heard something about the rebel-lion. But as Capodistria was far away, and rumors carried from mouth to mouth tend—especially when it comes to delicate matters in any way connected with politics—to be drastically altered and sometimes changed into their opposites, he decided to give him at the beginning of his letter a brief description of the events that, regardless of the fact that they were relatively short-lived, had resulted in his painting.

After the victory over far more numerous enemies at Anghiaria, there was a period of general euphoria, and Cosimo II Medici was temporar-ily absent, since he had gone off with his entourage, as he did every February, to his southern estates on a ritually compassionate trip to pick tangerines for the Florentine poor (a custom begun by his great-grand-father). The leaders of the families of Albizi and Peruzzi took advantage

of his absence to start a rebellion and attempted to turn over all power to the senate. It takes few words to explain how the rebellion failed. The city was full of corrupt adherents to the enlightened tyrant-demagogues, and the people were completely unprepared for democracy of any kind. Two of the rebel leaders were caught on the run, while the third managed to escape and hide in Rimini. A ceremonious public execution began the very next morning on the square in front of the Signoria, complete with fireworks and a procession. A catastrophic lack of coordination between the participants, as well as very limited imagination on the part of its organizers, made it obvious that preparations had been hasty. For example, no new banners were sewn; rather, the ones from the Medicis' last triumphal return into the city were used. The people ate tangerines.

The old Albizi died after only two hours, which saddened and enraged the crowds, whereas Peruzzi lasted almost until evening.

The Medici commission was something of a surprise. He was still young, with hardly any completed frescoes. Moreover, at the time of the execution, he had not been in Florence. Perhaps they were trying to get an idea of how fast he worked and how capable he was with a small project, so that later they might consider hiring him for something larger.

A clerk, who undoubtedly was just relaying the opinions of the chief Medicis, whose general concern for the people was in this case mixed to a certain extent with a feeling of wounded vanity, presented him with some concrete requests regarding the portrayal of the hanged, as well as a text, a verse of shame that was to be inscribed on the lower edge of the painting:

> *Crudel ribaldo, cavalier superbo*
> *Privato da mia schiatta e d'ogni onore*
> *Ingrato alla mia patria e traditore*
> *Fra costor pendo il più uniquo ed acerbo.*

> (Cruel Rebel, superb horseman,
> Without my family and any honor,
> Ungrateful to my homeland and traitor,
> Among these I hang the most unique and sad.)

Equally strange was their demand that all three of the rebel leaders be represented, even though only two of them were caught and hanged,

while the third was alive and well in Rimini, whence he sent them irate, yet also somewhat resigned, and in any case harmless promises of swift revenge.

To tell the truth, such brutal, didactic frescoes had existed in Florence earlier, but they never lasted long, since the first thing that rebels do after a successful or partly successful rebellion is to strip away, in a furious attack assisted by a mob, their adversaries' fresco-poster from the wall. The Medicis, in keeping with the significance of their latest triumph, decided that in size and ornateness this new fresco was to surpass all previous endeavors.

While his assistants prepared the surface of the wall, he made sketches, exploring the inner dynamics of that essentially static composition. At the very start, he rejected the idea of depicting them as hanging by their feet side by side. That would be too similar to the setup in a butcher shop. Presenting the bodies in perspective, with no possibility of using architectural details, he arrived at another type of composition. As the convicts' hands were tied behind their backs, and he could not and did not want to change this, all that was left for him to do was to resolve those three "blotches" in the context of the format and its internal relationships. The heads of the hanging men, by now almost purple from the blood flowing into them, reached the very bottom edge of the painting and led one's eye directly to the *cartello d'infamia* inscription.

Of course, it would have been inappropriate to portray the victims as already having expired. He needed to capture death at the very moment of its arrival.

As he had had occasion to learn from the Old Testament, hanging is, without a doubt, an accursed death. There is no hope for the hanged. First, they are humiliated, and death becomes much more difficult upon the painful realization that the souls of the executed, just like their bodies, will be eternally suspended between heaven and earth, condemned to wander through foggy marshes with no hope of final redemption.

But no matter how horrible all of this was, in the scene as a whole, in the whole act, there was also something amazing. They were hanging without a background; as he painted, he thought that it was actually entirely unimportant "who was guilty"—the episode surpassed all of them, as did his painting. Three shapes against the blank sky or marble; hovering, almost flying figures. Hanging by the feet, with the coarse rope cut-

ting painfully into his ankles, each of the convicts endlessly repeated to himself the sharp noise that the noose had made as it was tightened, a single and final tone, like that of a chord on an oversized guitar, that varied according to the weight of the victim.

The world was upside down; the tower of the Signoria hung down like a giant stalactite. The compactness of the tower was striking. For the first time, the convicts were faced with a world that at one moment approaches with great speed and then suddenly stops with the aforementioned noise and stands motionless two meters above eyes that bulge more and more with the accumulation of bodily fluids. If it were not for the ropes suspending them, the world would fall on their heads.

At that moment, the hanged men were left completely to themselves, like Torquemada's poisoning victim, but the experience was completely different. Death is like a forest, he thought. According to three different types of theatricality, he distinguished three types of violent death. The first category would be discreet death, an example of which was poisoning. Public executions would fall into the second category. The theatrics involved here were of a completely different type; such a death was to a large extent the experience of others and was divested of the seclusion of private chambers. When directing such a spectacle, one had to take into account the size of the audience, its demands and expectations; put simply, a suitable rhythm had to be found. Death on the central square was in a certain sense an event that remained to a large degree outside the central participant. Usually the accent was on something else. Only later would the fact of death descend on the dispersing crowd. Death by the blade, to which scenes of stabbing and flowing blood lent special erotic-aesthetic qualities, was in his system linked with the third category of violent death: death in war. Similar to the first group, death in war occurs somewhere else, somewhere beyond the reach of apparently uninterested glances, and is subject to the completely different, distinctly complicated rituals of martial arts.

Naturally, he wanted Albizi and Peruzzi to be incidental in the painting; he needed to capture the essence of death in its dialogue with the hanged men, the irrevocably private moment that escapes the audience's attention in the course of the public spectacle.

The feet of the hanged men were painted in entirely pale tones. There was almost no blood in them. The two ropes were taut, while the third

was slack, indicating a certain ricochet movement along the vertical axis. The fingers of their hands, clenched and entangled in the ropes, were in completely unnatural positions. With their open mouths, in which one could see teeth that had already turned blue, he wanted to suggest the subconscious desire of the hanged to be freed of their bodily fluids, which, so unnaturally distributed, caused them horrible pain. In the end, he was particularly pleased with how he had rendered the third convict, the fugitive. He had painted him with greater care because he was aware that the third one was where he could really test the true power and effectiveness of his artistry. Since that figure came out well, there could no longer be any doubt that, precisely because of the painting's convincing character as well as the power that he had put into it, somewhere in the streets of distant Rimini the fugitive would soon die a cruel, tortured death.

As soon as the scaffolding was taken down from the Palazzo del Podestà, the fresco began to spread terror in the streets of Florence. The agony in the painting exceeded by far the agony of the men who had actually been hanged; their suffering went almost unnoticed in the general frenzy. People took detours around the Palazzo del Podesta via neighboring streets, but the fresco caught up with them on other squares, and even in their homes, bathrooms, and beds.

He was not sure whether the the nickname that he had acquired, Andreino degli impiccati (Andy of the Ropes), had a scornful tone or was rather a form of recognition for a convincingly executed painting. He felt that the new name would surpass him; this was not a nickname that would be around for only a couple of days. He felt that he would carry those greased ropes everywhere he went, that they would enter cities he intended to visit ahead of him, coiling around doorknobs and other metal objects.

Translated by Stephen M. Dickey

Nemanja Mitrović

Nemanja Mitrović, born in 1960, published six collections of short stories: *War's Dream* (1980), *Races* (1983), *Pisces* (1987), *Souls and Objects* (1988), *Tales for the Eyes* (1990), and *The City Beside the World* (1994).

Mitrović's work is representative of postmodernist literature. He lives and works in Amsterdam.

IN THE MOUNTAINS

Fog extinguished the pulsating lights of the fireflies. Soon it would be winter; morning was much closer to evening than evening to morning. A fire danced in the fireplace as if there were no one else in the spacious parlor. Motionless and silent, the master of the castle watched his hands as they laid out a game of solitaire. He stroked the table a few times, then rose, setting aside the deck of cards. From the corners, the cats followed his movements with eyes slit by narrow pupils. He poured wine from a narrow-necked bottle; each sip could be heard distinctly in the silence. He clinked glasses with himself in the mirror, and this sounded as if two glasses had actually touched; the master was taking his leave, reconciled to the fact that the mirror's cold, servile surface would not remember him.

While the plants under their blanket of snow dreamed of blooming and the wind yearned for scents, frost covered the windows with a ghostly pattern of ferns the color of salt. Evening mixed the colors and turned them black. Covered with a dandelion-stuffed quilt, the master lay with his arms folded on his chest. His fists were the heavy, tired wings of a dove that had alighted on his heart and stopped it from beating. The cats played with the resonating strings of the harp; before the funeral, a silk veil had been woven into them so that no sound would disrupt the silence. The castle was deserted. The servants had dispersed without touching the valuables scattered throughout its rooms. All grew quiet. In the villages no one mentioned the name of the dead man. It was as if the frost were saving him from decay throughout the winter.

One night, as the full moon rolled across the sky, the cobweblike pat-

terns of his nerves began to shiver; lightning flashed, forking out through the darkness of his tissues. The master awoke. He had not been conscious of the previous weeks, but his last impressions before death remained under his eyelids, and he opened his eyes with the sensation that only a wink separated him from those final minutes. He found himself in the gloom and silence of the crypt, as if the end were coming that very moment. He had been far away, and now he awoke, calling out his own name, deaf and hoarse from a protracted, exhausting howl. Icy winds scattered the whispers of Gypsies through the mountains, and the rumor of the resurrection spread throughout the snow-covered villages. Everyone shuddered with fear, a chill they couldn't shake off, not even before a fire. Only large amounts of hot brandy erased the thoughts of evil. People crossed themselves quickly, as if some force might prevent them from doing so. And they worried about what had seemed irreversible.

It was known that the master never had contact with women; for centuries, his solitude had ripened through marriages contained within the same family. His existence was not justified by descendants, and the demands of his ancient origins would not give him peace, because with the death of the last descendant came the other final death of all his ancestors. Stepping after his resurrection into the parlor illuminated by moonlight, he grew dizzy: in horror, he had discovered that the mirrors did not reflect him. A shudder ran through his entire body as if he were not there, as if the bitter cold that filled the room had taken his place. When he had removed the mirrors, the room became dark and shrank to its true size. Before dawn, he was overcome by fatigue; it took away his strength so that he did not resist returning to the crypt. As if he were living in secret, from then on he awoke every day with darkness and went to bed before dawn.

The snow was melting, decaying, and for days the earth quietly lapped it up. The grass lay down under its weight like hair under a cap. Summer came, and the master, having left his crypt and feeling cold, laid his hands on objects from which the warmth of the sun was already fading. Days went by unseen and dust collected on everything, as if the very light, permanently glowing, burned out and settled into an ashy sediment. One windy night, he left the castle and ran to a nearby village in a fever, his face cut by branches. The victim's body was found near the outskirts of town the next day. The woman lay buried in the shrubbery of a ju-

niper tree with her head thrown back and her throat slit. She was gently covered with hoarfrost like a window fogged up by someone's breath. In her small, firmly clenched fist she held an amber button in whose clear depths hovered a motionless, perfectly preserved insect. The words of the Gypsies had been confirmed in a frightening way. When night drew its curtains, people, having closed their eyes, saw how the master advanced across fields starred with dewdrops, holding a dagger to his breast like a cross. He slept during daylight hours without dreaming and awoke as if he had shut his eyes only a moment before; in that way, his body rested but his spirit never did. He dreamed only during the full moon, each time the same thing, as if the dream eternally repeated itself or was continued: snow fell tranquilly and tides of spiders climbed up the wall of snowflakes, tirelessly wiggling their legs in place. Something rose up in him and led him; like a sleepwalker he visited the dozing villages and always returned before dawn, before the first stroke of the church bells shook off the dew that had collected on them overnight. It was said that he kissed his dying victims solemnly and drank their last breath. People were afraid, but another, much older fear did not permit them to leave and abandon the graves of their ancestors. Generation after generation appeared in the world, inheriting the same impossible, ever more uncertain hope of salvation. The forests grew old and it was as if the same snow covered the earth each winter.

The Gypsies were the first to meet the stranger. He arrived on one of those blue winter nights so cold and clear that the entire expanse of sky seemed devoid of air. For several days already, a deep frost had reigned, so harsh that it made one's teeth hurt even through one's cheeks, and he traveled quickly, sleepy from the beating of hooves on the frozen crust of snow. Exhaustion left his eyes feeling full of thorns. A camp illuminated by fire and moonlight appeared in a clearing before him. Someone helped him unharness the horses. Refreshed by bitter-tasting tea, he warmed his hands around the hot clay cup. He observed the wild, dark faces of the Gypsies, full of wrinkles through which shadows, like a dark residue, spread with each movement. The wagons were gathered around them in the shape of a horseshoe. The Gypsies traveled in winter, when roads disappeared under the snow. Without touching the earth, because it must not know where they were going, they wandered through clouds

in regions erased by fog and blizzards. The snow retained their tracks after they moved on, and when it melted the tracks remained where they had been, as if they had taken root there. They began a conversation in a strange mixture of languages. The newcomer was a large red-haired man with a fair complexion; his face and hands showed that he was entirely covered with freckles. The muscles of his face were permanently contorted into a tense and cautious expression that helped to hold in place a pince-nez trimmed with gold. His nose was wrinkled as if he were sniffing something, which reinforced the impression of short-sightedness, and his raised upper lip revealed his gums and protruding teeth. The sparkle of the pince-nez concealed the restless, bloodshot eyes of a man who was being pursued. The leader of the Gypsies sat beside him, old as a raven. His voice was hoarse, damaged from coughing, and Carl followed his words with effort. He spread his arms when he spoke, as if he were creating space for his words. Before the silent gathering he tried to persuade Carl not to remain in the area. He could join the Gypsy company, which was leaving at dawn . . . When he finished, he licked his lips and spat into the fire. Carl watched the curling silken swirls of the flames. For a moment he fell asleep with his eyes open and withdrew into himself before the panting, glittering mound of embers. The sharp, desperate screech of tiny creatures that had failed to awaken when the tree was felled rose suddenly from the flames. His face winced from exhaustion and began to twitch like the flesh of a slaughtered animal. On the other side of the fire, a young Gypsy quietly played the guitar. His fingers flew over the bars as if he were surreptitiously arranging dominoes under the strings. Carl closed his eyes, his eyelashes swept away all that he had been seeing until a moment ago, and he sank into himself.

He awoke in the sleigh where the Gypsies had left him before their departure, wrapped in a crude motley rug. Only wagon tracks and a circle of ashes in a wide crater of melted snow remained after the company had left. He stretched out his hand to take the reins, and the freezing cold immediately bit into his wrist between his sleeve and glove. Driven into wild, unfamiliar mountains, he avoided towns because the presence of a stranger, especially at this time of year, would arouse suspicion: sooner or later, someone would betray him. The story he had heard the night before had returned his hope for the first time after the feverish weeks of flight. The haunted place that the local people avoided with su-

perstitious fear would be an excellent refuge until the end of winter, until the manhunt subsided and moved away. Night fell; while the horses hurried up a frozen, snow-covered river, he let the wind burn the end of his cigarette and, staring at its glowing tip, tried to collect his thoughts. For the first time he was alone, far from friendly eyes that, like a constellation, had always offered him guidance. In the ravine it was as dark as in a chimney. The wind made his eyes water and drove tears up under his fur hat. Out of breath, the horses stopped before a huge cliff that suddenly shot up from the middle of the gorge. The uneven walls of a castle rose from a river island covered with ice; built from the cave ornaments of petrified waterfalls and springs, it appeared like something that had been arrested by frost during a thaw.

The many enormous rooms of the castle were covered with a thick, mossy dust. The fitful, trotlike ticking of many clocks had long since grown silent. Only the wind gusted in through the chimney and beat like a fire in the cold tile stoves. A lantern brought forth new chambers before him. He climbed up a wide staircase to the second floor, and checking to his left and right, he perceived a faint light at the end of a long, dark corridor. He extinguished the lantern and quietly approached the stained-glass door. After tapping on one of the panes with his fingernails, he opened the door and found himself in a warm, dimly lighted parlor. The entire room trembled with the restless gleam cast by a fire on the walls and objects in it. The fireplace resembled the gigantic, wide-open mouth of a dragon, full of sooty stalactites. From the table at the far end of the room, a man with a bloodless face, an albino, rose to his feet. His waist was tightly cinched as if a whip had coiled itself around it. His chin frozen, Carl barely managed to utter a greeting. As if from a great distance, the master of the castle answered quietly and, placing his hands on the back of an armchair, invited him to sit. He moved slowly and solemnly and dragged an enormous shadow after him. As if frozen, Carl remained in the doorway from which bitter cold flowed. How was it possible that in this remote place, at the other end of Europe, someone knew his language? Certainly he belonged to the posse. Carl did not dare act rashly; it must be that the others were also in the vicinity. He approached and sat without taking off his fur coat.

One end of the table was covered with a just-begun game of solitaire. The other end was full of battered books opened spread-eagle and laid

on their faces. Everything smelled of solitude and tranquility. The gleam of the gilded letters helped Carl to discern the titles of the books in the dim light. They were printed in different languages. In some places, letters of an unfamiliar alphabet were mixed in with Roman script. Finally he even noticed two titles printed in Gothic, resembling a garden fence of wrought iron. Evidently he had feared that he had fallen into a trap for no reason. Perhaps it was because he had not expected to find anyone there; in the story he had heard the night before, apart from the fact that there was a castle at the end of the ravine, everything had sounded like a fairy tale. It had not even occurred to him that someone might live here, forgotten amid the incredible stories that were spreading about him.

For weeks he had not met anyone with whom he could communicate and have a good talk. His host asked him no awkward questions; he was probably confused and frightened by this unexpected visit. Or his indifference regarding Carl's arrival simply justified not speaking about himself. Perhaps he too had accidentally stumbled upon this place for reasons similar to Carl's. His approval at first looked like an expression of courtesy, but it quickly became apparent that he was not indifferent. He spoke with eyes lowered, worried that his words might change their meaning after they passed over his lips. A smile warmed his face for a moment. Each of his words was a distinct echo of Carl's thoughts. The guest listened anxiously. He sat barely touching the chair, his muscles so tense it seemed they were all in knots. His hair, even more red in the flames' gleam, his fingers yellowed from tobacco, and his face spattered with freckles created the impression that his whole body was beginning to rust. He had not talked with anyone for such a long time that now every word naturally sounded friendly and familiar. He simply craved companionship and conversation . . . Why else would he have felt such a sudden and irresistible closeness to this pale gentleman he was seeing for the first time? In spite of the words that he uttered slowly as if he were counting them, Carl quickly and rapaciously scrutinized the master. He knew how to see through the years and see people not the way they wanted to present themselves, but the way they were, by patiently removing the many layers of veils under which the naked, vulnerable child cowered in fear and shame. But with the master it did not work; Carl's gaze could not penetrate past something that cut through this man's life like a rift. It was as if a cloak shrouded his inner self from view. Was it possible that

this man was the Master from the Gypsy's story and that death was what kept his past concealed?

Curiosity overcame fear, and Carl decided to put all his cards on the table. He confessed everything about his wanderings and his fall, keeping secret only the meeting with the Gypsies and the story he had heard from the leader of the camp. He told about his wife, about the distance that yawned between them, swallowing up days and weeks. From his pocket he drew a medallion with her picture and offered it to the master. His ruby eyes gleamed in the shadow of his long white eyelashes, thick like the strands in a feather. He had never seen a photograph; it was clear to him that such a thing could not be crafted by even the most skillful hand. This was no longer imitation, but rather the reflection itself, seized by a magic spell and preserved in the picture. Could he also in some similar, inconceivable way be deprived of his reflection? Suddenly he shut the medallion, hiding the picture from view. When he raised his eyes, Carl smiled at him, but the master remained cold, with a heavy expression on his face. Morning was near, the glow in the fireplace was diminishing. The master rose and twisted a large tree stump onto the film-covered embers. He began to pump a bellows that resembled the head of a pike, producing sighlike sounds. Then he bid his guest farewell and left the parlor.

Curled up as if being beaten, Carl slept like a dead man the entire day. When evening descended, he dreamed that he climbed through some dark corridor and went out into the night. The moon was full, but the earth was shrouded in darkness; as if from the depths of a well, he looked to its distant, bright opening high above. He started to run, led by the far-off barking of village hounds that turned to whimpers as it echoed. His clothing fluttered and seemed to breathe, puffing up and then clinging to his body as if it were wet. The barking was getting closer and more distinct. In their furious attack, the hounds pulled tight at their chains: they seemed to be dragging the entire invisible village toward him slowly. The lights were out. He passed by black windows. Winded and hot from running, he listened attentively to several men on a nearby square saying good-bye to each other and setting off for their homes. One was coming toward him, staggering slightly from drink and the icy street. Carl knocked him to the ground. Moonlight spilled over the snow as the man screamed with every stab of the knife. Carl straddled the body that rose

up in pain, trying with each spasm to free itself. The blade flashed and the man collapsed, choking on screams and blood.

He awoke with a howl; the insipid taste of blood became weaker. Under his skull a hot cancerous growth had sprouted. It seemed to him that he had slept for days . . . Dying embers in the fireplace reminded him of the previous night. The Gypsy leader's story had led him to become suspicious of the master, but this dream showed him that loneliness and fear had allowed this wild tale to have too strong an effect on his imagination. He was certainly going mad if he was ready to believe such nonsense; he was tense and could not stop thinking even in his sleep. For the first time since he had gone into hiding, he had slept in a warm room with firm walls, and as soon as he relaxed a little, several weeks of exhaustion overcame him. He did not even have the strength to blow out a match. As he paced from wall to wall, long wisps of smoke dragged after him throughout the parlor. Conversation would free him from the uneasiness that remained after his sleep, but the master did not appear. While waiting for him, he discovered that the books were difficult to remove from the bookcase; they were swollen, full of slips of paper covered with illegible handwriting, all of them messages written to no one. He couldn't help noticing that not one letter was crossed out. It seemed that the master never returned to correct anything in his notes. Evidently, instead of a definite goal, he had only immeasurable time stretching before him. Carl was completely electrified, as if someone had brushed his hairs without touching his skin. The impatience with which he awaited the master turned into fear. He had been drawn into a crime. He was not only his witness, but an accomplice as well; he saw everything through the eyes of the murderer. He would not let this go unresolved because of his fear; the fact that the master spared him would not stop him. He had to judge and redeem himself. Carl set the fire ablaze and began to feed the hearth with books, liberating lives that waited for someone's glance to illuminate them as they stood in the dark entrance halls to the human masquerade. How quietly and quickly, how submissively the paper burned . . .

As soon as the morning had overcome the distant, numerous nighttime suns, he took a lantern and set out to examine the underground passage through which he had gone out into the courtyard of the castle in his dream. Drunk with excitement, he staggered on. The corridor looked

as if the entire inside of a well first leaned, then collapsed. He passed several niches and stopped before one entranceway not covered by cobwebs. The master lay on a massive granite catafalque, with his arms folded on his chest. At the foot of the catafalque a wreath had been left long ago. Time had turned it into colorless dust, resembling the whitish ring of ashes that remains on the hearth around an extinguished fire. Shivering, Carl sensed the strong and intoxicating stench of horror. Yet all that he had dreamed about had also happened to the master at the same time, far away from him. With trembling fingers he removed the small mirror that doubled the lantern's light and, kneeling, held it to the master's lips. A moment before, the glass had been covered by vapor from his weak breath, he had seen the reflection of the empty pillow sullied by the turbid glow of the lantern in it. Blood rushed to Carl's temples and everything swam before his eyes. It was as if a falling drop had shattered the reflection on a still surface of water. The master was not seen in the mirror, like faces that, although they are present on silver-coated photographic plates, remain invisible until they are developed. What spell could summon his image, hidden on the thin layer of silver under the glass surface of the mirror? The Gypsy's whisper answered him; words that two nights before seemed mysterious and incoherent now fell into place. According to the legend, the master would die while looking at his reflection in sanctified water that had been cleansed of all evil!

The change of expression in the motionless, sleeping face was slow and imperceptible like dawn or the coming of night. His hair and brows became dark brown and his lashes black. Carl saw him in the weak light of the lantern as he had been before innumerable nights had turned his complexion white. But soon he began to turn pale again. Life had erupted in him only for a moment, more futilely and hopelessly from the short bliss offered by inebriation; nothing but nausea would remain after his awakening. Condemned to centuries of loneliness, almost deprived even of himself, the master's half-existence evoked in Carl simultaneous feelings of disgust and pity. He wrapped him in the crude rugs that the Gypsies had left him and carried him to the sleigh. The horses rushed, spurred by his agitation. Only a few hours remained until evening. Traveling down the road that in his dreams had been hidden in darkness, they should have long since reached the village. Now it was necessary to find some other town; only before dark! Covered with freezing foam, the

galloping horses threw their heads, trying to snap at and tear from Carl's hand the bloody whip that he wielded in his horror. Hoarfrost had turned the forest into white coral. The shadows were already losing their sharp contours, and the dusk seemed to emanate from them. The moon rose to the howling of wolves. Little buds bored their way up from under the snow and a lily bloomed in the moonlight. Finally the sparks of distant windows came into view. They passed streets that like fissures meandered between the houses and ended at the square in front of the church. The master awoke. He was still distant and sluggish, embalmed by the frost. Carl took his hand, tenderly, as if it were made of snow, and led him. He pressed down on the massive latch sticky from the frost, and with his weight he leaned on the doors, pushing them into the dark interior of the church. Inaudibly he stepped on the snow that the wind had blown under the door, then on the resounding stone floor. His warmth attracted the master, who followed in his footsteps with hushed movements. Intensified by the sparkling of the snow, the moonlight shone through the stained glass and the men's faces changed colors, swimming in the ghostly layers of a darkened, extinguished rainbow. They stopped before the baptistry, facing each other, with their hands touching the cold rim of the marble shell in which the water shone like an enormous, moist eye. The water had not frozen, and Carl received the portent with a slow, solemn bow. Copying his every movement as if he were completely immersed in them, the master bowed to him and in the still surface saw his own shining pale reflection. Carl was again overwhelmed from that moment on, possessed by the master's impressions and thoughts; they were again one. Petrified, the master could not tear himself away from his reflection, as if he himself were the moonlit face in the water. Everything blurred before his eyes because that other had surfaced only in order to look at him, then slowly sank back. Bent over the baptistry, he grew weary and faded away, withering with each hot, hoarse breath. The radiant surface of the water on which he had recognized his forgotten face with such longing and such a thrill reminded him of the empty mirror before which he had stood after his resurrection. Reconciled to the fact that he would no longer be able to see himself in a mirror, he accepted a life in which that possibility did not exist. Yet as soon as he regained himself, a memory that he had avoided was also revived: it was as if he were again stepping into the parlor illuminated by the tired, dejected light of the

moon and unable to see his face in the mirror. Reliving the horror, he awoke with a shriek. He found himself in a church, alone under the vaulted ceiling that rang with the sound of his voice. He didn't know how he had ended up there, because everything that had occurred in the intervening time had disappeared from his memory; all the sins of the other life were forgotten and forgiven. Out of breath as if he had just surfaced from deep water, he stood before the font for christening newborns, holding on to the rim with fingers numb and white from gripping so tightly. He hesitated for some moments, then bent over the water and in the dazzling circle made out someone else's unfamiliar face, distorted by the horror he felt within himself. Sinking down with his last breath, Carl collapsed on the frigid stone floor of the church.

Translated by Ann Clever

Vladimir Pištalo

Vladimir Pištalo was born in 1960 in Sarajevo. He graduated in law, but while he was still very young he started to write and publish in the avant-garde literary journals *Književna reč* and *Student*. He has written six collections of stories: *The Picture Book* (1986), *Manifestos* (1986), *Nights* (1986), *The End of the World* (1989), *The Stained Glass Memories* (1994), *Stories from the Entire World* (1997), and a novella, *Corto Maltese* (1990).

In his stories Pištalo dwells on both ordinary and peculiar aspects of life. He works and lives in Belgrade.

MAN WITHOUT A FACE

N ow I'm going to tell you a story about a madman," Mara said to Miloš when they were left alone in the pool room, surrounded by the ghosts of the haunted art colony Yaddo. Miloš was a composer; he wore his thinning hair gathered in a pony tail. In Belgrade they used to say about his compositions that the orchestra performing them didn't have to know how to play musical instruments. Mara was a playwright. Her story was interrupted by the sound of billiard balls as she changed positions and aimed.

"I lived on the Lower East Side and was rehearsing a new play. Someone in the apartment below listened to classical music. It didn't bother me, since I rarely came home except to sleep. Gradually, I began to realize that he had switched to jazz, and the music was louder. Finally he got stuck on a thundering religious station. When I could no longer bear the barrage of hymns and sermons, I went down and knocked on his door. He didn't answer.

"I slipped a note under the door: 'I'm your neighbor. My name is Mara. I live alone. Could you please be so kind to lower the volume, at least at night?'

"The moment the note slid under the door, the music stopped.

"The silence lasted three days.

"And then: The dead were brought to life! All hell broke loose, louder than ever!

"I had no choice but to tell the building manager. He went with me to

my neighbor's door. Nobody opened it. The manager adjusted his tie and pleaded with him 'to lower the volume for the sake of the others.'

"The air sucked in the music.

"The manager shrugged his shoulders.

"The pristine silence lasted three days.

"Then an explosion! Again I went to the manager's office. I learned that the one whom I thought of as a man without a face also came to complain. He griped that I was a spy, that I was following him. That I made his life hell and that I planned to poison him.

"From that moment on, I knew something was brewing in the apartment below. I spent the whole next day on the phone, discussing the new play. My doorbell chimed. 'Wait a minute,' I sang into the receiver to my husband, who had called me from Nevada. I peeked through the peephole. Distorted by the lens, a middle-aged person with a moustache stood there. Most likely I had seen him around.

"'What do you want?' I asked, without opening the door.

"The visitor turned and scurried down the stairs. I heard the door slam in the apartment below, and now I knew it was him. The man's appearance was so ordinary that even after I saw him, he remained the man without a face.

"Two more days passed. I was hard at work. The third day, as I was dragging a shoulder bag and a cassette player toward the elevator, the man without a face appeared without warning. He rolled his sheep's eyes and asked, 'Why did you do that, Mara?'"

Mara put down the billiard cue and stood up straight.

"Ordinarily I don't scare easily, but there was something about him and his voice that gave me a jolt of adrenalin. Like this, from my heels to the top of my head: Hoooosh!

"'Who the hell are you?!' I roared. 'What do you want?'

"He bent over and ran. Furious, I ran after him. He was surprisingly nimble for such a bald rat, and he disappeared in the maze of stairs. Running after him, I bumped into an acquaintance.

"'What . . . what's wrong with you?' She grabbed my shoulders.

"'Let me be! Some lunatic is after me.'

"'Come on, don't be afraid.' She touched my ear with her lips.

"Together we went to the police. Afterward, we paid a visit to the man-

ager. Two men were sitting there. First they looked me over, then they informed me that the man without a face had complained that I was following him.

"'Scuse me, this is crazy!' I couldn't catch my breath. 'Just a moment ago he was waiting for me by the elevator.'

"'He's not dangerous,' the younger of the two assured me. 'He's just a little strange.'

"'As a matter of fact,' the older one jumped in, 'he promised to move in two days. Because of you.'

"I rolled my eyes: cute!

"Actually, I did not really believe that he was harmless and I even thought that I should sleep somewhere else for a while. But I was running so much! I had an absessed tooth, but still I couldn't stop working. In the drugstore, for five dollars I bought a poultice that numbs your teeth like novocaine. The day the man without a face was supposed to move, I just wanted to sleep. But my cousin had a nervous breakdown. She called me to have lunch with me and talk. So, to be a good cousin, I went. Goodness saved me, as in a fairy tale.

"When I came back, firemen surrounded the building.

"'They broke into your place.'" My acquaintance squeezed my arm.

"'What did you do?' shouted a fireman when I reached my floor.

"'What did I do?'

"I saw they'd broken down my door and that all the windows were open. The air smelled of gas fumes. The radio roared from the floor below. The fireman ran through the rooms. Finally they ascertained that the gas had not been turned on at all in my kitchen.

"'It's coming from below!' someone shouted.

"The firemen broke into the apartment of the man without a face and entered hell. The volume on the television set was on full blast. The religious radio station thundered from the speakers nailed to the ceiling. The apartment was empty. The gas was on. Windows and doors were stuffed with rags. The deadly gas rose to my flat through the dismantled ventilation vent. Before he left, the tenant had left a burning iron and had lit candles with the intention of starting a fire."

Miloš stood with the billiard cue behind his back as if trying to improve his posture. It took him a while to grasp what she was describing and then a chill ran through him.

"My God! He tried to kill you? I wouldn't wait for that to happen. If I know anything, it is to split when I hear loud religious music."

The smile on his face didn't spill over into Mara's. Mara looked at him without blinking, as she had when he'd told her that her name, which she thought to be Jewish, was a common one in the Balkans. She shrugged her shoulders and continued.

"I didn't have to report the case. The firemen do that routinely. The manager had all the information about the man without a face. The police in New York were looking for him. I left my apartment immediately and now am sort of homeless. I don't believe the madman will really hunt me down. I think he was fixed on the space and not on me."

"The world is full of madmen!" Miloš touched his nose because he felt like someone had broken it from a distance. That day, he had heard that the beautiful Mostar bridge had fallen. Had the face of the Balkans been disfigured forever with that act? Instead of ironing the mourning band in his soul, he asked, "Does anyone know you are here?"

"No one does . . . ," Mara whispered, and looked at him without blinking. Two homeless people who had run away from madmen found themselves alone in a pool room in the middle of the forest. She snapped her finger as if to wake up, and said, "You are married and so am I. But imagine that life is a pebble thrown in the water. Circles widen around it—its traces and consequences. And when the last circles disappear . . . when on the surface of time no trace is left in the wake of our lives . . . what will our conventions mean then?"

She gave the composer a look that recalled the sound of the oboe while he snapped his fingers in a vain effort to awaken.

Translated by Charles Simic, with the author

Library of Congress Cataloging-in-Publication Data

The prince of fire : an anthology of contemporary Serbian short
    stories / edited by Radmila J. Gorup and Nadezdha Obradovic ; with a
    foreword by Charles Simic.
        p. cm. — (Pitt series in Russian and East European studies)
      ISBN 0-8229-4058-2 (acid-free paper). — ISBN 0-8229-5661-6 (pbk.
    : acid-free paper)
      1. Short stories, Serbian—Translations into English. 2. Serbian
    fiction—20th century—Translations into English. I. Jovanovic
    Gorup, Radmila. II. Obradovic, Nadezda. III. Series.
PG1595.E8P75 1998
891.8'230108—dc21   97-45345